SKETCH

Every Damn Day

52 WEEKS OF LESSONS, DEMOS,
PROMPTS, AND CHALLENGES
TO IMPROVE YOUR DRAWING SKILLS

SPENCER NUGENT

Sketch Every Damn Day

52 Weeks of Lessons, Demos, Prompts, and Challenges to Improve Your Drawing Skills

Spencer Nugent

Editor: Kelly Reed
Project manager: Lisa Brazieal
Marketing manager: Koryn Olage
Copyeditor: Linda Laflamme
Cover design: Aren Straiger
Interior design: Kim Scott/Bumpy Design
Composition: Kim Scott/Bumpy Design
Cover Illustration: Spencer Nugent

ISBN: 979-8-88814-144-1
1st Edition (1st printing, April 2025)
© 2025 Spencer Nugent
All images © Spencer Nugent unless otherwise noted.

Rocky Nook Inc.
1010 B Street, Suite 350
San Rafael, CA 94901
USA

www.rockynook.com

Distributed in the UK and Europe by Publishers Group UK
Distributed in the U.S. and all other territories by Ingram Publisher Services

Library of Congress Control Number: 2024937110

TABLE OF CONTENTS

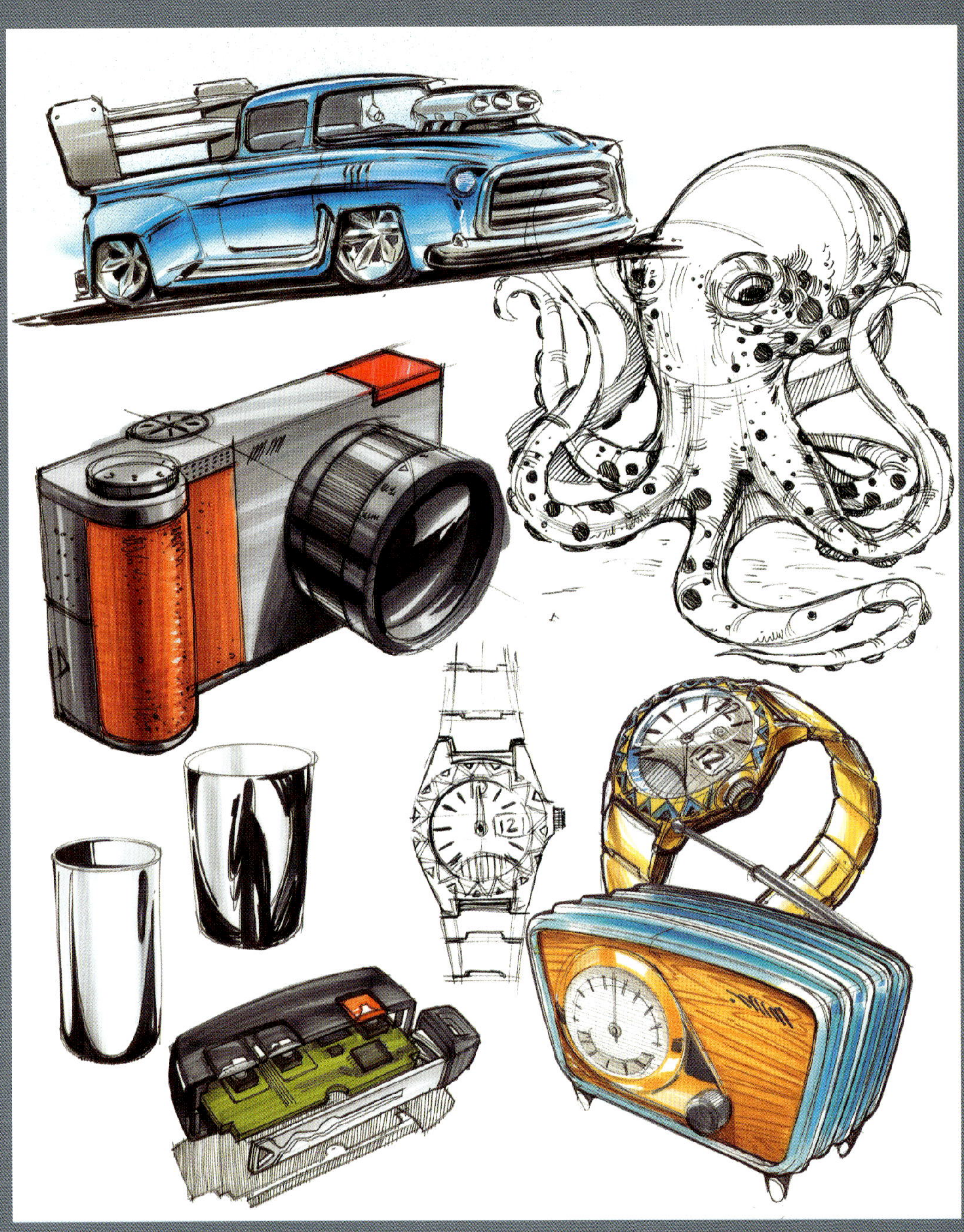

INTRODUCTION

"Sketch every damn day."

This simple phrase is my reminder that if I want to be great at sketching, I have to sketch every damn day. Only with consistent practice will you find greatness. Keep sketching, but be gentle on yourself, too. Just as you can't achieve your physical fitness goals overnight, your drawing skills will take time to improve, too. Focus more on the mindset of consistency rather than the minutiae of the practice.

This book is a guide—not a rulebook or a rigid framework for how to sketch. In it, I will discuss drawing concepts to help you improve your skills and also demonstrate how to apply these concepts to sketch a variety of objects. As you draw along with me through each exercise, you'll find images demonstrating key steps and reminders about important techniques you should practice. After each of the 52 exercise projects, you'll also find a challenge. Try to work through these challenges, practicing throughout the week. The challenges are meant to encourage you to sketch beyond the demonstrated projects. Don't be too hard on yourself, though, if some take you a bit longer than a week.

As an industrial designer, my expertise is in sketching physical objects and visualizing ideas using perspective, color, line weight, texture, and simple tools. I use sketching as one of my primary tools to visualize ideas and bring them to life. A sketch can express a lot, and it really is a cheap, low-commitment, and powerful way to capture and convey ideas.

Visualization through sketching can be a powerful skill, and learning it is like learning another language. Consistent practice over an extended period of time will help you gain fluency.

At the end of the day, what matters most is that you are striving to be consistent in work and effort. With that consistency, you'll see yourself improving. Be sure to sign and date your work so that you can look back and reflect on those improvements.

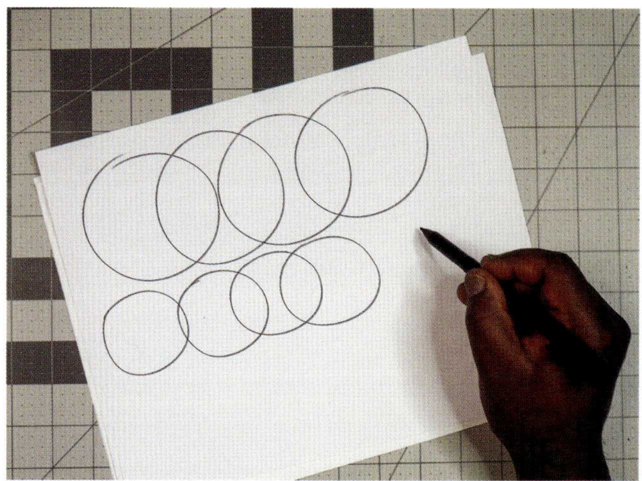

Embrace the Journey

You may not know it, but right now is the beginning of your sketching journey. Every journey takes many consistent steps along the way—and they may not all be easy. So, it was (and is) with me. As someone who is neurodivergent and has coped most of my life, I had to learn ways to help myself focus and channel that energy of hyperfixation into progress and improvement. Instead of looking at projects as an intimidating whole, for example, I learned to set goals and objectives each day. I make these small and manageable so that I don't feel overwhelmed or discouraged when I think about where I want to be versus where I am at the moment.

As you embark on your journey, don't think of mastery all at once, but understand that it takes time and effort. Trust the process and be consistent. Along the way, you may find yourself feeling stuck. You may find yourself feeling as though your skills aren't improving or aren't improving as quickly as you wish—and that's okay.

Rest assured that sometimes it takes your body a bit to catch up with your mind. In my practice, I, too, go through periods when I feel that I'm not improving. As long as I'm consistently practicing, however, patience never fails to pay off: It's only a matter of time before I see the big leaps and jumps in my ability to sketch and visualize.

You may find that in addition to these periods of seeming non-improvement that your creativity or your desire to keep sketching takes a dip. This is totally natural and normal. Even seasoned professionals go through slumps. Sometimes I find myself sitting and staring at a blank piece of paper, not knowing what exactly to draw or what to do. When this happens, just stop. I'm serious, stop what you're doing, and get away from sketching. Go for a walk. Do something you enjoy that might seem unrelated to drawing. Sometimes the step you take away is also a step towards rekindling that creative spark or creative spirit within you. Perhaps you find inspiration on your walk, or while playing your favorite musical instrument, perhaps you feel prompted to create and draw something new.

So welcome to your journey. Don't be discouraged. Remember, you have to start from somewhere, and whether you have just a little skill, are a professional looking to sharpen up, or fall somewhere in between, I promise that consistent practice is the answer to improvement.

You can do this.

Believe in yourself and trust the process. I promise good things await. Remember, your goal is to sketch every damn day—not to sketch something spectacular every day. Just keep your hands moving, your brain thinking, and your mind fed with inspiration, and you will improve. I believe in you, and I hope you believe in yourself too.

Your Toolkit: Essential Sketching Tools

The most essential tool for your sketching journey is your commitment to sketch every damn day, but you'll need a few other things, too. Just as a map, snacks, and good music can make a long road trip easier, the pens, paper, and more discussed in this section will help you reach your drawing destination.

Point of View

The first tool to put in your toolkit is not a physical thing but learning how you see things. When sketching an object of any kind, it's important to consider the point of view from which you want to sketch that object. *Point of view* refers to the relative position of the viewer (you or your audience) to the object you're drawing. Point of view can inherently convey scale, place, or context by virtue of how something is drawn. It is a powerful and fundamental tool that you can use to direct the narrative of your sketching, as you'll practice in Exercise 4 and throughout the book.

Pens

If you're new to sketching, I highly recommend you start with a pen. Although this may seem intimidating—pens are unforgiving and won't forget the last stroke you made—hear me out. I find this permanence comforting, because it reminds me to think before each stroke and to practice observing reality or visualizing before I sketch.

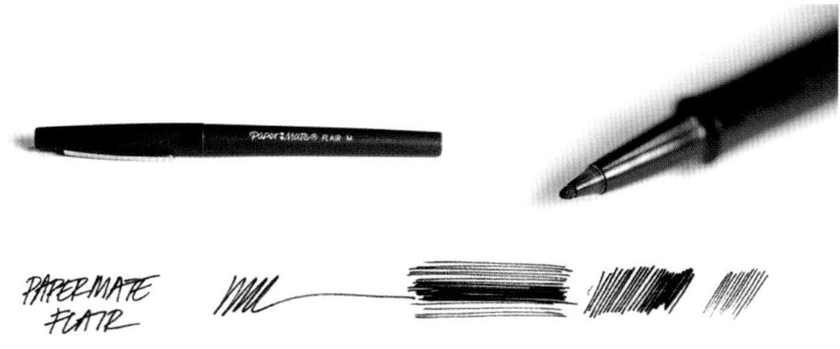

For this book, try a felt pen, such as a Paper Mate Flair, Sharpie, Pilot Razor Point, or similar. These pens feature a fibrous or plastic tip that transfers ink onto the paper. In some cases, they are pressure sensitive, but more often than not they will give you a whole line. *Whole lines* are lines that are consistent and decisive in their appearance. Using a tool like a felt pen or permanent marker is a great way to sketch whole lines. Take some time to explore which pen feels good to you.

Pay attention to how you hold your pen, as well. Rather than using a traditional writing grip, hold your pen halfway up the barrel as you draw. While you are growing and learning, sketching with a pen like this may feel somewhat uncomfortable. That is a good thing and an indication that you are indeed growing.

Until you gain some experience, stay away from ballpoint or rollerball pens. If you're unsure while you're drawing, these pens tend to make it a little too easy to hesitate. Without experience, this can lead to the development of some bad habits that ultimately will diminish the impact of your work. If you do choose to use a ballpoint pen, however, the BIC Cristal Xtra Smooth with a medium point is a fantastic pen that puts out a good amount of ink. However, just be careful not to get too comfortable and smudge your work.

Pencils

Although this book focuses more heavily on pen sketching, you can use pencils to achieve a variety of the effects in the demos. To try a variety of styles, consider getting a few pencils to sketch with. I prefer Prismacolor Premier pencils, which feature a thick waxy lead. Derwent pencils are also a good choice. If you plan to use pencils for color, feel free to get a set. Otherwise, just grab a white pencil to add highlights and a black or deep blue pencil for sketching until you gain an understanding of how to use pencil and colors. If you decide to pursue the medium, you can always upgrade to an expanded set.

Markers

In addition to pens and pencils, a set of markers is a good investment for this book— but not necessarily an expensive one. Markers have come a long way during my 20 years of experience, and budget markers are now a viable option. If you are just starting out, I recommend a simple set of budget markers. Premium markers include features that appeal to professionals, such as the ability to refill the markers or change their nibs, but at a much higher price. (At this writing, some are as much as eight times the cost of a budget marker.) Copic, Prismacolor, and Ohuhu all offer solid, tested markers that run the gamut of quality and features.

Should you get a full set of markers or just specific colors? Because I've been illustrating for a long time, I've accumulated hundreds of colors. I prefer to work in a single hue, however, using three markers of different values in the same hue range. For example, I might choose a light yellow-red, yellow-red, and deeper yellow-red marker. For this technique, you want a good value spread and contrast between each marker. A 20% to 30% difference will enable you to blend the markers together while shading and even create midtones (middle values) between marker strokes. A good way to start is to grab a 20%, 40%, and 60% marker in the same gray family. Although I don't go into depth on marker technique in this book, you can find additional advice in my first book, *The Perspective Drawing Guide*.

Paper

Lastly, you need paper. Although you could complete these exercises digitally, I find that sketching on paper with simple tools is a fantastic way to quickly sharpen up core skills. You don't need the fanciest paper to draw on, and you can complete most of the exercises on regular printer paper. I typically buy an inexpensive ream of paper as practice paper. If you plan to do a lot of work with marker or colored pencil, consider getting some marker paper, too. It is better at handling marker ink than cheaper printer paper, because it has a coating on the back to prevent the ink from bleeding through. It also has a smooth and subtle texture that enhances the look of shading with colored pencil.

Paper size is a matter of preference, but I recommend a minimum of 8.5 by 11 or A4, and ideally 11 by 17 or A3. The bigger you draw, the more you can use your shoulder and elbow as pivots to sketch. This, in turn, will help you create cleaner, more expressive sketches that appear much more confident.

And that's it. Those are the tools that you'll need at a minimum to work through this book. And remember, you don't need a super complex setup to practice and sharpen your skills.

TOOLS + TECHNIQUE

Tools matter, but technique matters more. The way you draw is often more important than what you choose to draw with. Remember to relax, draw with your shoulder, draw quickly, and be loose with your sketching. Try not to overthink as you sketch and lean into the feeling.

If you want to get really good at sketching, pick a tool, focus on that for a while, and then move on to the next tool. Find your "designated hitter," and then expand from there on.

To recap, here are some recommended brands:

- **Pens:** Paper Mate Flair, Pilot Razor Point, Sakura Micron, Sharpie

- **Pencils:** Derwent, Prismacolor Premier

- **Paper:** Bienfang or Canson

- **Markers:** Copic, Ohuhu, Prismacolor

Importance of Warming Up

Before drawing, it's important to warm up. If you followed along with any of my other content or previous publications, you'll know that each time I sketch I try to warm up first. Warming up involves completing a few exercises that will be both challenging and repetitive so that you can ready your mind and muscles to draw.

Draw with Your Shoulder and Elbow

Whether drawing or simply warming up, draw with your shoulder. In other words, use your shoulder and elbow as pivots while holding your tool of choice. (For warmups, I recommend a pen that will give you a whole line.) In addition, try to lock your wrist to avoid introducing unnecessary errors in your drawing. Finally, use a comfortable, relaxed grip on your pen while also holding it a bit higher up on the barrel than you would for writing.

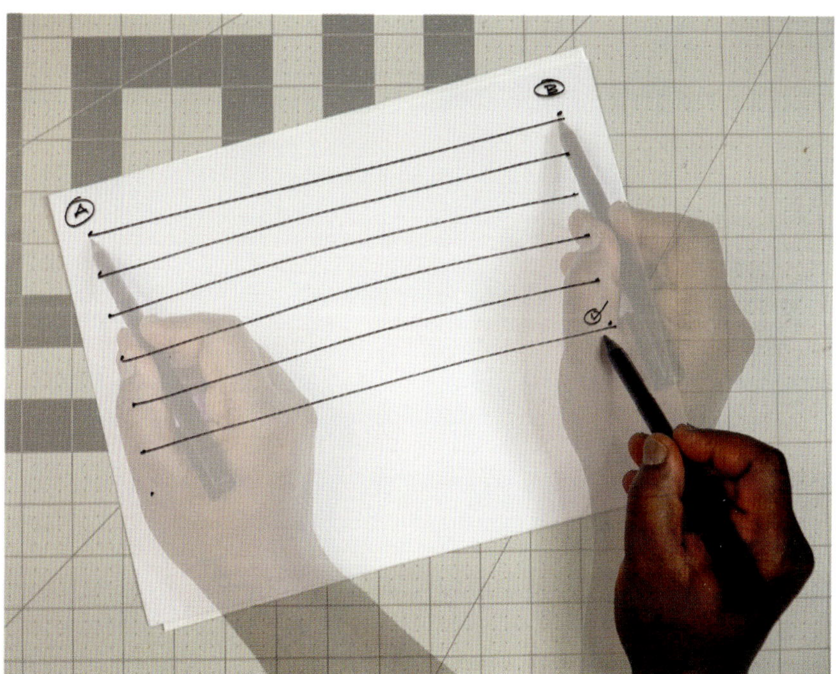

Warmup 1: Draw Straight Lines

The first exercise is to complete a series of lines. Rotate your paper so that the longest side goes from left to right and orient it at an angle that is comfortable to you. Place a series of dots along the left and right sides (short edges) of the paper. Starting at a left dot, draw a straight line to the corresponding right dot. To be more successful, focus on your objective (the ending dot) rather than where the pen tip is or where you started. Work as quickly as you're comfortable drawing but try to push yourself to draw a bit faster, as well. Drawing quickly will minimize the chances of error when completing this exercise.

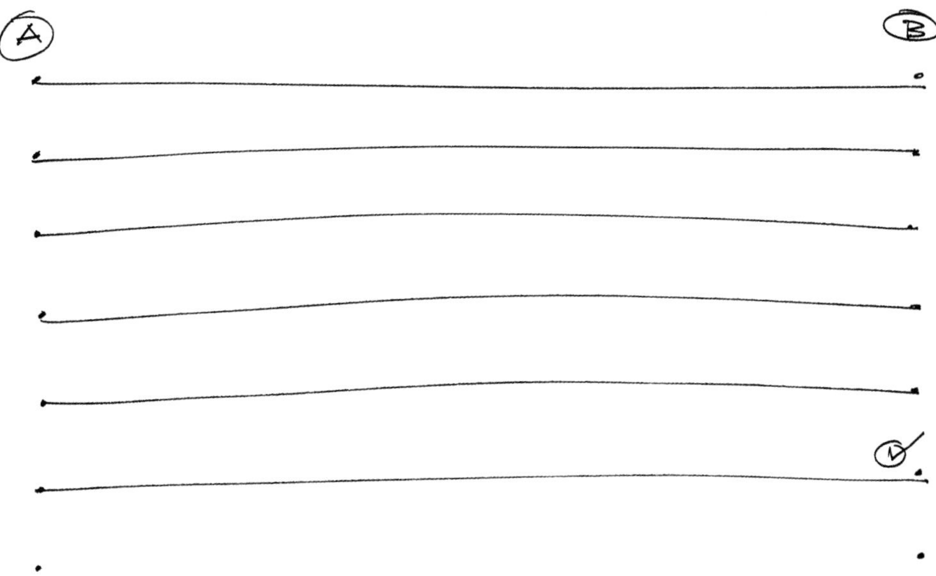

   SKETCH EVERY DAMN DAY

Warmup 2: Draw Circles

Circles are a simple but also challenging piece of geometry to sketch because they are effectively an infinite series of points that are equidistant from a given center. I'll put my math brain aside for a minute, and just say that a circle is a curved line that is equally spaced from a given point in all directions.

To sketch a circle, first think about the movement of your arm and also the proportion of a circle as you draw. Start by *ghosting over the paper*: While keeping your hand on the paper but not touching it with your pen, draw loose circles in the air to familiarize yourself with the motion of drawing the circle. When you feel confident (for me, that's usually after two ghost motions), lower your pen to the paper and continue the motion to draw the circle. Don't worry if your circles aren't perfect. After 20 years of drawing, I still do this exercise each time I draw—and my circles aren't perfect either. It's a great warmup to get those muscles moving.

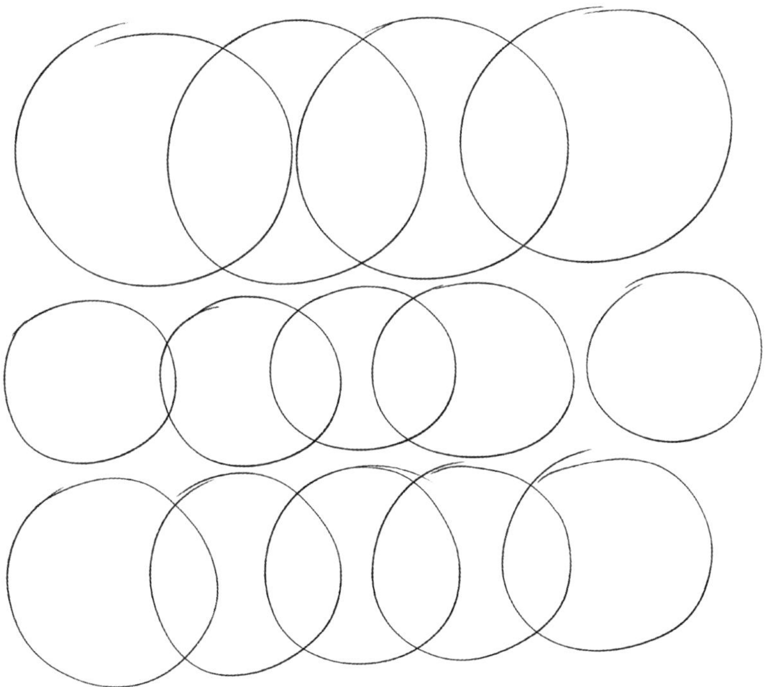

Warmup 3: Draw Ellipses

When is a circle not a circle? When it becomes an ellipse. Think of a circular object like the top of a soup can. When you view it from straight above, the top of the can looks like the circle it is. When you lower the angle of your point of view, however, that circle now appears to be an oval or an ellipse. At a shallow angle of view, the top of the soup can (and any) ellipse appears wider than when viewed at a sharper angle, just as a more distant ellipse will appear smaller than when you view the same object close up.

You need to account for this effect in your drawings, but two measurements can help. The shortest distance across the center of an ellipse is called its minor axis and the longest is the major axis. When you are drawing in perspective, the minor axis needs to be aligned accurately to reflect the point of view.

To warm up your ellipse skills, draw a series of ellipses at different sizes, ghosting over the paper first to familiarize yourself with the necessary arm motion. I like to start with a narrow ellipse and progressively open their degree (widen them) as a I draw more. Much like the circles, however, this is a difficult exercise, so it's more important to push through and work on the repetition of drawing a variety of ellipses than it is to get them perfect in one go. (For more ellipses tips, see Exercise 2).

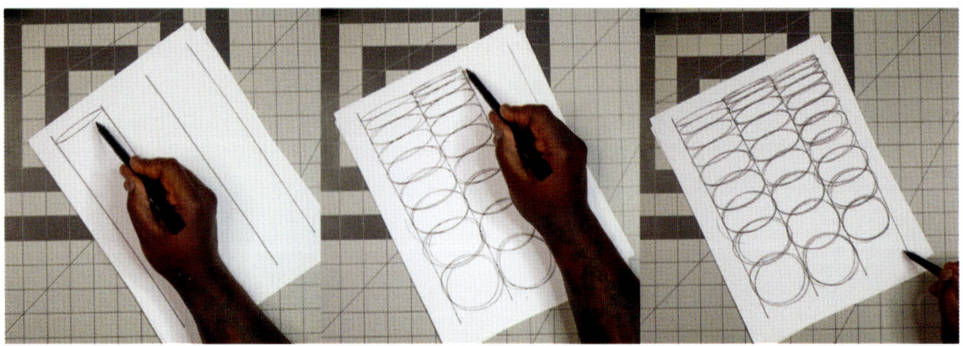

Additional Warmups

Beyond these three, you can come up with plenty more challenges to help you warm up. For example, sometimes I draw a series of squares, and then inscribe circles that touch each inner side of those squares. Or try dividing your warm-up circles into slices, much like slicing through an orange or a tomato. Exercise 2 includes more practice drawing fundamental shapes, as well.

WARMUPS

Warming up is key to getting good lines, perspective, and presentation when sketching. You can warm up by doing a few rough sketches or trying the following exercises:

- Sketch a series of lines between two points.

- Draw some circles, filling a page and focusing on precision and speed.

- Sketch ellipses in a sequential manner, opening the ellipse's degree for each.

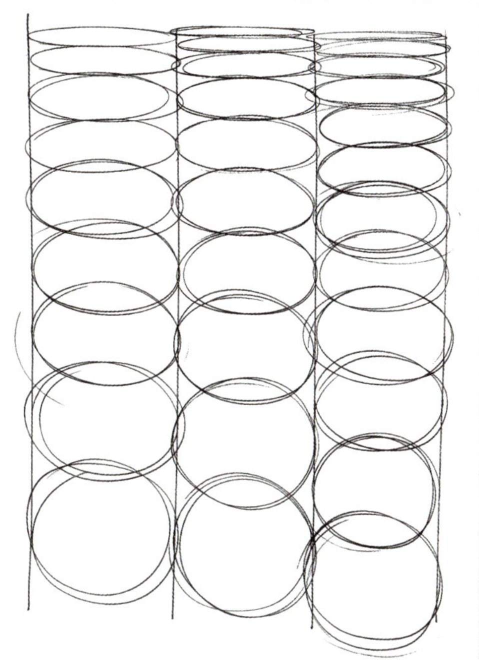

Daily Practice and Consistency

These warm-up exercises are great to do before you draw, but you also can take some time each day to practice them for practice's sake. When I was learning to draw, I would put on some music or a movie and do these exercises as much as I could. A good way to gauge your progress and check the accuracy of your lines, circles, and ellipses is by comparing them to shape templates. For instance, to help you with ellipses I've provided an example here that you can reference, or you can simply follow along with the book's photos.

Above all, remember that practice makes you better. In the following chapters, you'll find 52 exercises and challenges to practice—one for each week of the year—so, sketch every damn day. Be consistent, and you'll see the results with time.

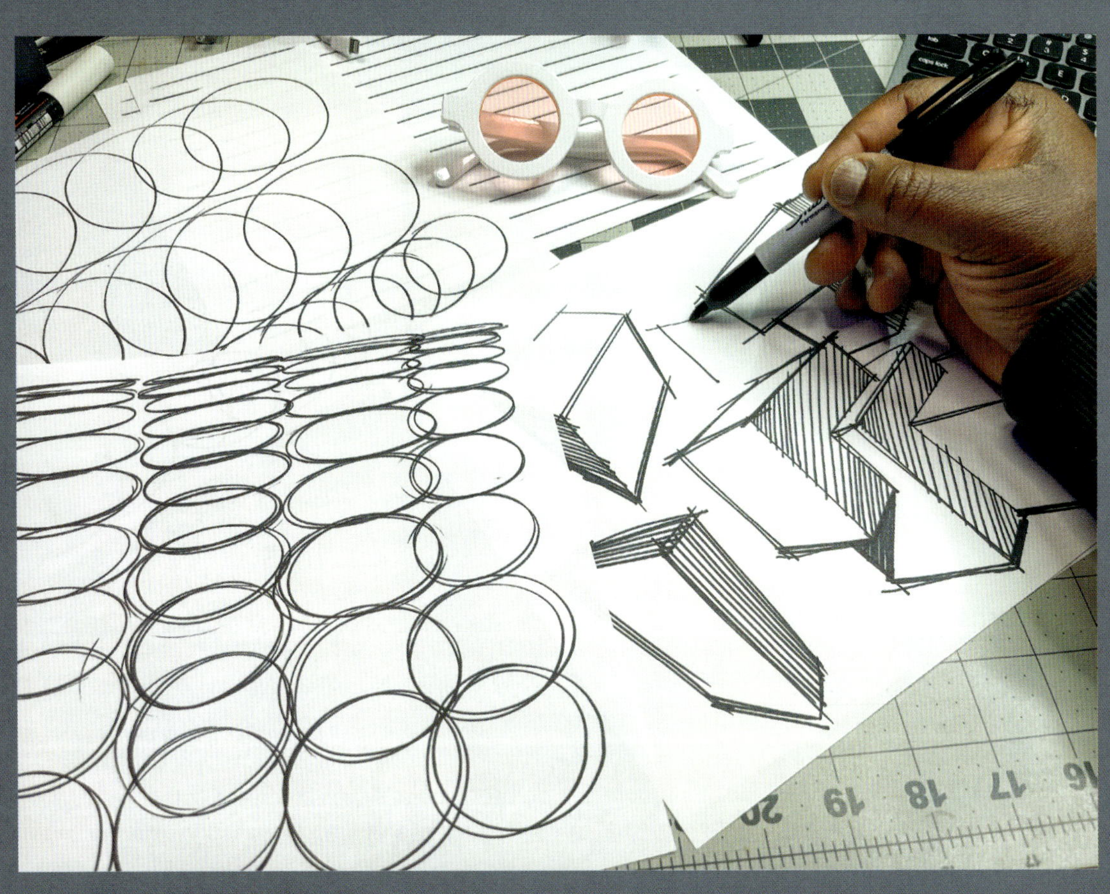

CHAPTER 1

GETTING STARTED: SKETCH WORKOUT

Think of this chapter as a bit like bootcamp. It focuses on the basic skills you need to be ready for the book's upcoming challenges. To get the most out of it, your emphasis should be on quantity and repetition. While working through these exercises and challenges, do your best but don't settle for it. Each time, push yourself to do even better than you may have done before.

As you progress and see improvement, feel free to revisit this chapter later on in your journey to practice a bit more and sharpen up. I've been drawing for most of my life, and I still find that revisiting the basics and fundamental exercises like these helps me sharpen up, improves my confidence, and helps me to think quickly, draw quickly, and be happy with the results. If I can do this, so can you. I know you can. You're here and committed, after all.

When you are challenging yourself to do something, it's important to have a vision for what you want and to commit to small steps that will get you there. Think of this chapter's exercises as your small steps leading to your vision of yourself as an accomplished artist. Remember, consistent practice will make you better, so sketch every day.

Here we go: Week 1!

A *cubescape* is a hand-drawn field of view filled with cubes in a variety of positions, and it's also the subject of your first exercise. Sketching a cubescape will help you sharpen your perspective drawing skills. Gaining a good understanding of perspective will help you draw the more complex challenges ahead in this book.

For the example, I used 8.5-by-11-inch printer paper and a Paper Mate Flair felt pen. You can use the same or choose another pen that will give you a nice crisp line. You could try this exercise with a pencil, but part of the challenge is developing confidence in your ability to start and finish lines at desired points. Completing this exercise should also help you feel more fluent and improve your hand-eye coordination when drawing.

Draw the Horizon Line

Start by drawing a horizontal line across the longest side of your paper. Position this line somewhere toward the middle of the paper vertically. This line is your horizon line. Imagine you're standing in an open field. The sky is clear, and nothing obstructs your view. Think of the horizon line as where the sky meets the earth. As objects get closer to the horizon line (and, therefore, farther from you), they appear smaller to you.

Establish Vanishing Points

Add two points on the horizon line, one on each end. These will be your vanishing points, the points to which parallel lines converge on the horizon. Label these points VP1 and VP2 or LVP and RVP. If you're new to drawing, these labels can help you keep track of where you want to draw your lines to. I tend to talk to myself while I draw, and I find this labeling helpful.

Draw the Initial Cube

Pick a point anywhere above or below your horizon line. From this point, draw a line to your left vanishing point and draw another line to your right vanishing point. Use my example as a guide.

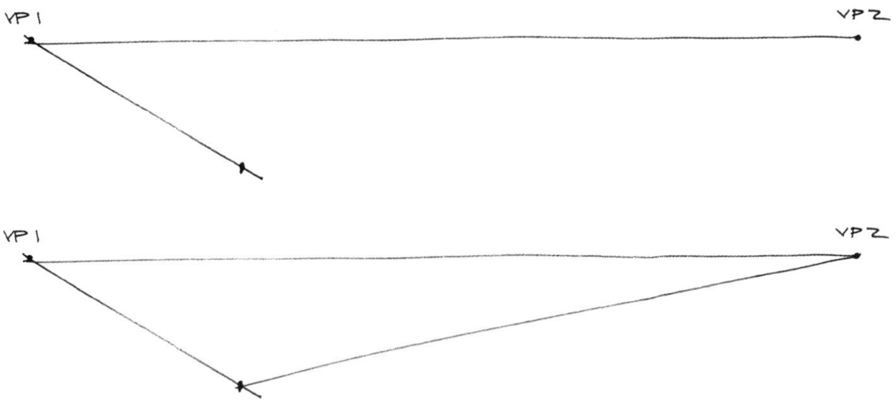

Next, draw a vertical line of any reasonable height from the first point (where your two lines now are connected to their respective vanishing points). On a letter-sized sheet of paper, for me this is about 2 inches or 50 mm. You don't want this line to be too tall as you will need additional room to draw other cubes in your cubescape. From the end of this new vertical line, draw lines that connect this point to the left vanishing point and the right vanishing point. Again, use my example as a guide.

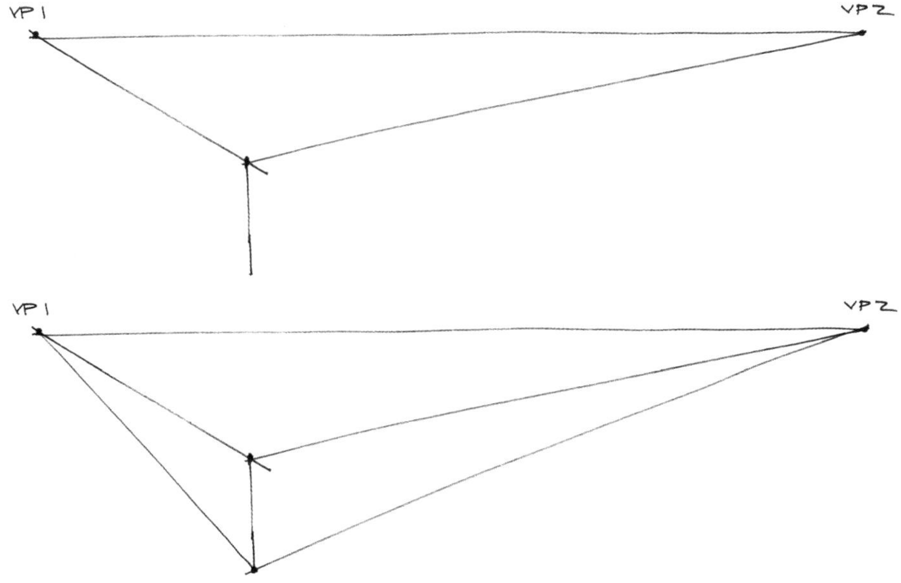

Form the Cube's Faces

Next, draw a vertical line to the right or left of the first vertical line. In the example, I drew the line to the right. Notice that this line creates the edge of a face of the soon-to-be cube. Try to estimate how far over to draw. You likely won't get this right the first time, but if you have a box in your environment, observing it can help you get used to estimating how far over to draw the line.

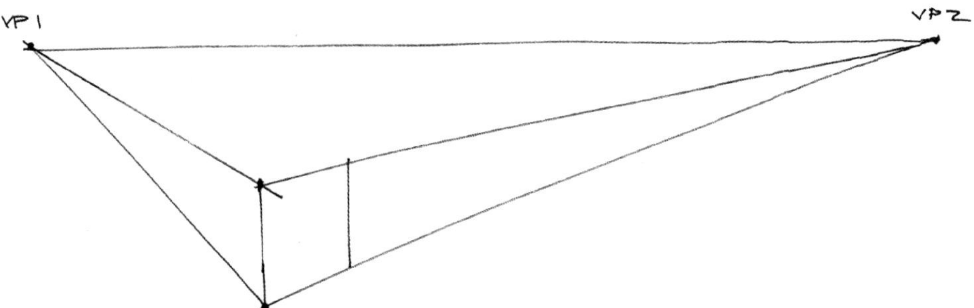

Connect the top and bottom points of your new edge to the corresponding vanishing point as shown. (I drew from the new right edge to the left vanishing point, VP1.)

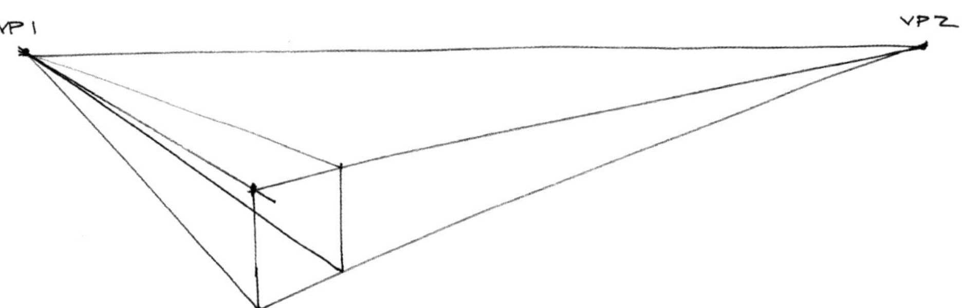

Continue by drawing another vertical line to form the other side face of the cube. You should have two new intersection points.

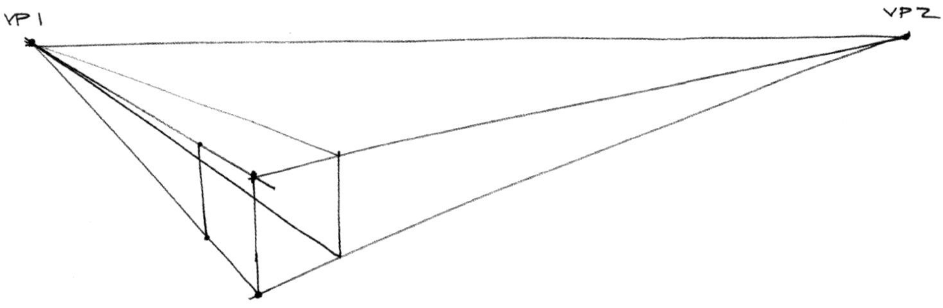

Connect these points to the corresponding vanishing point; VP2 in the example.

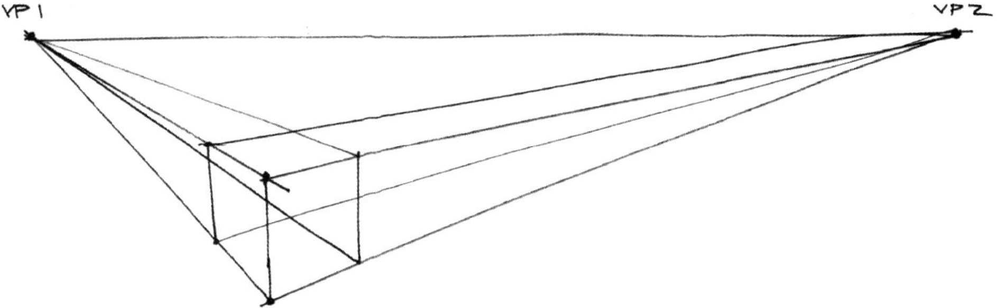

Darken the Cube's Outline

Now that you have your points of intersection, darken the outline to form your first cube.

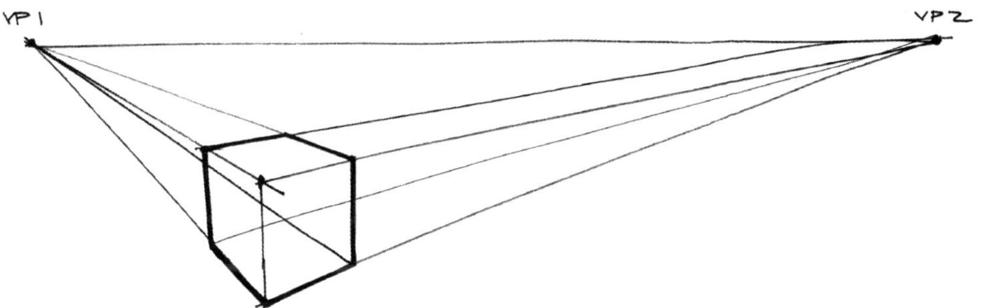

Expand the Cubescape

Continue drawing your cubescape, sketching cubes in a variety of places relative to your vanishing points and the horizon line. Although you start by drawing a cube below the horizon line, you don't have to place them all there.

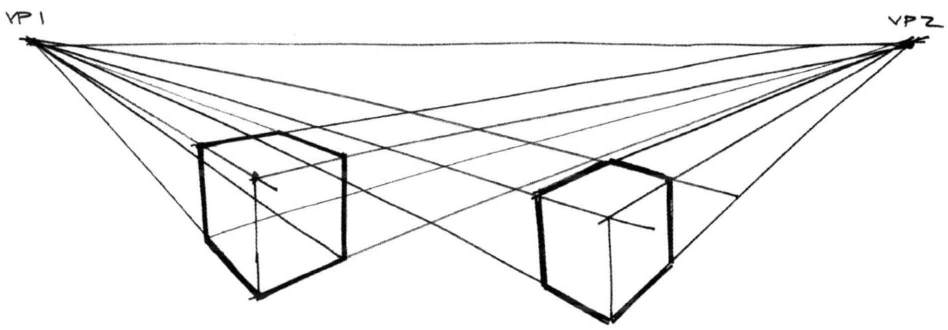

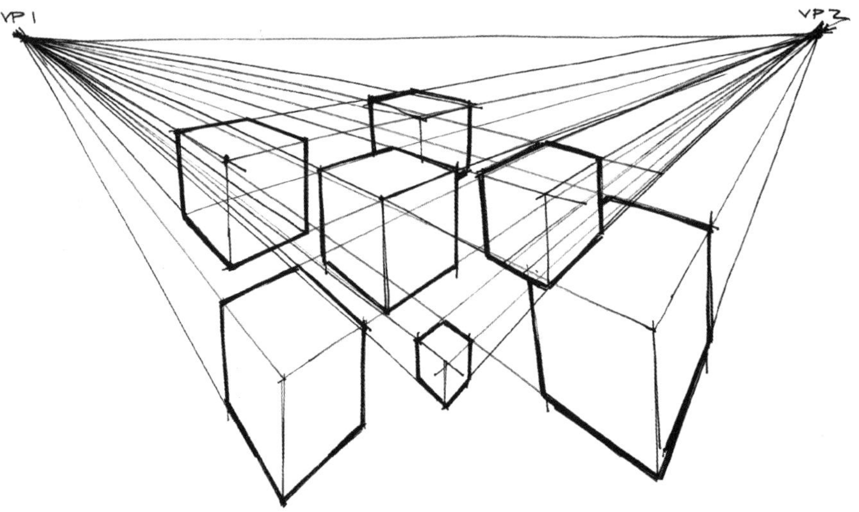

Try drawing a few above the horizon line. Repeat the process as for the first cube, just work from above rather than below the horizon.

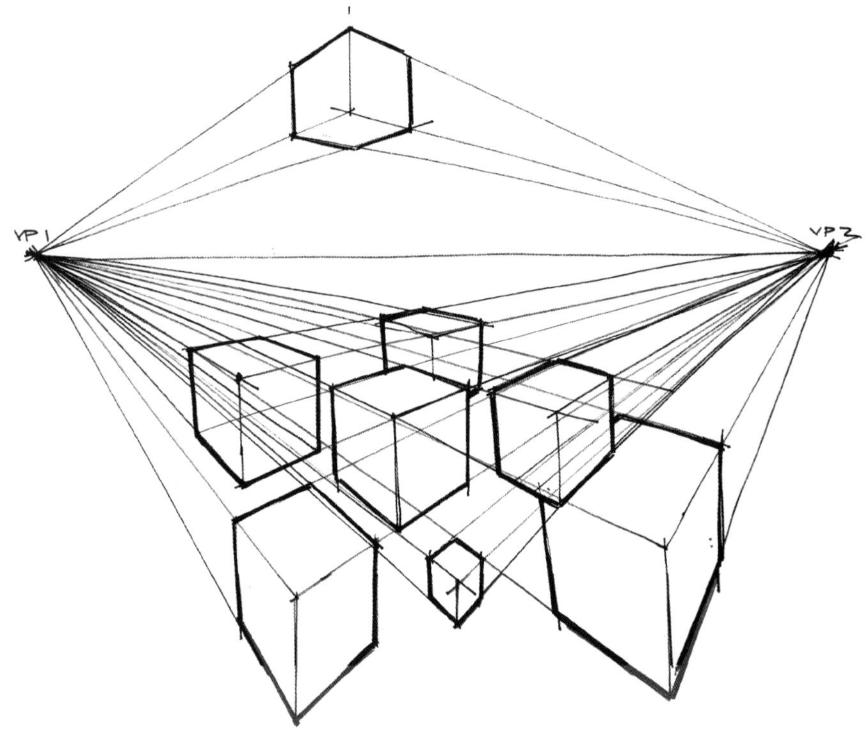

Observe Proportions and Shading

Pay attention to how the proportion of the faces of each cube changes relative to its position and distance from the vanishing points and horizon line.

Experiment with shading in one face of the cube using hatching, marker, or pencil shading to add depth to your cubes.

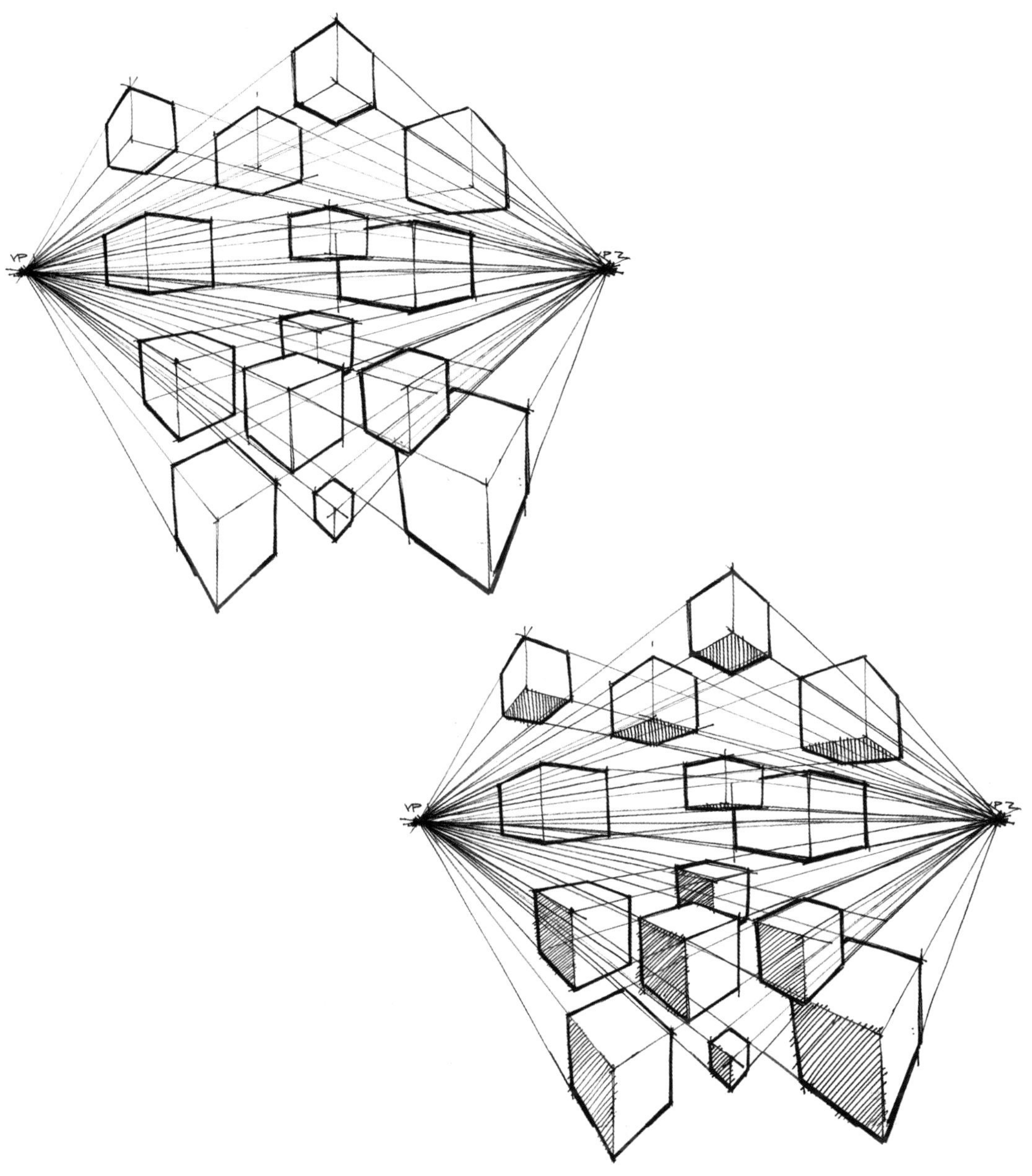

CHALLENGE

Try creating a few cubescapes of your own. Doing this will help you sharpen up your understanding of perspective and relative placement of a cube in a perspective system. If you get stuck, take a break and don't be too hard on yourself. The goal here is quantity over quality.

PROPORTION AND POV

Having the right proportion is important when sketching. How two objects look next to each other or how one object fits into a scene can make or break your sketch. In addition to proportion, point of view also affects the sense of placement and scale of elements in your drawings. Remember these tips:

- When something is drawn *below* eye level, the general feeling is that it is smaller than you, the observer.

- When something is drawn *at* eye level, the general feeling is that it is bigger than you, the observer.

- When something is drawn *above* eye level, the general feeling is that it is much bigger than you or flying above you, the observer.

Week 2's exercise is a collection of short exercises focused on *primitives*, which are the foundational shapes of most things you're going to sketch. Thinking of an object in terms of its underlying primitives makes drawing easier, because you're focusing on the building blocks of that more complex object rather than its details. I like to think of primitives as a bit like LEGO bricks, because they offer the potential to build more complex and interesting things. Like LEGO, primitives come in a variety of shapes and sizes: cones, cubes, cylinders, pyramids, and more. You can skew or transform these shapes into other shapes as well. For example, a cube has six equal faces, but you can build other objects from a cube by stretching or twisting it. Not only are primitives important, but you must draw them with the proper perspective as well. It's time to practice.

Fanning

This first exercise isn't so much a shape as an important technique to create the illusion of depth on a page. Think of railroad tracks for a minute: The rails are parallel, but as they stretch away from you towards the distant horizon, they appear to get closer together. In perspective drawing, you can mimic this effect by drawing straight lines that suggest they will converge to a singular point on your horizon line. Drawing lines this way is called *fanning lines*.

Practice fanning lines by drawing a series of lines that appear to converge at a single point. Do not draw the lines until they *do* meet (as you did in Exercise 1), but rather draw them in a way that suggests they will eventually meet. After you've drawn your lines, see where they intersect by extending your lines with the help of a ruler or by drawing them freehand. I find that using a different colored pen is useful here in showing the meeting of the lines as they are extended.

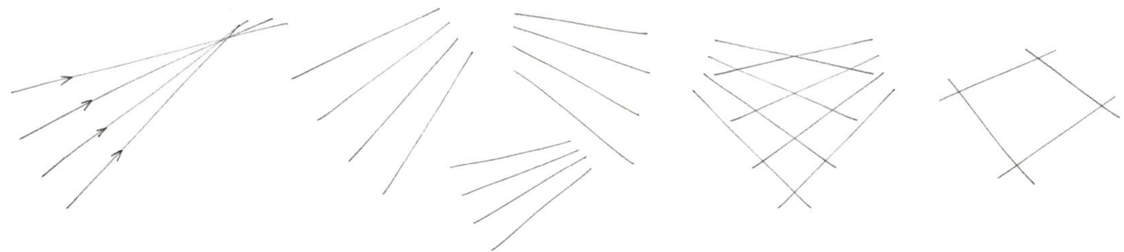

Cube

To begin a cube, draw four lines that intersect to form a diamond shape on your paper. This will be the top of your cube.

Opposite line pairs should appear to converge slightly to give the effect of perspective. If you were to extend them, they would meet at a vanishing point like the lines you drew in the cubescape. Remember, in perspective drawing, objects that are closer to you will appear larger than objects further away.

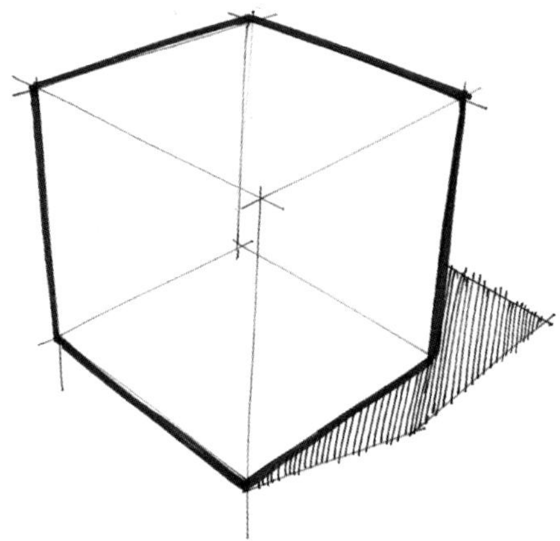

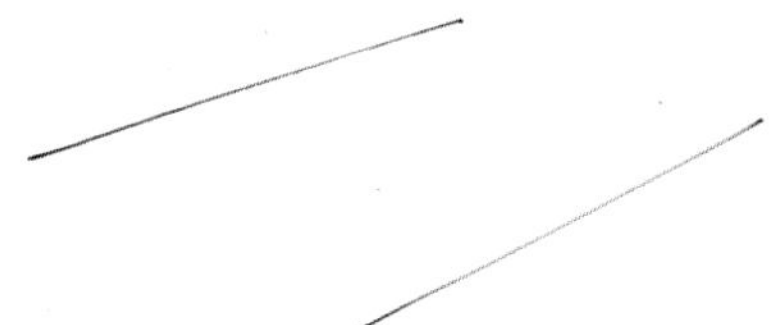

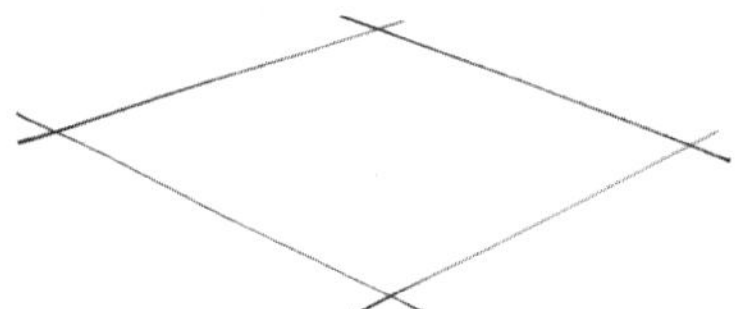

Next, draw three lines downward on your paper. Notice in the example that these lines appear to converge as well. This is the beginning of a three-point perspective cube.

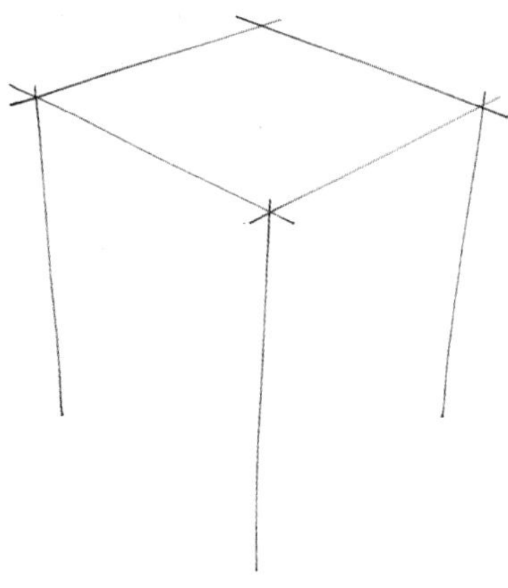

Draw through the top of your cube as well as complete the bottom portion of your cube by drawing another diamond shape. Remember, opposite line pairs should not be perfectly parallel but instead should appear as though they would eventually converge to a single point on either side of the cube. Look back at Exercise 1 if you need help visualizing this.

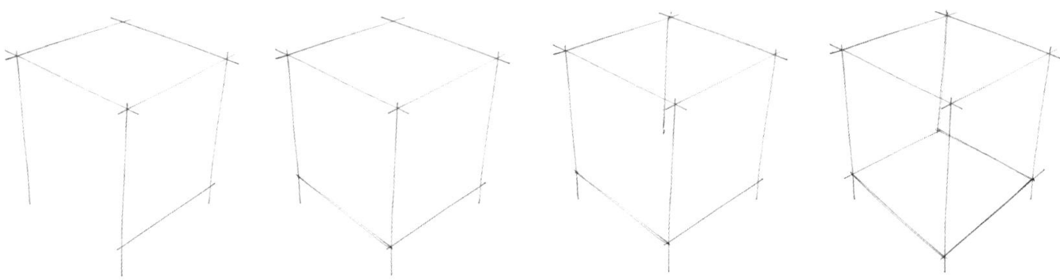

When you have completed drawing your wireframe for the cube, add some line weight. Draw a thicker line at the bottom of the cube, and then draw around the cube with the same heavier line weight. This will give your cube some presence on the page as well as help clean up any stray lines that you may have sketched.

To complete your cube, add a shadow by sketching in the projected shape of the cube onto an imaginary ground plane. You can then hatch or shade in the shadow with a series of parallel lines.

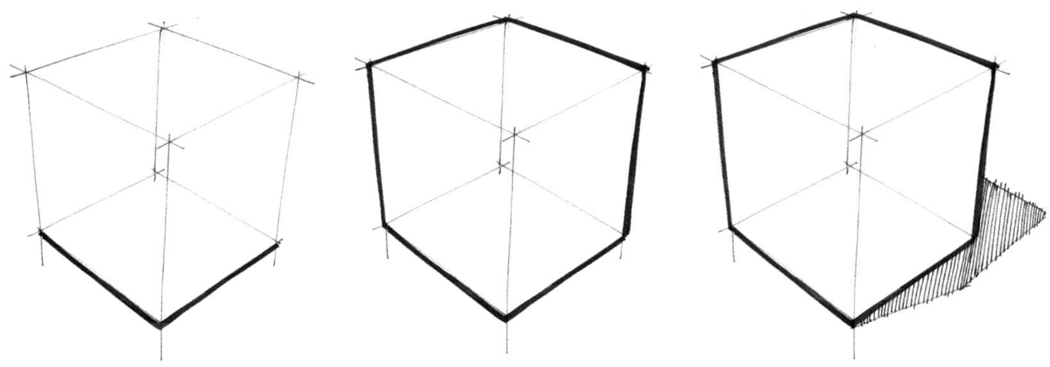

Cylinder

Before you draw a cylinder, let's review how ellipses work. As you remember from the Introduction, ellipses are simply circles viewed in perspective, and depending on the relative position of the circle to you, the ellipse may seem narrower and tighter or more open and wider. The top and bottom of a cylinder (like the Introduction's soup can) are parallel ellipses.

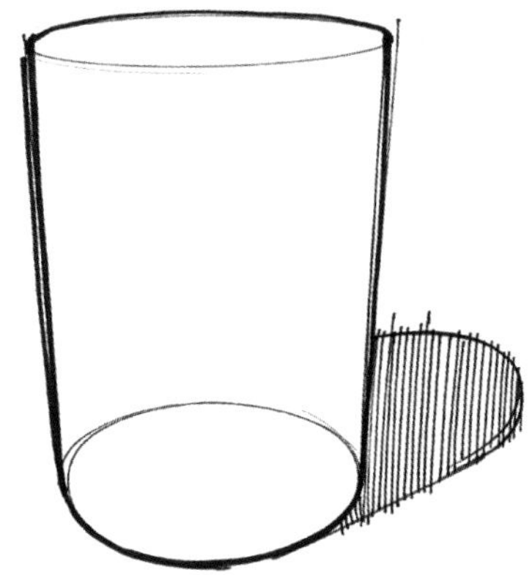

The minor axis of a cylinder's top ellipse (the shortest distance across its center) forms the top of a virtual line (or axis) that runs down the center of your cylinder and ends with the minor axis of the cylinder's bottom ellipse. Draw an ellipse as the top of your cylinder. Below it, draw the cylinder's bottom: a second ellipse that is parallel to but a bit wider than the first. The distance between them will be the height of your cylinder. (For more ellipse tips, see Warmup 3.)

Add the sides of the cylinder: Draw a vertical line from one end of the top ellipse to the corresponding point on the bottom ellipse, and then do the same on the other side. The lines should be tangent to the ends of each ellipse's major axis (longest distance across the center). Finish up by adding some line weight, and your cylinder is finished. Just like for the cube, feel free to add a shadow by sketching and shading in the region for the shadow.

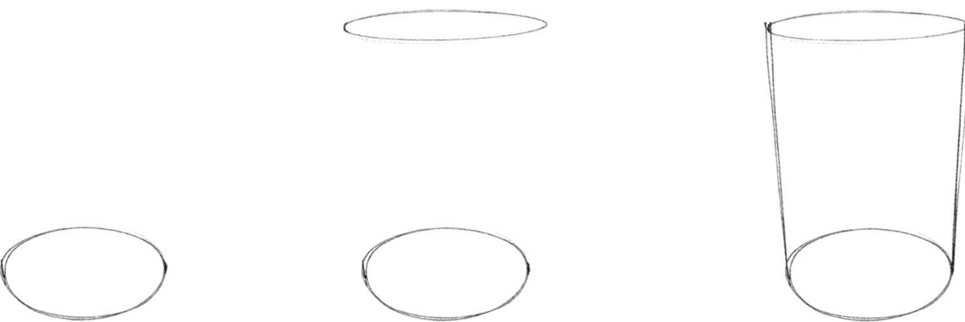

Pyramid

For a pyramid, draw a diamond shape to start. As for the cube, this diamond shape should have line pairs that appear to converge to common vanishing points to the left and the right in the distance. (If you're struggling to draw lines that appear to converge, practice the Fanning exercise above.) To find the center of this diamond face, draw lines from each corner to its opposite, creating an X in the shape. Where the lines intersect is the center of the diamond.

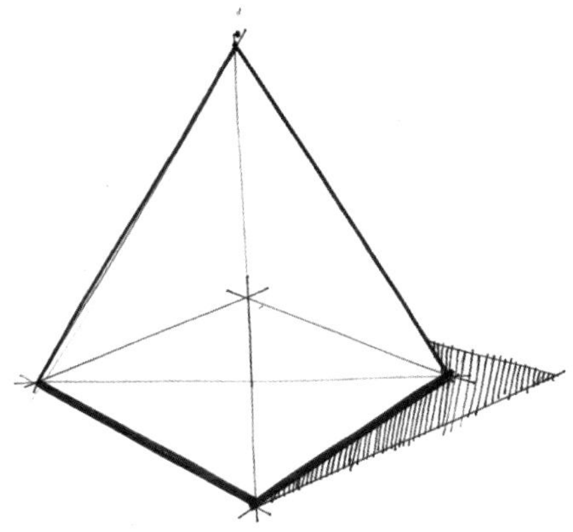

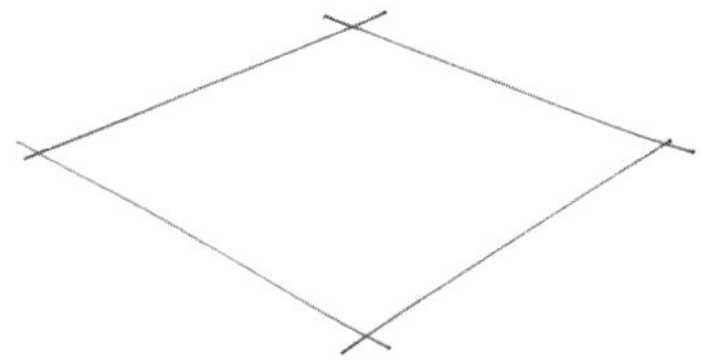

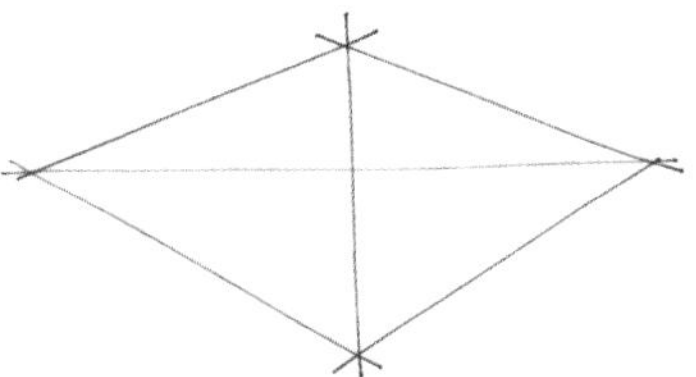

Draw a line from this center point upwards and away from the diamond. The line's top will be the tip of your pyramid, so draw the line as tall as you'd like. Connect the tip of the pyramid to each of the corners of the diamond shape.

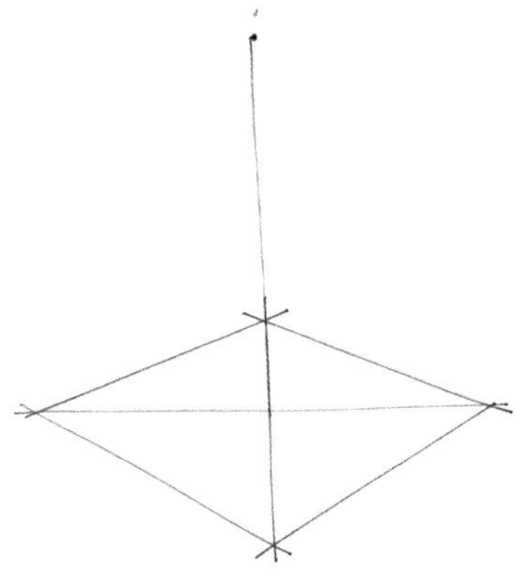

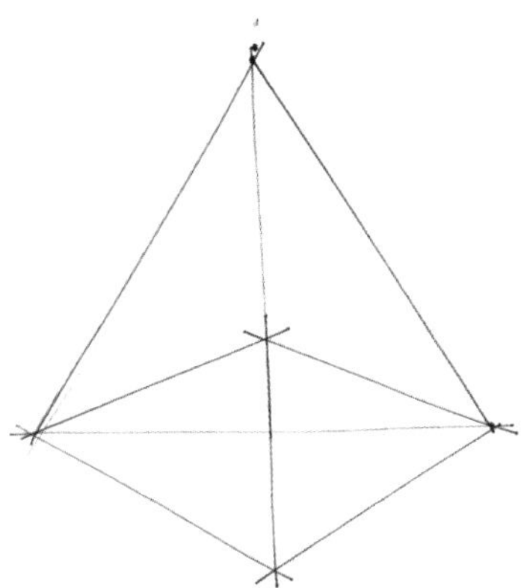

Add some line weight to help the pyramid pop on the page—have fun with it. You can apply this to the pyramid's outline with a separate pen or by simply drawing repeatedly in the same spot to thicken your line. Add a shadow, if you like.

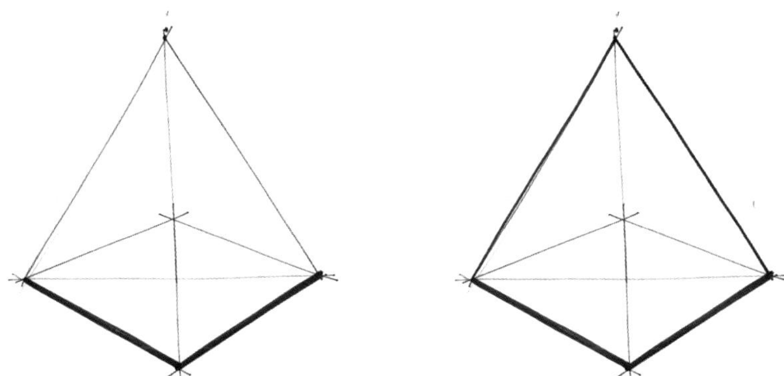

Cone

Drawing a cone is similar to drawing a cylinder with one key difference: The sides of a cone converge from a circular face (represented by an ellipse on your paper) to one point like a pyramid.

Draw an ellipse and locate its center (where the minor axis and major axis intersect). Next, draw a line from the center away from the ellipse. Pick a point that will represent the height of your cylinder and draw two lines from that point to the ends of your ellipse. As for the cylinder, these lines should be tangent and blend into the base.

Add an outline with more line weight for your cylinder, using either a separate tool or by repeatedly drawing in the same place to get a thicker line. Add a shadow to help ground and locate your cone on the page.

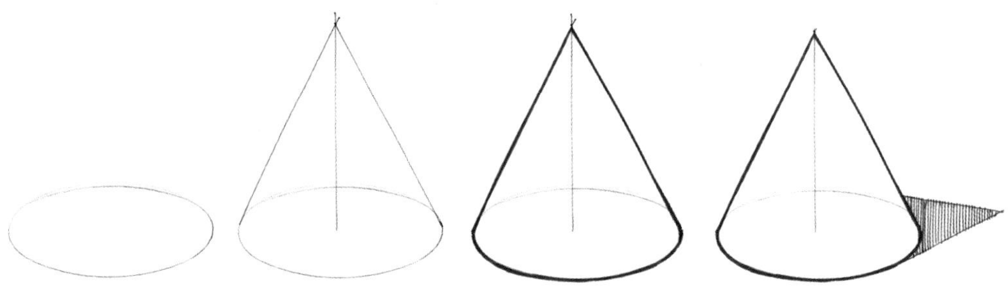

Sphere

Spheres are easy to draw, because a sphere is simply a circle when drawn in perspective. So, draw a circle. To give that circle dimension, you need to add shading, which can be tricky. One of the best ways to learn is by observation. Find a ball or other spherical object and pay attention to how the light hits its surface. The portion of the sphere that's closest to the light source will have a highlight. As you move along the surface of the sphere away from the light source, notice the *shadow core* (a slightly shadowed dark area) that appears.

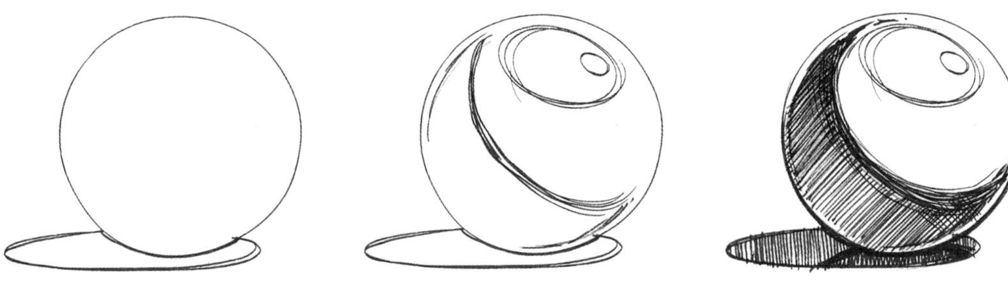

Drawing with a pencil is a great way to emulate this effect. If you're using a pen, take a moment to get creative and see if you can mimic this effect by shading with your pen.

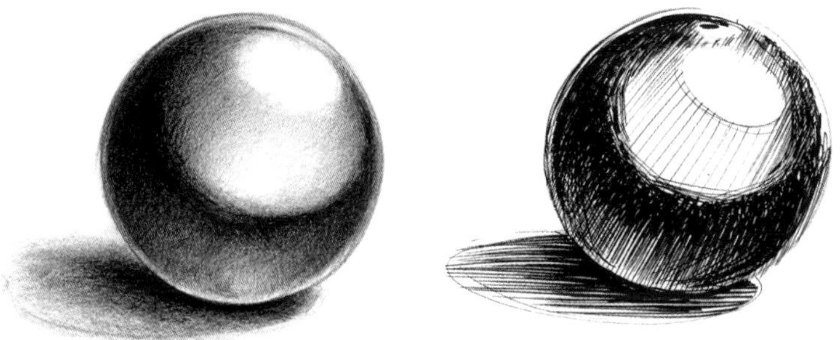

CHALLENGE

This week, focus on primitives. Primitives are the building blocks to more complex things. Pay attention to the objects around you and try to identify the primitives that compose them. Use the included images as references or find some objects that you can draw to practice first. Before you know it, you'll be seeing spheres, cylinders, pyramids, cones, and cubes every-where you look.

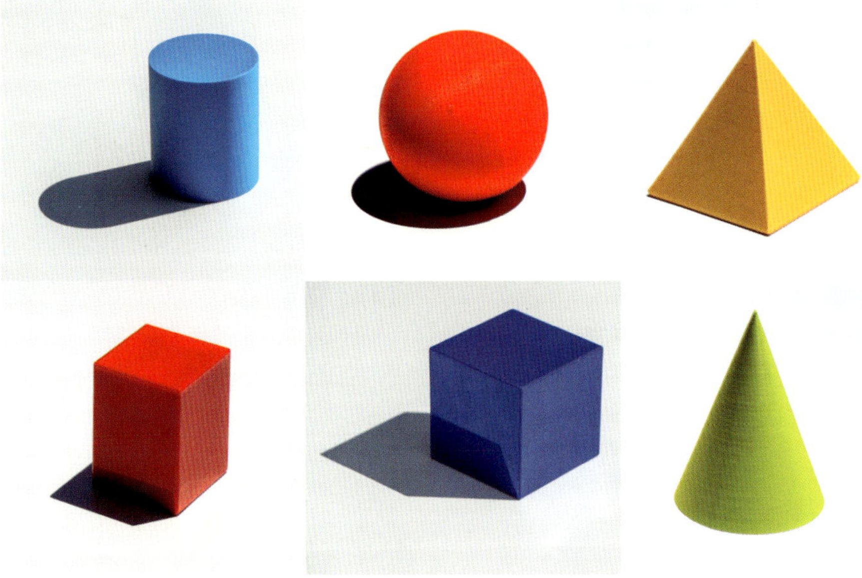

Combining forms is a great way to practice fundamental perspective drawing skills, point of view, and proportion, as well as to help you understand how to create more complex objects. Start small and try building from simple to more complex combinations.

Although you can complete this exercise with a pencil or even a ballpoint pen, challenge yourself by using a felt pen that will give you a solid line. A pen that never forgets will make you sweat, or something like that. My point is to have fun and push yourself to work with your mistakes. One of my tricks for corrections is to draw another line just as confidently as the first. At the end of my drawing, I resketch or add a heavier outline to clean up.

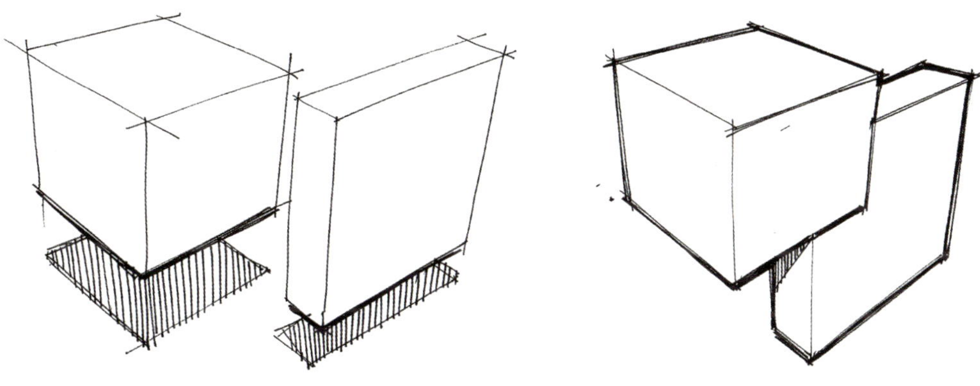

Decide on the forms you want to combine, then grab your pen and sketch these primitive objects separately. This will help you better understand the composition of your component parts. In the example, I sketched two rectilinear primitive objects (boxes) that differ in proportion (shown on next page). Combining these objects will create a new, more visually complex form with its own proportion and feel.

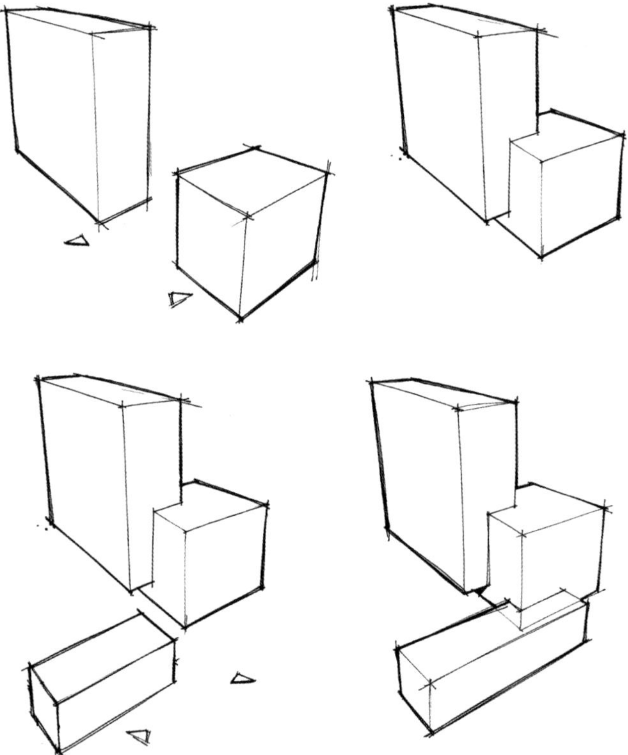

Now, draw your primitives in the combination you visualized. As you work, imagine the pieces moving together and intersecting. You can add, subtract, or intersect each form to create a new one. In the example, I added primitive curvilinear objects together to create new objects. Continuing to add objects will give you more complexity as well as test your ability to draw with more complex perspective setups.

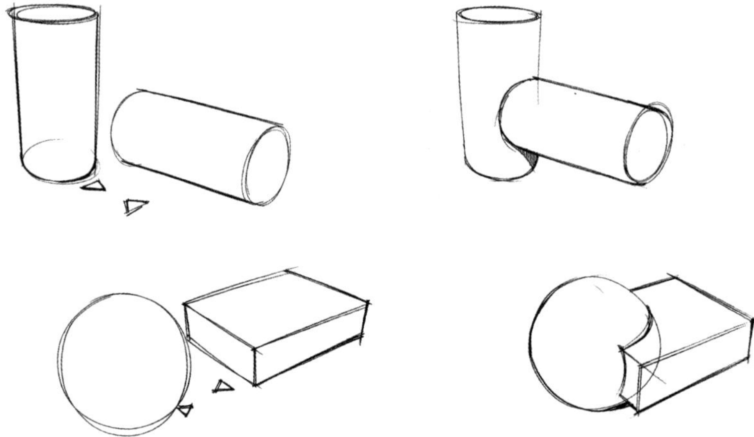

CHALLENGE

Experiment with drawing simple primitives in a variety of positions, then try combining a few of them. What might they look like when you subtract one object from another? What might they look like when you draw the intersection of the objects with each other?

PERSPECTIVE

Perspective is the visual effect of scale, color, and lighting relative to the position of an object and yourself. To help you draw in perspective effectively, here are a few tips to remember:

- Things closer to you will appear larger.

- Straight lines will converge as they approach the horizon.

- Think about the point of view and relative position of the horizon line.

- For lighting and contrast, darkest darks against lightest lights will communicate depth.

- Minor axes in ellipses will always follow the receding perspective line (central axis of a 3D object pointing towards the horizon).

- The degree of an ellipse is the relative angle between your eyes and the position of the planar profile of the ellipse.

When sketching objects of any kind, it's important to consider the point of view in which you wish to sketch that object. As you remember, point of view refers to the relative position of the artist or viewer to the drawing's subject. Point of view influences how you draw an object (think of the soup can lid) and can help convey scale, place, or context. In this exercise, you'll practice sketching a simple object from multiple points of view. Later in the book, you'll build on this foundation to draw more complex objects from a desired point of view.

Rotate a Box

For the example, I drew a progression of a simple box as it is rotated to the right and downward, relative to the viewer. To start a similar point of view progression, draw the first box in the upper-left corner. Next, rotate your box to the right along the vertical axis and draw it from this new point of view. Repeat this step as many times as you want phases in your progression. I drew four, but you can do more, if you like.

For the second row, again rotate the box to the right, but also rotate it down along the horizontal axis. In each new point of view you draw this time, you will be able to see more of the top of the box. Repeat this exercise again a third or fourth time by changing the vantage point in a progressively different way. As a bonus, add some hatching or shading to one side of each box to communicate depth and dimension.

As you draw each box, pay attention to proportion but don't get hung up on exactness. The focus of this exercise is to tune your eye and your hands to be able to draw from different points of view.

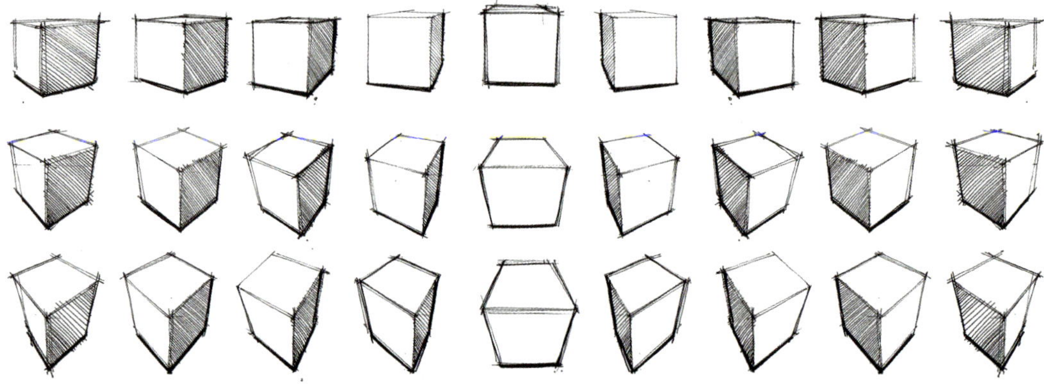

Point of View and Complex Objects

Take a look at how the exercise's concepts apply to a more complex object. Here I sketched a simple camera concept with a few details. In any given view, you're able to see only a limited portion of the object's many aspects. By using different points of view, you can show, hide, or emphasize certain features, leading the viewer to interpret your idea or sketch in different ways.

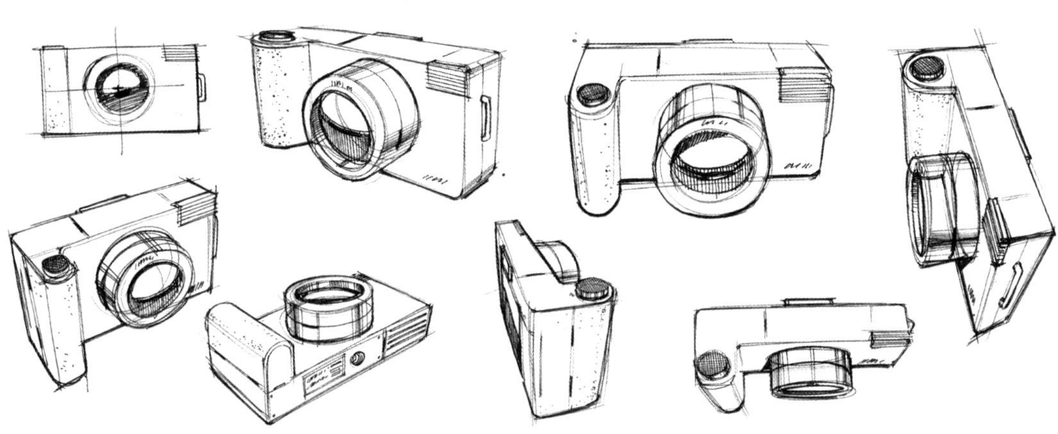

For example, with a more straight-on view, the viewer can see the details on the front of the camera but not the back. Even those details are somewhat simple. To communicate the depth of elements on the front or the camera's overall thickness, you'd need to sketch it from a different angle. Similarly, rotating the object and sketching a point of view that shows some of the camera's back can help communicate more about the camera. Sometimes it may be useful as well to sketch your object in an unfamiliar point of view in an effort to evoke certain emotions from your viewer. My example sketches combine to create a composition that shows many angles and aspects of this camera concept, enabling the viewer to gain a greater appreciation for the details, proportion, and elements that are unique to this model.

CHALLENGE

Pick an object and sketch it from multiple vantage points. This challenge will provide practice drawing from different angles, sharpen your perspective skills, and help you work on consistency from one view to the other. Pay close attention to where things are located, as well as their proportion, size, scale, and placement within your idea. If you are drawing from reference, pay attention to those details as well and try to be consistent across views. As you think about your composition, play with the placement and scale of items. If you mess up, don't get discouraged, just keep pushing through. Remember, these are sketches. They're not meant to be instant classics or masterpieces. Relax, and have fun with the process.

DETAIL

Deciding how much detail to include in a sketch can be tricky. When sketching, I try to balance the complexity of details with the overall appearance of what I am sketching. Sometimes, especially for objects drawn to appear distant, it is better to show a gesture of a texture or detail rather than a minutely accurate depiction. If you need to show detail for a part of a sketch, consider creating a new sketch that zooms in on the area you would like to showcase.

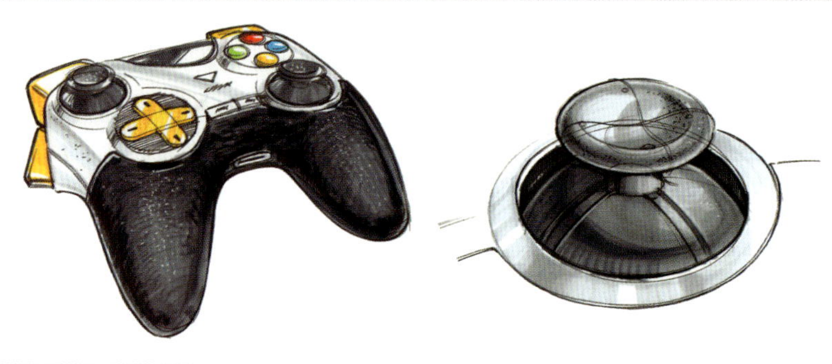

  SKETCH EVERY DAMN DAY

When you're sketching, how you use materials, color, and texture are important parts of conveying your ideas—especially when you layer these elements with perspective. In this exercise, I'll show you how to apply three materials to three cubes using some simple tools. I used a Paper Mate Flair pen and recommend you try the same or similar pen that gives you a whole line. After you try my examples, you can expand the exercise by thinking of ways that you could create versions of real textures using simple strokes or shading in your sketches.

Sketch the Basic Shapes

Start by sketching three cubes on a page. You can make these cubes the same size or different sizes. It's entirely up to you. (If you're already thinking of other materials to try, feel free to sketch an additional cube or two.)

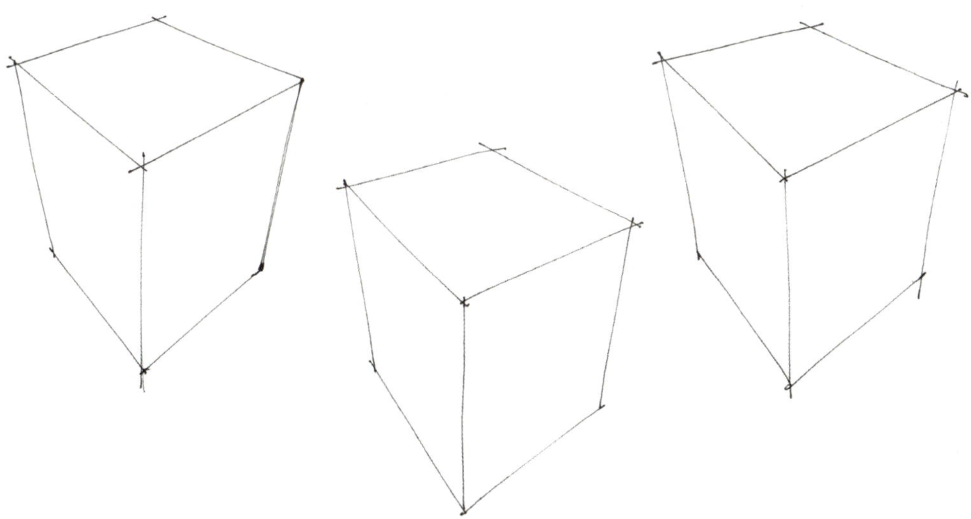

Create the Wood Grain

Next, identify key characteristics of each material you plan to apply to the cubes: wood, a shiny finish, and concrete. Let's start with wood. A cross section of wood will show annular rings on one face, and you can trace down each side from the corresponding ring where it intersects the edges of the cube on the top toward the bottom of the cube. This creates the beginning of a wood grain effect.

Create the Shiny Finish

I applied the shiny finish to the cube in the middle. When observing similar finishes in real life, notice that the smooth, polished surface acts like a mirror. To mimic this, include outlines for reflections on each cube face. In the example, I used straight lines, but you can get creative with the shape of your reflective areas.

Create the Concrete Finish

The third cube gets the concrete finish. For the example, I identified slight cracks as a key characteristic of that material. Add a few of these to your sketch to convey a sense of the material without having to do too much more lifting. Be sure to sketch lightly if you're not 100% sure about what you're doing. To do so, use the fine tip of your pen or a smaller, detailed pen to sketch these initial steps.

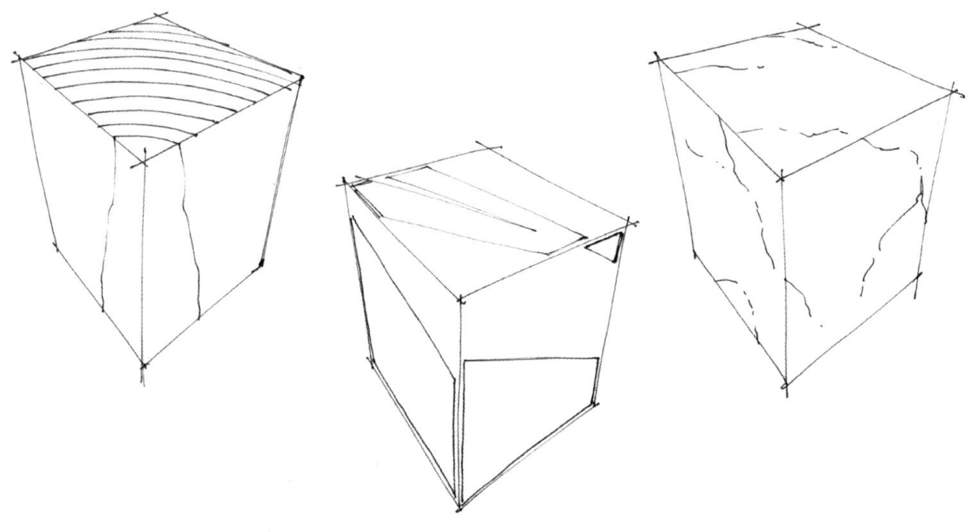

Detail the Wood Cube

Next, head back to the wood cube, and continue filling in the grain. Notice in the example that I hatched and shaded the center of the wood a bit. This darker area represents the heartwood center of a cross section of wood like this. Try to draw each grain line in an organic way that shows the grain corresponds with the wood's rings. For added effect, I added a few defects in the grain and shaded in one side of the cube as well with hatch lines.

Add Reflections to the Shiny Cube

Pay attention to objects around your environment, watching how the reflections change as you move an object. Now think about your shiny cube's environment and add some similar reflection effects. I imagined that the example shiny cube was in an environment that has some amount of black in it because I was using only pens. If you imagine your cube in proximity to something of a different color, add that color to the region I made black instead to get a similar effect. For more help with reflections, check out my book, *The Perspective Drawing Guide.*

Add Details to the Concrete Cube

The faces of the concrete cube need shading. Taking the direction of the light source into consideration, give each face different values. On mine, I drew squiggles with the very fine tip of a fine liner pen. Alternatively, you could select a pen with an even finer tip to execute this step. Notice that the spacing of the squiggles (closer together or farther apart) gives three distinct values to the faces of the concrete cube.

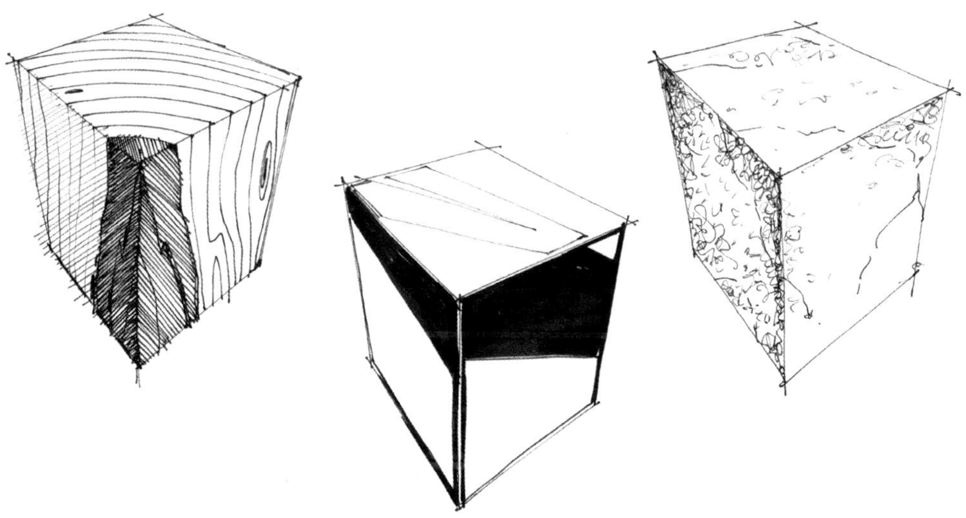

Enhance the Wood Cube

Making one last pass on the wood cube, continue to add details. For example, shade in each side of the cube left to right, making one side slightly darker. I am assumed that a light source was illuminating this cube so as to cast a shadow on the left side. I also included some additional details in the wood grain to suggest some separation in the grain and to help the block of wood feel more organic. If you like, add line weight to the outside of the block to reinforce its overall volume and shape.

Refine the Shiny Cube

Continue refining the polished cube's reflections by filling in dark areas and adding artifacts in those reflections to represent other objects in the environment or variations in the light source's reflection. It may seem counterintuitive to not shade the sides of this cube. When you look at a shiny cube, however, you will notice this pattern of reflections and the artifacts that are created as a result of each face being polished.

Finalize the Concrete Cube

For the concrete cube, continue shading each side by adding hatch marks and enhancing the squiggles. For the outline of this block, I chose to introduce some shorter strokes to make the block feel more natural and less perfect.

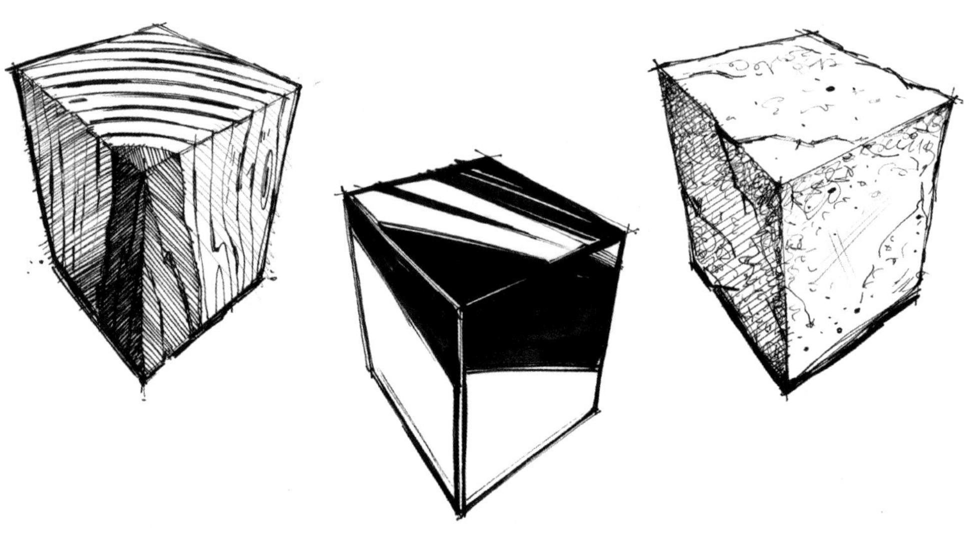

Additional Examples

You can apply simple texture effects to create a wide variety of materials, as these three additional examples illustrate. The block shaded with equally spaced straight lines could be indicative of a different type of wood or perhaps textured plastic. The middle cube could be a metal box with scratches, rusty areas, and rivets. The details help convey the material for this particular sketch. Using the squiggle shade method, you can create a texture reminiscent of a sponge, as in the third cube.

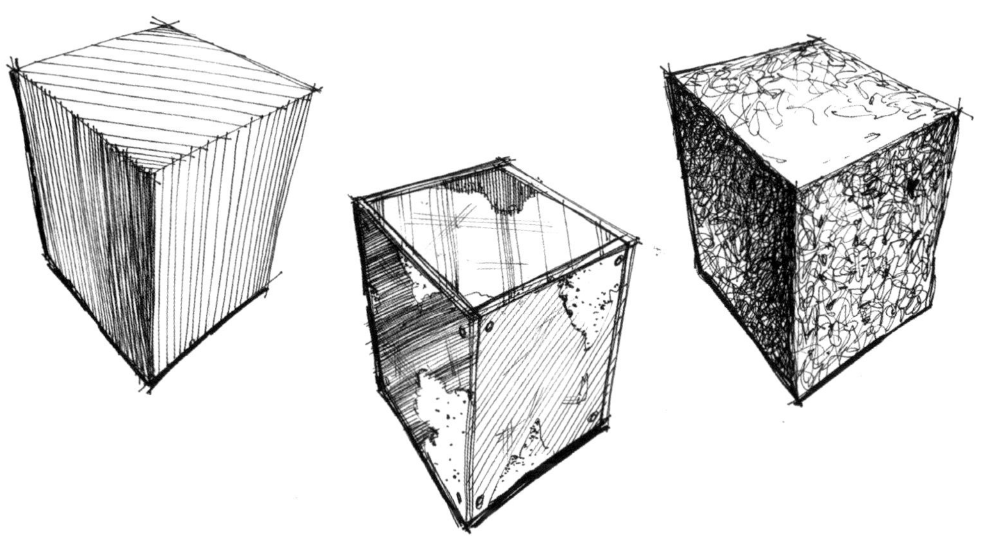

CHALLENGE

Get creative with materials and apply them to a variety of objects. Practice using simple primitives (cubes, cylinders, spheres, cones, and pyramids) to reduce the complexity of the object so you can focus more on creating the textures. If you're uncomfortable sketching in perspective at this point, you can also practice creating textures by filling in squares or other two-dimensional shapes to get the hang of using your pen to create the texture. So, get sketching, have fun with it, and remember to sketch every damn day.

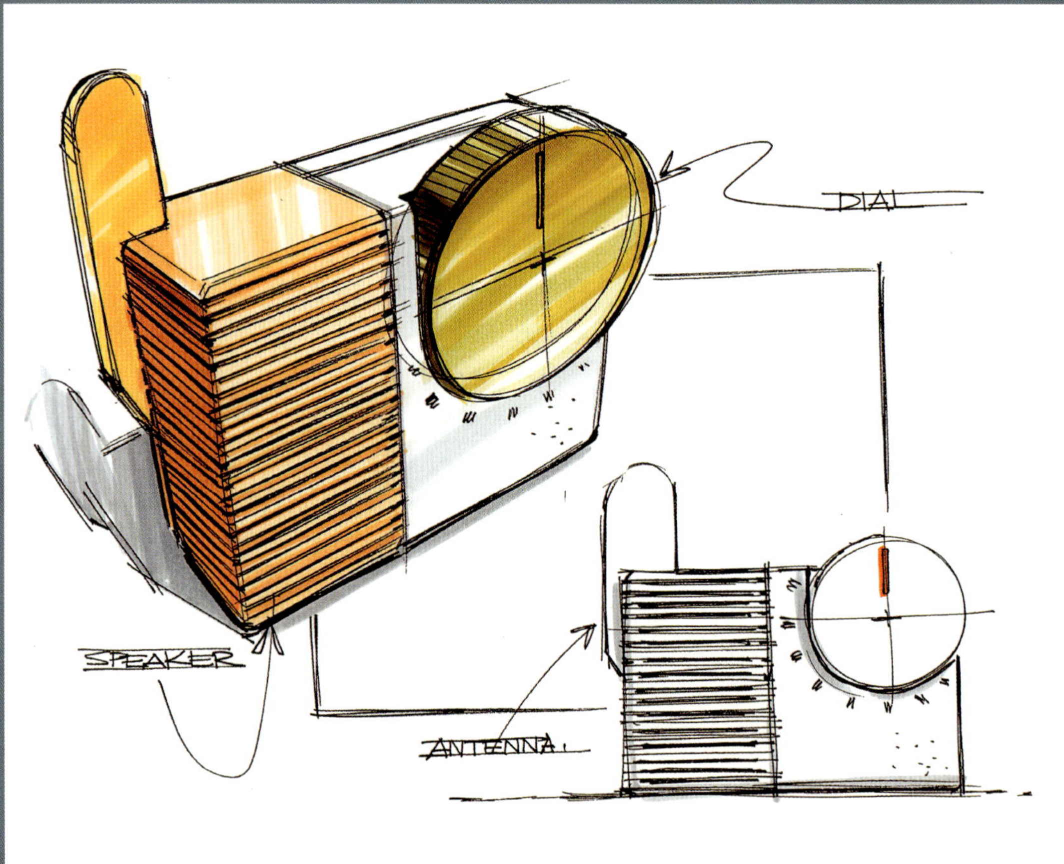

DIAL
SPEAKER
ANTENNA

CHAPTER 2

BASIC PERSPECTIVE

In this chapter, you get a chance to level up your perspective drawing skills, as well as practice creating complex objects from primitives. As we've discussed, perspective drawing is simply the way you geometrically represent three-dimensional reality on a two-dimensional piece of paper. As when you used shading to turn a flat circle into a convincing sphere, perspective drawing uses principles based on observed geometric effects related to how we see the world around us. Unless you take precise measurements, scale them accurately, and render them exactly, your drawings will be representative rather than literal, which is fine if you're drawing for enjoyment rather than commercial design.

For this chapter, simply focus on the quantity and quality of your drawings. The more you draw and the more you practice, the more accurate you will get. Trust the process and keep pushing through.

Perspective Principles Recap

As we discussed in Chapter 1, perspective drawing enables you to add depth and a realistic point of view to your work. Here are a few key tips to help you in this chapter and beyond:

- Things close to you will appear larger on paper (and in real life) than things further away from you. Parallel lines that recede into the distance in 3D space taper to a common point (a vanishing point) along the horizon line.

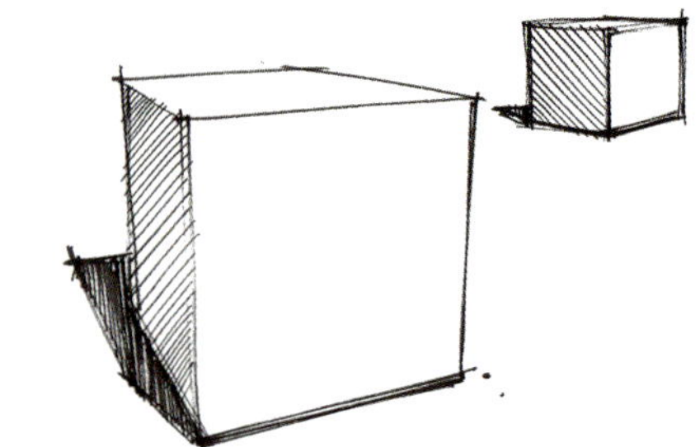

- Vertical lines, if parallel, will taper to a common point as they grow more distant as well, if you are drawing in a three-point perspective.

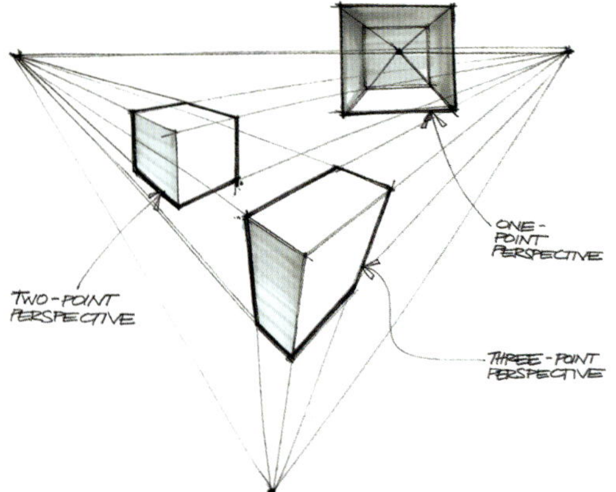

- Think about the point of view you're depicting and the relative position of the viewer and subject to the horizon line.

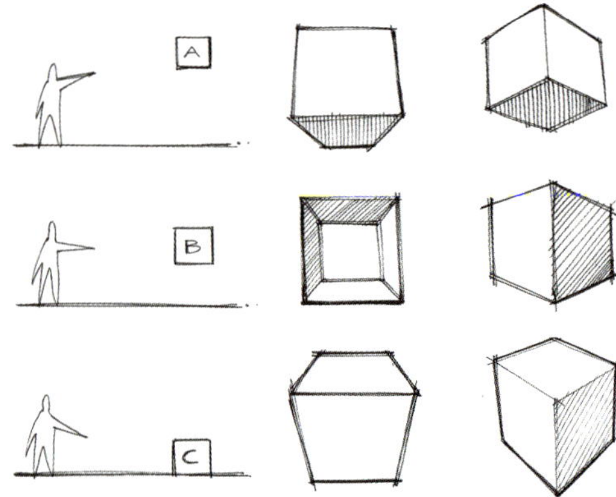

- Communicate depth through lighting and sharp contrast.

- The minor axis of an ellipse always follows the receding perspective line.

- The degree of an ellipse is the relative angle between your eyes and the position of the planar profile of the ellipse. Think of it as how narrow or wide the top of a soup can or glass might look at close to eye level versus a bit lower than eye level.

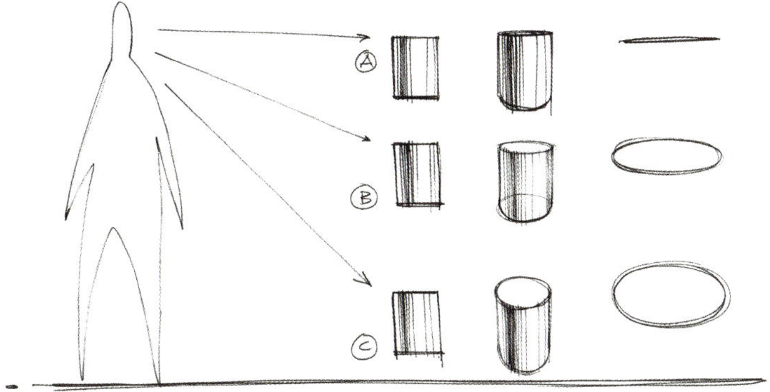

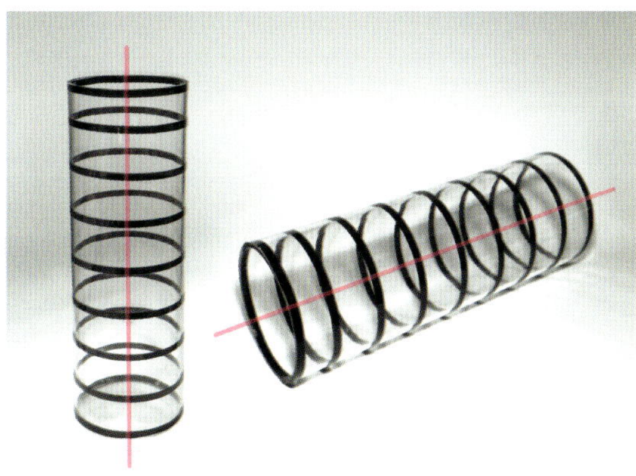

For Week 6, you'll focus on sharpening your perspective and line work skills by drawing a hammer. Perspective and line quality are fundamental to having good sketches that communicate your idea or concept so that others can understand what you're doing. Make sure to pick a tool that you are comfortable with, but more importantly, make sure to pick a tool that will give you a whole line. For the example, I used a Paper Mate Flair pen, which is one of my favorite pens to sketch with. Take some time to revisit your warm-up exercises and get ready to sketch.

Locate Your Subject on the Page

First, establish on your paper where you want to draw your hammer, and draw a vertical line with a couple of lines across it to mark the top and bottom of the hammer.

Place another line at the top to indicate the directionality of the hammer (mine will face towards the right). These lines will serve as a guide as you sketch, so pay attention to your reference points once you have chosen them.

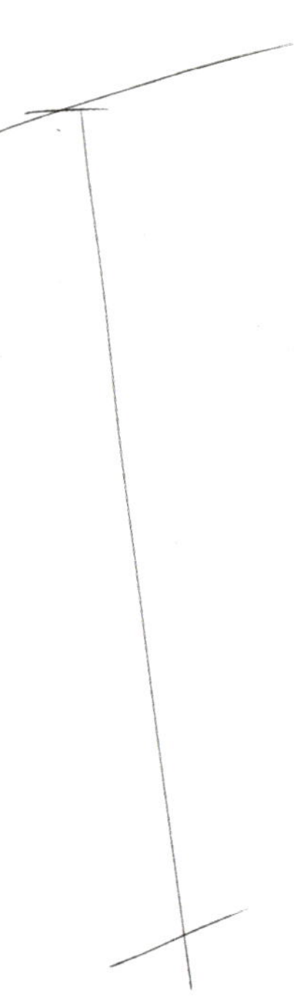

Build Your Scaffold

The next step is to create scaffolding around your concept. *Scaffolding* refers to lines and other elements that start to build out the shape of the object. Following the example, sketch in rectangles to represent the flat strike area of the hammer, the head, as well as an indication of the claw. Along the vertical line, draw shapes that represent cross sections of the neck and handle.

By representing the size and shape of a three-dimensional slice of your object, these cross sections will help you antici-pate how you will have to draw the next lines. Notice that the cross sections I drew respect the relative size of the hammer at key points, as well as indicate its ergonomic shape.

Sketch in straight lines and arcs to connect your cross sections, making sure the lines are tangent to the outside of your shapes. Don't worry too much about getting your sketch perfect. Focus on sketching quickly and decisively as much as possible.

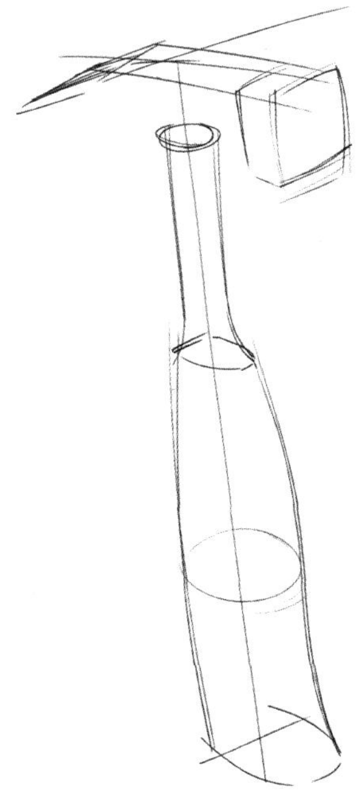

Build Out the Overall Shape

Continue to build out the shape of the hammer. Adding curves and reemphasizing lines helps bring out the tool's overall form, and it's starting to look more like a real object. If you're not sure about what details to add to a hammer or need a better sense of an ergonomic handle's shape, take a look at a real hammer or some reference images.

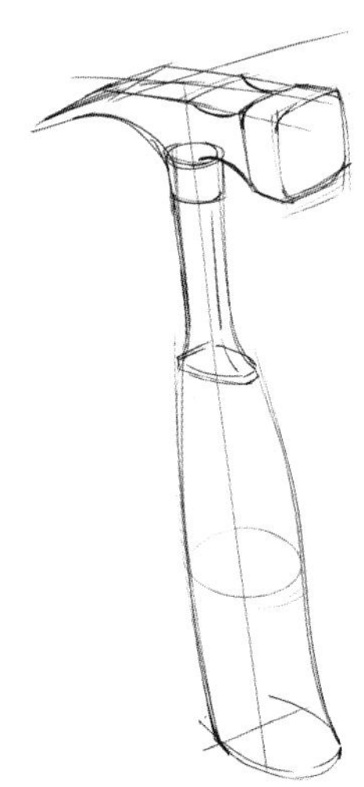

Add Details and Texture

With the hammer's overall form sketched in, add details to define its various sections. For example, to suggest a non-slip grip area on the handle, you can sketch in some diagonal grooves. Detail the claw by increasing the line weight in that area.

Texture is one way to add realism and enhance your sketch. Where might you want to introduce some texture into your hammer? On mine, for example, I added hatch lines on the strike area and emphasized the grip area's texture.

Next, continue shading by adding hatch lines where needed. This will help round out the hammer.

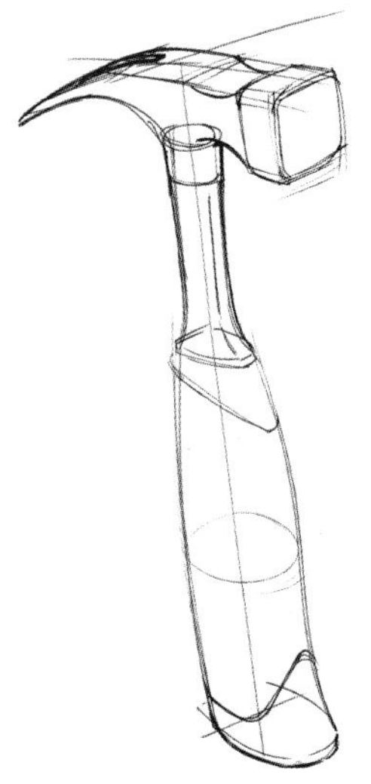 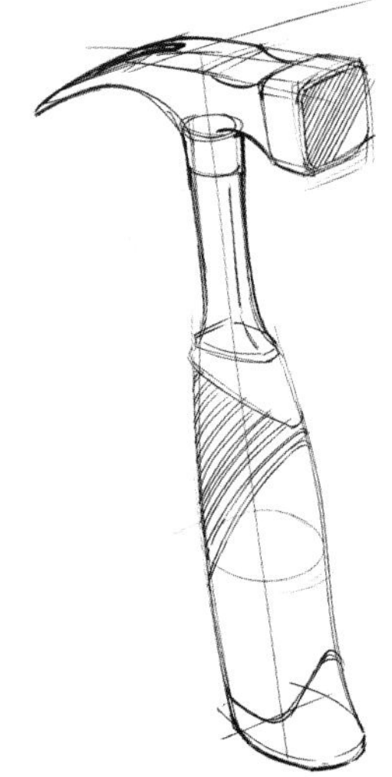 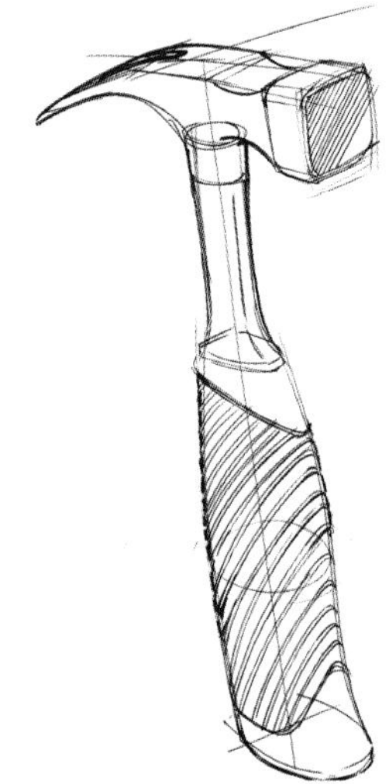

Add Shading and Shadows

As this is a simple sketch, try to focus on your lines and the quality of those lines, including their gesture and flow of those lines. If your sketch is a little messy, you can always apply some extra line weight to the outside perimeter of your sketch because this will help ground your drawing on the page a bit more.

Add shadowing to the overall shape of the hammer in the form of parallel lines to help communicate the three-dimensionality of the hammer. On the outside left and right edges of the handle, for example, add a few lines slightly spaced from each other that follow the overall contour of the handle. Additionally, add similar lines on the hammer's neck, as well as some hatch marks where the head of the hammer connects to the neck. These simple lines are a quick way to show lighting and three-dimensionality in your sketch. Small details like this can really help your drawing pop.

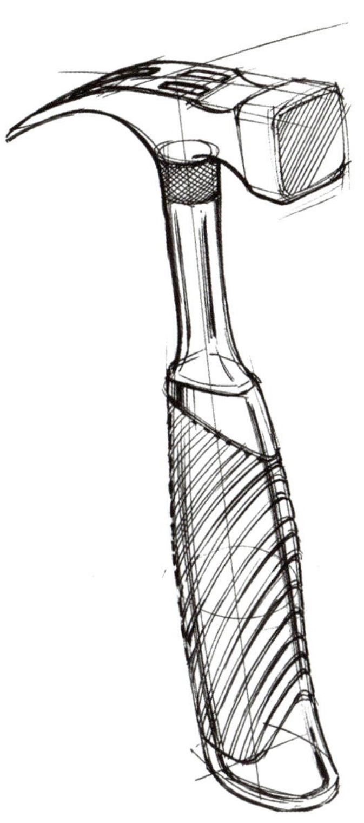

CHALLENGE

Create a series of sketches of a tool or object that you can break down into simple elements and draw in a similar fashion to the hammer. Stick to simple tools, and sketch quickly, drawing with your shoulder. If you're struggling to feel more confident with your sketches, don't worry, it happens to all of us. Remember, these are sketches to help you learn and progress, not showpieces for an exhibit. Keep practicing and be confident.

Drawing a chair may seem complicated but remember that once you understand its structure—or the structure of any object—you have the blueprint for creating it. In this exercise, you'll draw a wooden chair with cushions. I used a Paper Mate Flair pen for the example, but you can use a different tool if you'd like. (For an added challenge, try a tool that you're not used to using on a regular basis.) You'll also need markers to add color to your sketch. Stay loose, warm up, and have fun!

Sketch the Initial Shapes

Start by drawing four horizontal, straight lines, representing the top of the chair back, the seat's back edge, the seat's front edge, and a ground line where the front legs will sit. Make sure all your lines are consistent with the overall proportion and perspective of the chair. If you extend them, they should seem to converge to a common vanishing point in the distance. If they don't, then your drawing will feel like something is off. You can pick any point of view in which you'd like to draw the chair, as long as your lines appear to converge to common vanishing points off in the distance.

Connect your lines to create a basic rectangle for the chair back and another for the seat (again, if extended these new lines should appear to converge on a vanishing point). Add four vertical lines to represent the legs, making the front legs straight, but the back legs slightly angled.

Add Cushions, Legs, and Details

Build out the volume of cushions or any other prominent features in the chair design. In my design, I sketched wedge-shaped cushions.

Don't get too hung up on making the lines perfect at this point. If you'd like a clean result later, you can use heavier line weights for the outline or draw a quick overlay to clean up the drawing (more on this option shortly).

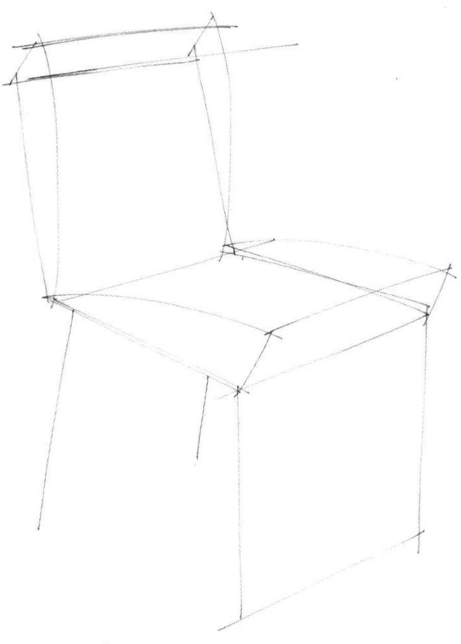

Block in the shapes and volumes for the legs. I wanted the wooden base to have a mid-century design feel, so I tapered the legs with rounded blends into the frame.

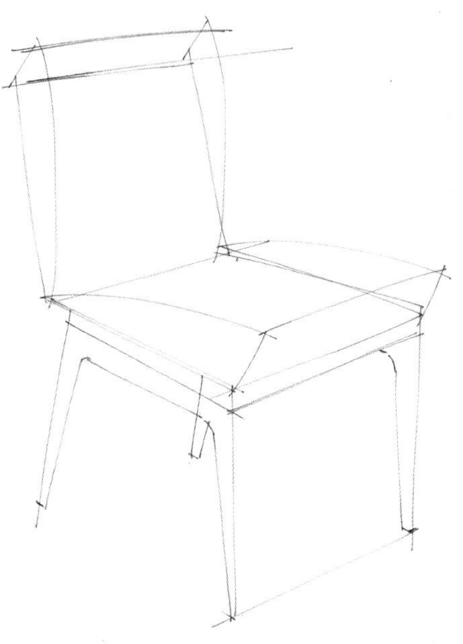

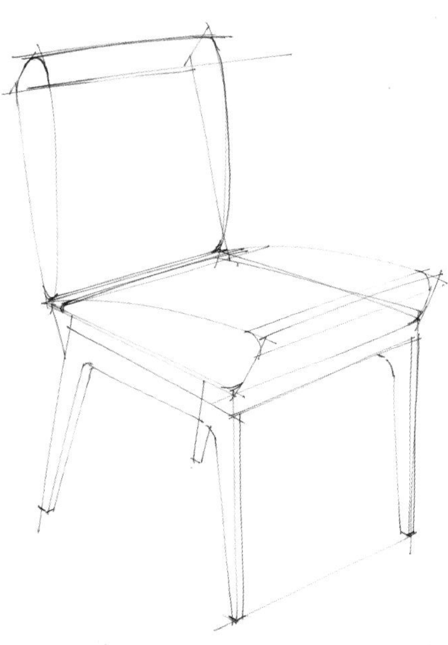

Continue adding details as you sketch and think about the parts of the chair. If desired, add wood grain (see Exercise 5 for tips), fasteners, buttons, or any features that may be a part of your design. Or you may want to keep things simple as I have for now.

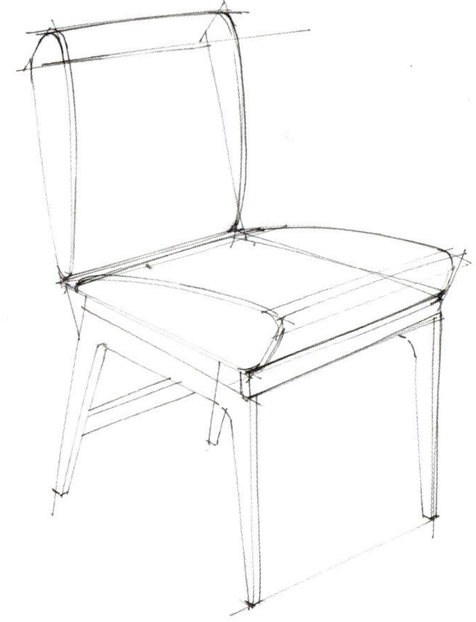

Create an Overlay

At this point, you have a decision: Complete the outline of the overall sketch, or create an overlay of the underlying sketch? An overlay gives you more flexibility to tweak your drawing and correct mistakes by re-sketching. I decided to create an overlay of my chair, and suggest you give one a try too.

To create an overlay, place translucent paper over your original sketch and re-sketch your lines on that second sheet, using the original sketch below as a guide. Alternatively, you could place your sketch on a light table, then place a thin sheet of paper over it. The light shining from below will enable you to see through to the underdrawing.

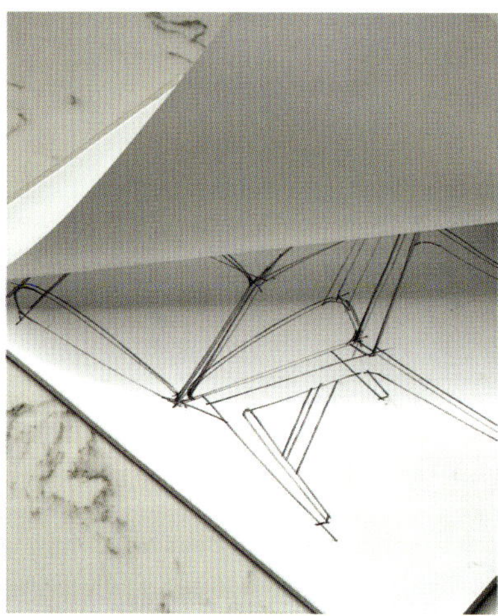
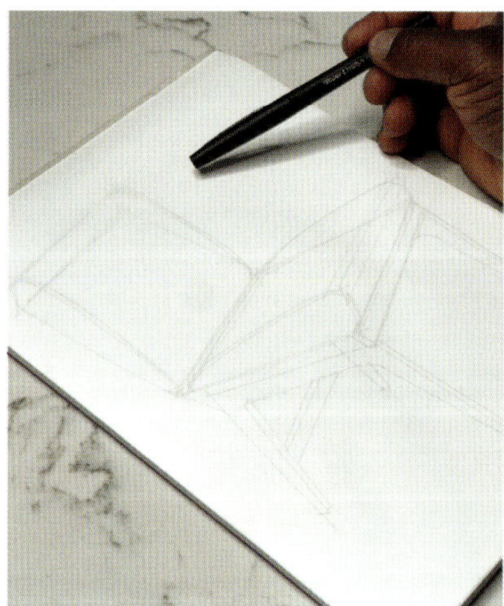

Don't think of this process as rigidly tracing your first drawing. Tracing tends to be slow and nerve-racking as you try to precisely match the original lines. Re-sketching, however, gives you the freedom to refine things as you go. You'll end up with a new drawing that has more life and energy to it. If you're nervous about making mistakes while re-drawing, remember that you can always grab a fresh sheet of paper and start again—your original sketch is safe underneath!

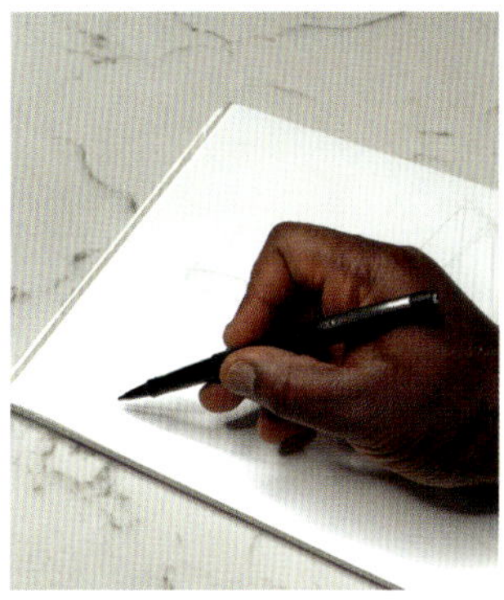
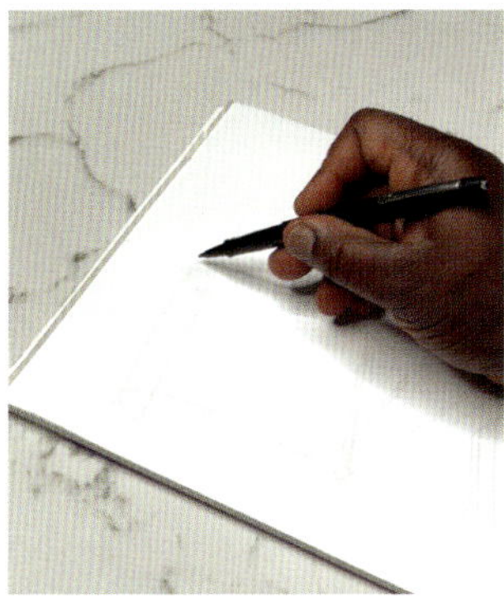
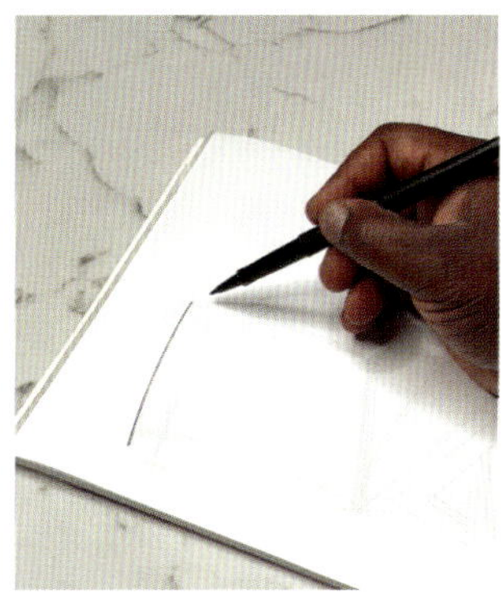

You can always do this step a few times until you're happy with the final output. Plus, you can add a few new details, such as the peg connectors (the circles) I added to the chair's back legs. Relax and have fun.

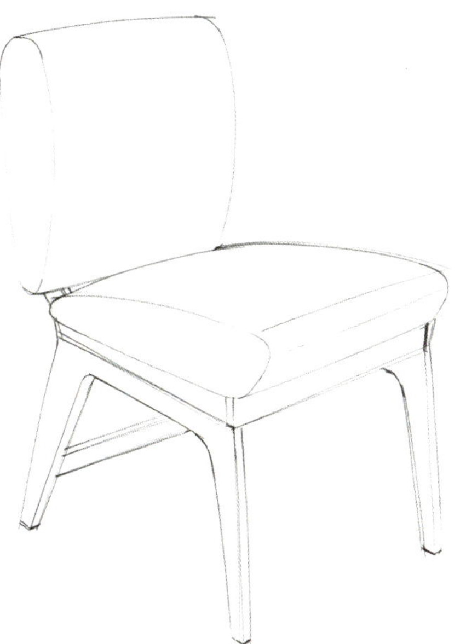
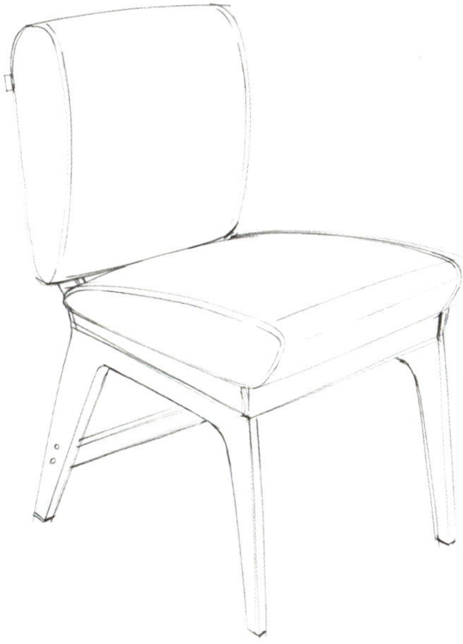

Add Color

With a few markers you can quickly add color. (If you prefer to use colored pencil or some other medium, that works too.) Start by using your lightest marker to create an outline of each of the main parts of the chair. For the cushions, I used a light-yellow marker. For the wood base, I picked a warm brown marker.

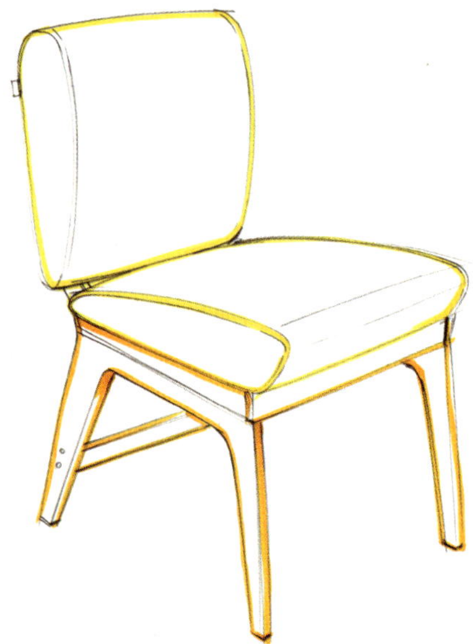

Once your outline is complete, fill in each of the outlined areas with the colors you chose. I find it easier to work this way when using markers because my colors tend to bleed less outside of the lines I've sketched in. I'm not sure if this is simply a mental thing or practical, but either way, it works for me. Take note of what works for you and think about how to implement it in your workflow. Whatever your method, follow the contours of the chair section you're shading. Notice I used a different stroke direction for the cushions' faces than for their sides in the example.

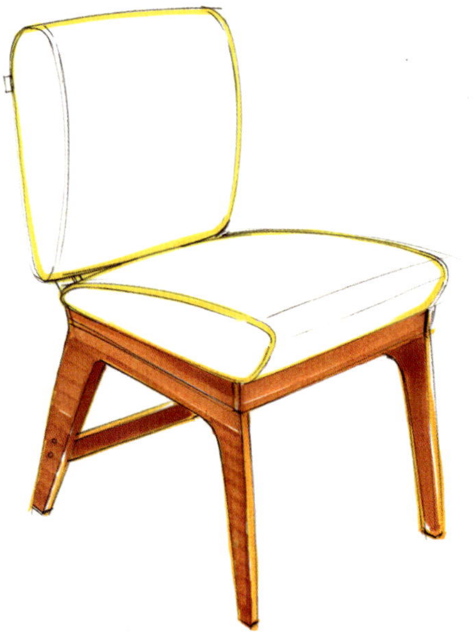

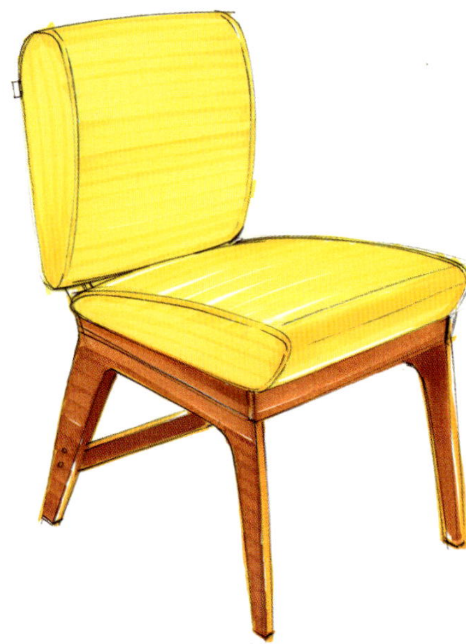

To add depth, think about the light position in the chair's space. In the example,
I pictured the light coming from the
top-right in the scene. Because of this,
the left side of the chair should appear
darker than the right side. The amount of
contrast you use is up to you. The more
contrast you use, the harsher or stark the
drawing may seem. The less contrast you
use, the less depth you may achieve in
your drawing, and it may be hard to see
details. Placing lights against darks will
help you achieve depth in your drawings.

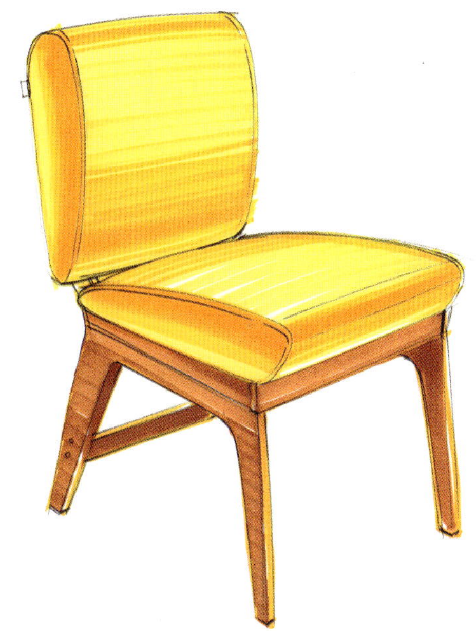

Refine the Contrast

Continue to build contrast and depth by
allowing the marker to dry somewhat,
then reapplying the same marker to the
areas you are coloring. When you can't
go any deeper or darker in value, consider using another marker to add more
deepness to the color. For the example,
I shifted to darker yellow and darker
brown marker to add contrast and value
to the colored areas. The shape of the
colored dark areas also will help you
communicate the shape of the cushions
or legs. Be sure to think about each
surface and its orientation to the light.
Your drawing is the guide for coloring
and contrast. Try not to get too lost in
the details, and always remember the big
picture.

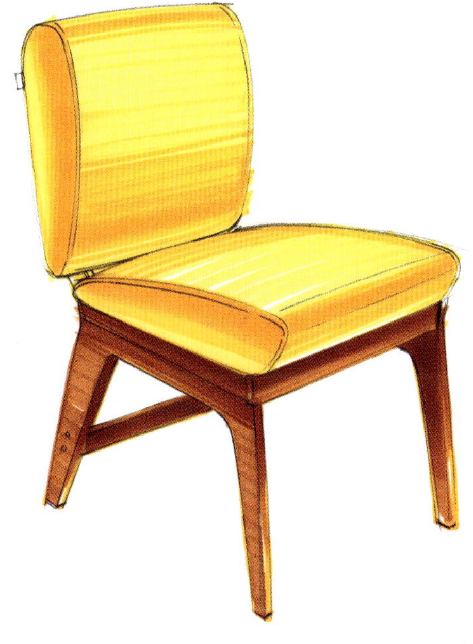

If desired, you could finish your drawing by adding texture with a pen, marker, or pencil (you'll get lots of practice with this in Chapter 7). You could also add a shadow to ground the chair or a background to help contextualize it (Chapter 8 covers backgrounds in more detail).

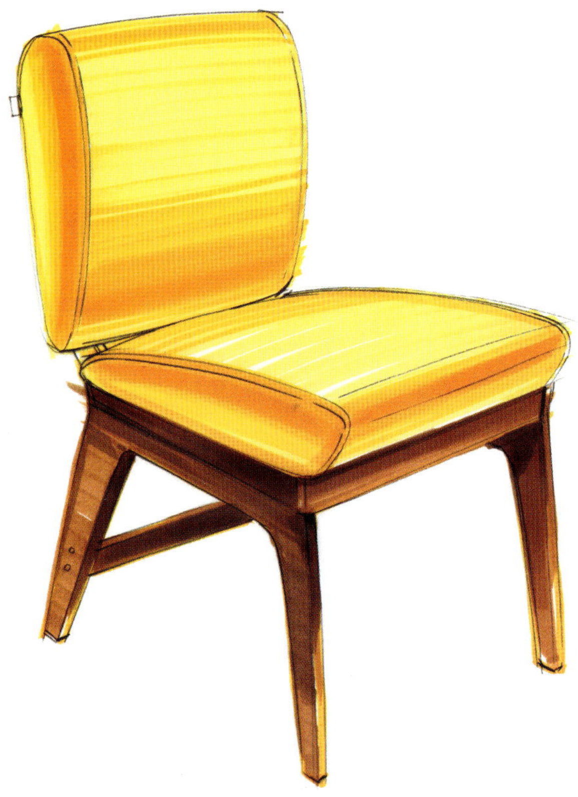

CHALLENGE

Design and sketch your own version of a chair. Remember to think of the overall idea and use the strategies outlined in this section to build volume step by step as you sketch. Experiment with creating overlays (tracing over your previous sketch) to clean up your drawing if needed. Think about lighting details, and use markers to build contrast and depth in your drawing. Get creative! There are no wrong answers, and the only right answer is to keep pushing and practicing every damn day.

Drawing furniture, especially large pieces, is a great way to practice basic perspective. In this exercise, you'll explore drawing a couch in accurate perspective while also being expressive with strokes, textures, and line quality. Grab your favorite pen that gives you a solid line (I used a Paper Mate Flair), and warm up.

Outline the Proportions

When drawing in perspective, it's good to start with a simple plane or object to help orient yourself as you draw. So, draw the top plane of a cuboid to serve as a guide for the overall proportion of your couch.

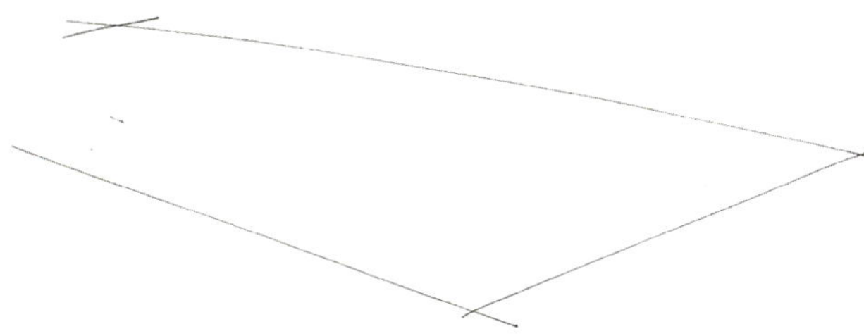

To represent the couch's volume, create the full cuboid. First, extend four lines down from the corners of your plane, making them a reasonable height for your couch, and then complete the cuboid with a corresponding plane. If you'd rather, you could draw the top and bottom planes and then connect each corner with lines to create the cuboid.

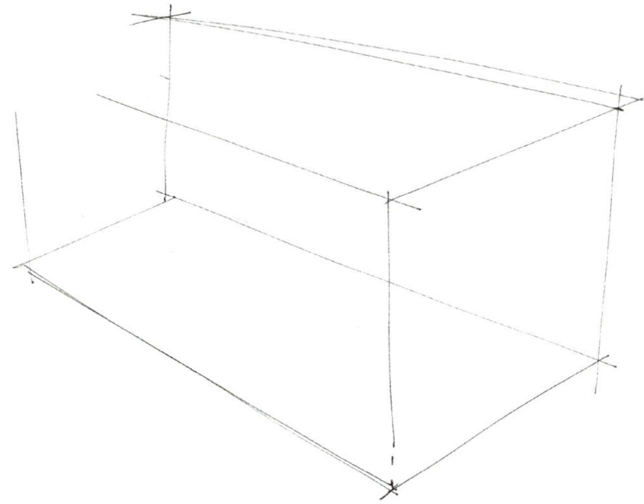

Sketch in the Functional Elements

With the overall proportion of the couch set, you can divide the couch into functional bits like a seat, legs, armrests, and so forth. In this step, sketch a mid-plane at a slight angle to establish the seat of the couch.

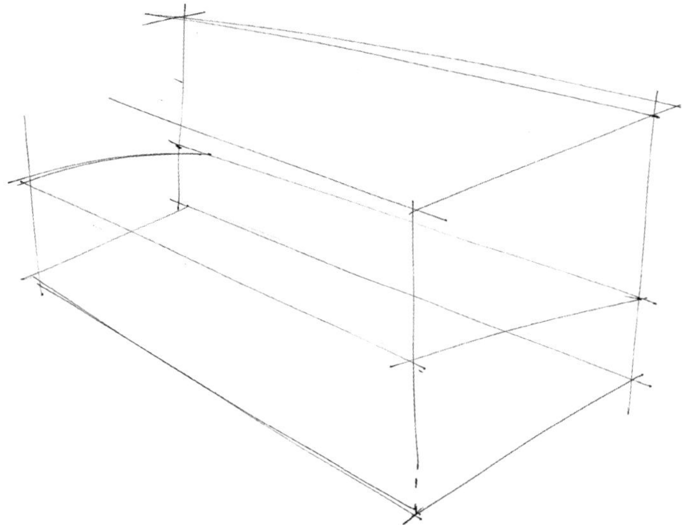

This plane will function as a guide for placing cushions or other elements. Next, sketch in armrests by extending lines up from the seat of the couch and extending toward the back of the couch.

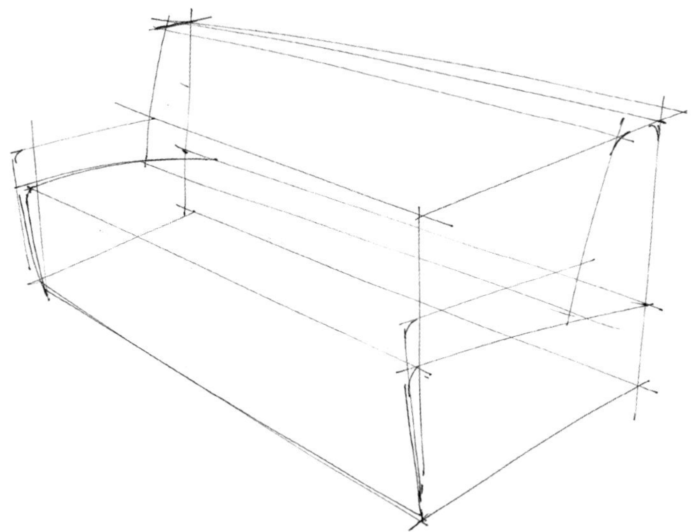

Then, divide the shapes and add depth to the armrests by offsetting your initial sketch lines. If you make a mistake, don't worry, you can always extend your sketch a little bit as I had to. That's right, even seasoned professionals make mistakes. The important thing is to work with them to create a good sketch.

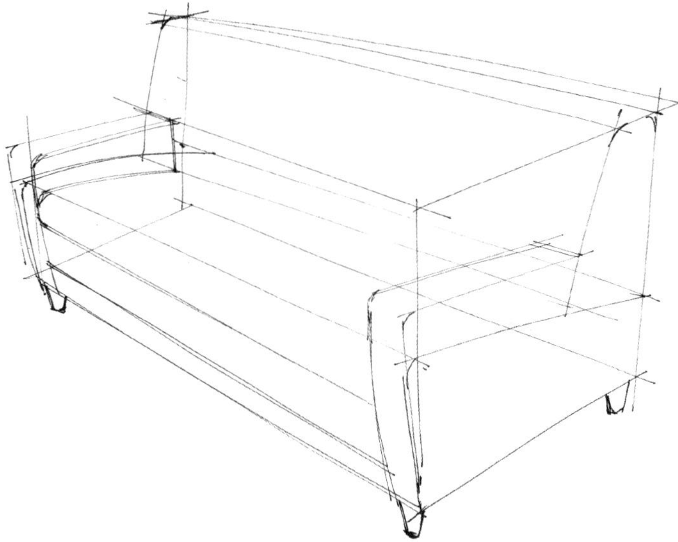

Be mindful as you work out your details to sketch quickly and be expressive with your lines. I decided to divide the seating area into three cushions. Notice that the divisions follow the general curvature of the seating area I initially sketched. This is an example of how your construction geometry can help guide the rest of your sketch process.

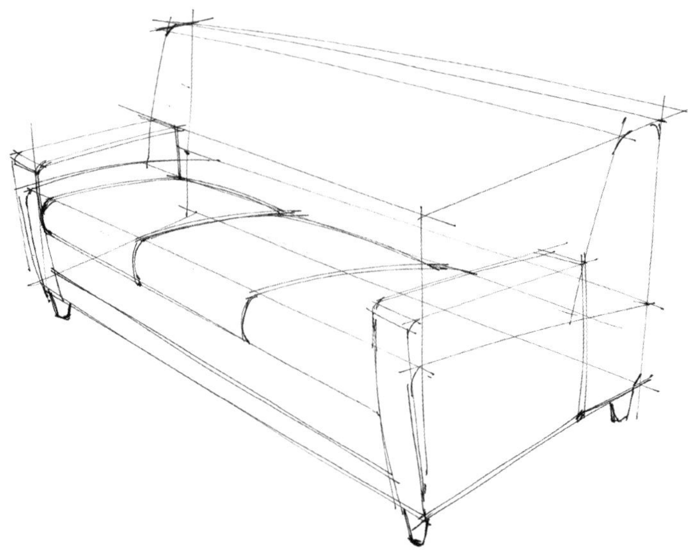

Introduce the Outline

If you have one pen, sketch over the outline of your couch to enhance the line weight by drawing the same line multiple times. If you're concerned about the accuracy of repeatedly drawing a line, you can switch to a pen or marker with a thicker tip that will give you a nice clean outline for the couch. Notice as the outline is introduced that the construction lines (your initial reference and scaffolding lines) in the sketch become less visible, distracting, or concerning.

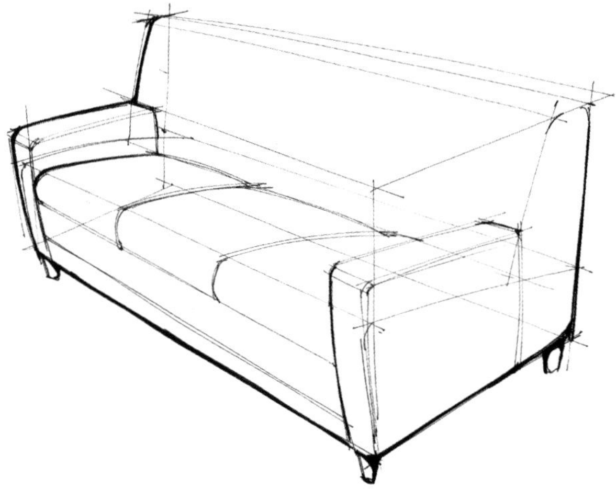

Create an Overlay

Despite having the thicker outline in the previous step, I decided to create an overlay of the couch. To practice the skills you learned in Exercise 7, create your own overlay: Place a translucent sheet of new paper over your couch and re-sketch it, cleaning up mistakes and refining your design as you go.

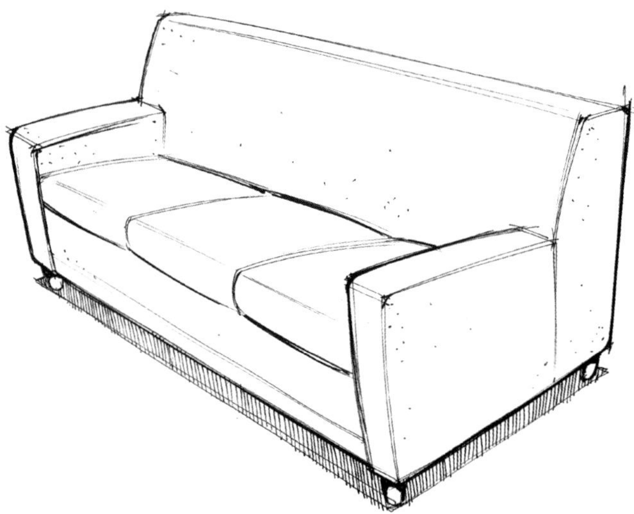

For finishing touches, consider shading a shadow, as well as detailing the couch's legs on the overlay, as well. You could also add a few stippling marks by tapping on the paper in a random order to create a pattern to suggest a fabric-like texture or convey materials by adding some color with pencils or markers, as I did.

LINE QUALITY

Lines are the limits of what we can see when drawing. You can combine lines to create a different feeling in your sketches. Lines can be short, long, parallel, or converging. They are also a great way to create textures, using simple scribbles, gestures, and strokes with a pen or pencil. The exercises in Chapter 6 dive deeper into the expressive power of lines.

CHALLENGE

Create a series of sketches exploring different furniture styles. Focus on accurate perspective as well as line quality. Pay attention to the convergence of your lines as you sketch them. Remember, they should appear to be converging to a distant point.

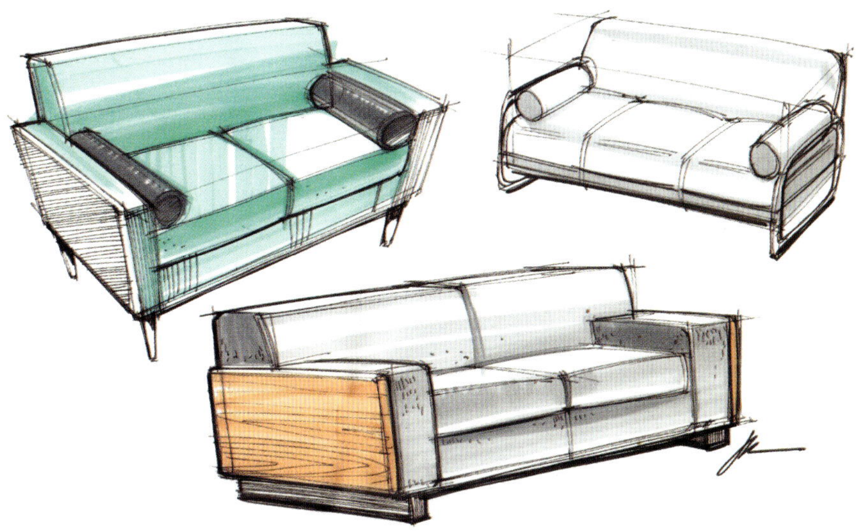

A great way to practice and understand perspective is by drawing interior spaces with small objects or elements in them. This way you get an appreciation for the different approaches to scale and composition. For this exercise, you'll draw a long room or hallway with a few features on the ceiling and repeated features on each wall. For the example, I use a Paper Mate Flair pen and printer paper. You can use whatever tools you'd like, but make sure to warm up first and sketch as loosely and confidently as you are able to. Sometimes the attitude with which you approach a drawing translates into the drawing itself.

Rough Sketch a Thumbnail Version

Start by sketching a thumbnail version of the room you envision. Does it have doors, windows, overhead beams, maybe pictures on the wall? Sketching a thumbnail allows you to plan out your drawing before committing to a more detailed version of it.

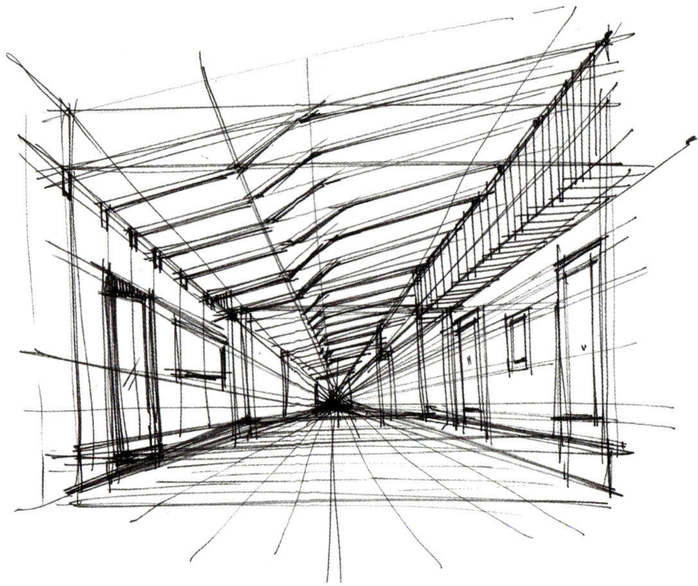

Set Up the Room and Reference Lines

The room drawing will be a one-point perspective drawing, meaning all lines that recede away from the viewer will converge to a single point. All other lines will be either vertical or horizontal relative to the viewer. To see a real-world example of one-point perspective, stand at one end of a long hallway and observe how the corners of the room above and below appear to converge to a single point in front of you.

To help you draw your room in perspective, you need to set up a few reference lines. Draw a horizon line and place the first vanishing point at its center.

From this line, extend four lines out. These lines will form the basis of the room or hallway that you're sketching. If you make a mistake, it's okay. I made one too, but we'll work with them as we go.

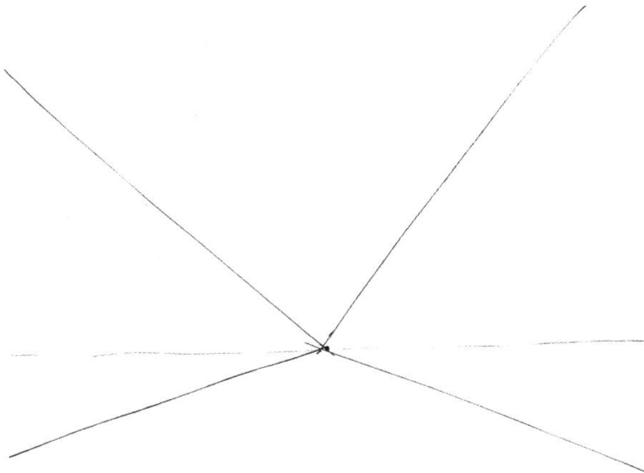

Draw two horizontal and two vertical lines that intersect the lines that radiate out from the center of the horizon line. The new shape these create is a virtual plane that you can use more effectively to render perspective as you draw.

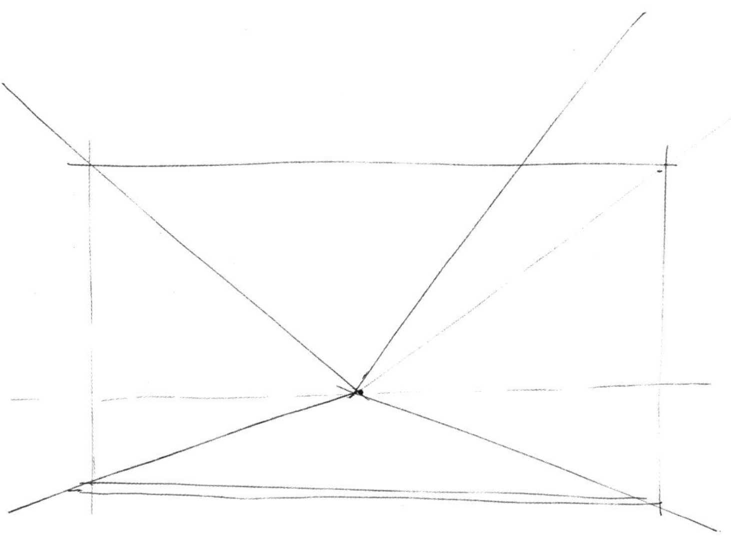

Next, draw additional lines as needed emanating from the center at the vanishing point. For example, on the left side of the long room, I extended a line from the vanishing point toward the viewer. Later, you can use a line like this to establish the height of doors or other aspects of the room as they recede away from you.

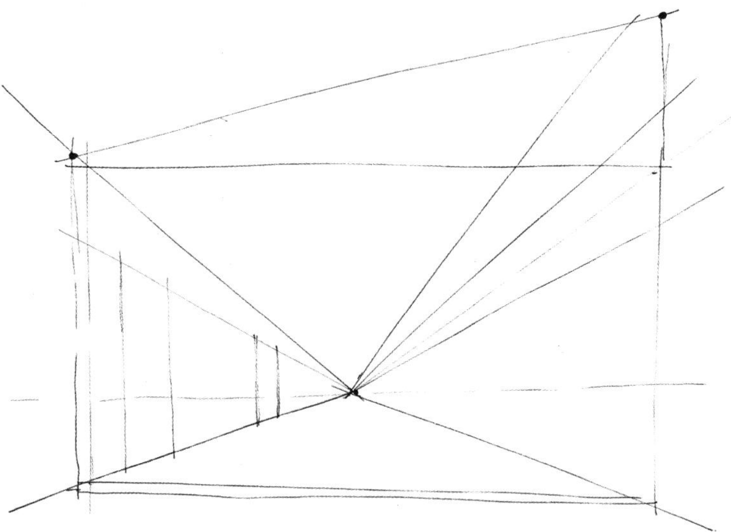

Draw a line from the vanishing point upward and another to the right. These lines form the structure of the ceiling that you will eventually be sketching.

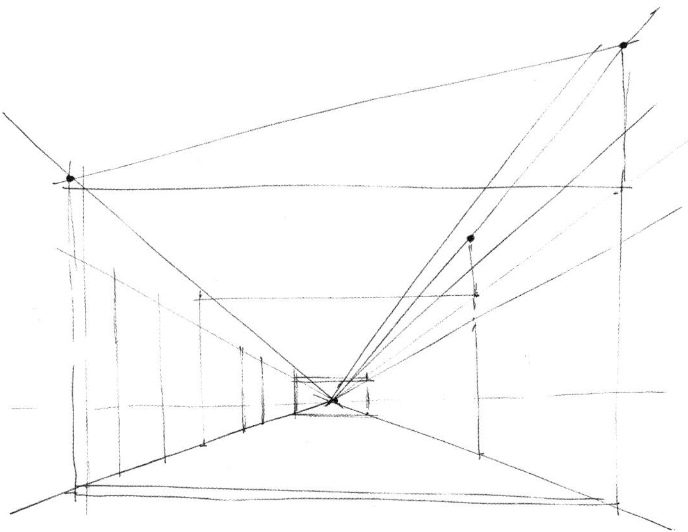

Continue to add lines that define structural features in the room as needed. To measure a distance in a scene like this, simply estimate the distance and sketch lines or points to use as reference. It may take some practice but pay attention to how distances change the further away they are from you. Remember in perspective that objects closer to you will appear larger than those further away. As you are working out the overall drawing, be sure to not overemphasize single elements at this point. Rather, sketch lightly when adding construction lines and figuring out where objects will go in the environment.

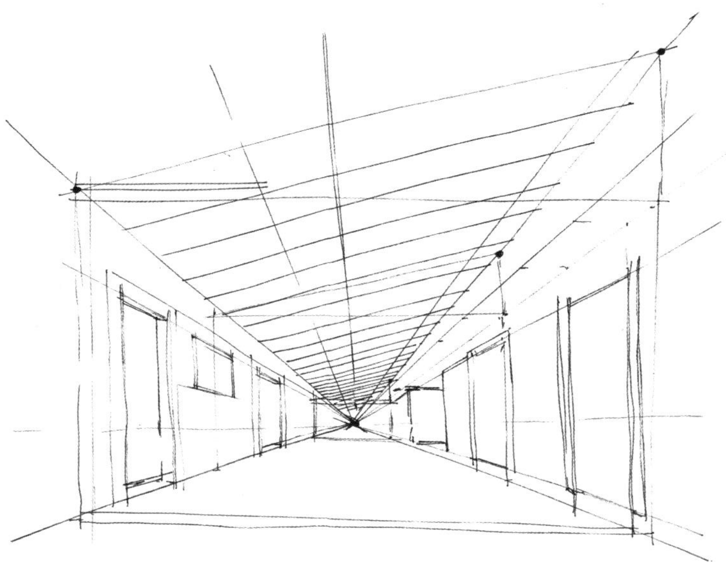

Add Architectural Details

With the structural elements in place, continue sketching by adding details such as door frames, windows, or items on the wall. Notice that with the construction lines emanating from a single vanishing point, the effect of perspective works to make items that are roughly the same size appear smaller as they recede away from the front virtual plane.

In addition, add some details like a few lines on the roof-like ceiling that may indicate some sort of repeating structural element. Notice that these lines on the angled ceiling appear closer together the further away from the virtual plane they get. Add additional lines as needed to show the thickness of elements along the ceiling or on the walls.

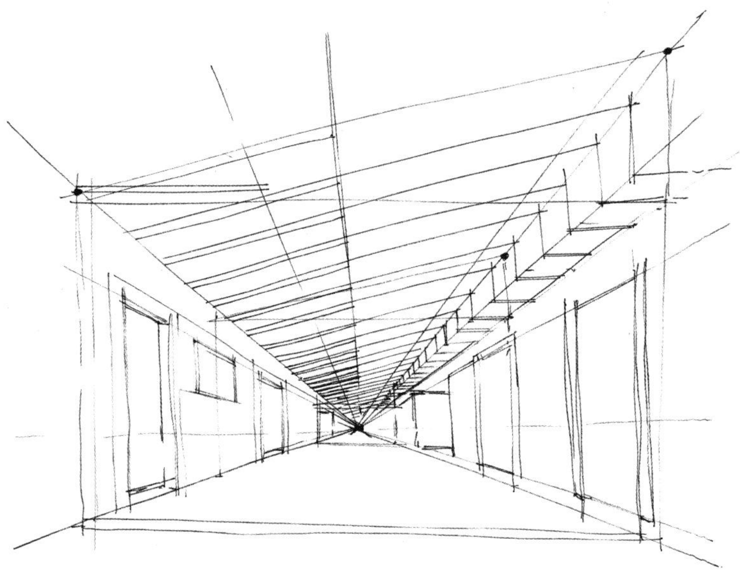

Use Shading for Texture and Volume

Much like when sketching textures with a pen and adding those textures onto smaller objects, you can use hatch lines and repeated strokes to show shadows or textures in this scene. On each door, for example, I shaded using vertical lines, somewhat equally spaced, to represent a material for the doors. For shadows down the hallway, try drawing parallel horizontal lines in a consistent fashion.

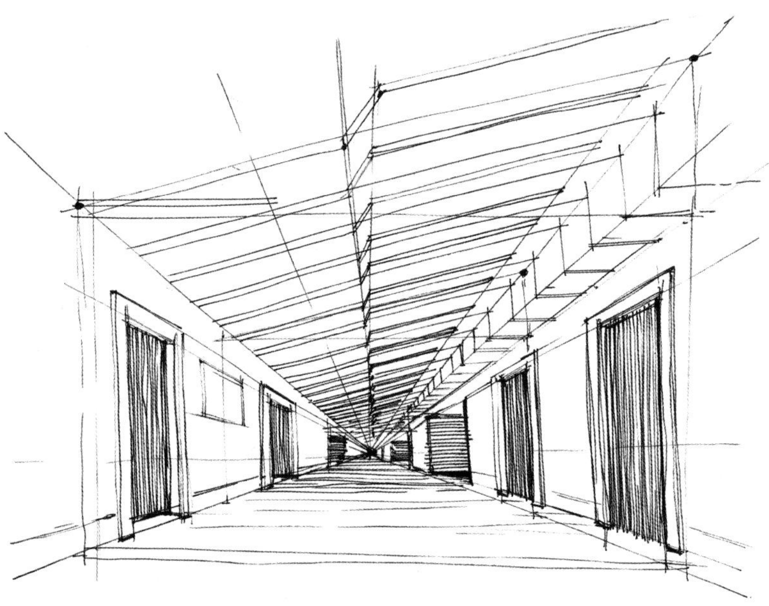

Introduce Line Weight and Clarity

On the ceiling, carefully count the spaces and thickest lines that are used to determine the size of these beams. Adding a heavier line weight to the outside of the beams will help them pop on the page. If other items in your room need emphasis, judiciously add line weight to create emphasis where necessary.

Finally, continue to bump up your line weight and introduce clarity into your sketch by drawing repeatedly in the same spot or by using a different pen that has a wider tip. By doing so, you can emphasize aspects of importance or clean up troublesome areas of your drawing (like my mistake during setup). Notice that even though your initial construction lines are still visible, they do not command your attention as much as they once did. This is the power of using line weights quickly and efficiently in your sketches.

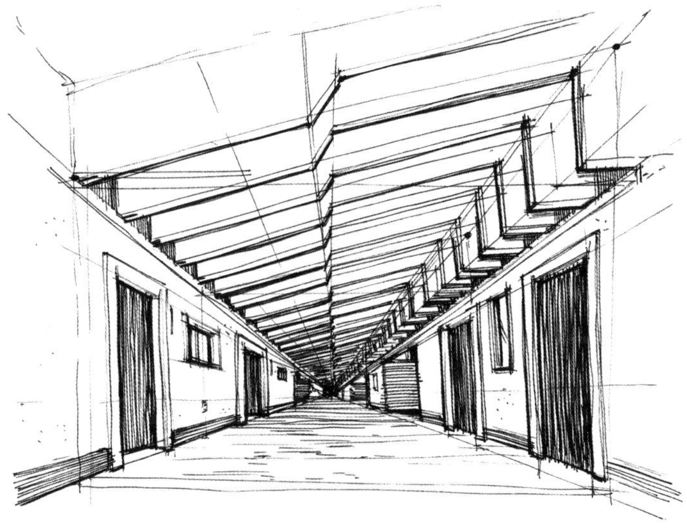

CHALLENGE

Draw some spaces outside your comfort zone. At the same time, you can practice drawing from observation. Look around you, and draw as best as you can the room you're in or one close by. Pay attention to all the elements in the room as well as what's happening with the corners of the room due to your perspective. Use a pen like a Paper Mate Flair, and remember to draw with your shoulder, lock your wrist, and use your elbow as a pivot.

Drawing modern homes is a fun way to build on the concept of using form combinations to come up with interesting things to draw. Structures like this are some of my favorite things to draw, not only because I have a chance to dream of something I've always wanted, but it's also a fun exercise in perspective drawing using simple tools to create interesting compositions and striking sketches.

You can think of a modern home as a simple, clean, but interesting combination of cubes and cuboids, and this exercise is an extension of Exercise 3 with the added details of windows, wall textures, and so forth.

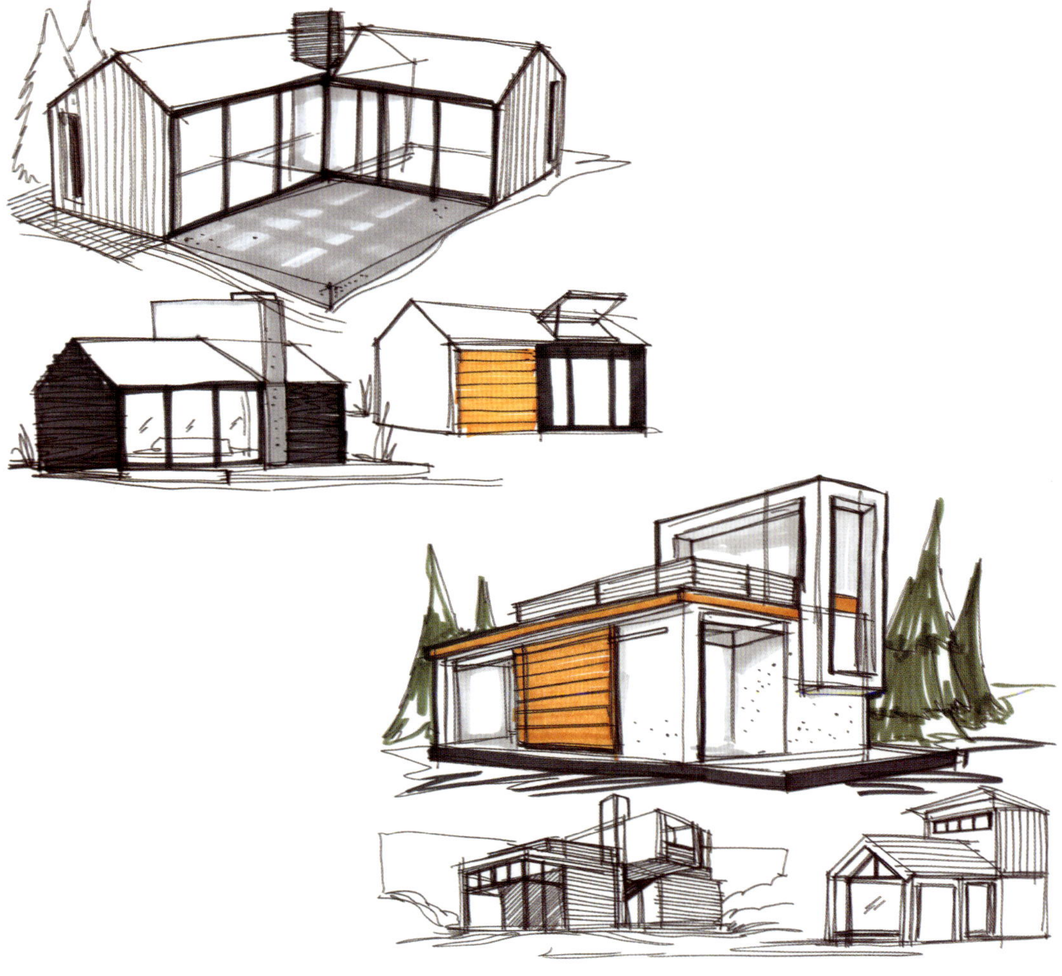

Set Up the Sketch

To start, sketch a simple horizontal line and decide where your baseline for your structure will be. You could also use this horizontal line as the horizon line for your scene. Construct another line above the horizontal line that's slightly angled. This will be the front edge of your structure. If you are working from a thumbnail, you can pay attention to the overall look and feel of your thumbnail to decide where to put these lines.

Next, complete the base object by sketching to the right and completing the base cuboid. Above the base, sketch additional lines to represent the upper floor of the structure. This can be a simple cuboid or any other shape you decide. The important part is to follow the general perspective flow of the base cuboid. Notice in the example that the roof lines and the lines of the concrete structure above follow the perspective of the base object. This includes the overhangs as well as the cut-out portion of this section of the structure.

Continue breaking up the base shape by drawing vertical lines and adding roof or deck elements to the structure. To add a roof or deck element, simply sketch a rectangle in perspective and offset your lines to show the thickness of that shape. These first few steps of the sketch serve to create construction geometry that you can build on. For example, I added a deck to the upper right of the structure, indicated by horizontal double lines sketched to represent railings.

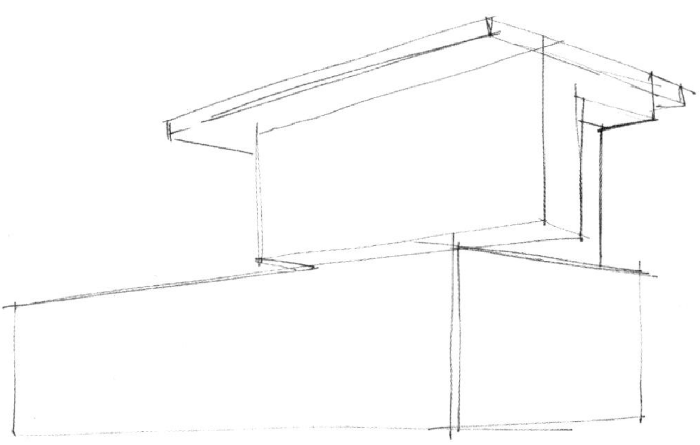

Add Functional Elements

Now that you've largely established the construction geometry and have a sense of place along with the topography in front of the structure, divide the faces of the geometry into functional elements. To the lower right of the unit, add a window so the homeowners will have a large picture view. To the right of it, sketch in a recess with possible wood cladding and quick stairs.

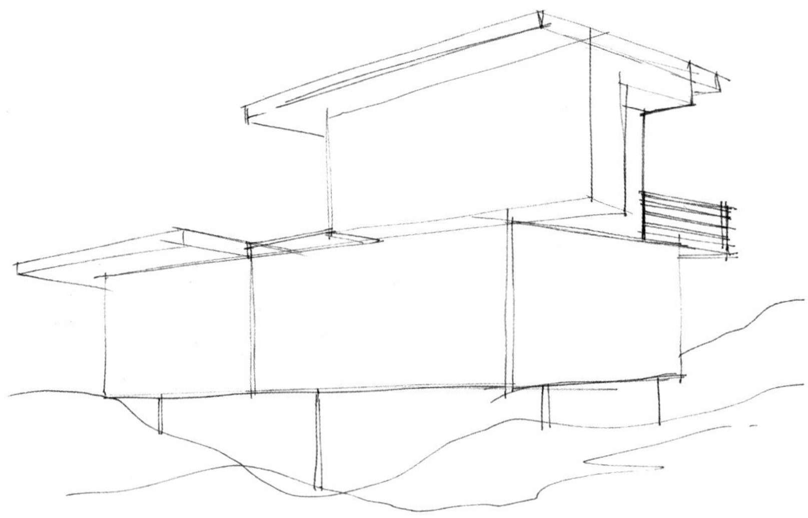

To sketch these stairs, draw two slightly converging angled lines from the base of the structure down towards the topography and the scene. You can terminate these lines wherever you please, thinking about your sense of place and where these might end and meet the ground. If you need to pause and practice before committing to the sketch, feel free to do so at this point.

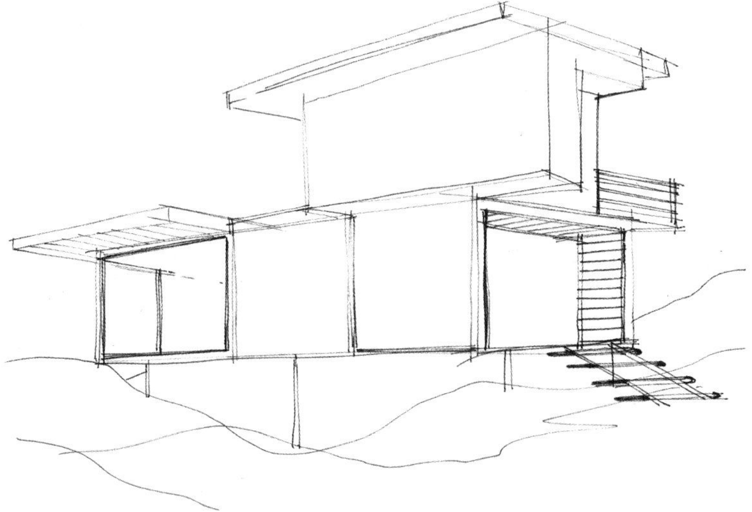

With the functional breaks in place, I decided to add details in the middle of the structure next, such as a cut-in recess. I added a door to the right side of the structure by loosely sketching lines that follow the perspective of the wall.

On the underside of the upper portion of the dwelling, you can add a texture to create value in shading and suggest a shadowed area. You can even plant a bit of foliage using quick and simple shapes to pepper the landscape.

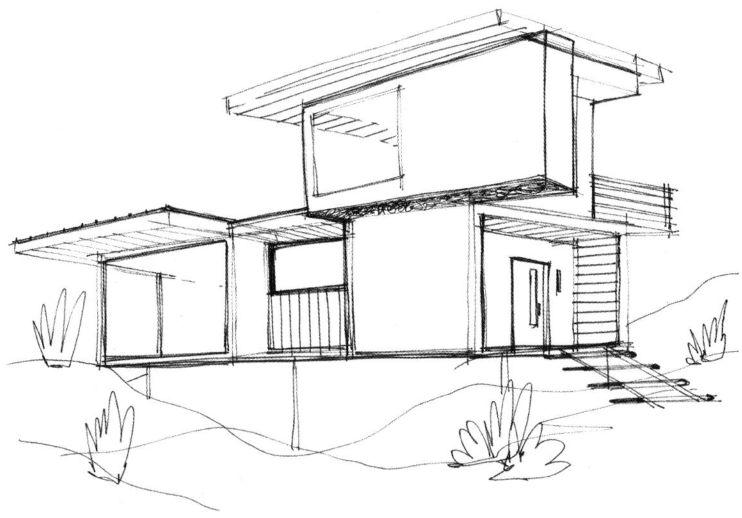

Detail with Hatch Lines

The next step is important as we are using simple tools to sketch the structure. When using just a pen, hatch lines are a great way to communicate texture, shadow, and detail in your structure. At the base of the structure, sketch vertical lines that are slightly spaced to create an even and striking base for the modern structure. By keeping these close together, you can establish a darker value as well as a textural contrast in the structure.

In the left-most windowed section of the structure, add hatch lines to suggest a window covering. On the upper portion of the structure, add horizontal lines that follow the general perspective of the structure to create an effect commonly found on modern homes. This effect is the result of forming concrete with planks of wood instead of smooth metal forms. Additionally, add stippling and small cracks to communicate concrete material where needed.

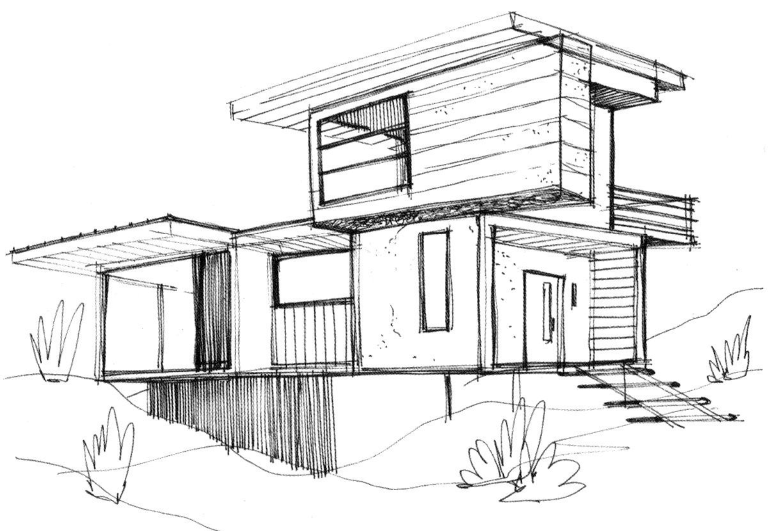

Add Final Touches

To finish up, complete hatching and shading in the base of the house by darkening this area, allowing the upper portion of the structure to shine a bit more.

Notice on the left side of the example structure that the ceiling is visible through this large picture window. This helps lighten up the structure somewhat, but also notice that the direction of the hatch lines contrasting in orientation helps reinforce a sense of depth.

Add any final touches you like. I added a window to the front right of the home and sketched in subtle details on the inside of the upper window as well as the windows on the main floor. As a final touch, I added clouds to function as background elements to add interest to the sketch.

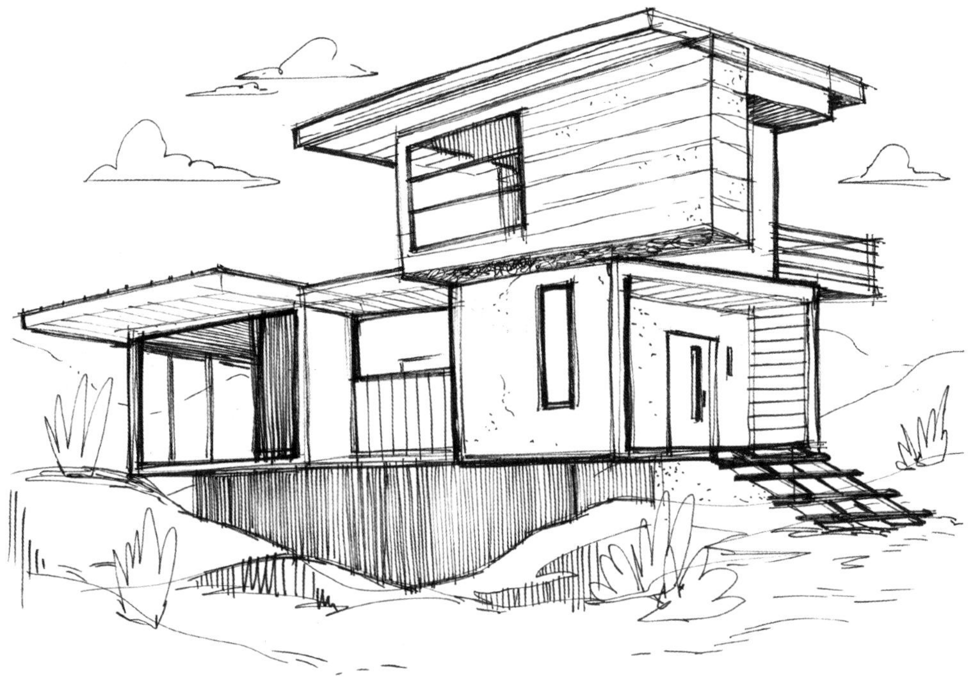

Adjust Line Weights

By adding line weight to the overall structure, you can make your sketch pop a bit more, which in turn makes the construction lines fade to the background. When adding line weight to your sketch, be mindful of the impact of a heavier line with a dark value. Typically, think of three line weights in the sketch: the outline, the construction or thin lines, and lines that are somewhere in between. The outline establishes the silhouette of the shape, and the construction lines help set up your sketch. The in-between lines are typically found inside the silhouette of the sketch. If you take a closer look at the final example sketch, you will see these three line weights used to show overlap, outline, and texture all within the same sketch.

Where applicable, add more lines to the landscape to suggest texture and shadow. Try not to overdo the shading on the landscape, however, as the subject of the sketch should be the structure itself.

CHALLENGE

Now get creative and explore form combinations that could be used to sketch more modern homes. Play with the proportion of different elements and their placement. Seek out inspiration to understand any architectural trends that might help spark some ideas. Dream big, and have fun while exploring.

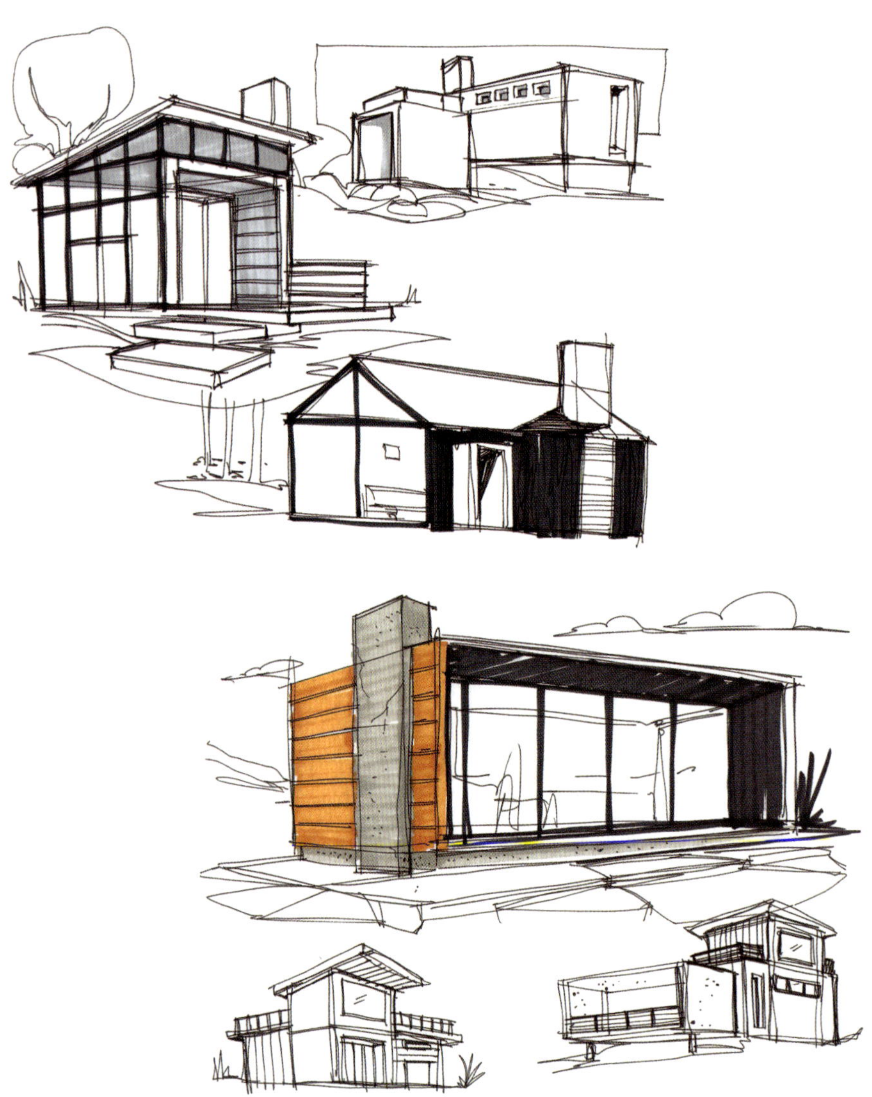

Practicing simple objects is a great way to bolster those perspective drawing skills you have been working so hard on. This week, you'll get a chance to do just that by drawing a printer. You'll sketch its simple form, breaking it down and adding details. I call this "silhouette, shape, substance" in my book *The Perspective Drawing Guide*.

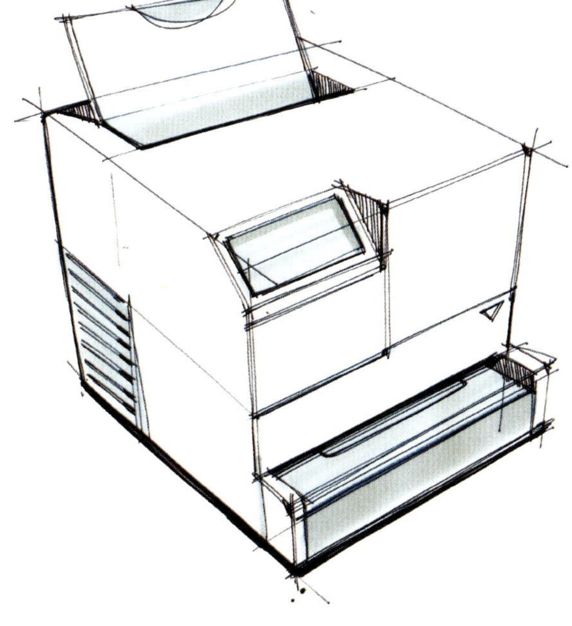

Grab a felt pen or similar pen that will give you a solid line, and first warm up by sketching straight lines as well as practicing fanning your lines.

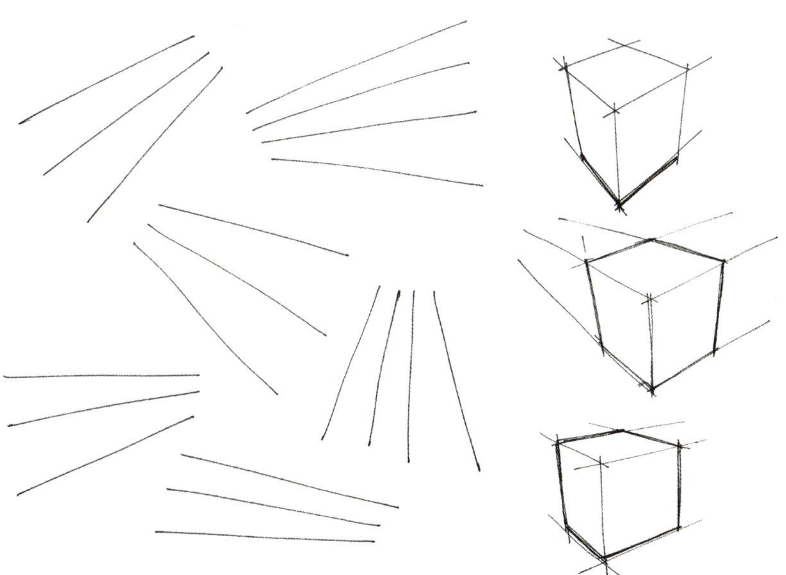

Start with a Box

Sketch a simple rectilinear box in whatever point of view you choose. Make sure that the lines on corresponding sides of each face of the rectilinear form would converge to a common vanishing point if extended. This sketch should be simple and without details. Focus on the overall shape, placement, and proportion of the printer. Remember to draw with your shoulder quickly and confidently to get the best lines.

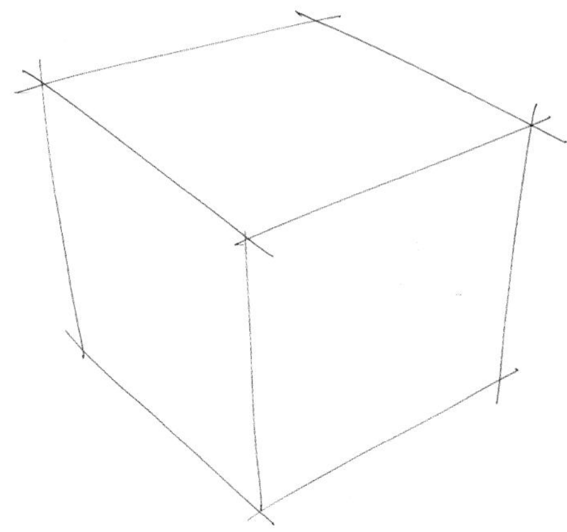

Add Details

Think about the functional parts of the printer—paper trays, screen, vents—that you would like to include. Add those to the overall form by sketching in lines to break up the faces of the form. Add any additional features that help communicate the design of the printer in your sketch. If you need to block in additional details, now is a good time to sketch in rough geometry to act as construction lines.

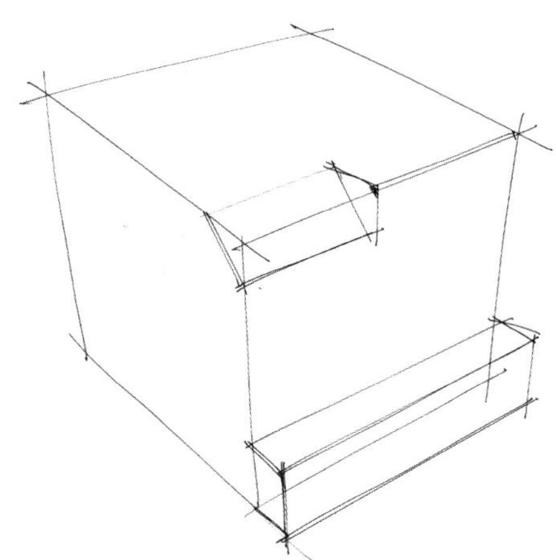

Enhance Line Weights

Once you are feeling confident about the details in your sketch, start adding heavier line weights to your sketch lines to emphasize and clarify the detail you're sketching in. In the example, notice the heavier line weights I added around the screen and tray areas of the printer to highlight functional breaks. These heavier lines provide contrast that will make parts of the printer pop out when someone is looking at the sketch.

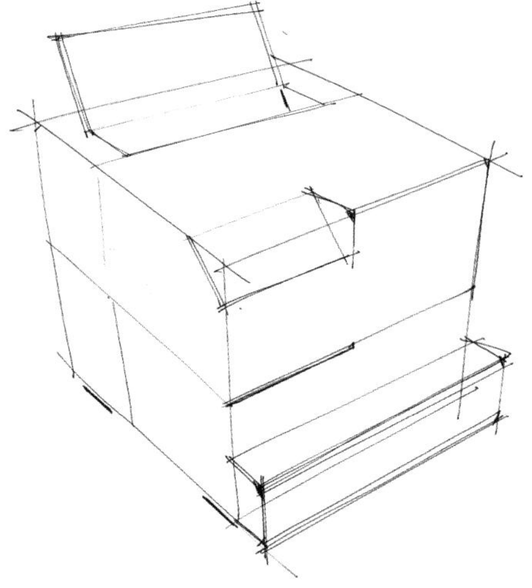

Add Texture and Refinements

If you want, add additional texture or details. Add line weight to the outline of the printer as needed to help pull out the final design of your printer. For example, I added a tab for the input paper tray, lines to define a screen, and details on the printed output paper tray.

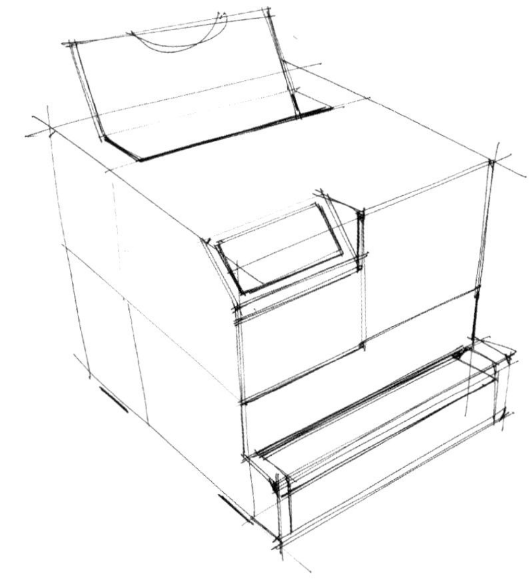

Continue to refine the details around the screen and trays by sketching a bit more carefully. Add hatch lines for shading to help communicate more depth in your sketch. While shading, be sure to consider the perspective of the view and the orientation of the face you're working on. Notice that the lines I used in shading follow the general direction of the face they're on. This way, the shading complements the face, rather than distracts from the perspective in the sketch. At this point, also consider adding a simple background, shadow, or a power cord to help flesh out the idea.

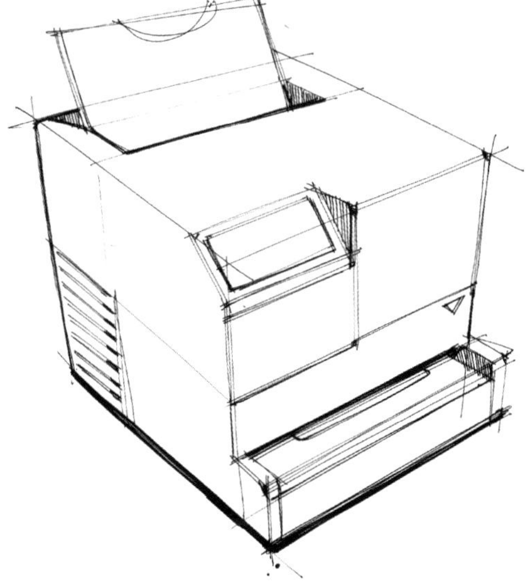

Enhance with Marker

For the example, I used very light cool gray marker to shade over the pen lines that I had already sketched as a subtle shadow on the left side of the printer. Adding marker like this builds on the perspective and the hatched lines used for shading. Keep it simple and try not to overwhelm or distract from the line work you have in your sketch. Managing the balance between clarity and shading may take some practice. Eventually, you will find yourself being more confident about how much shading to add to your sketch.

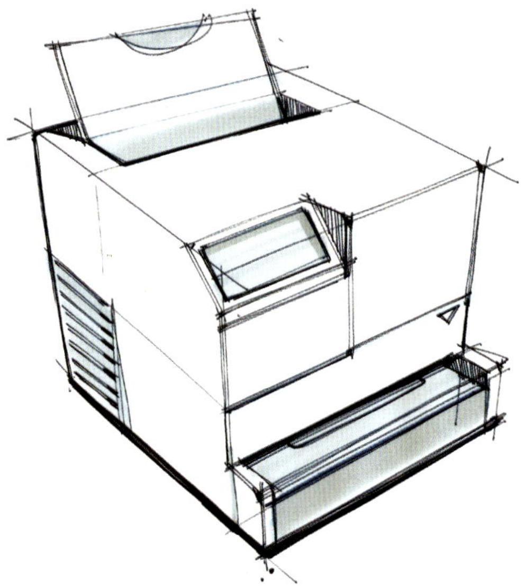

CHALLENGE

Sketch a few printers or similar appliances or electronic devices around your home. Pay attention to details as you sketch. Start things off with simple shapes and build up to the final drawing as you go.

I love furniture design, and drawing furniture is a great way to practice basic perspective skills, texture, and overall composition of an object. In this exercise, you'll sketch a sideboard.

Make the Initial Sketch

Think about your design, and sketch in the top face or a few lines of your object. Next, complete the top portion of the sideboard by sketching in additional perspective lines to create an elongated cube or cuboid. This cuboid will serve as a frame to guide the rest of the sketch process.

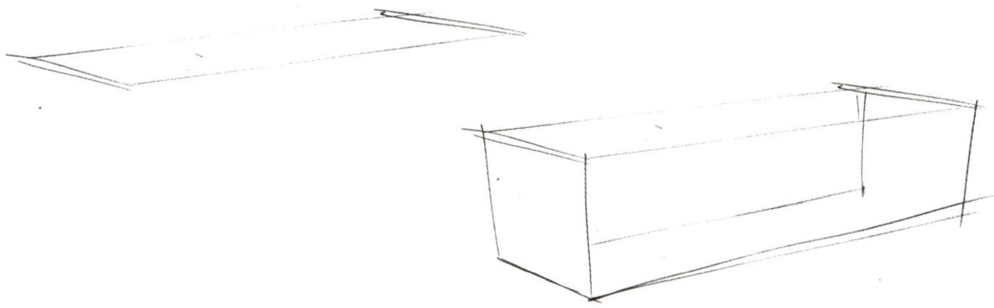

The sideboard needs legs, so sketch in four vertical lines, as well as additional perspective lines if you need help with placement. Much like for the top of the sideboard, these lines will serve as construction lines to help with placement, proportion, scale, and the functional breakup of the sideboard.

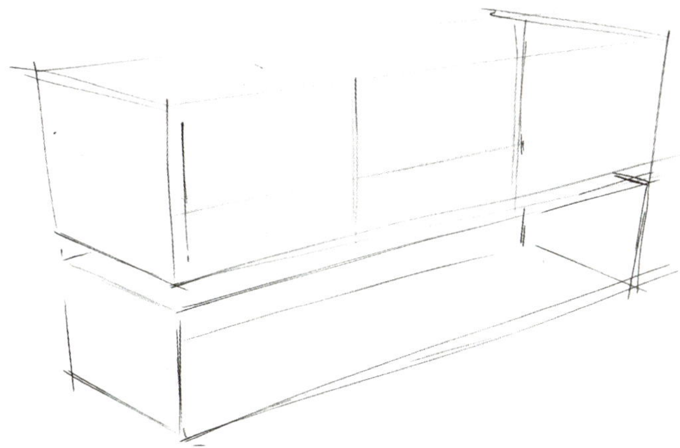

Add Defining Details

After you've established your proportional construction lines, you can now start designing and sketching the rest of the sideboard. For my design, I decided to have drawers on either side and a central section. To follow this example, divide the front of the sideboard into three roughly equal sections. To maintain perspective, each section should be slightly smaller than the previous one because it's more distant from the viewer.

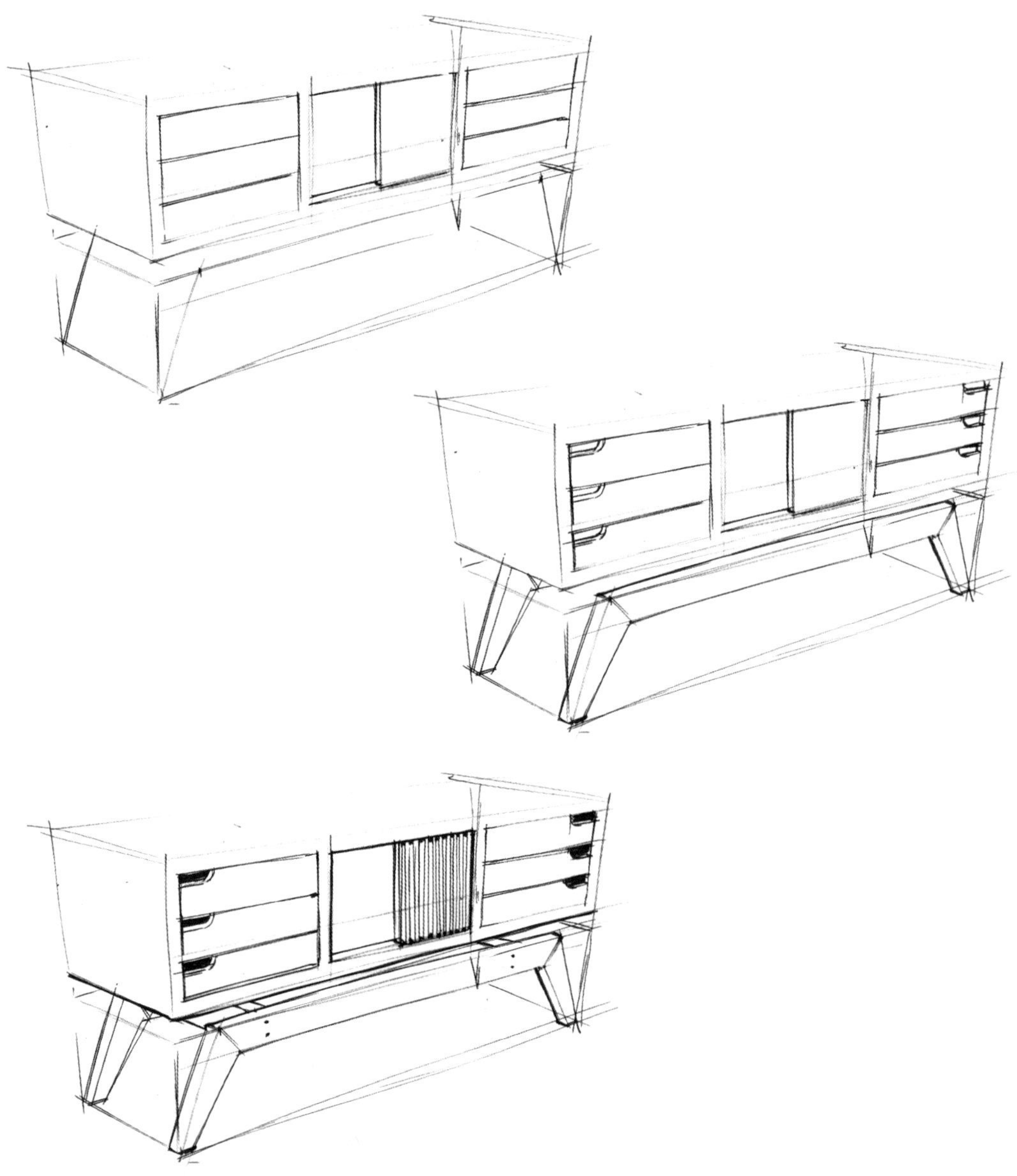

Sketch in drawers, doors, or whatever other details you would like to include. Additionally, sketch in lines that represent the angles of the legs for your sideboard. If you choose to do vertical legs, that's fine. If you choose to do angled legs or some other shape, however, think of a creative way to transfer dimensions from one area to the next. I like to use tick marks or dots to help with proportion, matching, and placing lines where they need to go. Continue adding details to your sideboard, such as drawer pulls or the shape of the legs for the unit.

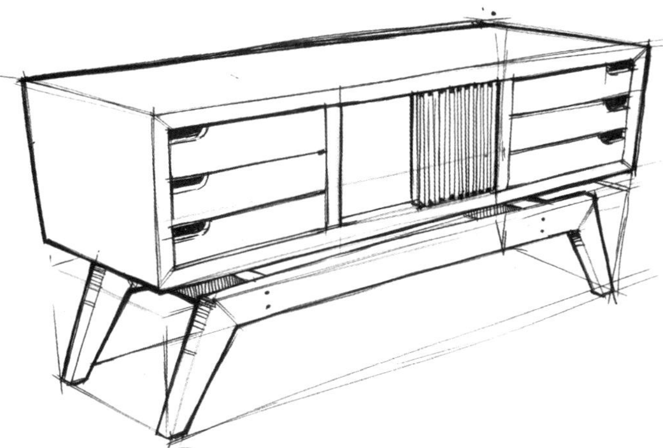

Add Line Weight, Texture, and Shadows

Add some line weight and definition to bring out the overall look and feel of the sideboard. Consider adding texture to a door or adding some value to the cutouts for the drawer pulls. Add line weight to the outline of the sideboard, to help establish the furniture piece and its placement on the page. If you were to compare this step and the previous step, you should notice that with the additional line weight, the sketch has a different look and feel and commands more of your attention. This is the power of using lines confidently in your sketches.

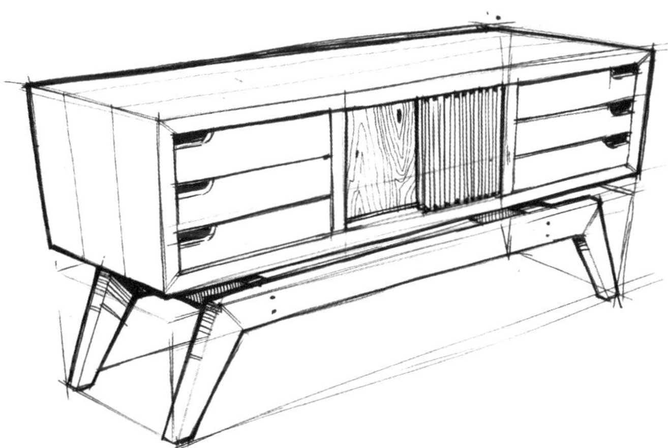

Add shadows and texture, if needed, to your sketch. Shadows will help reinforce the depth within the sketch and help convey a sense of interpreted realism. Because this is a wooden piece of furniture, I decided to showcase a bit of texture work on some of the wood paneling. On the front of the example, you can see a series of lines drawn in a way that conveys a wood-like texture to the door. Continue applying texture to the rest of the piece as needed.

With the texture of the wood shaded in and some shading applied to the shadow under the piece as sketched, the sideboard really takes on a life of its own. As you can imagine, adding color to this sketch would definitely enhance it as well. Right now, however, focus on getting familiar with applying textures to actual objects using simple techniques such as drawing your lines in a consistent and familiar pattern to create wood grain.

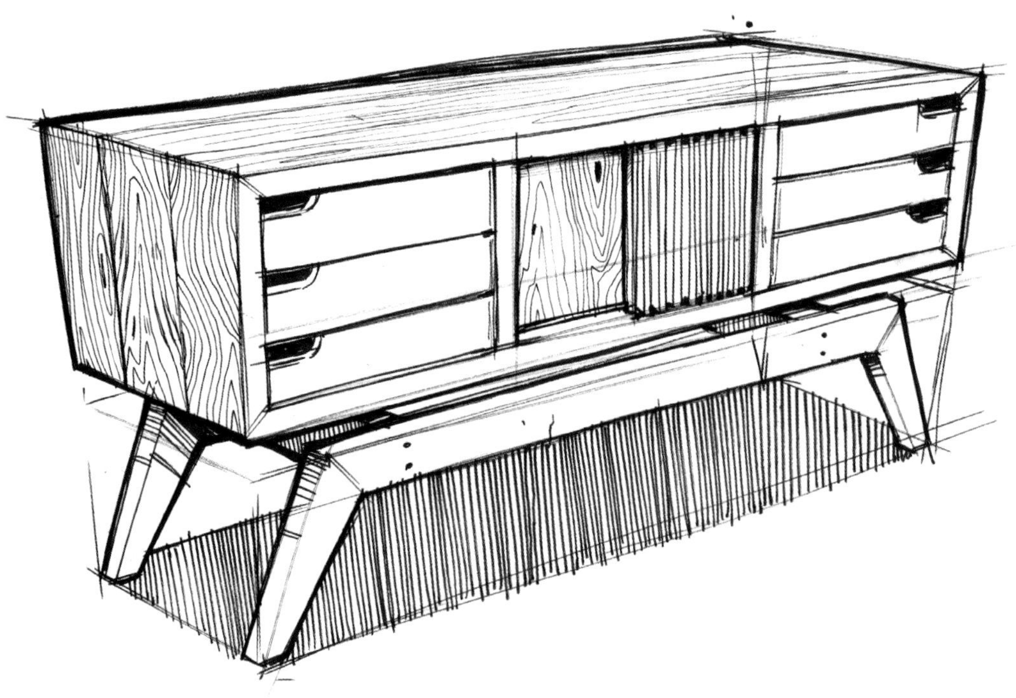

CHALLENGE

Draw other pieces of furniture, focusing on your line quality, shading, and texture creation. As a bonus, try to draw an item that has an interesting texture or one that requires you to draw a few longer lines. The challenge here is drawing consistently straight lines in perspective that appear as if they would converge at a single point.

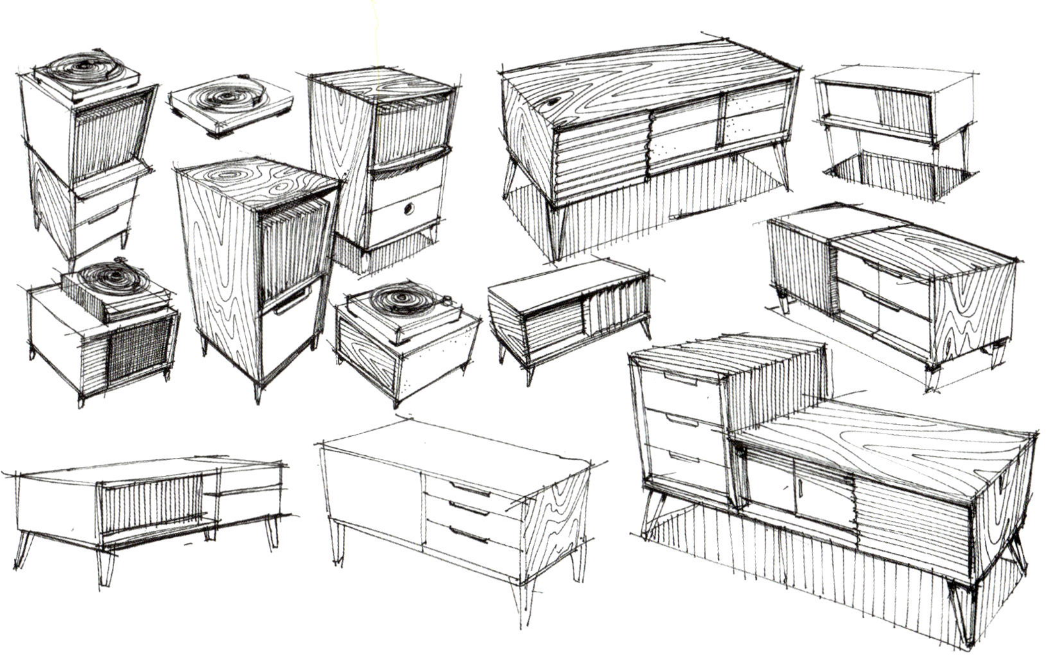

One of my favorite things to draw from my imagination is spaceships—well, besides robots, but we'll get to those in Chapter 4. Drawing a spaceship may seem complicated; however, if you break things down into simpler objects, it becomes a lot easier to draw. Consider this simple spaceship, for example. What primitive shapes can you see?

Its general form is made up of a sphere, a wedge, and two cylinders. By practicing form combinations, you can quickly develop aptitude and fluency in drawing more complex shapes. (Chapter 4 will give you lots of practice.)

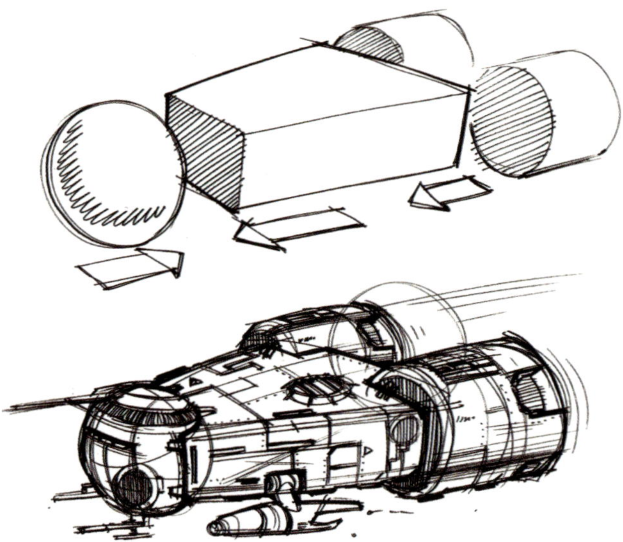

For the example, I used a light gray marker, a Sakura Micron pen, and marker paper, because I find that marker paper does a much better job of handling the marker ink than cheaper printer paper does. You, however, can use any paper and any pen that will give you a nice confident line. Remember, a pen that never forgets will push you to think about what you want to draw as you draw. It will also help you be more precise with your strokes. Stay loose, warm up, and have fun doing it!

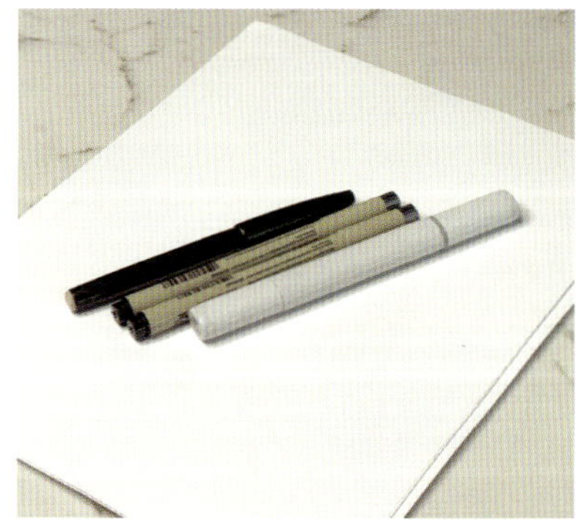

Strike a Centerline

To begin, grab a light gray marker or very light pencil. Decide where you want to place your spaceship and draw a line that represents the center of mass of the ship you want to draw. Think of this line as a bit like the central axis of a cylinder or the centerline of a shape, drawn in perspective. Because you drew the line with a light gray marker, it should not show up prominently in the final drawing.

With the centerline drawn in, imagine a flat, transparent piece of paper on which you are drawing the outline of the spaceship in perspective. Another way to think of this is by drawing a simple shape that will be the cross-section outline of your spaceship, using the first line you drew as a line of symmetry. You don't have to match the outline of my spaceship exactly. If you'd rather draw your own design, just keep in mind the overall feel that you desire and think of the simple objects that make up your spaceship.

Draw the Basic Shapes

Start drawing rough, simple shapes with your light gray marker. I added a wedge shape toward the front of my concept, for example. Pay attention to the convergence of lines that make up the overall spaceship design at this point. Paying attention to perspective in the early stages of your drawing will pay dividends later; when you add details, you'll be in a good position to follow the perspective framework of your drawing.

Rough in Details

Add details, like boosters or wings, in a
rough way. Because of the gray marker,
you should be able to "draw through"
(drawing the parts you wouldn't normally
see) to the other side of the spaceship
if you would like to check placement of
your boosters or other details.

Using the gray marker or a light pencil, continue to add details, like panels,
hinges, vents, antennas, or whatever
other details come to mind. As the
marker dries, the marker lines may seem
lighter than they did initially. If you need
to add additional emphasis, simply wait
for the marker ink to dry, and then reapply the same marker in the same spots
where you need additional darker values.

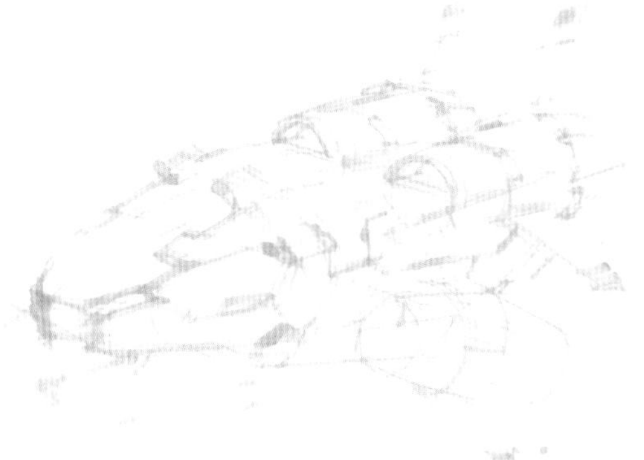

Increase Contrast with Pen

Now that the rough sketch of the
spaceship with details is complete, start
drawing with a pen to define the spaceship with additional clarity based on the
light gray sketch lines. At this point, you
may notice that there are issues with
your perspective or design intent for
your concept. Take some time to think
as you draw and correct any issues with
your pen. Notice that the pen lines are
much more visible than the light gray
marker lines. Contrast is your friend!

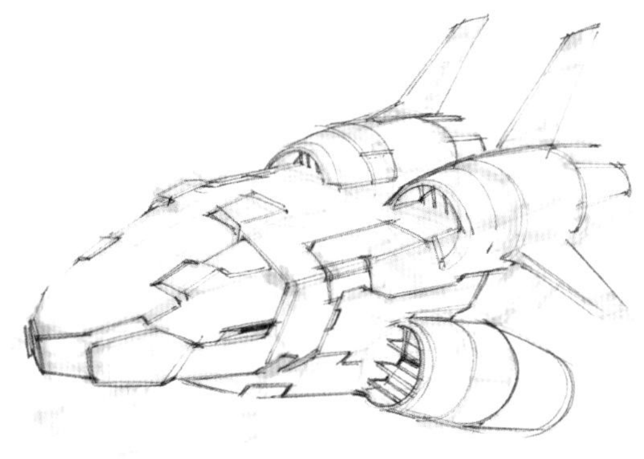

Add Final Details and Definition

If you're having trouble thinking about details for your spaceship, take a look at photos featuring aircraft or rockets, and pay attention to their details. Notice the panels, rivets, and even exposed mechanical parts at times. As you sketch, try to mimic these details, where possible. Double lines, small dots, and even drawing along the surface of the spaceship will help make its construction interesting and somewhat familiar.

If desired, add hatching, or stippling, as you sketch. At times, I find myself working all over my drawing rather than completing one section and moving on to the next.

As you work on adding details and definition, start to add more emphasis to the lines that make up important parts of your spaceship. Add lines to convey value or the three-dimensional geometry that makes up your spaceship.

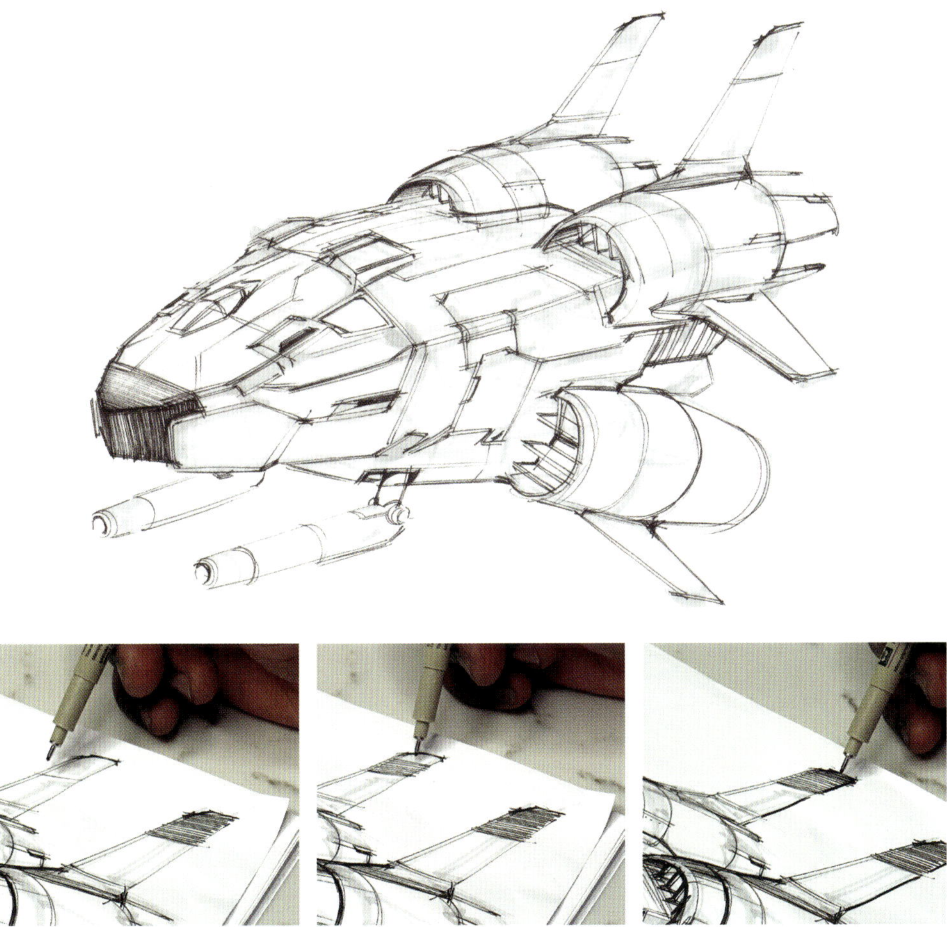

To finish, beef up the outline of your spaceship with additional pen strokes. A wider nibbed pen will give you a thicker line to help emphasize the final design of the spaceship. As a bonus, you could add text, symbols, scratches, or other details to your spaceship to give it a more interesting, realistic feel. Along the way, correct any perspective issues using a heavier line weight. If you missed it, notice the differences in perspective and symmetry between the second to last and the final sketch in this step.

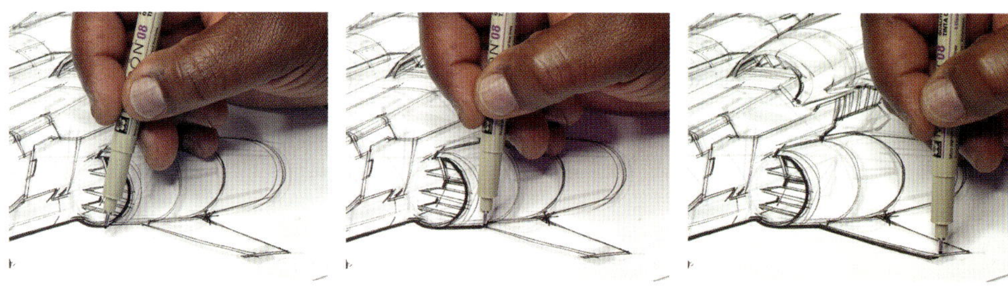

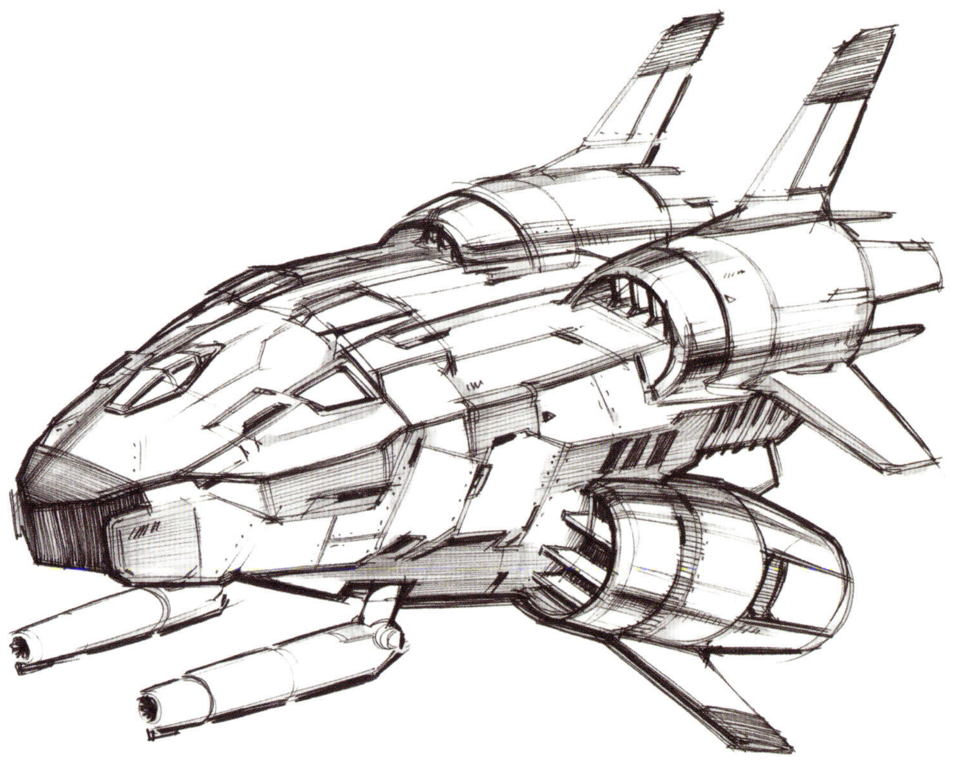

CHALLENGE

What interesting shapes and objects can you combine to create your own spaceship? Whichever you choose, focus on correct perspective. If you need to check perspective, show your drawing to a friend. They may notice something is wrong, even if they can't explain how to fix it. Work on including details in your spaceship to make it feel, well, more "spaceship-y." For detail inspiration, check out some real-life aircraft and spacecraft.

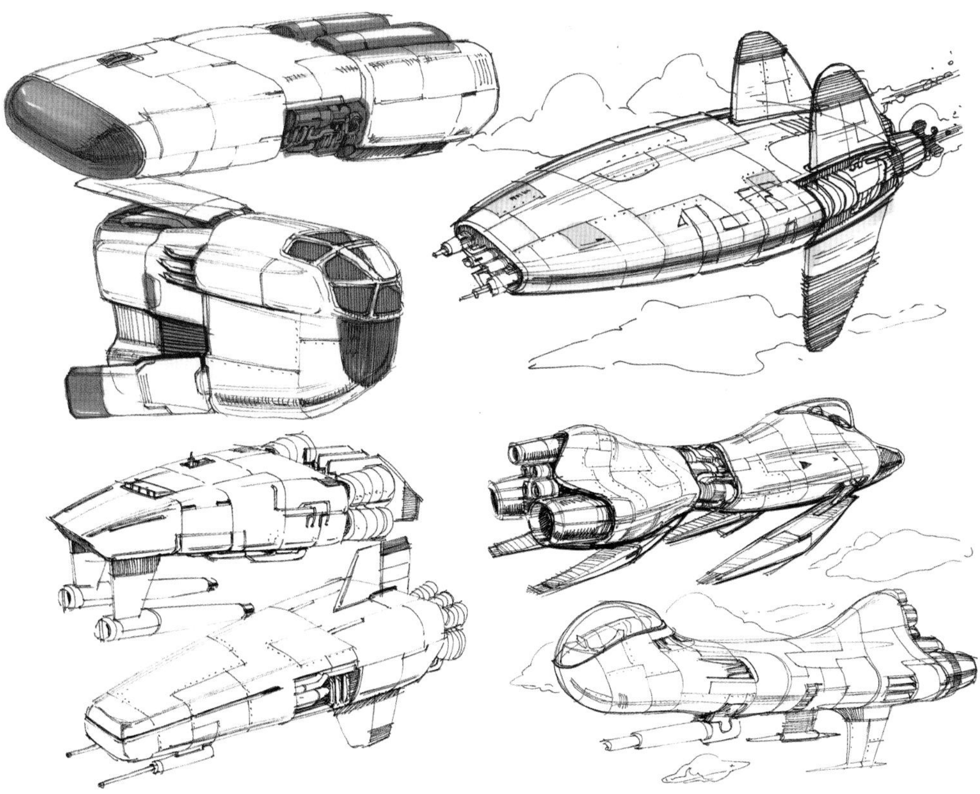

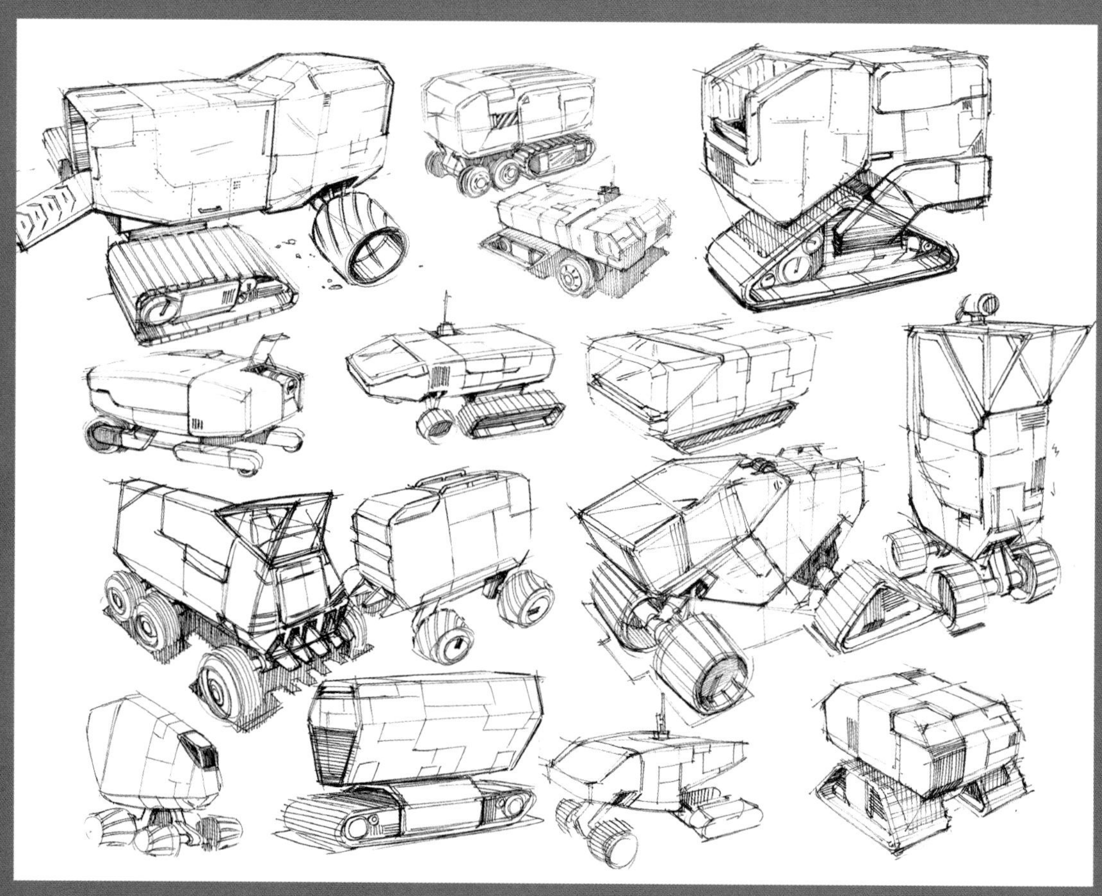

CHAPTER 3

SHADING AND ENHANCING DEPTH WITH SIMPLE TOOLS

You don't always need a full art studio to create something interesting when drawing. A simple felt pen, for example, is a powerful way to quickly capture ideas and is versatile enough to add textures and other enhancements to your sketch. Plus, the simple tool approach to drawing is a great way to sharpen your skills and become proficient with a particular tool before moving on to the next one.

Like the designated hitter or that clutch player the entire baseball team can rely on, a simple felt pen can deliver results when you need them most. When you practice with a specific tool, learning how to draw and shade with it, you and your designated hitter are taking batting practice, so to speak.

This chapter gives you an opportunity to do just that: You'll be drawing primarily with pens and black colored pencil. I encourage you to approach them with curiosity and excitement, trying to simplify your drawings by simplifying the tools you use. Let's get started.

 # ELECTRIC TOOTHBRUSH

Available in a variety of colors, a ballpoint pen is a convenient and versatile tool that you can take anywhere. Depending on the pressure you apply while drawing, it produces a lighter, thinner line or a thicker, heavier line. Plus, you can darken values by repeatedly applying it over a consistent area. Give a ballpoint pen a try this week to draw an electric toothbrush. For the example sketch, I used a simple BIC Cristal Xtra Smooth ballpoint and regular printer paper.

Mark the Axis and Proportions

To start, sketch a central line on your page in whatever orientation you wish to sketch your toothbrush. (I opted for one slightly angled away from being perfectly vertical.) This line is the central spine or axis of your toothbrush. Next, create marks that proportionally divide your line into a region for the head of the toothbrush and the handle. These marks will serve as a guide for the next step.

Sketch the Basic Shapes

Next, lightly sketch or block in ellipses or cross-section shapes for the handle of the toothbrush, then lightly sketch the head and area for the bristles. Remember, using less pressure with the ballpoint pen will give you a lighter construction line as you work out these details.

Refine the Outline

Begin filling in the overall outline of the toothbrush. If necessary, check a reference image (or make a quick research trip to your bathroom sink) before completing the silhouette. Continue enhancing the line weight of the toothbrush around the overall outline of the silhouette and up to the head of the toothbrush.

Next, work on refining the outline, including adding details that hint at the head of the brush having bristles. Notice the slightly jagged line at the edge of the bristles in the example. Additionally, consider adding a power button or switch. I sketched an elliptical shape in perspective with a slight offset to indicate where the button would go, along with a slight pill shape below to show where potentially there could be a light.

Continue cleaning up the sketch by sketching repeatedly and essentially shading in a darker line with the ballpoint pen. Creating a darker value for this outline helps the toothbrush have a sense of place on the page, and essentially shading this line in is a neat way of ensuring that you have a clean outline for your sketch.

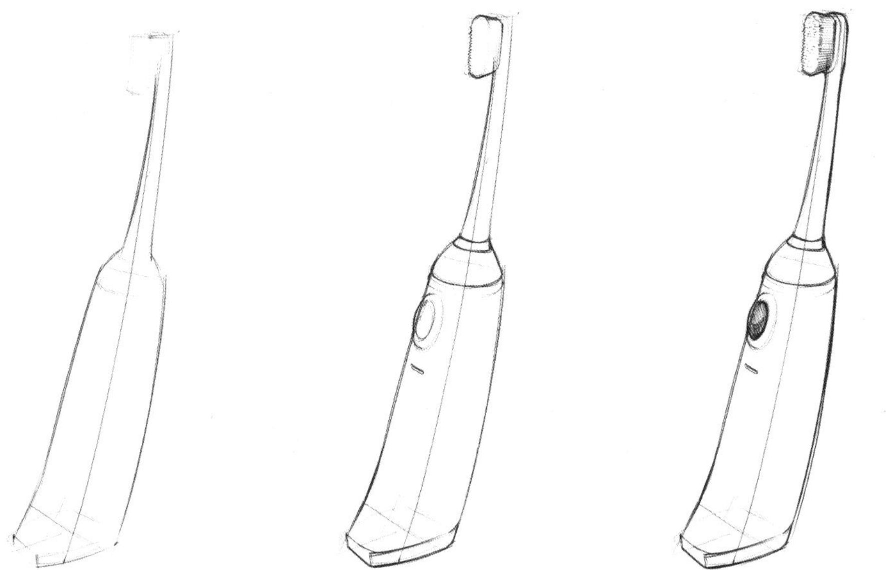

Add Shading

Shading with a ballpoint pen is similar to shading with a pencil because of its pressure sensitivity. Unlike a pencil, however, a ballpoint pen is limited in terms of the angle at which you can hold it to draw on the paper. Therefore, shading with a ballpoint pen is a matter of creating a slight gradient in the resulting lines by varying the amount of pressure you use.

To add shading to the toothbrush, think about your
light source in the scene. Start with the handle, lightly
sketching in a series of lines toward its left and right
sides. Depending on the orientation of your toothbrush, you may need to adjust the direction of shading
you choose. To create a shadow core, create an area of
intensity at the center of these lines and slightly reduce
the pressure as you move away from this core shadow.
By sketching your lines in this way, you can create an
effective gradient using your ballpoint pen to communicate surface finish as well as materiality.

Continue shading up the neck of the brush. Notice in
the example the shading applied above the handle to
the transitional surface into the neck is a lot starker and
has a darker value than the handle. This portion of the
toothbrush is likely a different material, such as shiny
metal. Remember to keep it loose and fresh as you
sketch. Try not to overthink and move quickly.

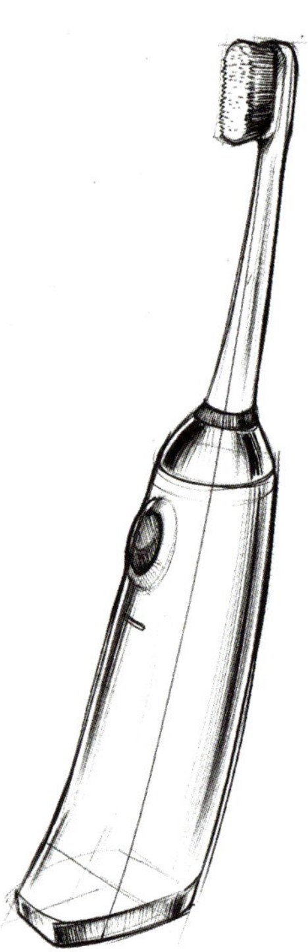

THE SQUINT CHECK

Remember, contrast is your friend when shading. If you're not sure of how
much contrast to add, try squinting your eyes while looking at your sketch. This
technique reduces the amount of complexity you see and allows your eyes to
focus on the values in the drawing. By squinting, you can more accurately evaluate the amount of contrast in your shading without distractions.

CHALLENGE

**Practice shading with a ballpoint pen or pencil. You can start out by shading
simple shapes, or if you like, try your hand at sketching a few toothbrushes or
similar objects. Work on varying your pressure to vary the shading tone. Pay
attention and observe the differences in your results. Compare and connect
the results with how you were drawing previously.**

In this exercise, you'll use a colored pencil to sketch a simple utility flashlight. You can get a lot of expression out of a single pencil. Depending on the pressure you apply, your pencil's lead will produce a thicker, thinner, or more gritty line. Angling your pencil and shading with it will give you a completely different stroke as well. Take some time to familiarize yourself with how your pencil reacts to pressure and sensitivity at different angles before you begin the exercise. I used a black Prismacolor Premier pencil for the example.

As you work, keep in mind that because of the way pencils transfer material onto the paper, rubbing your hand on your sketch can cause smudging. Colored pencils are more resistant to smudging than graphite or charcoal pencils, but the possibility of getting your sheet of paper a bit dirty from an inadvertent rub or hand placement still exists. Stay loose, pivot from your elbow and shoulder, but always be mindful of where your hands are to avoid smudging your work.

Sketch the Axis

First, sketch a line to represent the central axis of the flashlight. This line will help locate the flashlight on your paper and set up the angle at which you're drawing. To set up the perspective, sketch a line above and below the axis so that all three appear to be converging towards a single point in the distance.

Add Ellipses

Lightly sketch three ellipses. You can either sketch these in part or whole, depending on your comfort level. In the example, I have sketched the front ellipse and the rear ellipse in whole and then partially sketched the third to represent the flashlight's trim. You will use your three ellipses to guide the rest of the sketch. The ellipse toward the front will be the lens where the bulb of the flashlight is located.

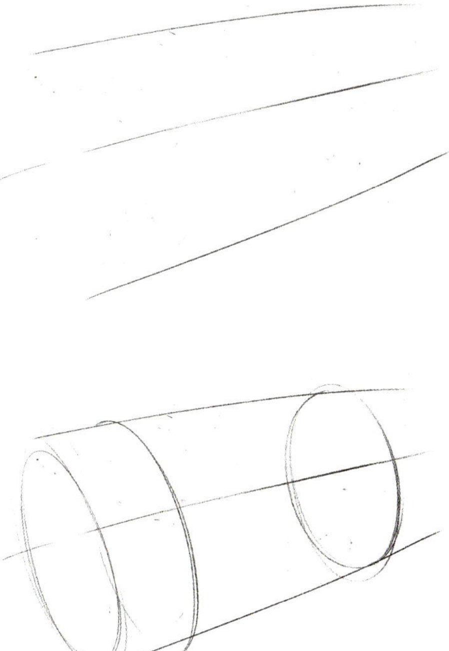

Rough in the Body

To provide another reference for the handle, sketch a simple plane that intersects the central axis. For construction line work like this, be sure to use only light pressure. Continue sketching the handle and other details on the flashlight. If it helps, you can draw with straight lines first and then curved lines. In my process, I went ahead and sketched curved lines in lightly to act as construction lines for the example flashlight. Here you can see the handle and the body beginning to take shape.

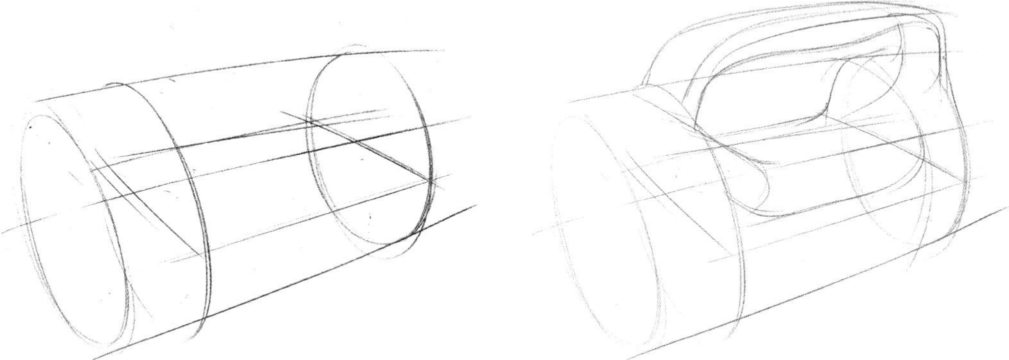

Add Details

Continue adding details like a power button, material breaks, or part segments in your flashlight sketch. You can offset ellipses toward the front of the flashlight to create a sense of depth for the bezel or trim of the flashlight. Additionally, obscuring part of the offset ellipse toward the front creates a nice spot for a bulb or LED array for the flashlight. Feel free to add any details like an accessory strap or battery door, or whatever comes to mind.

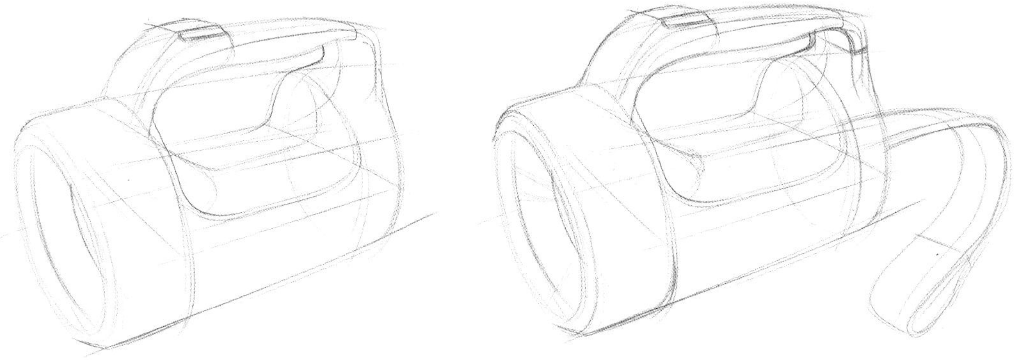

Emphasize Line Weight

Begin to define the flashlight as an object by enhancing the line weight. To do this, simply re-sketch over your existing construction lines with the same pencil and push a little harder. You can rotate your pencil as you draw to maintain a sharp tip as you sketch. The more pressure you apply, the more quickly the pencil's tip wears down. Don't forget to rotate or pause for a quick sharpen now and then. Of course, you could also sharpen a few pencils ahead of time so that you could simply grab a new one rather than break the flow of your work.

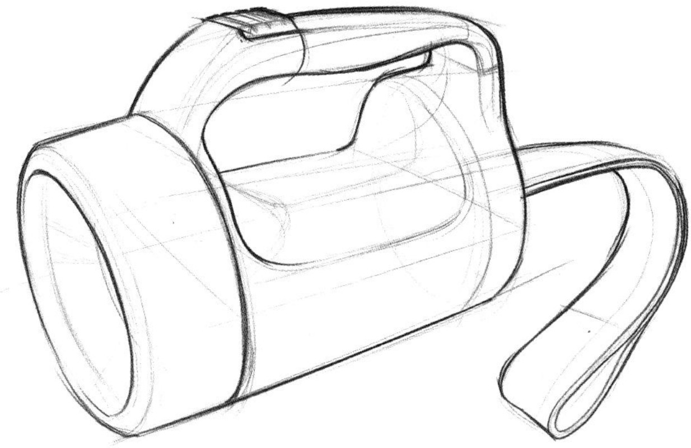

Shade the Shadows

Think about the light source in your scene. Where is the light coming from, and how is it interacting with the flashlight? In my example, the light is located somewhere to the right and above the flashlight, which I indicated by highlights on the bezel.

Add an appropriate highlight to your bezel. A highlight is where the light is most intense on a part of your sketch. Think about the relative position of the light (somewhere to the right and above the flashlight) and place a highlight in line with the light source. This can be done by leaving an area white as you shade or using something like correction fluid, paint or white pencil to add some white.

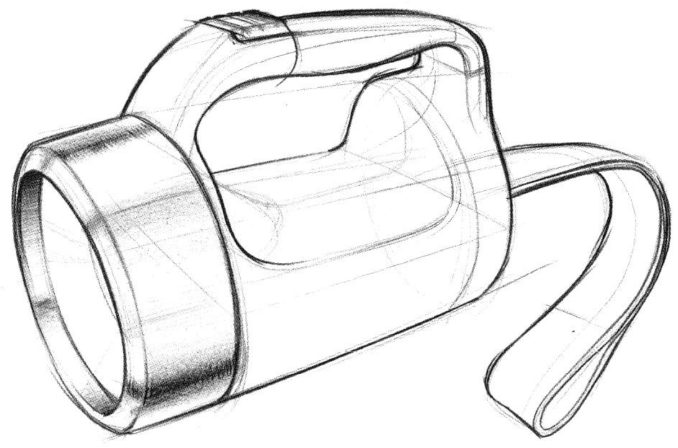

Because there is a shadow on the recessed lens, you can shade a little heavier to create the effect of a recessed area. Toward the bottom of the bezel, introduce a shadow core to help communicate the roundness of the flashlight. You can add a secondary shadow core to your flashlight toward the top or simply focus on leaving a highlight in that spot. Regardless of where you put your highlights and shadow cores, be sure to work light until you get it right. Go easy on the pencil. The more confident and familiar you become with the tool, the quicker you'll be able to shade in details.

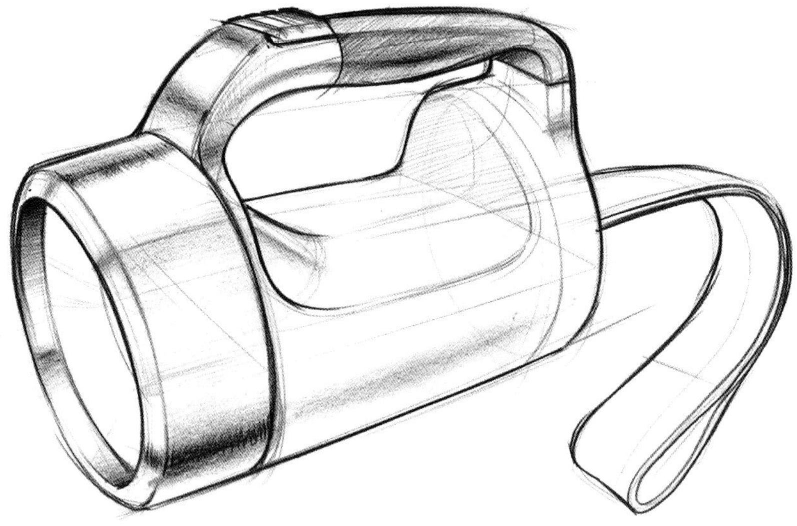

Continue shading the rest of the flashlight by tilting your pencil to the side and covering larger areas than you would be able to with the tip. However, on the handle grip, I chose to shade with the tip of the pencil to create a different kind of texture. This way, I can get two effects from the same tool. Add any subtle shadow cores or shadows as you shade your flashlight in.

While you work, remember to try a squint check (Exercise 14). Whether working in pen or pencil, it is a good way to check whether your object feels three-dimensional or whether you need to introduce some additional deeper values and contrast in the sketch to reinforce the three-dimensional perspective drawing.

Introduce Texture

Lastly, think about ways to introduce texture where applicable. For example, on the strap, I added a series of strokes meant to convey a fabric-like texture, as well as shading to show depth and shadow where applicable. On the flashlight's reflector, shade in a couple of dark areas that are punctuated by white spots. This effect is common and familiar in appearance and is a quick way to show a shiny chrome-like reflector as a part of the flashlight. Touch up any areas as necessary on the outline or any other shaded-in areas by revisiting them as you finish up. And there you have it: You completed a flashlight. Give yourself a pat on the back, a high-five, or just smile really big.

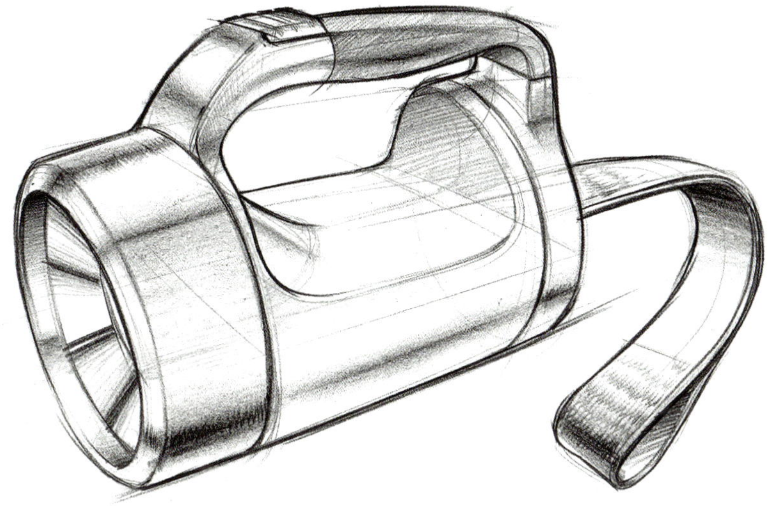

CHALLENGE

Continue to sketch your own flashlight designs. Pay attention to the construction of your lines, shading, and the cleanliness of your work. Represent textures and definitely look at visual reference if you need to as you sketch. If you're feeling adventurous, apply the techniques you learned in this exercise to some other product ideas as well.

For this exercise and challenge, you'll be sketching some tea kettles. By now, you should be used to sketching objects in a few views. Sketching a product in different views gives you an opportunity to practice perspective and point of view, as well as allows you to pack more information into a single sketch page.

Choose a marker or pen that will give you a solid line (I used a Paper Mate Flair pen on printer paper), and warm up by practicing drawing lines, circles, and ellipses.

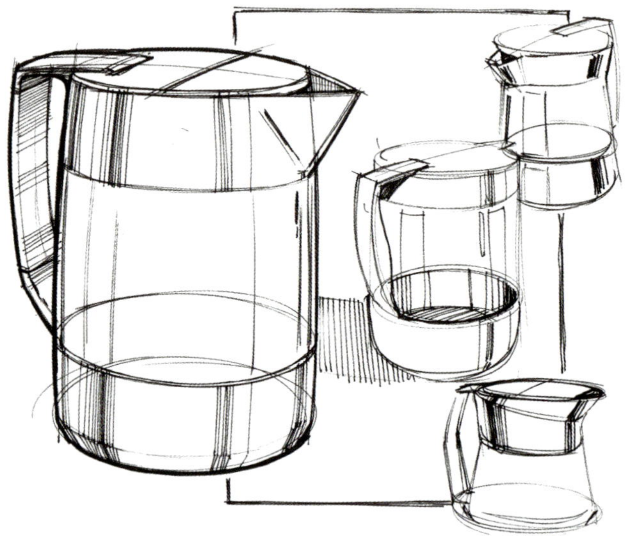

Sketch the Basic Forms

To start, sketch two ellipses, one above the other. Make the top one a bit narrower than the bottom one, because the angle between the top of the kettle and your eye (the point of view) is shallower than the angle between the bottom of the kettle and your eye. Don't despair if this is difficult. Ellipses are among the hardest aspects of sketching to master. For some tips to help, see Warmup 3 and Exercise 2. Next, sketch a centerline across the top to help you locate the spout later.

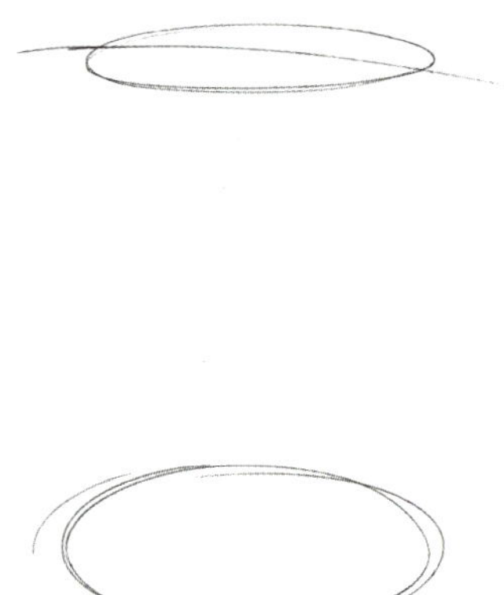

To establish the overall shape of the kettle, draw two arcs that connect the top and bottom ellipses tangentially. This serves to establish the overall shape of the kettle, which has a slightly convex, cylinder-like surface.

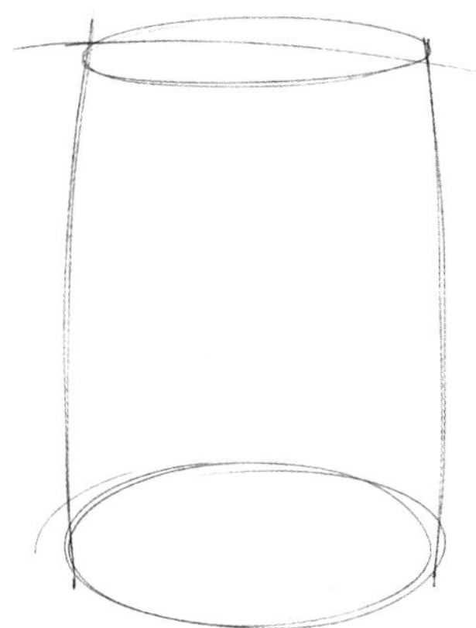

Add the Spout and Handle

Sketch in the spout oriented with its point on the centerline and add a part line to indicate where the kettle widens at the base. Notice that in the example I used the initial line at the top of the kettle to locate the end of the spout. If you wish to change your design or do something different, you can use a similar technique by placing a centerline elsewhere on the top of the kettle. Also, notice that the bottom of the spout is not coincident with the outside line of the kettle, because the centerline at the top does not intersect the vertical boundary of the kettle as you can see.

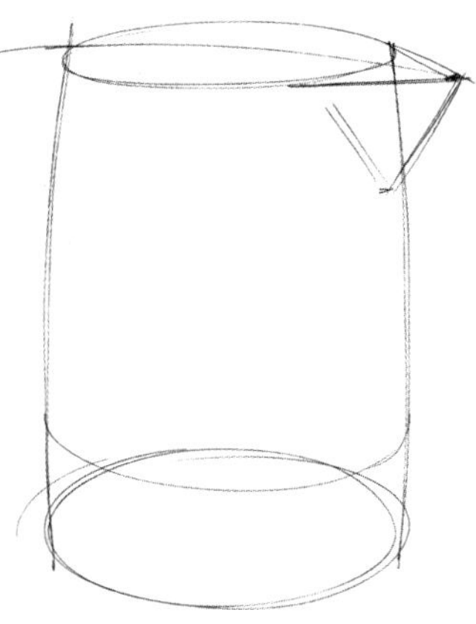

Will the body of your kettle be transparent or opaque? To leave your options open, use the centerline at the top again to roughly sketch in a handle, but stop your strokes before the outside edge of the initial kettle shape.

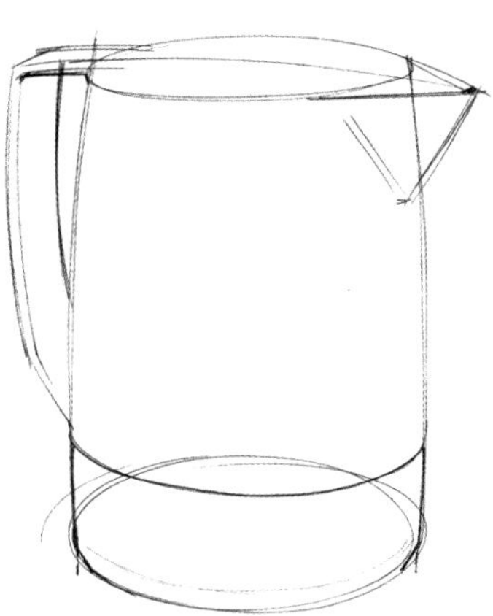

Next, continue to break up and define parts of the kettle by sketching in additional lines. Adding a bit of line weight here will also help pull out any relevant details in your kettle. As you can see, I added line weight to the handle, spout, and overall perimeter of the kettle to enhance the visual appearance of the example kettle. I also added a double line to its body to communicate some materiality and translucency in the design.

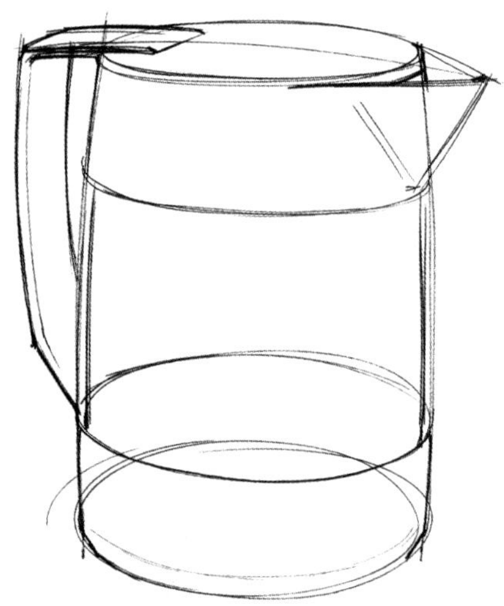

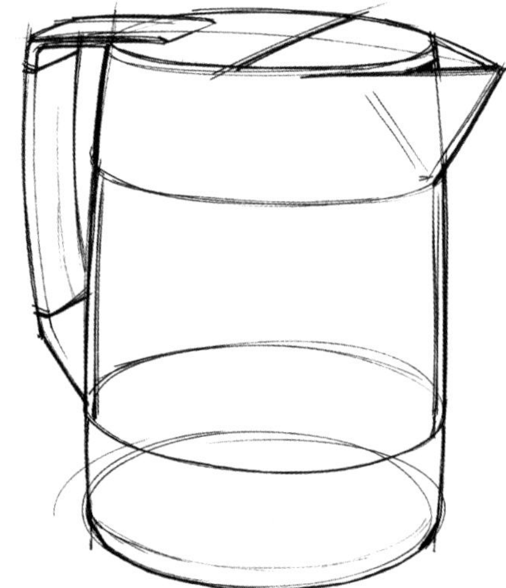

Hatch in Shading

Finally, add some hatch lines to your sketch. Notice that the hatch lines in the example are complementary to the surfaces on which I sketched them. I shaded this way so as not to undermine or counter the perspective and the nature of the details I included in the sketch. If you're running into difficulty trying to decide where to put sketch lines, just remember that shadows are the absence of light, and you can observe a lot of examples of reflections in shiny materials by looking around you.

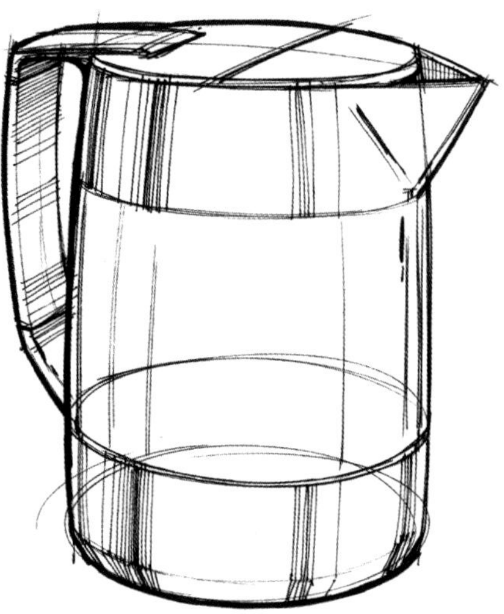

CHALLENGE

Try drawing a few kettles from different perspectives. Use simple tools
and focus on the structure and perspective of the kettles. Think about the
composition on the page and where you'd like to place objects. Try to vary
the scale, position, and details in each concept as you practice and work
through the challenge. Don't worry about color or using other materials; the
goal for the challenge is to work on line quality, shading, and using a single
simple tool.

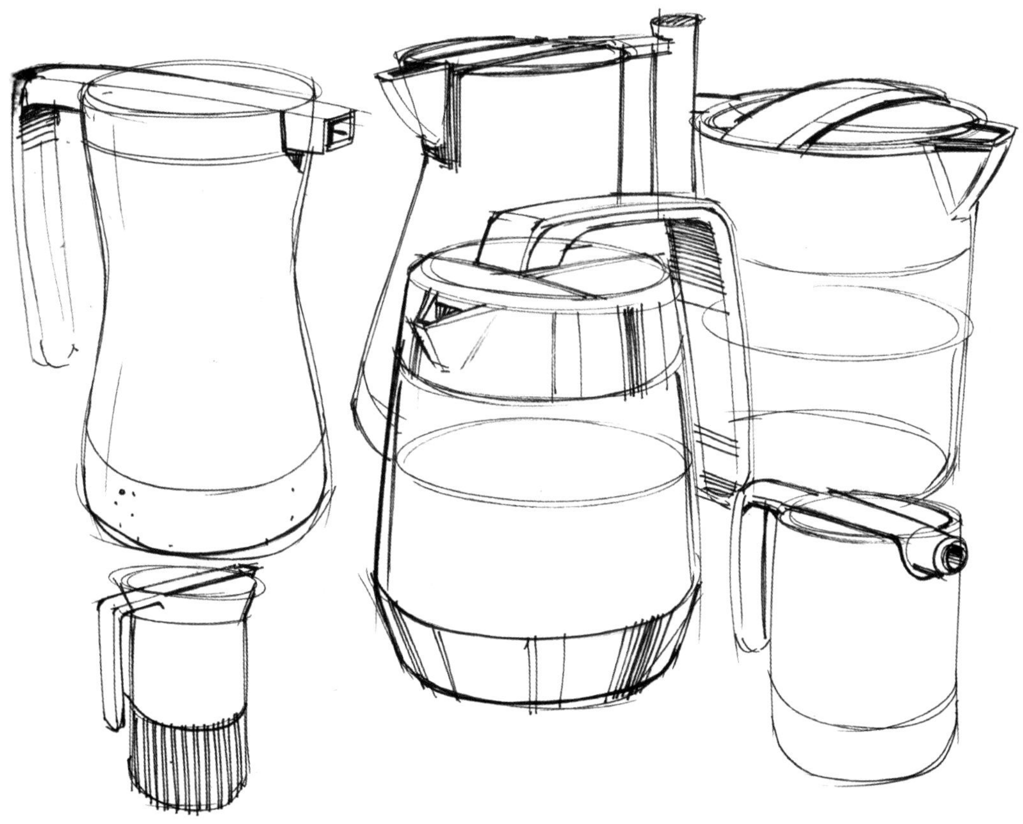

For this exercise, you'll sketch multiple views of similar keyfobs on the same page. When sketching multiple items on the same page, you need think about the overall composition. To make an interesting one, you need to include a reasonable amount of variety. Think of music: Listening to a piece with the same beat and tone on and on gets boring eventually. The more interesting compositions have a balance of beats and harmony throughout. Think of your sketches as beats. How do each of these beats fit and balance in the overall composition on your page?

Sketch Boxes

Start by drawing boxes in a variety of views in perspective. These will serve as wireframes for your sketch concepts. These boxes represent the overall volume of the ideas and will serve as a guide as you sketch and add details. In each box, sketch in elements for your ideas. These boxes could be the same keyfob if you choose, or you can lean into your creativity and sketch a variety of designs. Rough in major elements and work light until you get it right, building up your ideas without stressing too much about perfection.

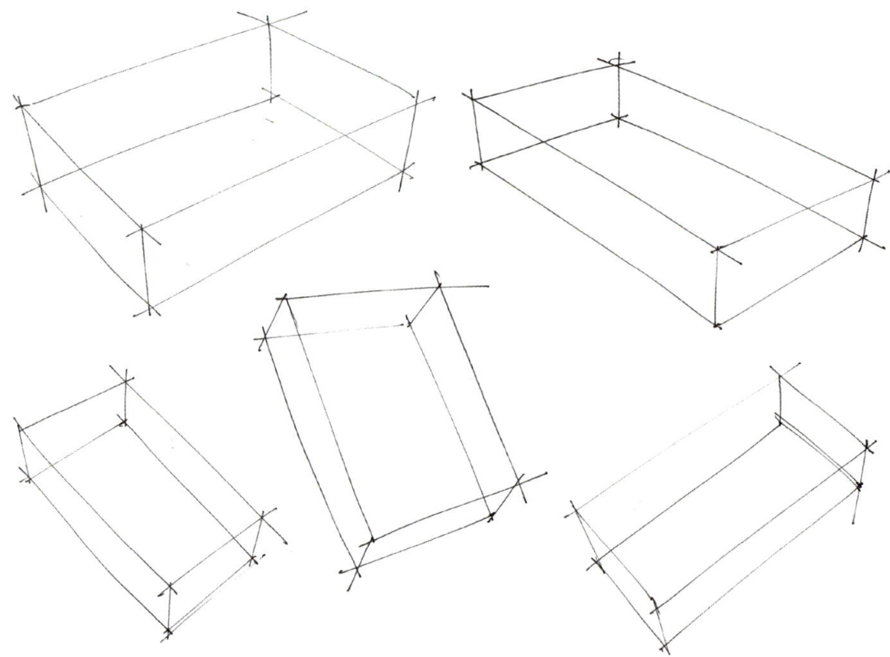

Add Line Weight

Notice that my construction lines are showing at this stage. As I sketched, these lines overlapped and intersected to create boundaries and perimeters within each sketch. Adding line weight and other details to the views will clean up these lines. So, add some line weight to each of your sketches.

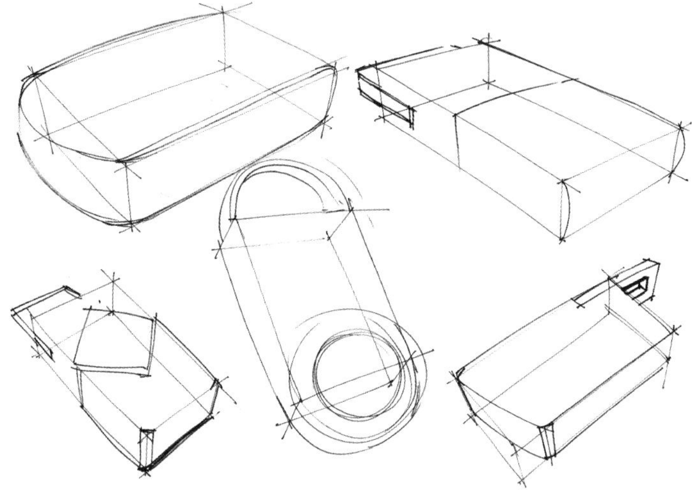

Consider the Light Source

Although you could think of one consistent light source for a composition like this, I oftentimes vary where light is coming from for individual sketches. Understanding where the light is coming from will tell you where to add shadow, and in this case, where to make hatch lines more or less intense.

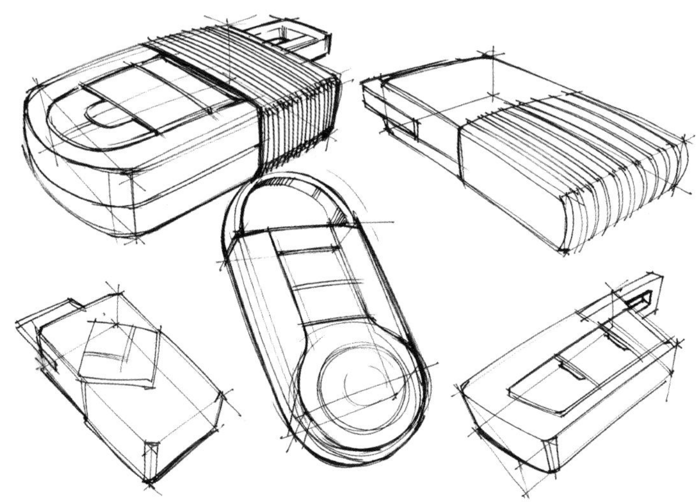

Add Texture

Adding texture to concepts by drawing a series of lines close together or further apart is a great way to quickly pump up and enhance a sketch. Notice that two concepts in the example have distinct linear textures that draw your eye.

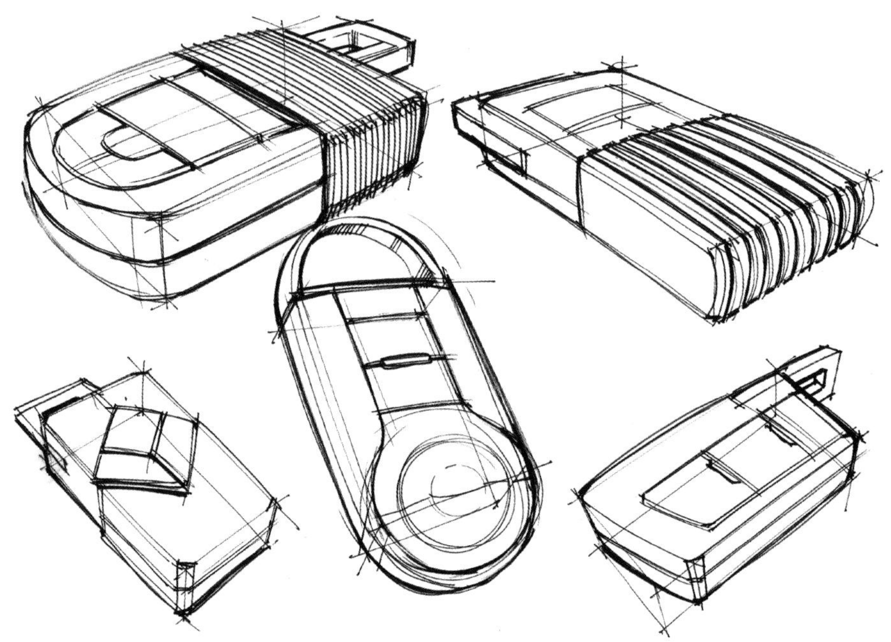

Enhance Dimensionality

Continue to add line weight and define and refine each drawing. By adding line weight, immediately areas of interest are created, and fidelity is added to these sketch concepts. You can enhance line weight by drawing repeatedly in the same spot or by switching to a pen with a wider tip.

Add vertical lines on the rounded corners, as well as periodically on faces, to convey three-dimensionality, that the surfaces are not perfectly flat, or that they are also interacting with the light. Sketch in a shadow under each of the fobs you wish to highlight. Use your judgment here and decide for yourself where you would like to place some emphasis with shadow. To sketch the shadows in the example, I opted for a simple drop shadow. To create one, project the contour profile of the object downward until it hits the ground plane below each keyfob.

This can be tricky if you're not used to visualizing, so observe how the shadows of real-world objects project onto a flat surface. Move the position of the light source and notice how the object's shadow changes on its ground plane. By projecting and observing the shadow of a real object, you can learn much about symbolically representing shadows in your sketches.

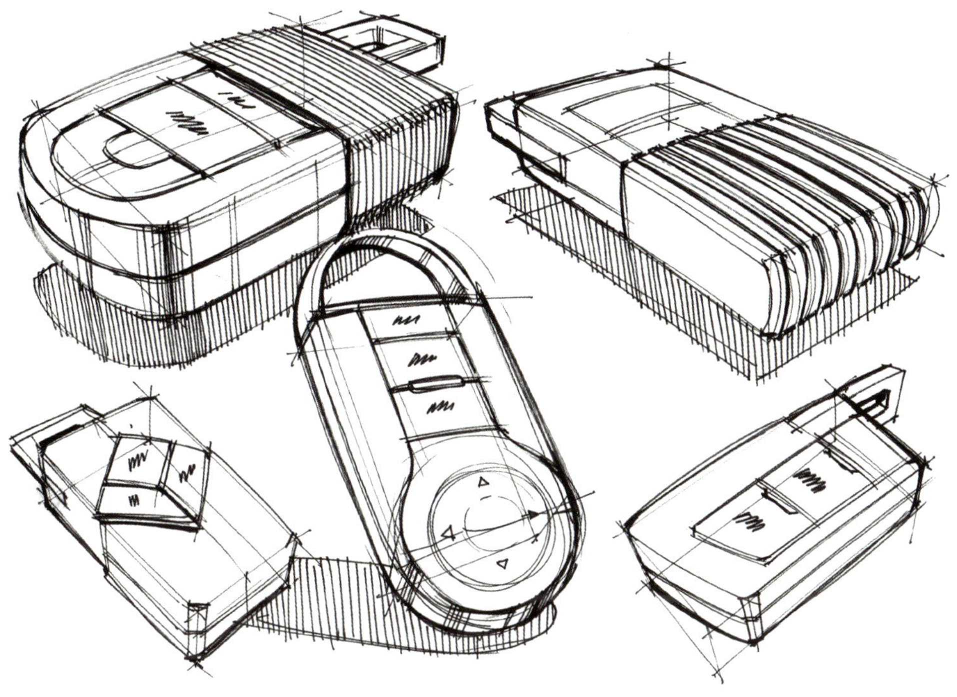

CHALLENGE

Sketch objects from a similar family in multiple views. Sketching in multiple views will help you get quicker at perspective drawing as well as create more interesting compositions. Sometimes we all (even professionals) get into ruts and patterns, so it's important to mix things up. Observational drawing from different views can help you break the habit of being too comfortable with drawing the same way you always do.

Sketching natural objects can be a nice departure from sketching rigid, man-made objects. To sketch organic and natural objects, you need a slightly different approach, as you'll learn in this exercise. Let's take a look at sketching some rocks.

I recommend some very fine point pens. If you want to produce a variety of strokes, consider purchasing a set of Sakura Micron pens with very fine tips to thicker tips. A brush pen may also be useful for sketching organic objects like these rocks. I used printer paper for the example. If you want to apply markers or another medium like watercolors, you may want to use cold press watercolor paper or Bristol board instead.

Draw the Initial Sketch

Start by sketching the outline of the general shape of these rocks. Draw from your imagination, take a walk where you can study rocks or boulders as reference, or seek out some reference imagery.

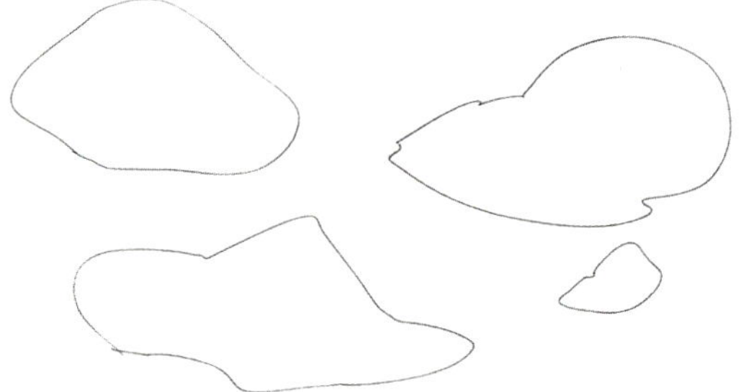

Use Crosshatching for Shading

When you're satisfied with your silhouettes, start sketching in a few lines slightly inset from the outer silhouette of each shape. These lines are the beginning of the shadow core and are a concentration of the texture that you will be applying using crosshatching: Sketch a series of parallel lines that follow a similar flow to each other and the surface you're shading.

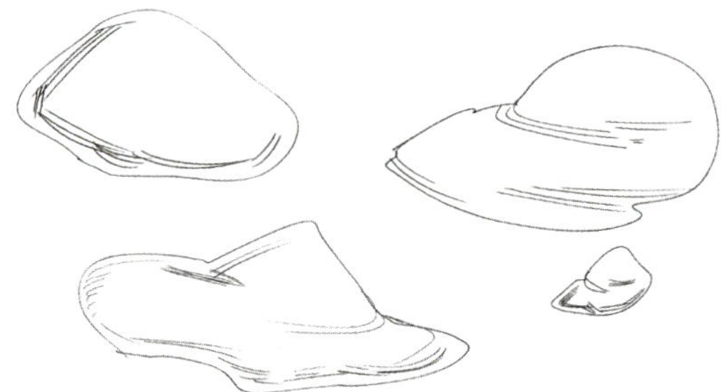

To decide on a crosshatching angle, simply consider the direction each face of the rock might be facing and any details that might be present on the rocks like cracks or bumps. Don't overthink it, though.

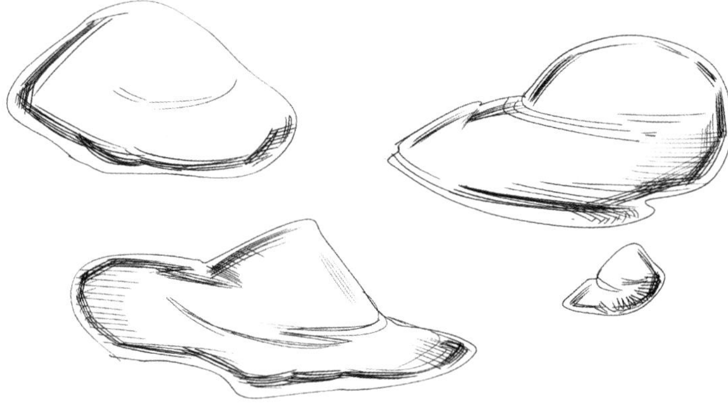

Continue darkening by placing additional lines in the same area close to the perimeter of the rocks. Notice that the shadow core is now a bit darker. Additionally, to simulate texture, add hatch lines by sketching at an orthogonal angle to the sketch lines that are present. This introduces a secondary value through the use of lines that are spaced slightly further apart but give the overall area a texture of sorts.

Continue crosshatching and shading by changing the direction of the lines you sketch in. Be mindful of the imagined topography of each of the rocks and hatch lines in accordingly. With a fine pen, it may take several overlaps of crosshatching to get the deepness and tone that you are after.

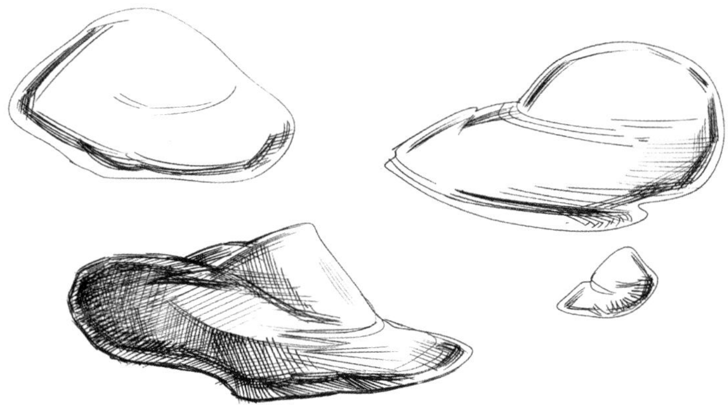

Add Texture

After crosshatching to create some light texture and value in your rock, emphasize the outline by sketching with a slightly thicker pen or sketching repeatedly in the same areas. As this is an organic object, short strokes and a looser drawing style work well. For the remaining rocks, follow the pattern of the first rock by enhancing the shadow core and adding crosshatching.

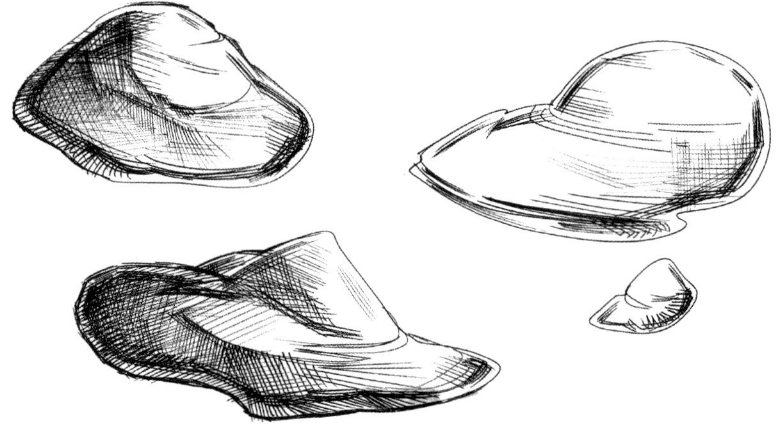

Add Shadows

When you're satisfied with your crosshatching of the deepest values, lightly outline a shadow for the ground plane. I drew the shadow with my thinnest stroke as this area will be filled in the last step. To help your rocks feel a bit more realistic, consider adding stippling or spots. Remember to consider the lighting in your scene when placing your shadows and shading the rock with hatching.

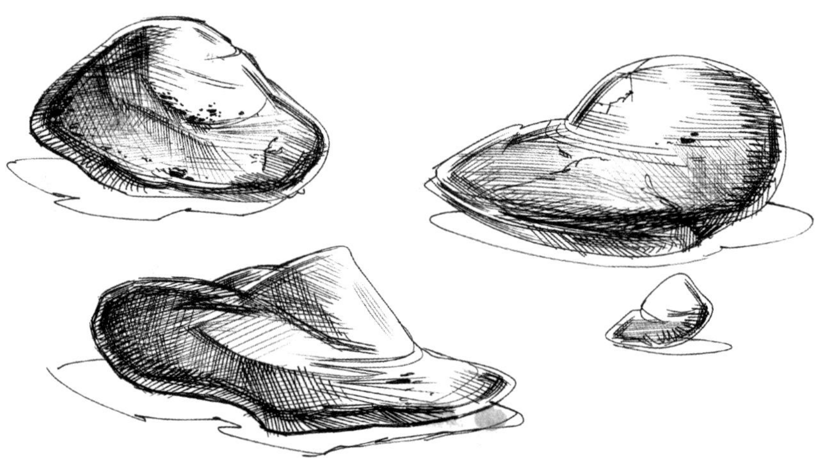

Add Final Touches

To finish up, either grab a marker or thick pen and hatch in your shadows such that the shadows have the darkest value of black on your page. Adding a dark shadow like this will help the rocks really pop and also give them an added element of three-dimensionality.

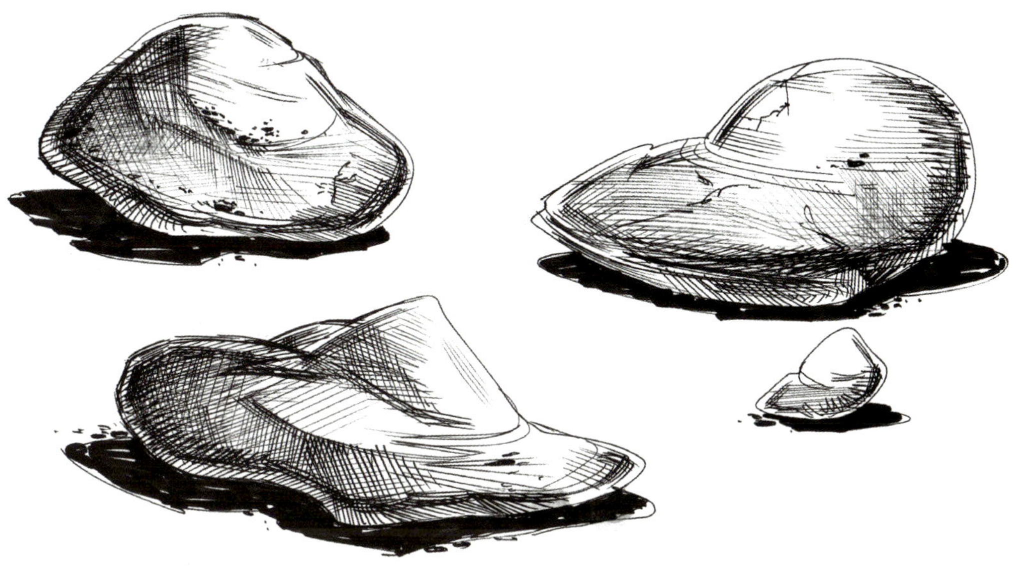

CHALLENGE

Play with organic shapes and shade in using crosshatching and textures to create rocks of your own. This should be a fairly simple exercise but an enjoyable break from more structured sketching. I find it helpful to first lay out the shapes I'd like to sketch, and then work to fill in those shapes with the shading and other textural details as needed.

Let's stay outside for Week 19 and sketch a leafy deciduous tree. You can apply the techniques demonstrated to any shape of tree you decide to create. The focus for this exercise is on texture, gesture, and the structure of the trees themselves. To start, identify where you want to draw your tree on the page, and imagine or visualize a ground plane on which to plant your tree. If it helps, you can always consult some reference imagery. With an idea in mind, grab a simple pen and get started.

Sketch the Basic Structure

Sketch a few lines to suggest a general direction of the trunk, as well as a circle and two ellipses to represent the eventual clusters of leaves that will make up your tree. Thinking of the tree as being made up of simpler geometry should give you a sense of how to shade these clusters of leaves and branches as well as the trunk of the tree. For example, the trunk of a tree can largely be described as a combination of cylinders or a cylinder that has been squished or stretched into the shape of the trunk.

Add Branches

Next, using the initial straight lines as a guide, lightly sketch in branches for your tree. Now would be a good time to look at references if you haven't already, or just take a look out the window at a leafy tree near you. Notice that as the trunk transitions into the main branches of the tree, the branches diminish in diameter as they get progressively further away from the main trunk. Understanding this

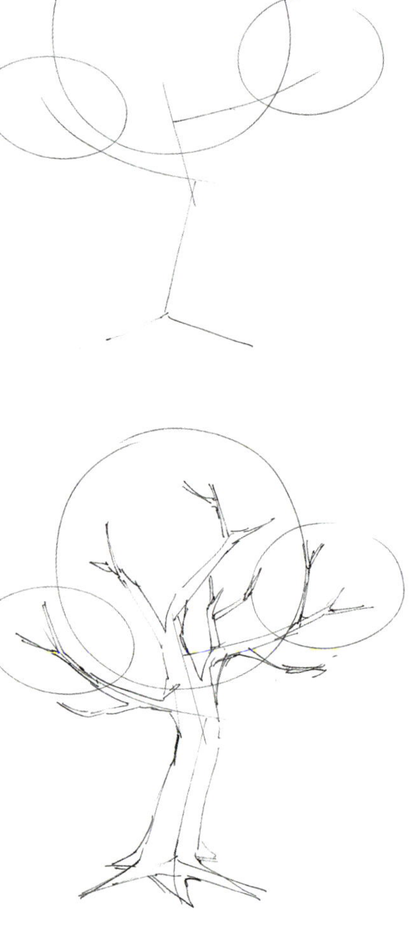

detail makes it a lot easier to draw branches that look and feel realistic. Additionally, you may want to take some time to look at how the branches in a tree tend to be arranged. Remember, sketching isn't always about creating a perfect re-creation of what you see, but rather identifying patterns in what you see and replicating those patterns on paper.

Sketch the Foliage

Now that the branches are in place, move on to sketching in the foliage of the tree. Using the ellipses and circle as a guide, sketch a very squiggly, continuous line around each shape. I sketched the squiggles along the path of the initial circle and ellipse by moving my hand and fingers in an erratic pattern. This is a good point to pause and practice creating a squiggly stroke of your own through experimentation and exploration.

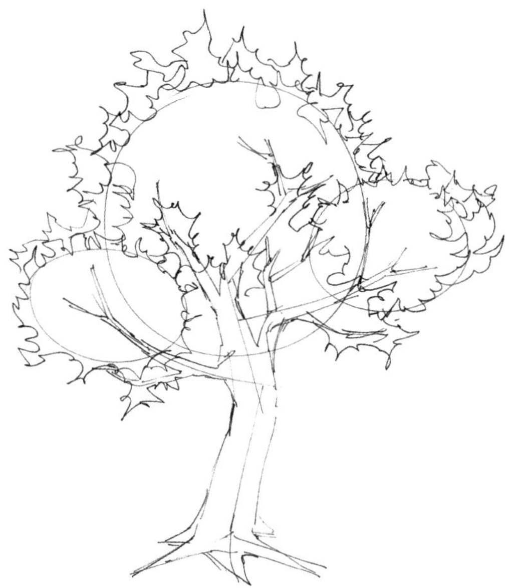

Shade the Foliage

With your squiggles in place and several leafless pockets sketched in, begin hatching the shadowed portion of the pockets in the foliage. Remember to hatch in a consistent direction. If you take a look at a tree, you'll notice that the leaves are arranged in layers. These layers will feature leaves that appear brighter on the outside and darker toward the center of the tree, especially on a deciduous tree such as this. The hatch line shading you use here is meant to convey that depth without your getting bogged down in the details of sketching every single leaf. This is an example of editing while sketching to prioritize the effect over the specific detail and realism in a sketch. If you have the time or motivation to sketch individual leaves, go ahead but follow the same technique for shading them.

Finalize the Outline and Add Texture

With the pockets shaded in using parallel line hatching, move on to the outline of the tree and trunk itself to create this outer limit rather than using a whole line. Use short strokes to create a sense of roughness on the tree trunk. Be careful not to overdo this step; instead, carefully build up to the final appearance of your tree. Remember, it's a lot easier to work light until you get it right, and doing so makes it easier to correct or work with mistakes along the way.

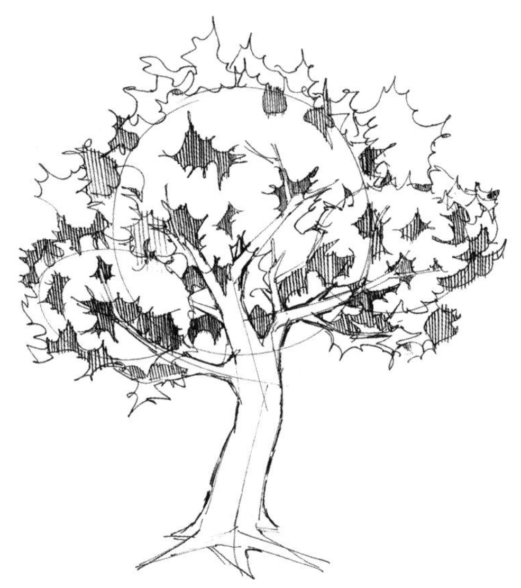

Complete the Tree

Next, add texture to the tree trunk by scribbling lines where the shadow core might be located, such as where the branches blend into the foliage of the tree. Use a denser arrangement of hatch marks to communicate shadowing. Because you started out by sketching the general gesture of the tree with straight lines, you can use those as a guide to understand the direction that the tree trunk is growing in. When you understand the direction, it becomes a lot easier to place hatch marks. If you think about the trunk like a cylinder, it should become a bit clearer where to place your shadow core. Think about a light source in the scene, whether directly above or slightly to the left or right and arrange your shadows in that way to complement the position of your primary light source.

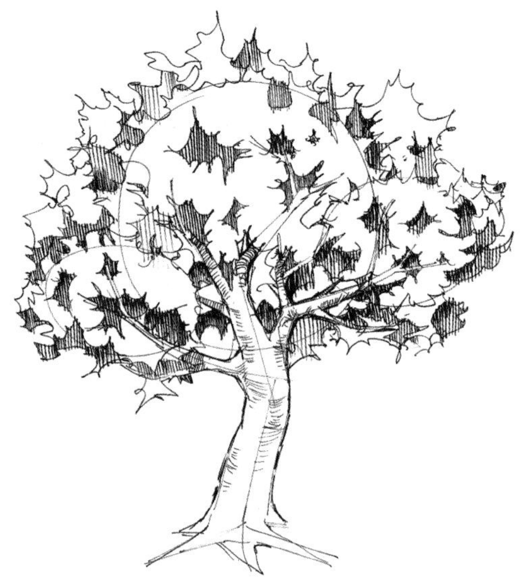

Review and Refine

To finish up, focus on the shadowed portions of the foliage on the tree. If you squint your eyes and look at this final sketch, you'll notice that the contrast between the shaded-in areas and the areas that have been intentionally left white creates a lovely three-dimensional effect on the foliage. It is important that as you sketch the foliage of a tree like this, that you exhibit some restraint; don't shade in every white spot on the tree. Additionally, shading in this way allows for the possibility of adding color to the sketch without having to compete too much with hatch marks in the sketch. Continue darkening the shadows by hatching these pockets with your pen. By repeating the stroke, the value of the shadowed areas is deepened. Additionally, you can add shadows to the trunk where roots are further away from the viewer. The tree is complete, and as you can see, sketching a deciduous tree is a lot easier than it might appear at first glance, thanks to this simplified approach.

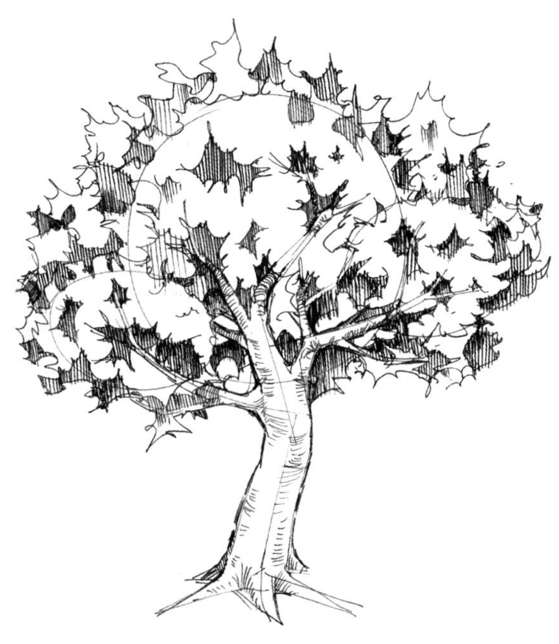

CHALLENGE

What other trees can you dream up using this technique? Get creative and keep your arms moving—the more you sketch, the better you'll get.

If you're in need of inspiration, you can always check online for examples of different deciduous trees or go for a walk. Pay attention to all the different shapes, sizes, and details of the trees you observe. Eventually you'll feel confident enough to come up with your own versions of these trees. Use your imagination to dream up something really cool.

 # EVERGREEN TREE

After leaf practice last week, it's time to try your hand at needles. For this exercise, you'll sketch an evergreen tree. I used a Paper Made Flair pen and some simple printer paper.

Sketch the Gesture of the Tree

As with the deciduous tree, decide on a point of view, try to identify the overall gesture of the tree, and sketch it lightly. For example, I started by drawing a triangle bisected by a vertical line extended down the page. This arrangement of a triangle and single straight vertical line will serve as the underlying structure for the tree.

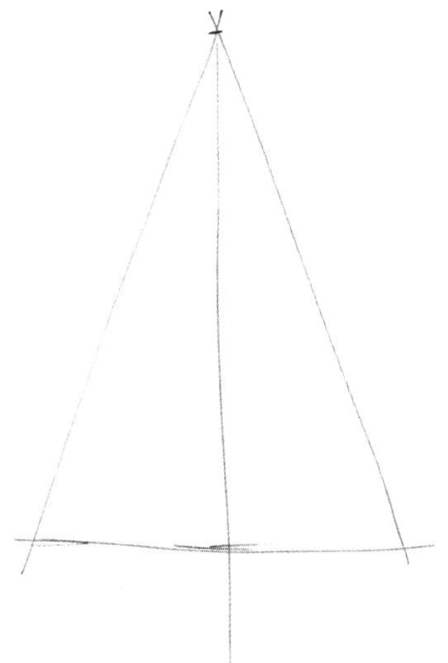

Add Layers of Foliage

Next, sketch in several tick marks moving upward toward the tip of the tree to indicate where layers of foliage will be sketched in. You can skip ahead to see what this might look like or simply find a picture of an evergreen tree and note how the foliage is layered with the branches. These tick marks will serve as a guide for placement in subsequent steps.

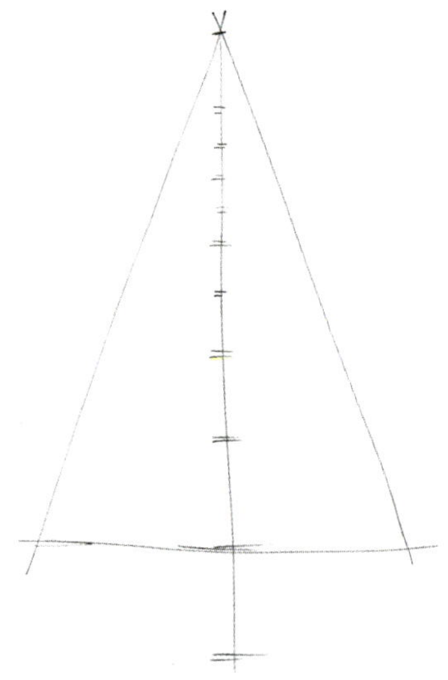

Sketch the Branches

Next, sketch a series of curved lines that become more acute in angle to each other as you move up the tree. Starting at the bottom, sketch two arcs that extend outward from the center of the tree to the corners of the triangle. It's not important to specifically hit the corner of the triangle but rather sketch in the gesture so that there is a point of reference for the foliage and branches. Once you have sketched your arcs in, fill in the gaps on the left and right sides of the tree, following your arcs. At the tips of each of these curved regions, try to add a few additional strokes to feather the shape created by these arcs. At this point the tree is starting to take shape. Be sure to sketch in a rough shape for the trunk that you will shade in later.

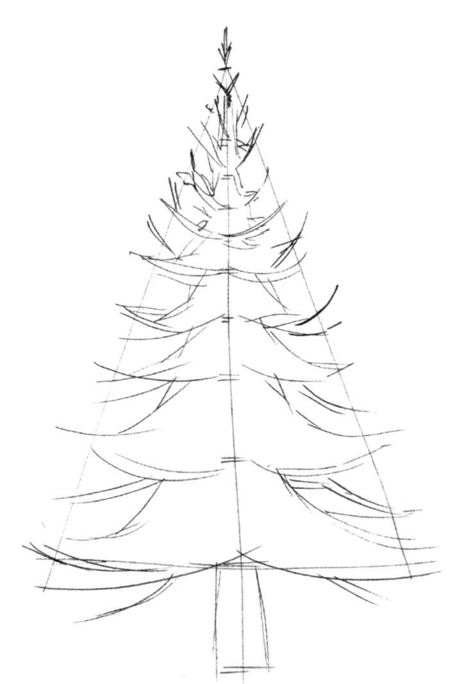

Outline the Foliage

With the underlying construction lines in place, you can start to add a bit of squiggly variations on the edges of these shapes. Similar to the process with the deciduous tree, follow along the contours and add a squiggly perimeter to the outside shape of the tree. The squiggles are what will create the overall outline of the tree as you work toward filling out these shapes with textures. Start on the left side and continue to fill out the tree on the right side as well. If you want a more natural feel for your final tree, be sure to not exactly mirror left to right all the strokes you've made, but rather re-sketch and embrace the variations that naturally will occur from left to right. Continue squiggling your lines around the perimeter of these shapes until the entire tree has been outlined with these lines.

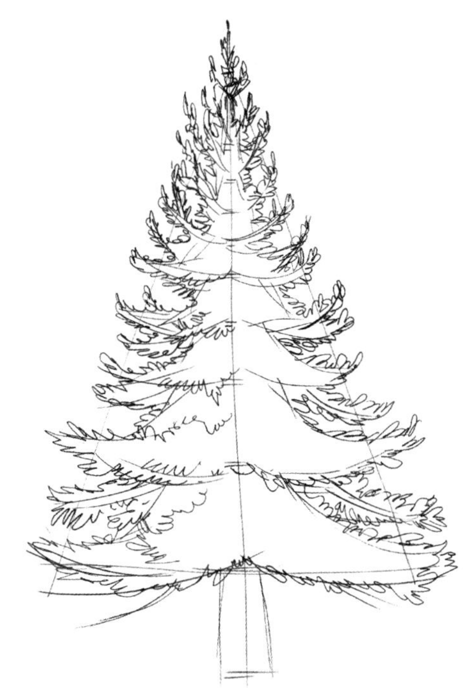

Layer Squiggles and Shadows

Once your base squiggle lines are in place, continue to fill out the foliage in the gaps with smaller squiggly lines. These squiggly lines will help create a basis for shading, similar to the gaps in the deciduous tree. For the example, I added more layering of foliage within the curved regions of the foliage and progressively filled these regions within the tree to indicate the layering of branches.

To mimic the appearance of the foliage on this evergreen, start by sketching in the shadowed areas underneath each layer. Simply scrape with your pen back and forth and follow the contour of the squiggly boundaries you sketched. If you need to, pause and practice on the side before committing this texture to the tree. Or if you decide to go ahead, just remember that you can always start over, and you'll have some extra practice under your belt. Use a squint check to determine if there is enough contrast or too much contrast between the blank areas in the foliage and the rest of the tree.

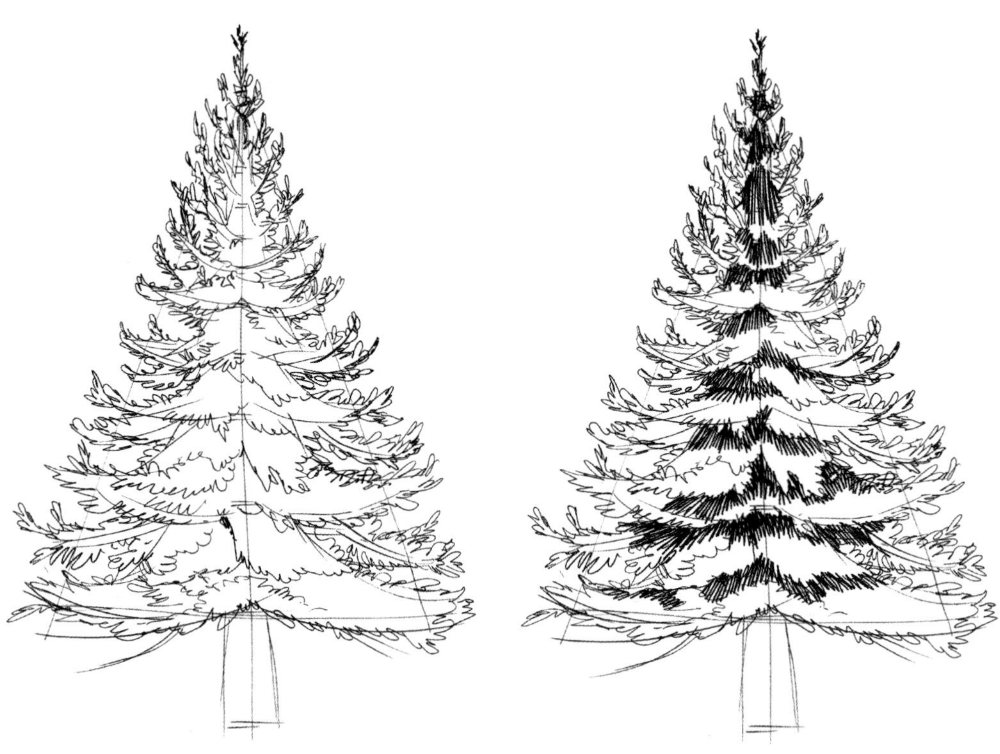

Add Midtone Textures

Next, add some midtone textures by sketching longer lines that are parallel and radiate from the center of the tree outward to fill in regions of foliage on the tree. These longer lines should contrast from the deeper shadowed areas right under the overlaps where layers of foliage rest on top of each other. Try to sketch these lines quickly and energetically so that the tree has a bit of balance and life to it. As you progressively shade in the foliage with this midtone value, your tree should start to take shape and come to life. Continue shading in with this midtone value until the entire tree has been shaded. If you'd like to add some dynamic lighting to the tree, now is a good time to deepen the value of your shadowed areas as well as modify any regions that have been shaded in with hatch lines representing a midtone. The interplay of shadow and light on a sketch like this will give it a degree of three-dimensionality even though the view of this tree is largely head-on.

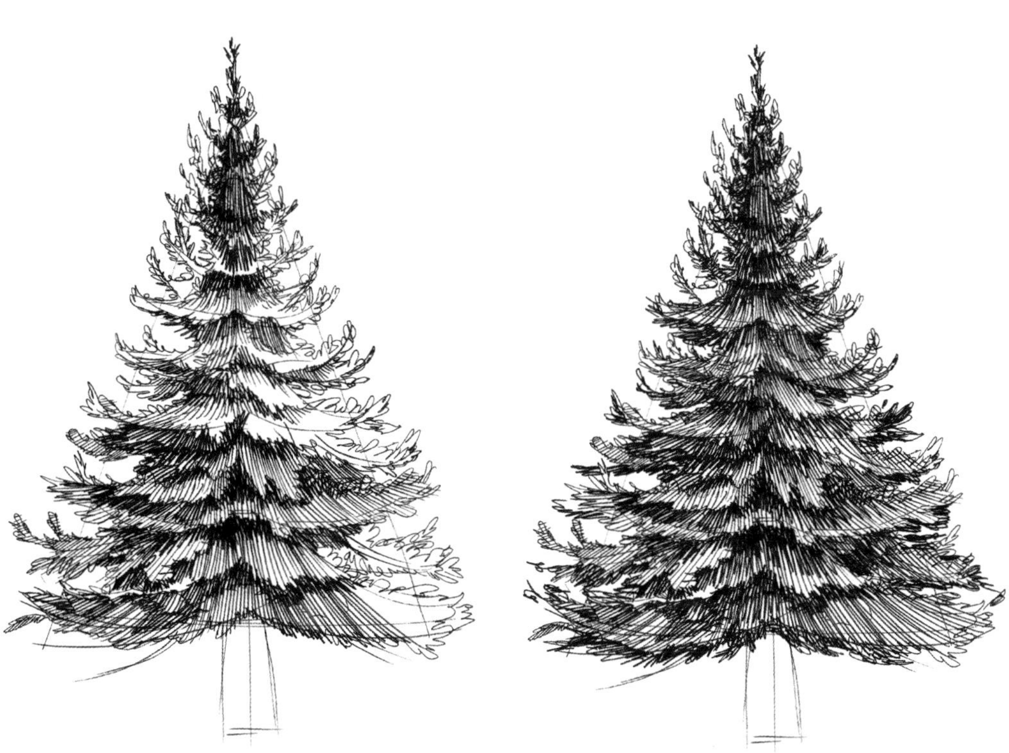

Review and Refine

To finish up the tree, fill in any gaps in the foliage as you see fit by adding a few squiggles here and there as well as dark and light regions around the perimeter of the tree. I shaded in the trunk with vertical lines quickly at first and then transitioned to hatch lines along the far-left side of the tree trunk. Add a ground line and sketch it in to give the tree a sense of place on the paper. Lastly, to round out the three-dimensional appearance of the tree, add a shadow on the trunk just below the last row of foliage closest to the ground—and you're done. Take a minute to compare the approaches to these two types of trees. What similarities and differences do you notice?

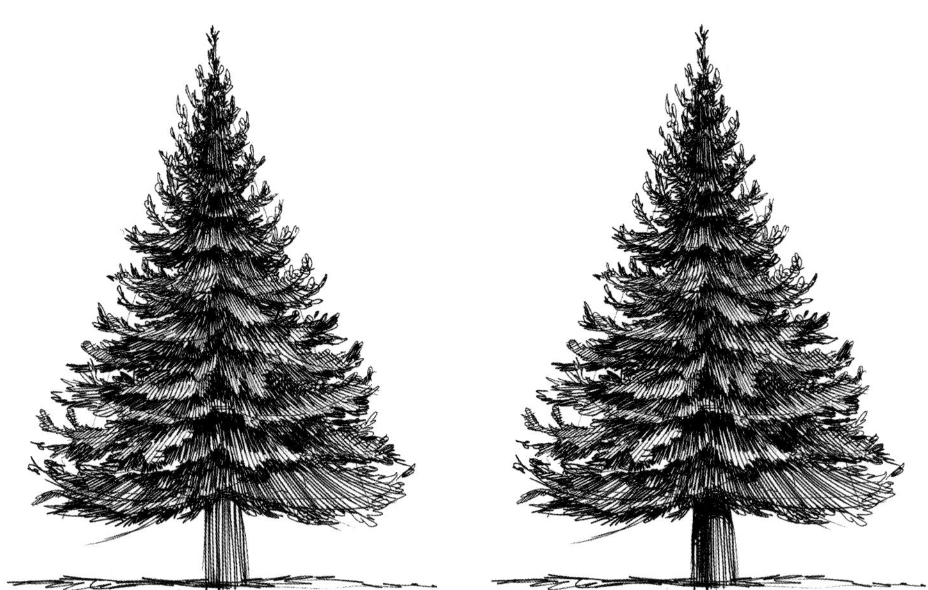

CHALLENGE

Draw some trees from observation and others from imagination. Drawing from observation will help you build a visual vocabulary that you can refer to when you're called upon to draw from your imagination. If you have a sketchbook, go for a walk outside and pause to draw a few trees along the way. If you can't go for a walk, try looking up some reference images or find the closest tree to you and see if you can draw it from different points of view. Try to focus on the expressiveness and looseness of your lines as well as practice textures and shading with just a pen. Once you're comfortable sketching a few trees, you could try your hand at adding some color to a tree or two.

ATHLETIC SNEAKER

In this exercise, you'll sketch an athletic sneaker in pencil. When sketching a more complex form like this, remember to sketch lightly so that your construction lines and scaffolding elements don't negatively impact the overall presentation. I recommend a black colored pencil; I used a Prismacolor Premier. Although you can use a regular graphite pencil, I find that a quality colored pencil, such as the Prismacolor Premier I used, leads to less smudging as you work. For the example, I sketched on marker paper, which has a smooth and subtle texture that imparts a lovely look and feel when shading with a colored pencil.

Start with the Sole

You probably see your sneakers a million times every day, but take a moment to analyze one now. What basic shapes do you see? One way to simplify the sole of the shoe is to sketch two ellipses. Using straight lines would work just fine as well, but the ellipses provide reference geometry for the shoe.

Draw the Outer Contours

Next, use these curves to guide you in drawing the outer contours of the sole, respecting the curvature of the ellipses but also trying to mimic the shape of the outsole. These curves form the medial side of the shoe. Complete the profile of the shoe by lightly sketching slightly curved lines as shown in the example. These lines loosely follow the foot that would fit in the shoe. Imagining someone actually being able to wear your shoe and sketching it accurately in perspective will lend credibility to the drawing.

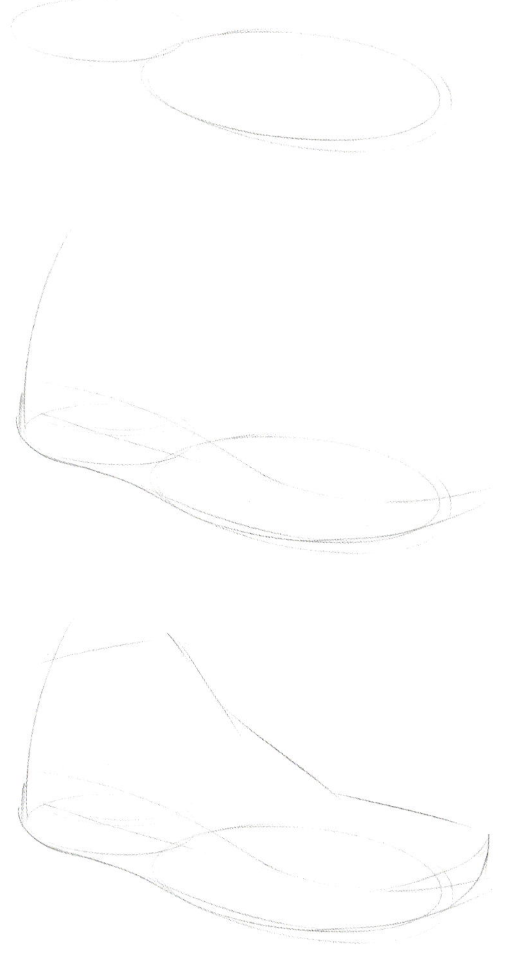

Divide the Silhouette

Having established the shoe silhouette, divide it into functional overlays and parts. Take a look at the example to see how I sketched in the quarter overlay, tongue of the shoe, and vamp. Keep these lines loose, fluid, and light. The more pressure you apply, the thicker and more visible your pencil lines will be. Continue dividing the upper of the shoe and adding details on the outsole by sketching in lines as shown in the example or following your own design.

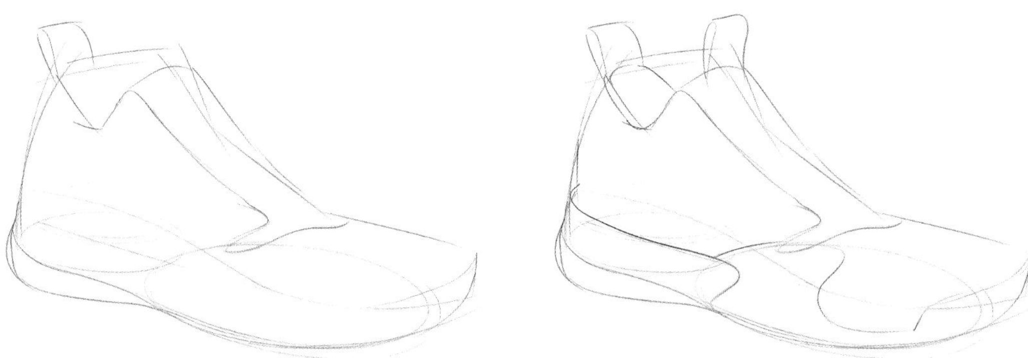

Add Details

Sketch in the collar of the shoe and identify a tab to be sewn onto the upper portion of the tongue. Add a strap to the upper of the shoe that is integrated into the tooling and outsole. Detail the rear quarter panel and add laces to the tongue along with eyelets on the quarter and quarter overlay. Finally, give your shoe some traction by sketching lugs on the outsole. Use a bit more pressure to give heavier line weights to the outline of the shoe and areas where there may be overlap or shadowing.

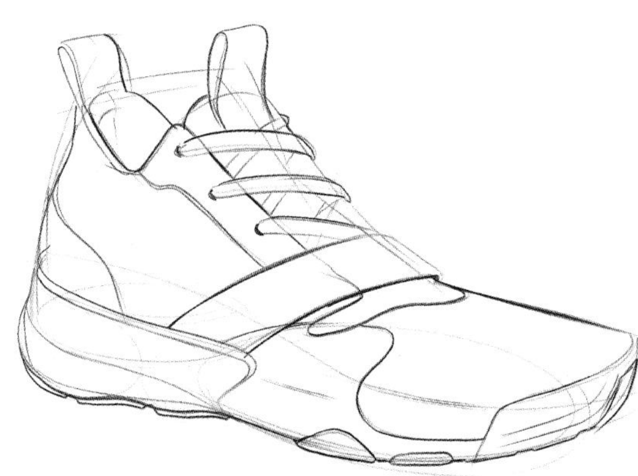

Apply Shading

As you know, shading enhances the materiality of your sketch. You can shade with pencil in two ways: You can hold the pencil more upright and shade in a way that almost creates hatch lines, or you can tilt the pencil on its side and apply pressure on the tip to shade a wider area. Use both of these techniques to shade in material blocks and shadows on the shoe. For the quarter panel, I used a more upright grip on the pencil, giving it a consistent and almost flat feel.

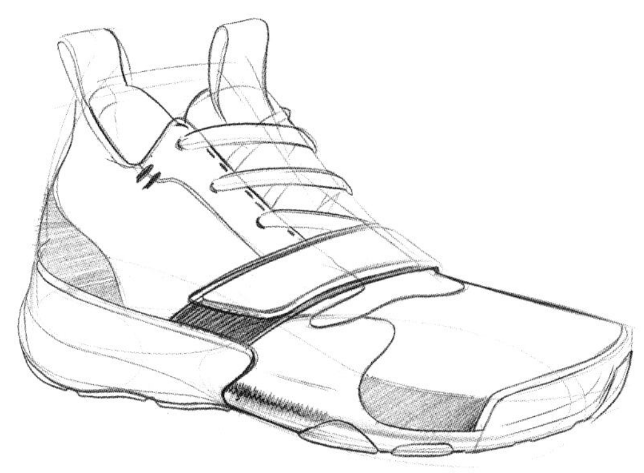

Finalize the Sketch

Take another look at your sneaker—on your foot and on the page—with an eye for details that would add realism to your sketch. For instance, I broke the strap on the example into two visual parts: one being the hooks and the other being the loops. I also added stitches to the quarter overlay and quarter panel at the collar, as well as cleaned up the tabs at the collar and tongue. If you feel the need to practice shading a bit, now is a good time to pause and experiment.

Just past the toe box on the outsole, there's an overlay panel wrapping into the tooling. To shade this shadow core, turn the pencil on its side and move it back and forth to create a shadow core with a bit of texture. Sketch the shoe's toe cap and define it with slightly thicker lines and a bit of shading. If you want to add color to your shoe, this is the perfect time to do so, as there's not too much pencil applied to the paper and still room to fill in colors and materials.

Consider the Light Source for Shading

To wrap up the shoe sketch, continue shading while thinking about primary and secondary light sources in the scene. To strike a balance between realism and communication in sketching, try to imagine a singular light source rather than multiple light sources. As shaded, the example shoe suggests that the light is positioned to the top and to the right. The shadow core at the heel transitions to midtones and lighter areas toward the back of the shoe due to reflected light in the environment.

Similarly, I shaded the upper and quarter panel to show a visible shadow core. I shaded the top of the toe box with a light shadow core to suggest that the upper of the shoe is rounded in this area. Think of this region as a bit like a cylinder, and shade it to communicate three-dimensionality and depth. Shade the lining of the sneakers fairly dark to provide a nice contrast between the upper, quarter, overlay, tongue, and tabs. Contrast is your friend: It reinforces the perspective in your drawing.

Refine with Final Touches

Add squiggles to the strap to suggest some type of text. Squiggles are handy shortcuts for including text elements without committing to a specific word or phrase. In the example, notice that the initial construction lines play little to no role in the final sketch. The sketch itself is well shaded and defined, and the line weight of the outline takes attention away from those initial construction lines.

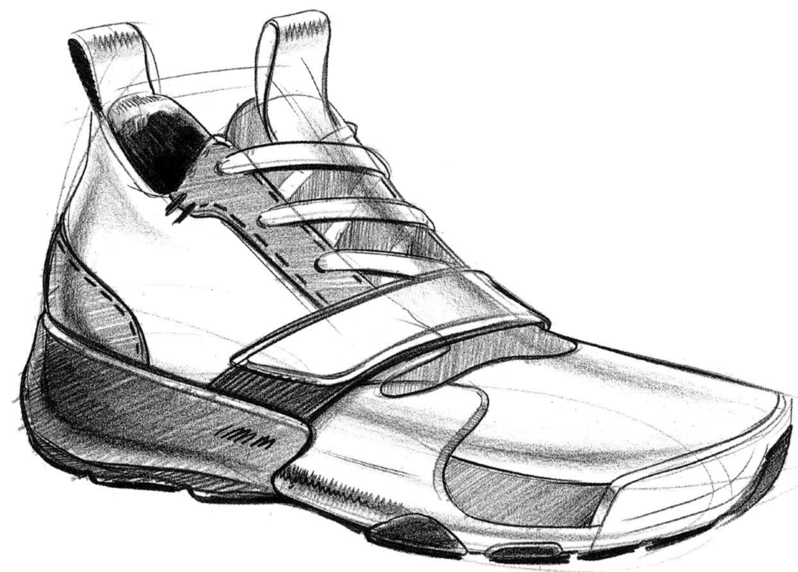

CHALLENGE

Keep sketching shoes. If you're rusty on perspective, revisit prior exercises to sharpen your skills. Have fun, and experiment with your pencil to improve the quality of your drawings.

In this exercise, you'll practice your pencil shading while drawing a utility knife. With a little bit of pencil work, you can make a flat two-dimensional drawing pop and communicate dimensionality. Remember, turning your pencil on its side and shading along the contour of the shape you're drawing gives it depth and presence on the page. While working on your drawing, imagine what the cross section of its shapes would look like if it were three dimensional.

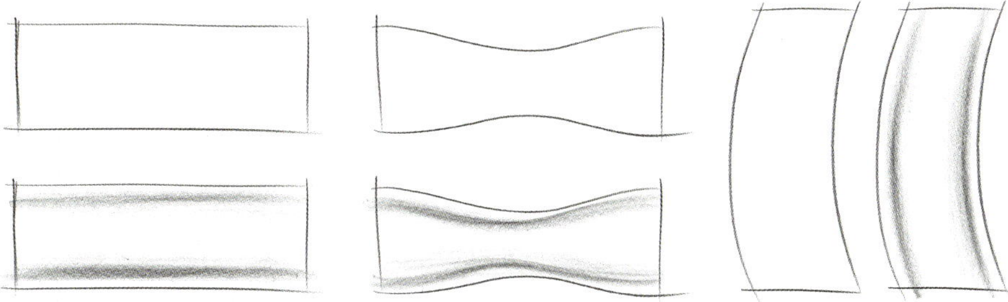

Draw the Outline

Imagine what a utility knife would look like from a side view, and then create an outline of it. For this example, I lightly sketched in some lines and even extended a few lines to define the overall profile.

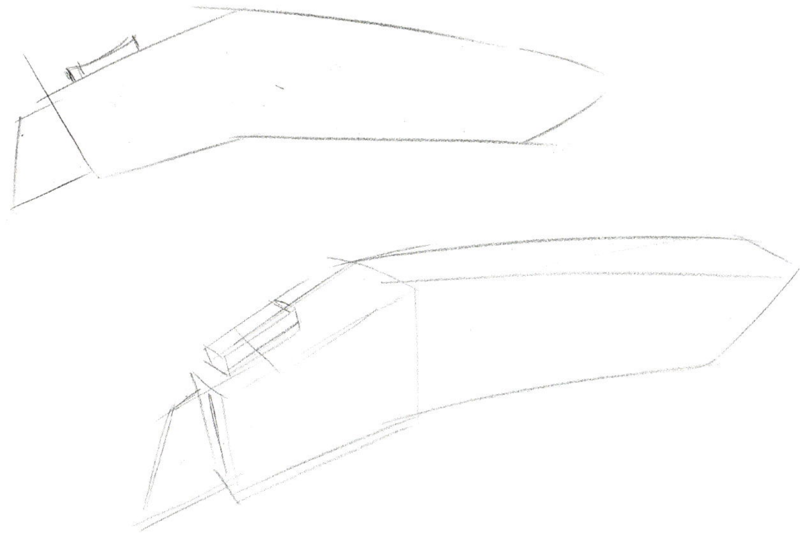

Add Details

Think of how the knife might function. Does it have a retractable blade or some ergonomic feature that you'd like to incorporate into your sketch? Don't stress about mistakes; instead, focus on the overall design of this object. In the example, I made a mistake at this step, but I didn't let that get in the way of my drawing or overall vision. I also added a few details on the knife's grip and an affordance for finger placement, which help make my design feel more functional. Be sure to shade in any part breaks and functional details you add.

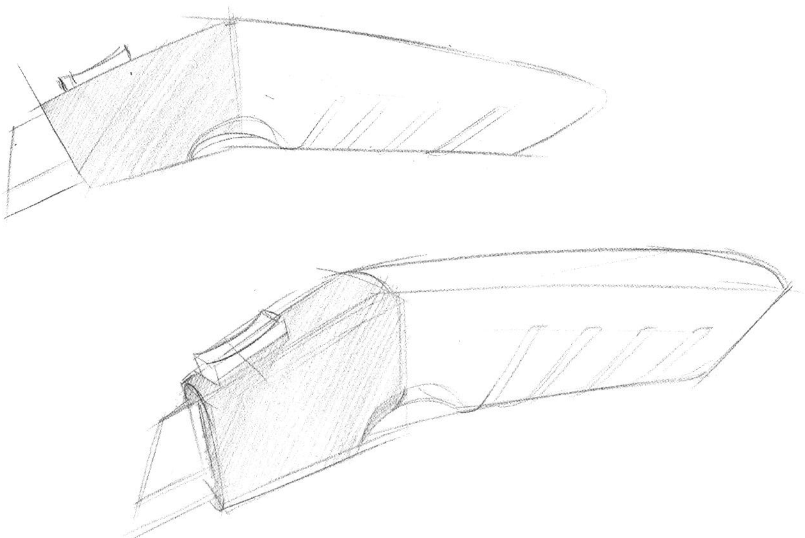

Work on Shading

Adjusting the pressure you apply with your pencil will help you control the amount of contrast in your lines and help you work in a bit of gesture and expression with your sketch lines. Remember to rotate your pencil so that you're not consistently drawing using the same part of the pencil. This will in effect sharpen the pencil as you sketch so that you have a sharper tip as you go. Take this opportunity to emphasize any three-dimensional details in the knife by turning your pencil on its side and shading in core shadows and highlights.

Notice in the example that the lightest lights are against the darkest darks, which helps give the impression of three-dimensionality where it matters. You can really create a lot of expressiveness with a pencil. As you work with this medium, play with the amount of pressure you apply to the page. You'll learn the most when you're willing to explore, make some mistakes, and see what works for you in that process.

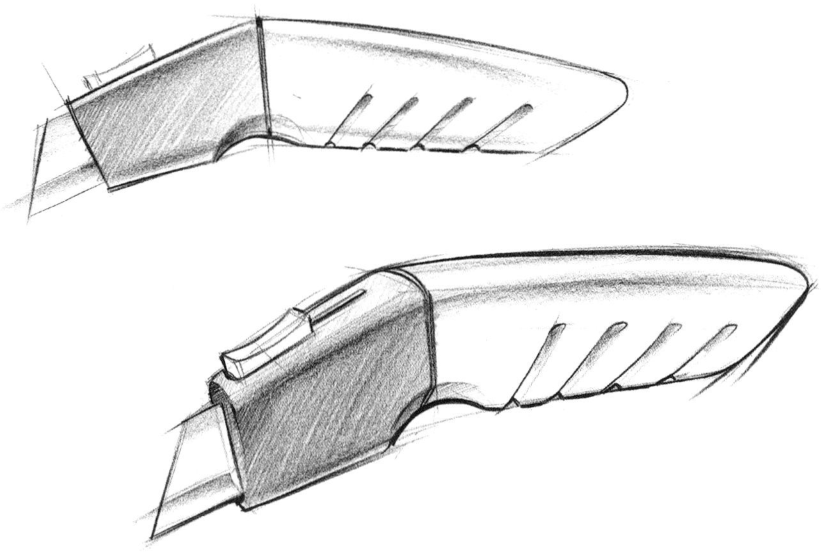

CHALLENGE

Try sketching a few knives of your own using a similar technique. Get creative and experiment with pencil to see how it feels and how you can shade your sketches. Quantity matters, but also try to focus on getting it right in your own way.

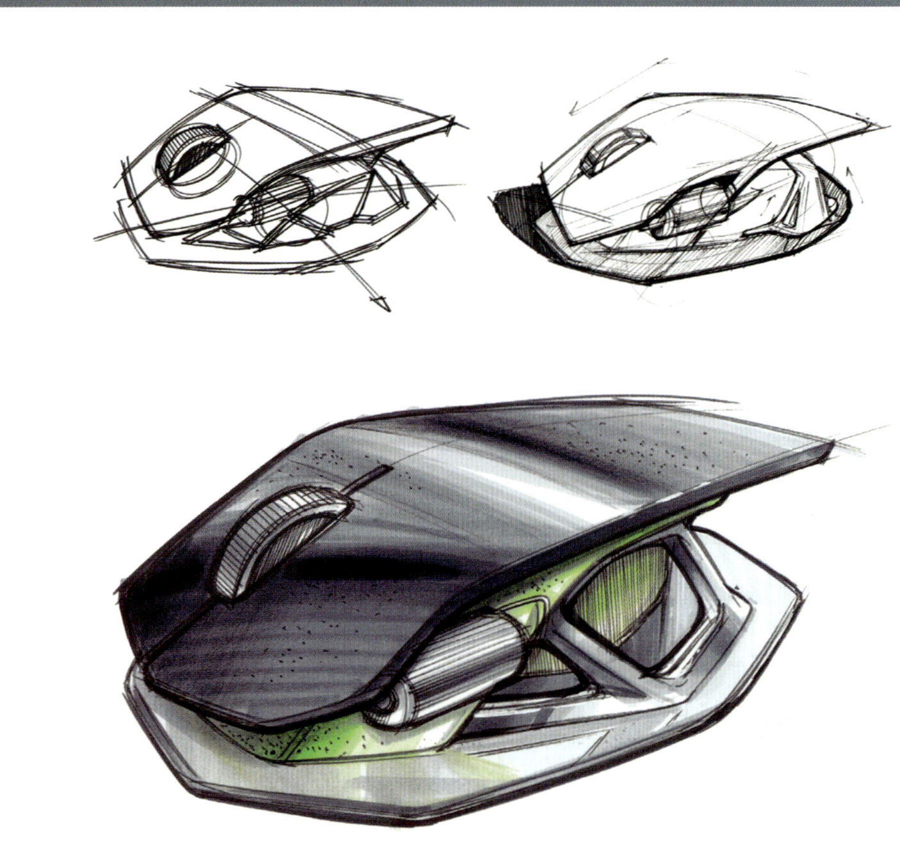

CHAPTER 4

FORM BUILDING

As you remember from Exercise 3, *form building* is the process of creating complex drawings by combining simpler elements. Form combinations can involve the addition, subtraction, intersection, or blending of two distinct forms. For example, you can replicate a cube to represent an elongated object. If you bend a cylinder enough, you can draw hoops, loops, and squiggly three-dimensional shapes. Another way to build form is by analyzing *cross sections* of an object's overall structure. Think of a sliced loaf of bread. When all the slices are in place, it is clearly a whole loaf. If you were to remove some of the slices, you would still be able to recognize its overall loaf shape and identify it as bread. Plus, the slices you removed (tasty cross sections) would give you a better understanding of the bread. So, it is with drawing more complex shapes; understanding a few key cross sections will help you draw something more complex and interesting.

Form building can be an intimidating process, but this chapter's exercises will help you gain more skill and confidence. Here are three quick tips to keep in mind throughout:

- **Always work light until you get it right.** In other words, use light lines to begin, and then finish your drawing with a thicker line to emphasize the final shape.

- **When in doubt, rough it out.** Create an underlay quickly to capture the overall shape and gesture of what you intend for the final drawing. When the rough sketch is complete, you can then create an overlay by re-sketching your idea. This way, you preserve energy and visual intent, and the result is an expressive drawing that feels more interesting. (See Exercise 7 for tips on creating an overly.)

- **Observe substance, structure, and silhouette.** If you can observe and figure out the structure of something, you can then divide that into functional or visual parts and finish up by applying style and substance to the sketch. Drawing more complex objects becomes a bit easier with this approach, as you can go into an exercise with an idea of a process that will get you the results you need. (For a more thorough discussion of this approach, see my book *The Perspective Drawing Guide*.)

For this exercise, you'll sketch an angle grinder. When sketching a more complex object, it's always helpful to take a minute to analyze the object and decide on a strategy for sketching. I familiarized myself with the general part makeup of angle grinders before sketching the example. If you like, study a few reference images, then grab some simple tools and paper. For the example, I used a Paper Mate Flair pen and alcohol markers with marker paper.

Create the Initial Sketch

To start, sketch a series of lines that represent the directional axes and critical features of the angle grinder. Notice the four lines I began the example with. The longest is the central axis that defines the majority of the tool's body, including the handle and the grinding head. Next, block in rough three-dimensional parts of the angle grinder. Keep these shapes elementary as they are meant to be used as reference geometry. At this step, you can also include cross sections for the handle or whatever other elements you decide to include.

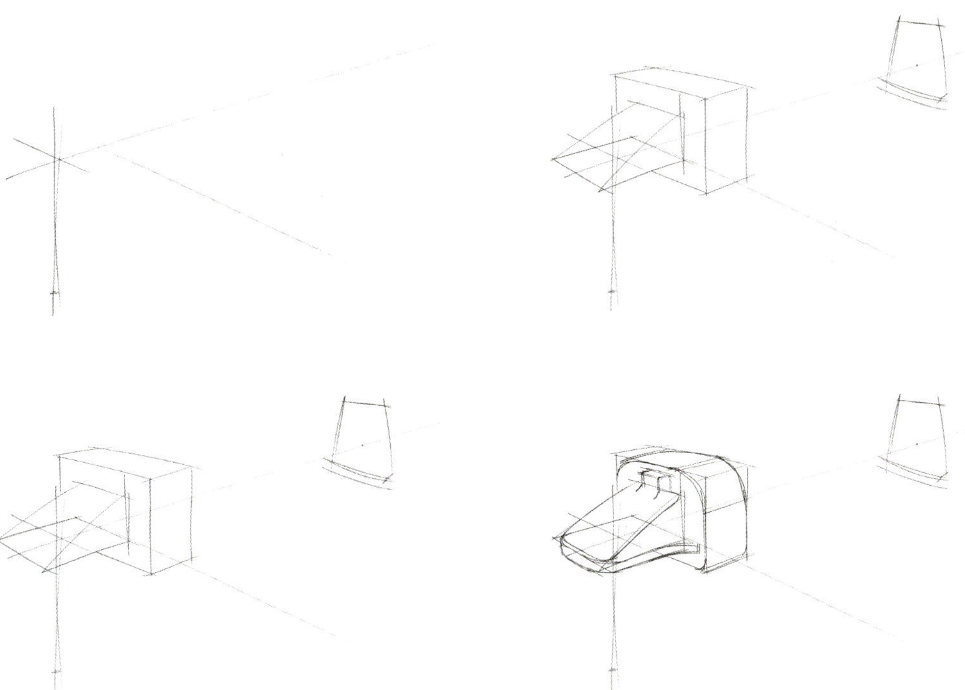

Add Details

With the rough construction geometry in place, sketch in transitional surfaces for the motorized head of the angle grinder by adding fillets and small transitional surfaces. Next, sketch in a series of ellipses at the head of the angle grinder to represent the rotary components, including the motor. Position the ellipses along one of the initial construction lines that serve as an axis and a visual point of reference (check the example for placement).

To form the basis of the grinder's safety guard and grip handle, sketch in a large and small ellipse along the axis placed at 90 degrees in perspective to the longest axis. The larger ellipse should be fairly large to prevent the operator's hand from slipping into the grinding disc. The smaller ellipse, meanwhile, defines the overall diameter of the auxiliary grip. In addition to adding transitional surfaces and ellipses, sketch in a curved or undulating profile for the grip of the angle grinder. For my purposes, I included one cross section. If you need additional guidance, feel free to sketch additional cross sections on planes along the primary axis of the angle grinder.

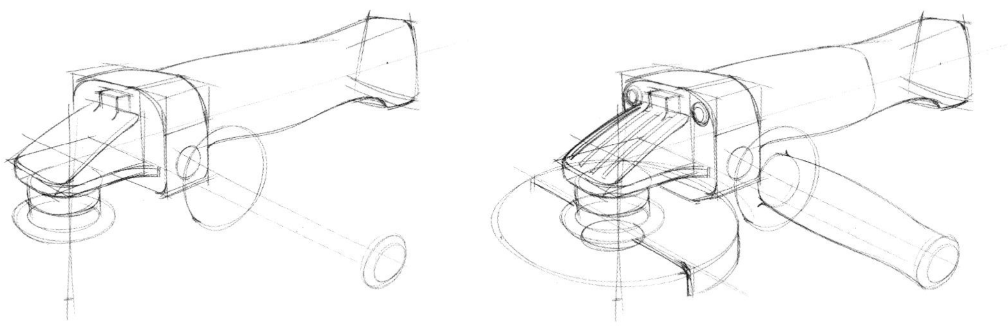

Refine the Sketch and Enhance Details

With the tool's basic building blocks in place, you can begin detailing the overall sketch. For complex objects like this, I find it helpful to tackle things in sections. If you prefer to bounce around a sketch a bit to finish areas that may not necessarily be related to each other, that's fine too.

For now, turn your attention to the business end of the angle grinder: the motorized head. Where you initially sketched ellipses along the short axis, now sketch a larger ellipse to represent where the grinding disc and protective cover will be located. Sketch this ellipse using a double line to suggest thickness, or simply lightly sketch it in to function as construction lines. Add fasteners on the motorized head and refine your details by enhancing line weight to some degree. Don't forget to add transitional surfaces on the handle of the angle grinder. As you can see in the example, they will provide a better sense that this is an ergonomic handle meant to offer better control of the tool.

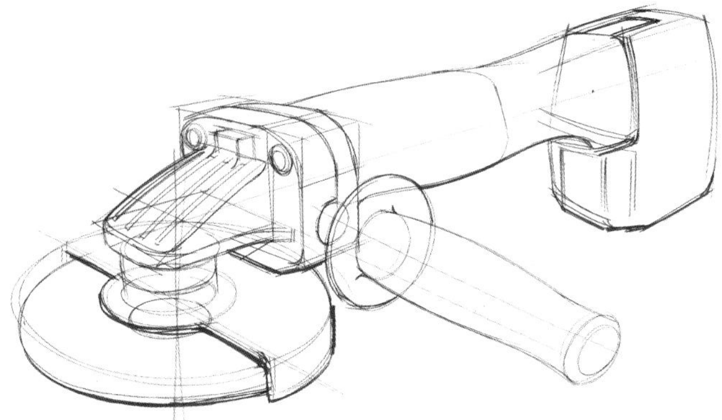

Add Line Weight and Final Details

Keep adding line weight and defining things a bit more. For example, I added some line weight to areas that overlap the grinding disc, the motorized head, and the main grip, as well as more details to the handle. I decided to make this angle grinder battery-powered and sketched in a rough battery pack affixed to the end of the unit. I continued by sketching in additional line weight and details using my Paper Mate Flair pen.

Within the silhouette of the angle grinder, add part breaks to the handle along with venting for the motor. Make corrections as necessary. You can see I made a few errors on the example's head that I planned to correct when I added color. See if you can spot them. Notice how color affects the overall presentation of this idea. Where applicable, add hatch lines to shade in regions where there might be a cast shadow, such as on the protective cover for the grinding disc and on the battery pack toward the rear of the grinder.

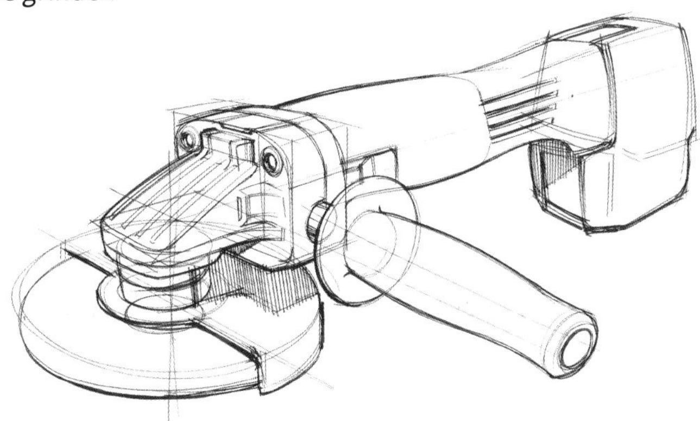

Apply Color

It's time to apply color as you continue to refine the line work in the sketch. Grab some markers and decide on a single color and set of grays that you would like to use. To color the angle grinder, start by outlining an area with which you'd like to apply the lightest color in your set of markers. Creating this outline will help you shade more. Use your gray marker to fill in any metallic or gray plastic areas on the angle grinder as you see fit. Additionally, shade the grinding disc using multidirectional strokes or bunches of strokes oriented in a way to mimic the randomized texture of the grinding disc. These groupings of short strokes create a texture on the disc as a point of interest and a textural contrast for the rest of the sketch.

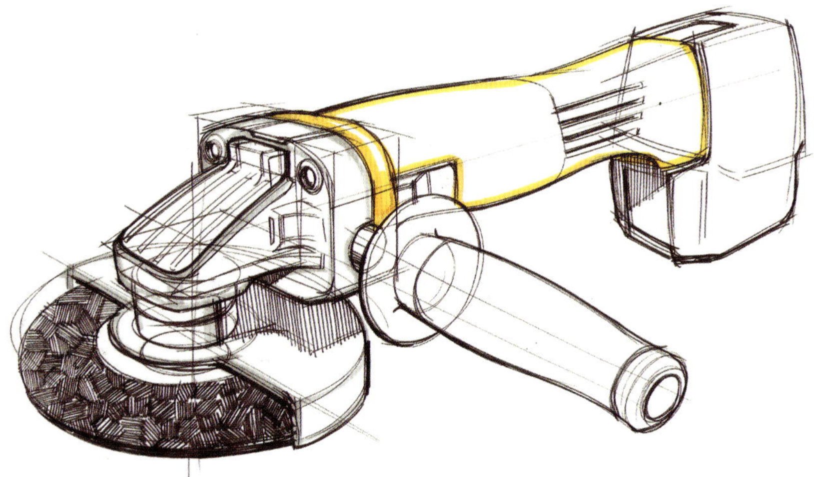

Next, once the marker has dried in the yellow section, reapply the marker to emphasize and deepen the yellow along the shadow core of the handle. Also shade the motorized head slightly yellow for an insert along with the end of the auxiliary handle. Even though you're coloring with marker, try to apply the same looseness and confident technique that you use for drawing lines so your marker sketches will take on life. Using a midtone gray marker, shade in additional shadowed areas, emphasize reflections on metallic parts, and add some gray to the grinding wheel to showcase the difference in material. You can shade the battery pack with the midtone gray along with the lightest gray. Notice that with the addition of color, many of the construction lines in the sketch become deprecated in importance by way of color and contrast. Also, take a minute to refine any of the form's outlines.

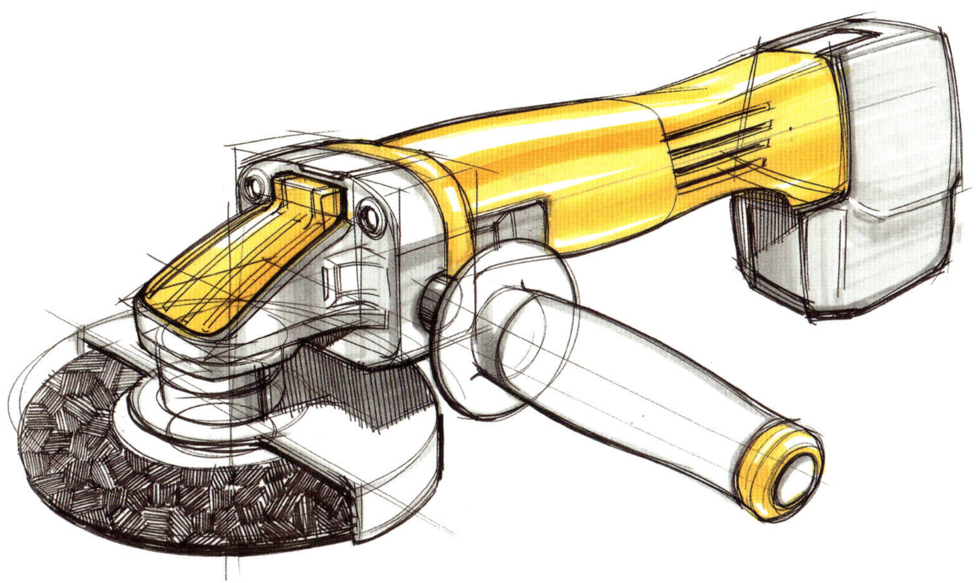

COLOR AND VALUE

When using color, remember these tips:

- Always try to work light until you get it right.

- If you're struggling with identifying the right color, take a minute to pause and scribble to the side to check color application. When sketching, I use markers primarily. With these, it is always a good thing to take a minute to test your colors before drawing.

- Generally speaking, warm colors will appear closer to you or the viewer, and cool colors will appear further from you or the viewer.

- Try to stick to the same color family if you are blending. However, if you're trying to blend colors that are very different from each other, consider using a texture to create the blend.

Add the Final Touches

To wrap up, I further enhanced the shadow core of the handle with my deepest yellow marker, as well as shaded in any shadowed areas on the head of the tool. If needed, use your midtone color marker to soften the blend from the intense shadow core through the body of the marker. With a 70% marker (or whatever your darkest marker is), shade in the rubberized parts of your angle grinder. In the example, I shaded in the auxiliary grip shadows and added a bit. The grinding disc is covered by the protective cover at the motor head. Shade in any button, screws, or other elements to round out the sketch. As a bonus, you may consider adding a drop shadow under the angle grinder or adding a background to the sketch to help it pop a bit more on the page.

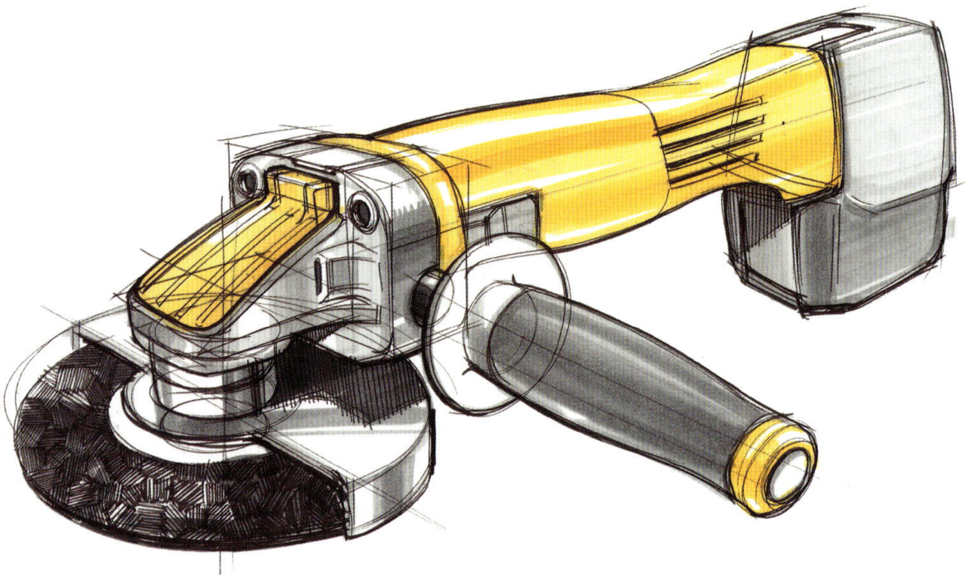

CHALLENGE

Practice sketching complex objects using pens and markers, while focusing on the methods of constructing the complex objects we discussed. As you sketch, work light until you get it right by keeping your construction lines thinner and lighter than the rest. Remember to use line weights to help pop your sketch from the page. As exciting as color is, try to calmly and confidently apply colors in your sketch.

Deciding on the right strategy when sketching a complex object is important. In this exercise, you'll draw a soft backpack, which may not have a clear and easily identifiable structure at first glance. In cases like this, I try to establish perspective first on the page and then fill in the rest. Think of it as sketching in the overall silhouette and position of the object and then dividing it into its parts and adding details (remember, the technique of silhouette, shape, and substance). Taking this approach allows you to relax a bit rather than think about all the details and elements all at once; start with the overall shape, then add substance within that silhouette.

Establish Perspective Lines and a Shape

Roughly sketch perspective lines that define the overall shape of your backpack. In my example, I sketched the upper and lower corners of the backpack that are closest to the viewer. Think of this as the upper and lower portion of a cuboid that is positioned at eye level. Connect the upper and lower portion of these sketch lines to the lower portion to complete the overall shape. It's okay to sketch these lines in lightly and loosely as they are merely guiding the process as you establish the overall shape of the backpack.

Next, start sketching in elements of the backpack that are part of the straps. Toward the top left, sketch in four curves that will define the shape of the straps and, toward the lower corner of the backpack, a small, truncated triangle to indicate where the straps will interface with the backpack. Remember to draw with your shoulder and keep things loose and fast as you sketch. Next, with a few curves, loosely sketch downward from the upper portion of the straps to define the remaining shape of the straps. Also connect the straps to the truncated triangle flap attached to the lower-left corner of the backpack.

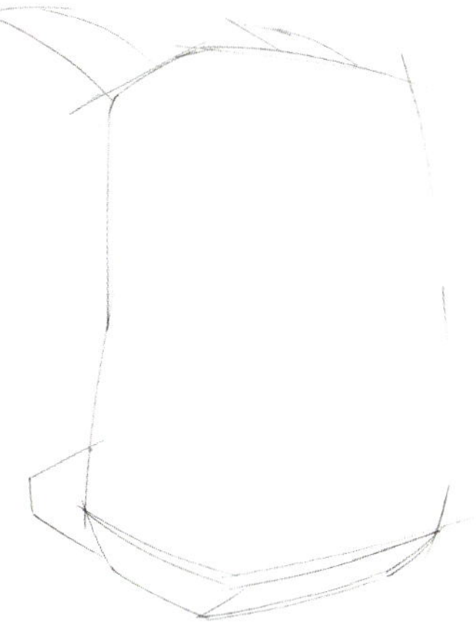

Divide the Silhouette into Functional Sections

Within the main backpack silhouette, begin dividing the shape into functional areas. For instance, sketch a few curves to indicate side pockets as well as a panel on the front of the backpack. If you have a specific design in mind or thumbnail sketch, you can refer to this as you include these details. What's important is that you think about the overall shape of the backpack as defined by the original perspective lines and try to sketch as if you're sketching on top of a three-dimensional shape.

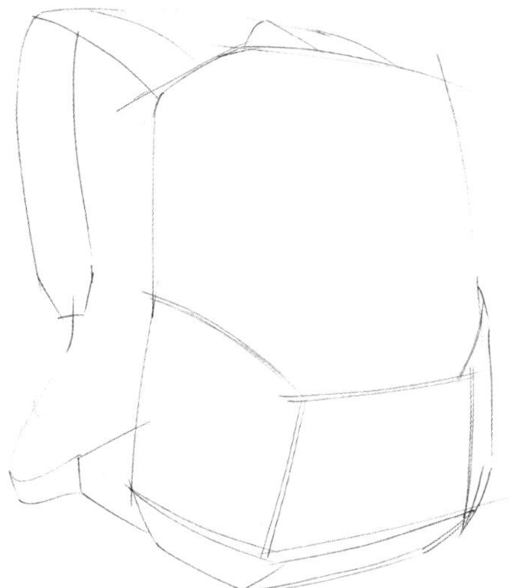

Another thing I like to do is use double lines where two panels on the backpack meet. This way I can create the effect of there being piping or a slight separation of materials where these sections meet. It's a subtle detail that can have a big impact on the overall appearance of your backpack.

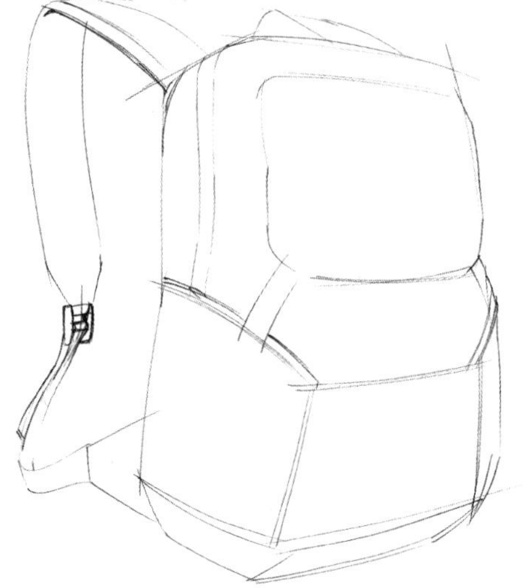

Continue Adding Shape and Substance

Next, add some thickness to your strap by sketching in an additional line just below the initial curves you used to define the strap. As you move down the strap, add details and definition like hardware for adjustment. On the main body of the backpack, begin to separate the overall shape by adding a zipper and additional details like straps or further breaks in the design to indicate a panel or pouch up top. Because the underlying sketch was a bit more rigid at this phase, when including additional details like texture or hatch marks with a pen, try to be a little looser and more organic. Give the front pocket of the bag a texture by slowly sketching in some lines that undulate to create a wavy appearance. It may take a few tries to get the look and feel that you want. If necessary, pause here and create some sample textures on scrap paper to find out what works best for you.

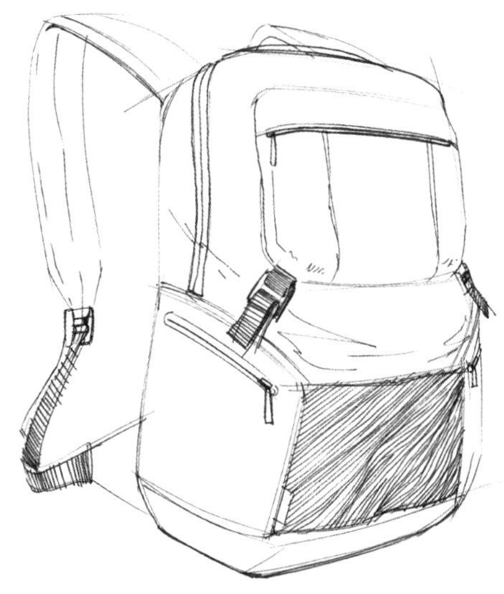

I tend to keep the zippers simple by drawing a line dividing the zipper and also including a simple shape to indicate the zipper pull. On the top portion of the example backpack, notice that the area outlined as a pouch now includes a zipper as well as further separations with double lines. The buckles and straps in the front are also now shaded to convey a feeling of being made from webbing. I added wrinkle lines as well as zigzag lines on the front of the backpack to help reinforce and convey a sense of a fabric-like construction for the overall bag. On the strap, notice the somewhat broken line just inset from the outline of the backpack, which is meant to show that the strap has some thickness.

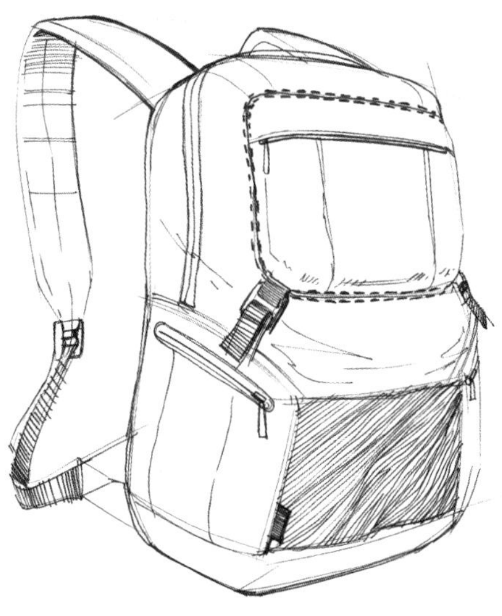

Add a dash line where necessary to show stitch marks if that is a part of your design. Follow along the outline of the upper pouch by offsetting the initial sketch line and drawing a dashed line that follows this profile. On the strap, shade in quickly with a pen to show shadow where the strap points downward. Next, enhance the line weight and outline of the backpack by either using a separate pen or repeatedly drawing over the outline with the same pen. At this point, I switched to a black Copic marker as a way to quickly add a drop shadow as well as outline the backpack itself.

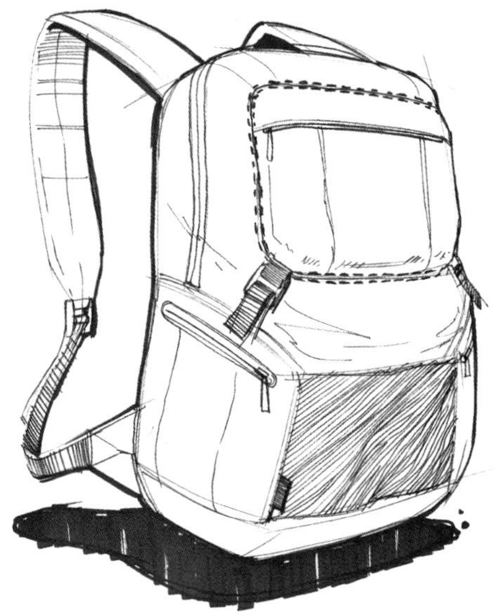

Create Texture and Shadow

To further add texture and detail to the bag, use your pen to stipple along any areas that may need some textural indication. Hatch in the bottom of the backpack to suggest a material change and add any additional stitch lines or part lines at this point. While this is a complete sketch and could be presented as a new product idea, for example, you could do a little more to help make it pop.

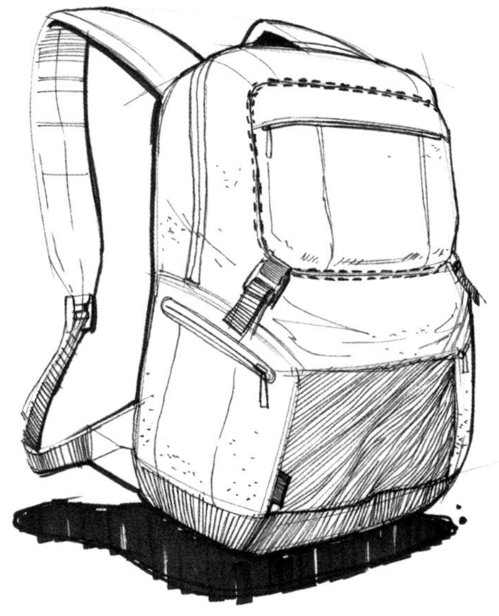

For the final step, grab a gray marker and a color marker. Use the gray marker to shade any subtle shadow areas on the backpack and use the color marker to highlight interesting design details. In the example, I applied a red marker to the zippers and used the gray marker to shade in where there might be shadowing caused by the wrinkles in the bag. Applying the marker in an organic, slightly erratic way that follows the areas you wish to shade as shadowed helps reinforce the overall look of the backpack as being made from fabric.

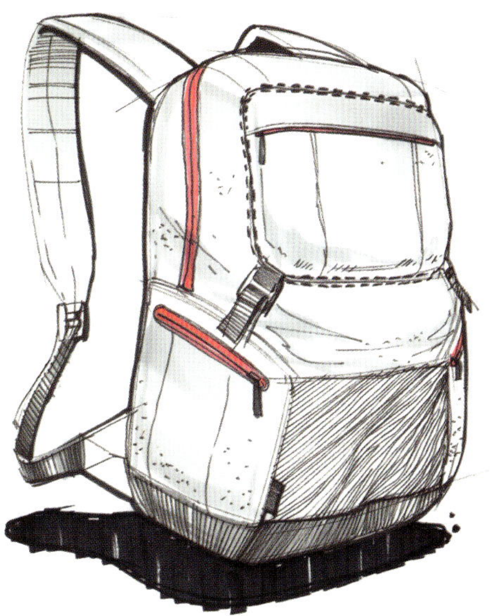

CHALLENGE

Try using this week's technique to sketch other items that are made of fabrics or textiles. If you'd like, draw a variety of backpacks in different points of view and see what creative techniques you can come up with to mimic the textures you see in those fabrics. Try not to get too bogged down with using markers at this point. However, if you are comfortable and confident with using markers, feel free to add a splash of color to enhance your textures and the overall appearance of your backpack. Remember, don't stress about having the perfect sketch, but rather focus on consistent practice and output. It's about consistency, not perfection in the end.

 # CUTE MONSTER

I love sketching monsters, because it gives me a chance to be creative in a free-form way and come up with some pretty crazy ideas as well. In this exercise, you can explore your wild side, too. Use a light gray marker to sketch the rough shape of your monster and a felt pen to sketch in the details. I used a Sakura Micron pen for detail work and Copic and Ohuhu markers.

Rough in the Shapes

When sketching a creature, it's helpful to begin with a vision in mind, then draw a few shapes that loosely represent the creature you're imagining. Sketch two circles: a large one for the head and a small one for the pelvis. I imagined a round head, thick legs, and proportions a bit like a gorilla for my monster. If yours has different proportions, adjust your circles accordingly. Next, sketch two ellipses to represent the two front arms or feet and continue sketching with the gray marker to rough in the overall body shape.

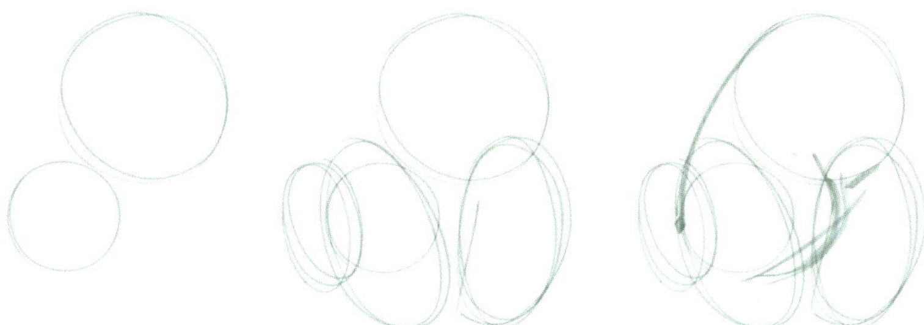

Detail the Face and Body

When the outline of the body shape is in place, begin scribbling on the face to sketch in a mouth with a very thick lip. Detail out the feet to have nails or claws of some sort. (Let's call them nails since this is a cute monster and not something terrifying.) Continue using the light gray marker to sketch in any details you'd like to include. I sketched two circles for the eyes and connected those circles to the body with a few curves. This gave my monster eyes that are a bit like a snail's.

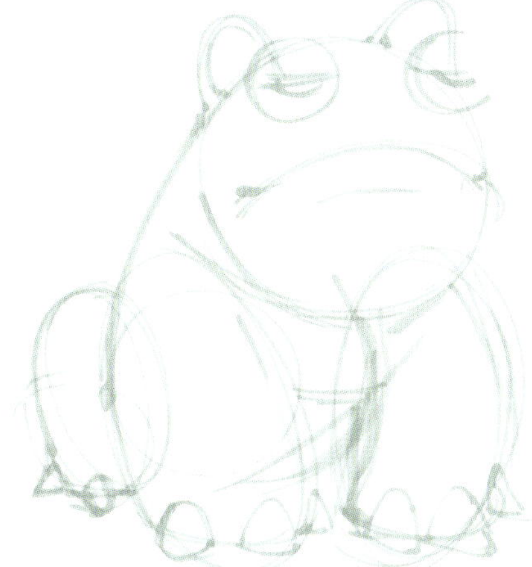

Add Texture and Finalize the Rough Sketch

By now the overall silhouette should be loosely sketched in, but continue to add details. If you pause to allow the marker ink to dry before sketching over your lines, your marker lines will be a bit darker. This is a good way to work sequentially and light until you get it right. I added irises and pupils on the eyes and made a couple of tweaks to the main body and front leg. Because I worked with a light gray marker, it was easy to change the position of a leg and modify other details on the monster.

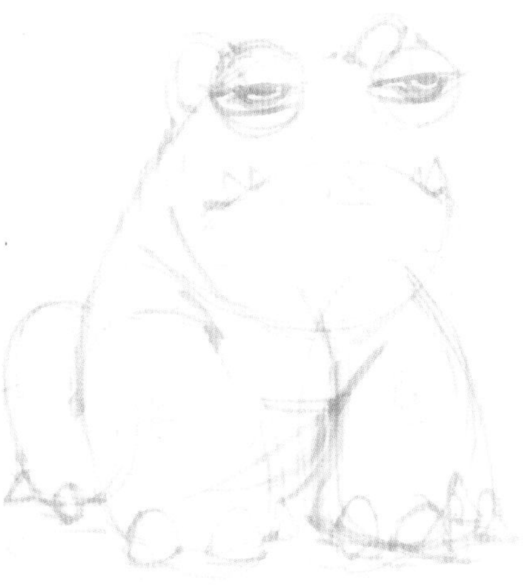

Outline with Pen

Using your pen, begin sketching in the outline of the monster. Remember, you're not simply tracing but re-sketching using the gray marker as a guide. By re-sketching, you can introduce fresh energy into the sketch that otherwise might be lost if you methodically traced everything. For added effect, I used my Micron pen to create dots and wrinkles and stipples on the skin of the monster to give it a more realistic feel.

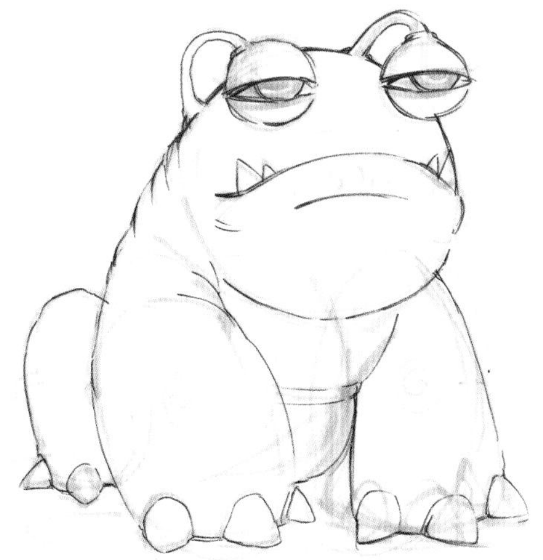

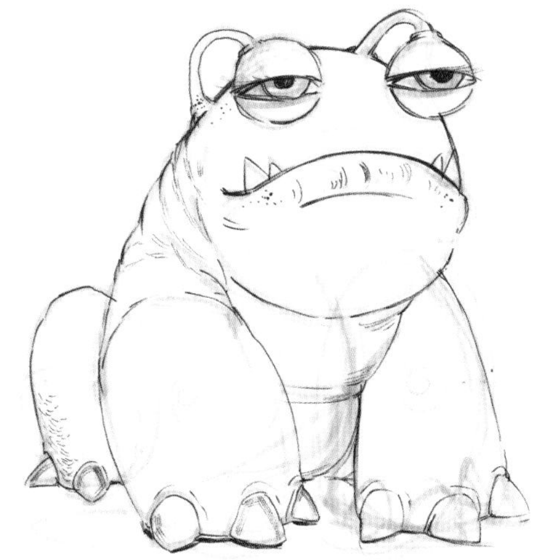

Add Texture and Shading

Next, using the fine tip of my Micron pen, I created a subtle texture on the skin of the monster. To achieve the effect you see in the example, draw very short curves in roughly a C or U shape. Together, these small curves will give the monster's skin a scale-like or bumpy appearance. As you shade in the texture, try to concentrate the density of the texture along areas of the monster that normally would be shaded with a shadow core. Using texture in this manner reinforces the three-dimensionality of the monster and saves you from having to cover the entire monster in the texture.

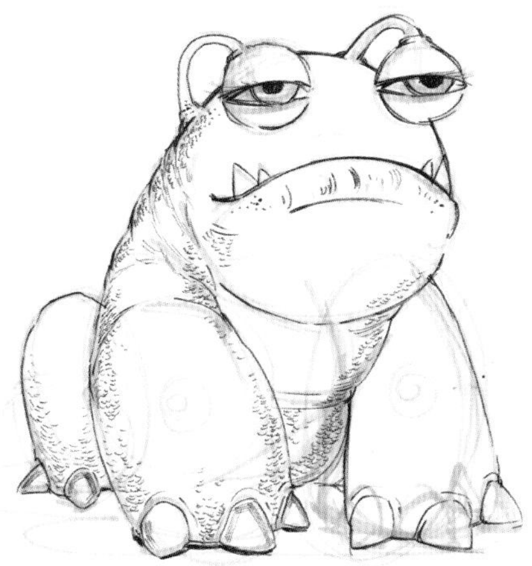
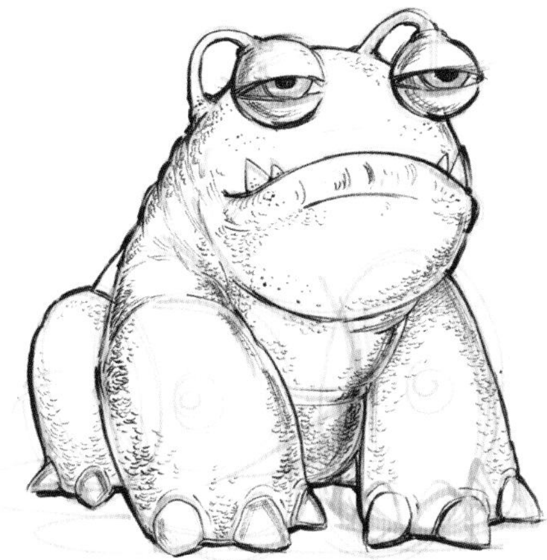

Finalize the Line Work

With the texture in place, your rough sketch is almost done. Add a bit of line weight to the outline of the monster using a slightly thicker pen or even a brush pen for a more expressive outline. If you like, capture a picture of your sketch at this point, remove the gray construction lines, then print it, or simply create an overlay to get rid of the gray marker lines that might affect the appearance of color. Regardless of which path you choose, make sure that you use paper that can hold up to coloring with markers, receive ink well, and make your colors pop.

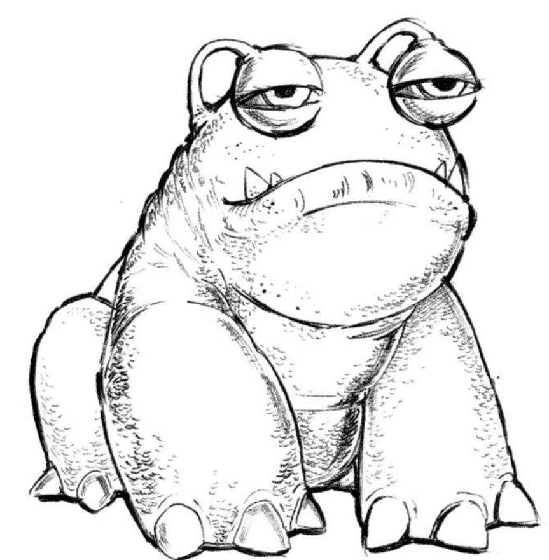

Add Color

Now that the line work drawing is complete, have fun adding color to your monster. I picked a very pale pink marker to outline mine, as well as outline a few spots on the legs. I find it an effective way to ensure that my marker stays within the bounds as I color. I next switched to a teal marker to shade in the spots. Choosing colors can be tricky, but since you're drawing a monster, go ahead and pick something with a fun contrast.

When working with markers, especially in color, make sure that you have a 20% to 30% value difference between each marker. This will make sure that you have markers that are light enough and dark enough to help create a good depth perception in your sketch. Some marker brands have numbers on the caps that indicate hue, saturation, and value to help you choose. Get to know your markers a bit, and test color combinations on scrap paper, if you like.

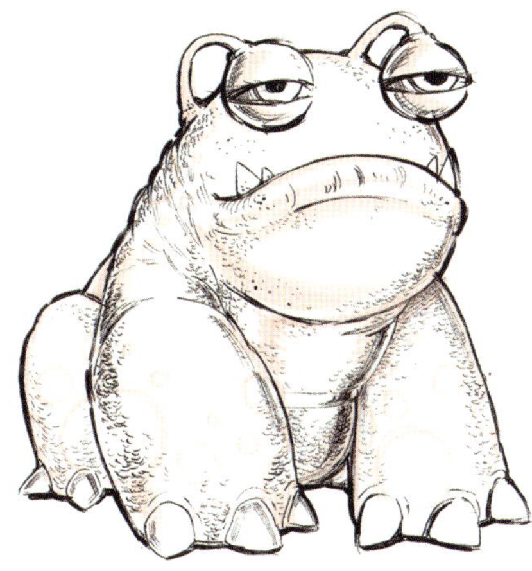
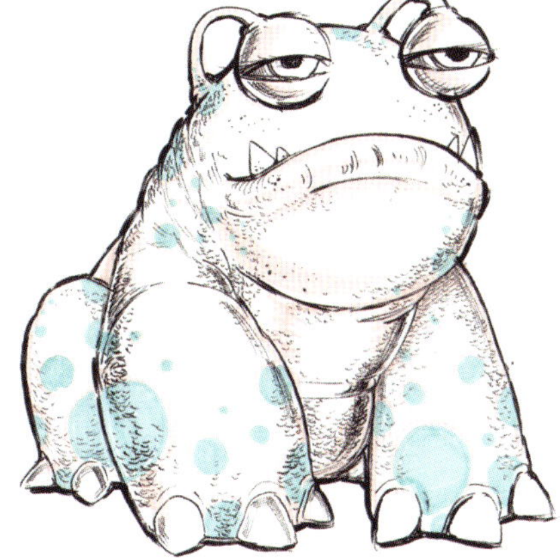

Add Shading and Detailing

Shade in the body of the monster (I used light pink), being careful to exclude areas that might receive some light. Notice that to the upper and general right in the example, I intentionally left blank, white spaces because I did not want to over-work the sketch and bog down the paper with super-saturated colors and details up front.

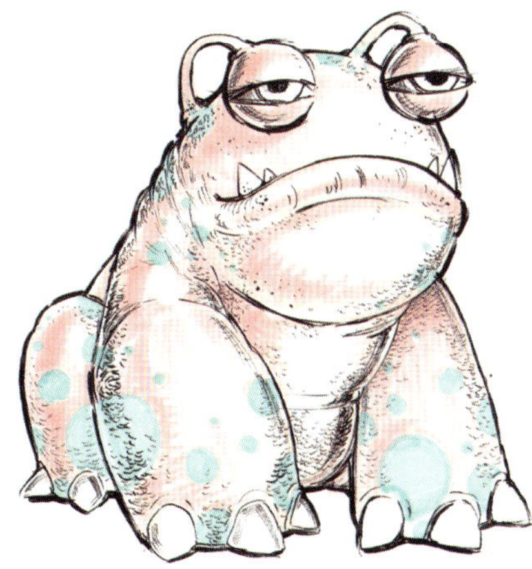

Next, work to build up color and saturation to create a three-dimensional look. Switch to progressively darker markers and focus on the shadow core on rounded areas or other areas of the monster that may be obscured in shadow. Once you have a good base color down, you can move to other areas in the sketch. For example, I shaded in the spots on the monster with a teal marker and used a darker teal to shade and enhance the appearance of texture. Rather than flooding the area with marker ink, use short strokes to mimic the texture you sketched with your pen. This way, the line work, texture, color, lighting, and perspective all work together to create a cohesive and compelling appearance for your monster.

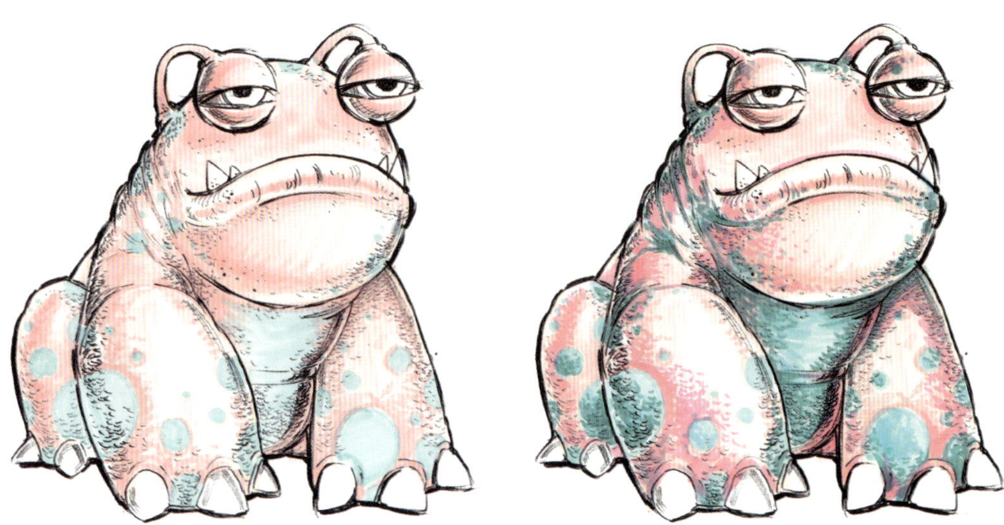

Refine with Finishing Touches

To finish up, I grabbed some deep reds and red-violet markers to shade in the shadow cores on the legs, belly, and body of my monster. Notice how I used the green and reddish pinks in close proximity to each other to show textural contrast as well as lighting. The line weight on the outside of the monster is also intentional but considerate of its overall look and feel. Add your own final touches to your monster. This may take some practice in exercising restraint; however, give it a try and see how expressive you can get with your outline without overwhelming the subject of the sketch.

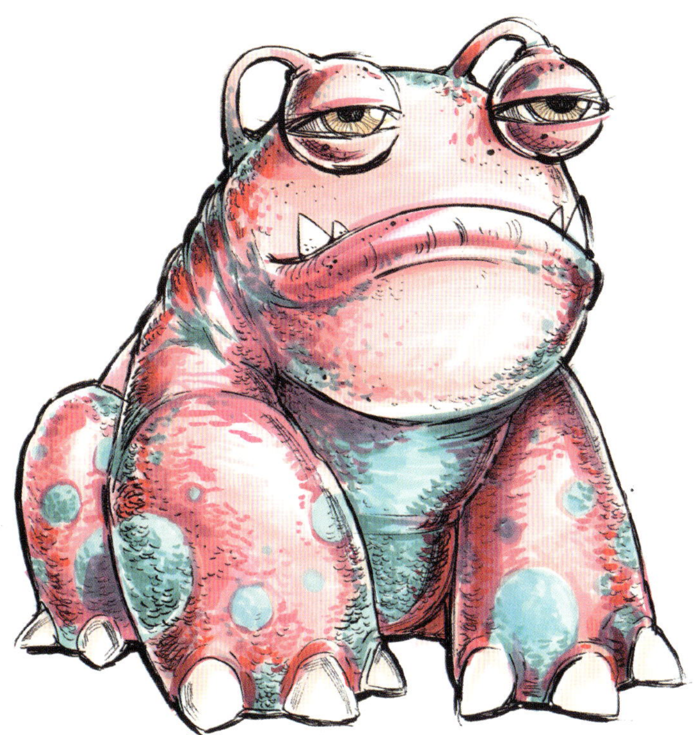

CHALLENGE

Keep mining your imagination and sketch more monsters to practice the techniques you learned this week. Start with simple shapes and see if you can interpolate and use these shapes to make up the body of a monster. I tend to sketch cute monsters, but you could try your hand at something a bit scarier or, better yet, combine a monster with something else you've already drawn. What about a monster holding a cube or wearing sneakers?

Welcome to Week 26—the halfway point! I hope your sketching journey is progressing well, and you're sketching every damn day.

One way to construct complex geometries is by breaking them down into simple planes and shapes as you sketch. Another is way is what I call the "blob method," which involves placing a shape on the paper that is close to the final shape of the object you're sketching. In this exercise, you'll try both methods to draw a computer mouse. Grab a felt pen or your favorite tool, and let's jump into it.

The Planes Method

At first glance, a computer mouse may seem more organic or complex, but a closer look will show that there are simple elements that you can use to sketch it. Take a look at the bottom of a mouse, for example, and you'll notice simple arcs, lines, or shapes you can translate into three-dimensional planes as you sketch.

First, establish a point of view by sketching a central axis line on your paper to help you orient yourself as well as the object you're about to draw. Think of this as the centerline through the mouse along its bottom.

Next, draw two ellipses: one smaller toward the front of the axis and one larger toward the back of this line. The ellipses will form the basis of the shape of the bottom of the mouse. Remember, these are construction lines, so don't stress too much about getting them perfect as you sketch. If it helps, you may start with a two-dimensional sketch of the mouse or use a reference object to check proportions as you sketch.

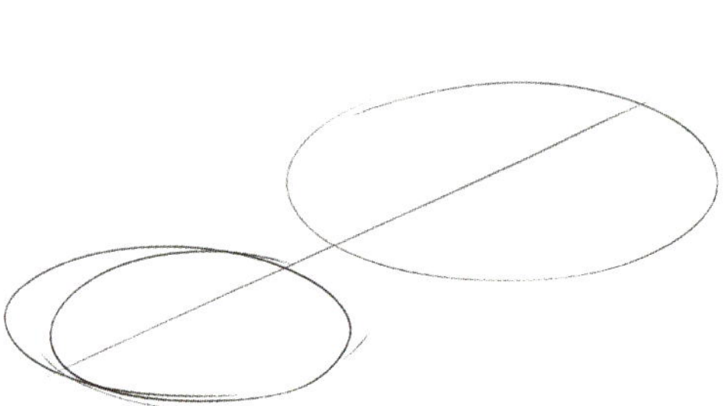

Identify and mark proportional breaks along the central axis for the base of the mouse. For example, the line toward the front or lower left of the example drawing indicates the front of the mouse, and the line toward the middle indicates a point of transition in the width of the base of the mouse. Lines like these help me orient myself as I sketch so that I don't have to guess where to put my next few lines.

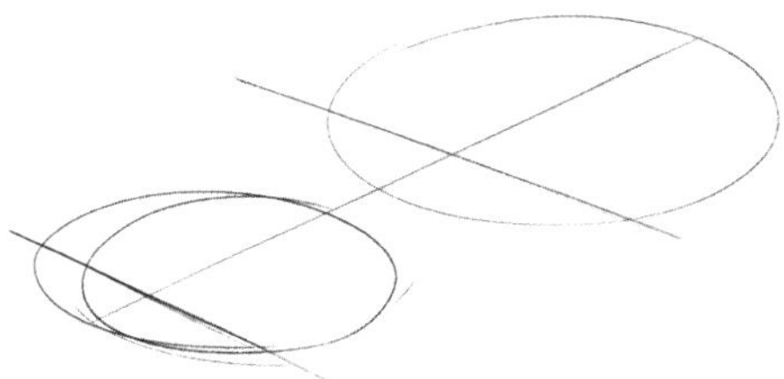

The next step involves a little bit of gestural sketching: Toward the back of the mouse, sketch a sphere or circle, and toward the front of the mouse, start adding horizontal and vertical lines in perspective. These lines and the sphere are meant to represent the overall volume of the mouse. Notice that I sketched the vertical line toward the front such that it intersects the central axis. The sphere toward the back is also centered around this axis.

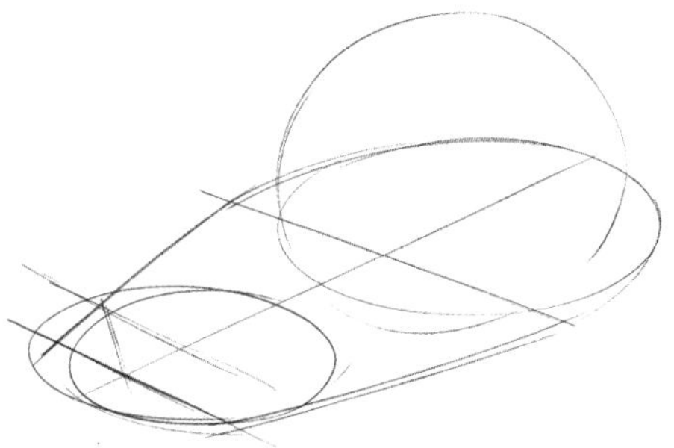

Next, roughly divide the volume of the mouse into functional details and complete the outline. Sketch these lines roughly but lightly. At this point, you could include things like an indication of where buttons may go or if there is any sort of transition in the shape of the mouse along the side. Once these key elements are in place and you have a general idea of the proportion and placement of elements on the mouse, you can move on.

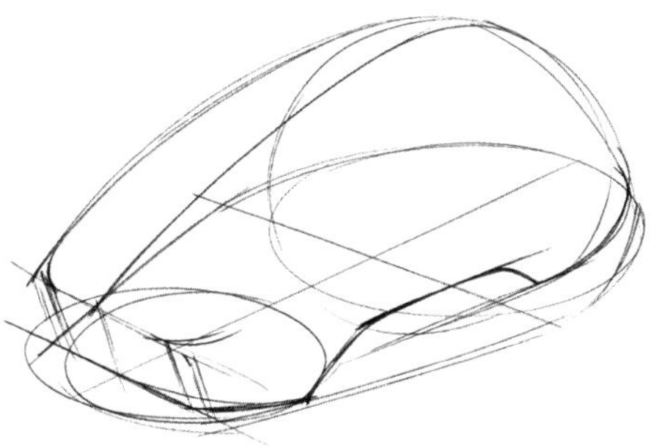

Add details like part breaks for the but-tons, the scroll wheel, and any surface transitions along the side or bottom of the mouse. If desired, add some quick shading and line weight to help clean up the sketch. As you near completion, notice the vertical hatch lines I added toward the bottom of the example mouse as well as the vertical shading lines toward its front corner. These lines quickly establish a material change as well as give the impression of roundness on the corner of the mouse. Adding a few lines to the wheel of the mouse along the surface profile also helps communicate the roundness of the wheel.

Next, if desired, create an overlay of your initial sketch to refine it. Remember to re-sketch using free and expressive strokes rather than slowly trace with trepidation that saps the energy and expression from your drawing. (For more tips on overlays, see Exercise 7.)

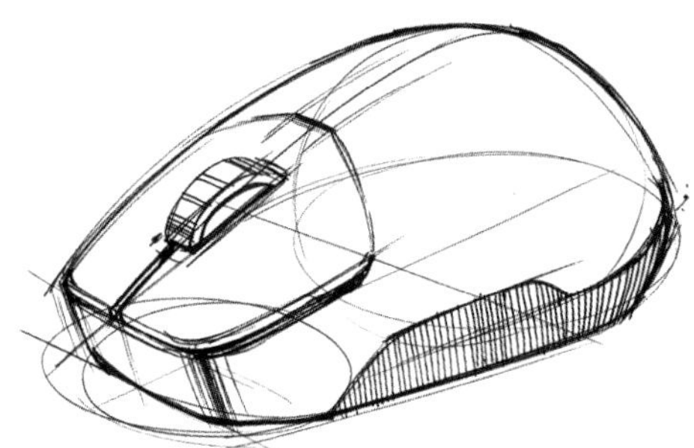

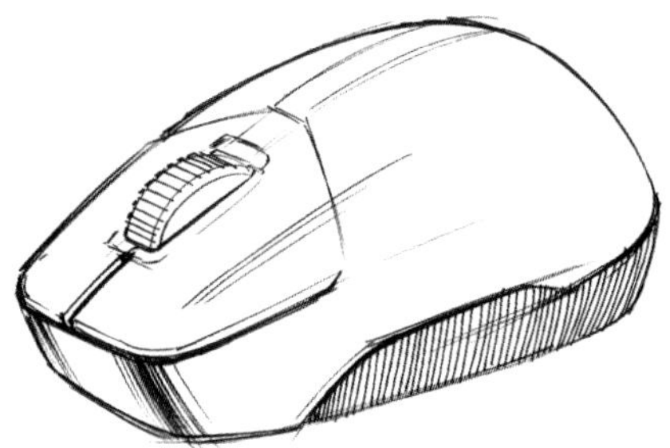

The Blob Method

Using this second technique, you'll first place a simple shape (or blob) on your paper that is close to the final shape of your subject. Look at your reference mouse again—ovalish, thicker on one end than the other—and decide on the per-spective from which you'll draw it.

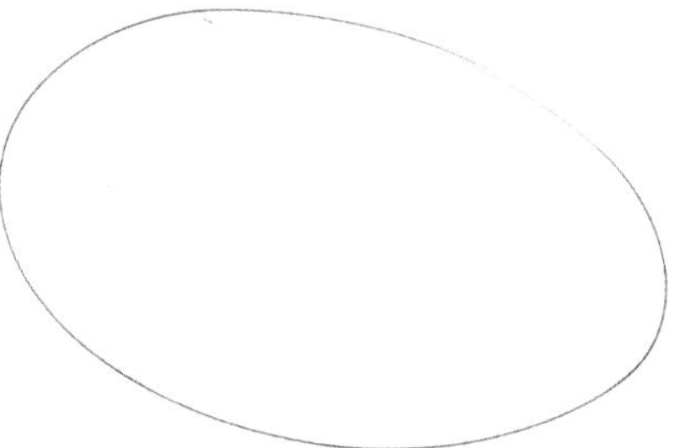

Sketch an egg shape or ellipse, orienting the "egg" in your desired perspective. I drew mine in the same perspective as the central axis I drew for the first mouse, with the front of the mouse pointing toward the viewer's right. If it's helpful, you can draw the centerline or any other reference lines as well. However, I find the blob method to be fairly quick and a touch cleaner than using several construction lines.

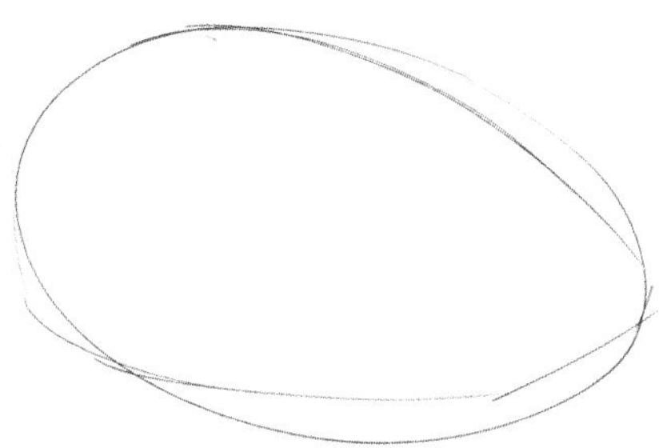

Next, using this reference shape, create subtle adjustments to block in the overall shape of the mouse. If you are able to visualize the final sketch in your mind, you can start by tracing the outline with your pen quickly and gesturally. Don't get too caught up about the initial shape being distracting, as you will handle that with some enhanced line weight later. Getting the hang of it may take a few tries; however, you can use this technique for a variety of complex forms, including things like shoes or automobiles.

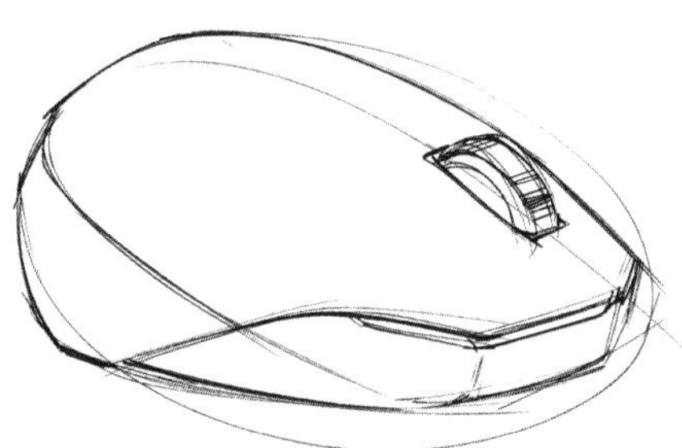

Following similar steps as for your first mouse, add details like buttons, part lines, surface breaks, and material changes by sketching gesturally. Notice that with the enhanced line weight, the initial egg shape appears diminished on the page. When using simple tools, line quality and line weight are critical in cleaning up a sketch like this.

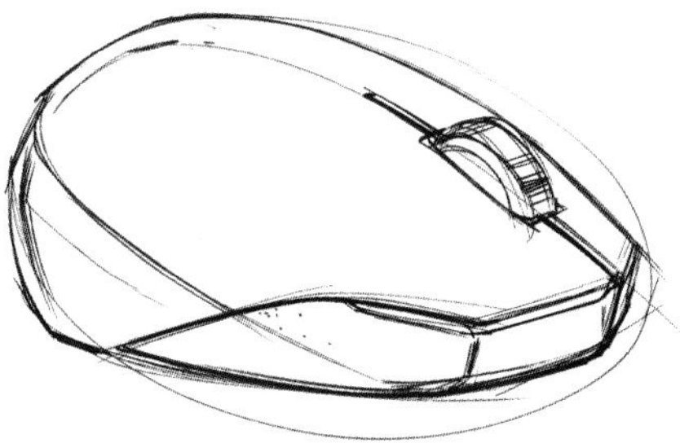

Finally, continue to refine the sketch by enhancing the outline of your mouse. Notice that I added a heavier line weight toward the bottom of the example mouse and divided the top surface of the mouse, giving it two functional buttons and a scroll wheel. I indicated surface details by lines within the sketch profile, such as toward the lower left of the mouse and along the top.

Blob method sketches are good for quickly thinking through ideas, and both techniques are very effective for sketching complex forms. With the help of an overlay, you can create a cleaner version of both of these, then add color, line weight, texture, and materials.

CHALLENGE

Use both the planes method and blob method to sketch other somewhat-organic objects: bottles, headphones, handheld objects that are ergonomic, or if you're feeling exceptionally confident, a car. (I'll show you how to draw a pickup truck with this method in Exercise 36.) Remember to keep your tools and approach simple, and don't be too hard on yourself. As you push through this challenge, you'll find yourself gaining confidence in your ability to analyze objects and sketch more quickly and efficiently.

This exercise ups the form-building complexity: You'll sketch a humanoid robot. You can take inspiration from construction equipment, automated manufacturing robots, or research robots, such as MIT's Humanoid Mini Cheetah. Look at the joints and articulation points to get a feel for the shapes and movement of the parts as they work. When you have your own design in mind, gather some gray markers and felt pens, as well as brush pens to create texture, tone, and shadow.

Draw the Initial Sketch

Sketch a few light lines to establish the positioning of your robot on the page. An arrangement of lines in a rough skeletal form makes a good guide. Next, lightly sketch in the silhouettes and shapes of the pieces of your robot with your gray marker.

I used a warm gray 30% marker to block in shapes to get a feel for the robot. Don't be afraid to be a little exploratory as you draw. For example, the position of my robot's head was in line with the main body at this point, but I wasn't convinced that was quite what I wanted.

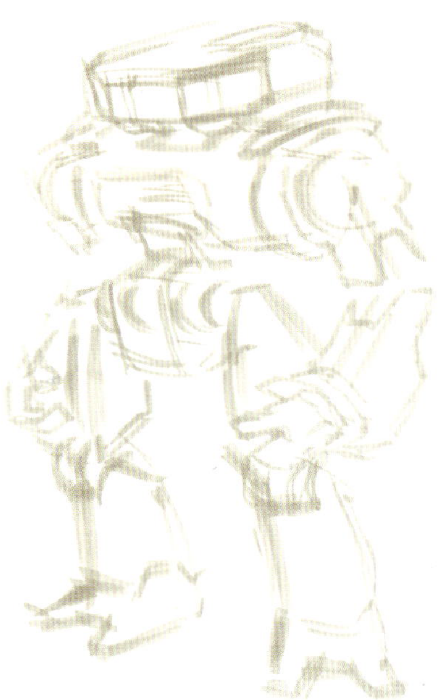
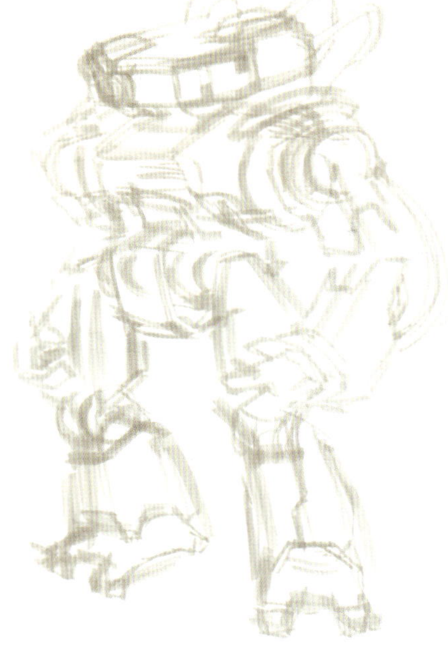

Define and Refine Details

Grab a felt pen of your choice and start adding details to define the shape of the robot. Because you did the under-sketch in gray marker, the contrast of the felt pen helps pull out the final silhouette and shape of the parts. This, in turn, means that changes are easy to make. In this step, I changed the position of the head to a bit more interesting pose.

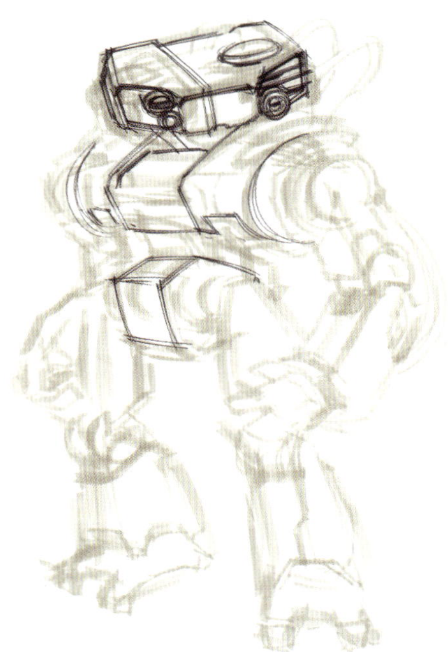

Continue sketching in things like the arms and details related to articulation. You can take creative liberties with the proportion and placement of elements as long as they look like they could work. This is an imaginative piece after all, so have some fun. Continue refining details with your felt pen.

At this point, if you wish, you can use a thicker felt pen to start blocking in the outlines of the silhouette of your robot. I chose to sketch over the silhouette a few times to get the line weight that I wanted.

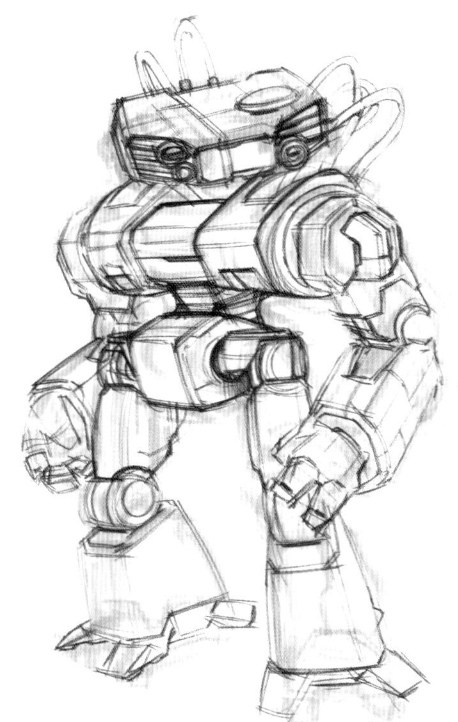

Add Shadows

Using a fine pen, add hatch lines where you want shadow on the robot. In my example sketch, the right side of the robot is generally closer to the observer's position. With this in mind, I tried to make the right side of the robot lighter than the left. You can use this trick of making one side lighter than the other to establish depth and placement of an object as you sketch.

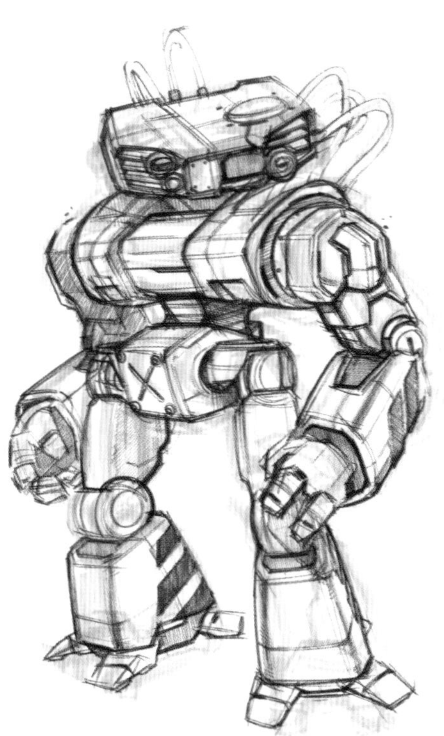

Shade with Markers

With the shadowed areas of the robot hatched in, use a darker (but not your darkest) gray marker to shade in the shadowed areas a bit more. I used a 50% gray marker. Combining a marker with the felt pen helps create not only a textural detail but also set up the contrast in these areas to make them pop. Take some time to add breaks in the metal panels, fasteners, vents, and other details. You can also add graphics or other visual elements to the outside of your robot to help it feel a bit more finished and rounded out.

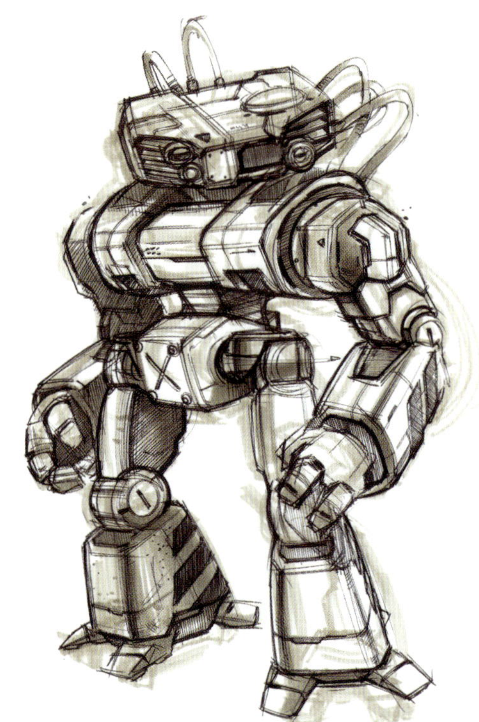

Increase Contrast

Now that the midtone shadows are in place, use your darkest gray marker (a 70% for me) to increase the contrast of these areas. Placing this darkest gray next to lighter grays or white areas helps establish contrast that will give your robot perspective. Perspective is not just about scale and proportion, but also about your use of contrast, lighting, and saturation to convey a sense of depth.

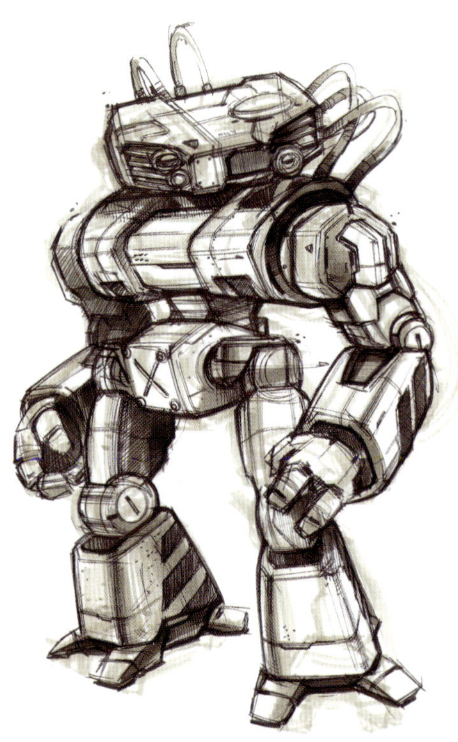

Complete the Final Details

When you're satisfied with the contrast and depth, consider what other details or enhancements your robot needs. Be as fanciful or traditional as you like. For example, I drew rivets, fasteners, and other body details with a fine pen, added some more pen work to the shadowed areas and outlines, and cleaned up the joints, fasteners, and cable connections. If you'd like to clean up or adjust your sketch even more, consider making an overlay or even scanning it in to Adobe Photoshop or other editing software.

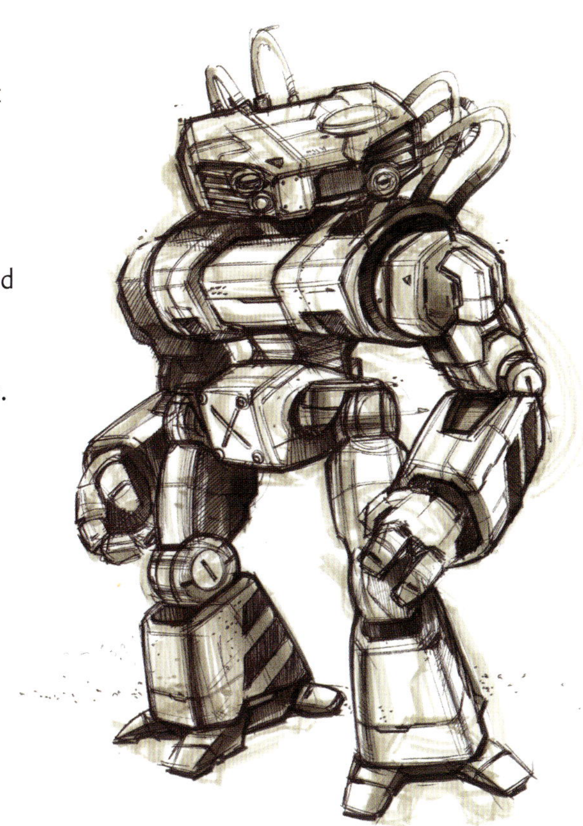

CHALLENGE

Get creative and sketch more robots of your own—humanoid or not. Remember to work light until you get it right. Use a gray marker for roughing in the overall design, then apply ink on top to sketch your final idea. Or use a light graphite pencil to scribble in the shape of your robot, and then finish up with a marker. Push yourself to do several concepts and poses, changing the look and feel of each robot. Before you know it, you'll have your very own robot army ready to go.

Sketching a vehicle of any kind can be a daunting challenge given that the perspective tends to be a bit more complex. As always, however, using some sort of reference on your page at the outset will help you locate your object. In this exercise, you'll start small by sketching a simple Vespa-like scooter with a ballpoint pen and markers. (In Exercises 33 and 36, you'll graduate to cars and pickup trucks, respectively.)

Establish a Proportional Frame

The first step is to establish a proportional frame for the scooter: Sketch a rectangular elongated shape in perspective at whatever angle you choose. If it takes a few tries, that's okay—you'll get it. Add reference shapes along the central axis of your rectangle. For the example, I added squares in perspective to the front and the rear of the flat rectangular shape, as well as a lightly sketched a few additional planes. Ballpoint pens react to pressure a lot like pencils; applying less pressure produces a lighter line, while applying more leaves darker line. Depending on the pen, you may also get a thinner or thicker line as well.

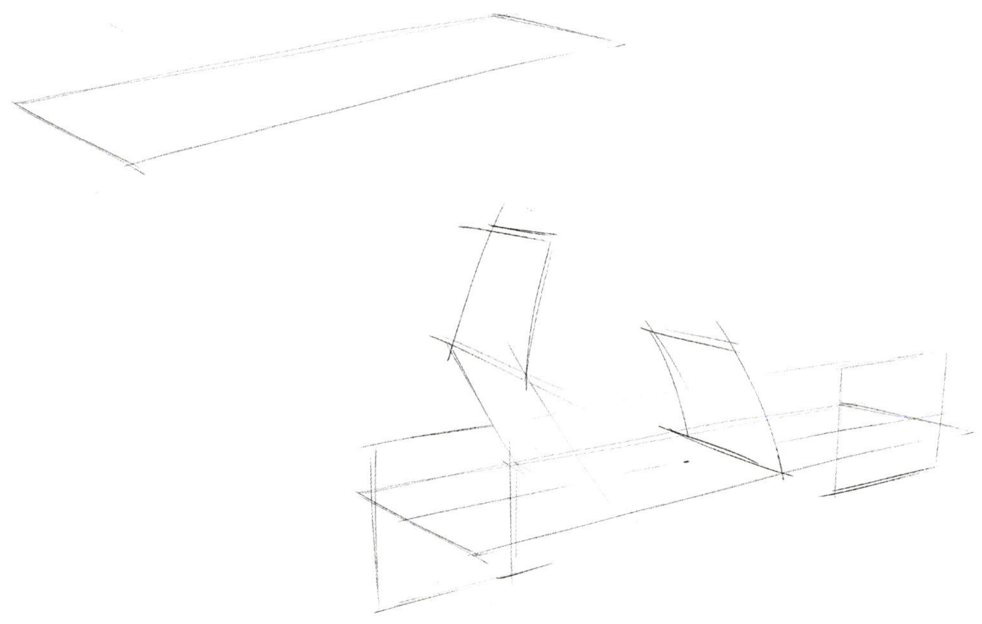

Rough in Major Components

Sketch reference lines for the scooter's handle bars and seat area, as well as a reference line for the rear housing. Definitely consult a reference image or real scooter if you need to understand some of the details, placement, and proportion you need to portray. Sketch an elongated cylinder to represent the handlebars. Sketch another cylinder to represent the headlight. Draw an offset ellipse to block in the trim or bezel of the headlight. At the front and rear of the scooter, sketch in two ellipses to represent the wheels. Additionally, adding curved lines toward the outline of the scooter helps establish the overall silhouette as you go.

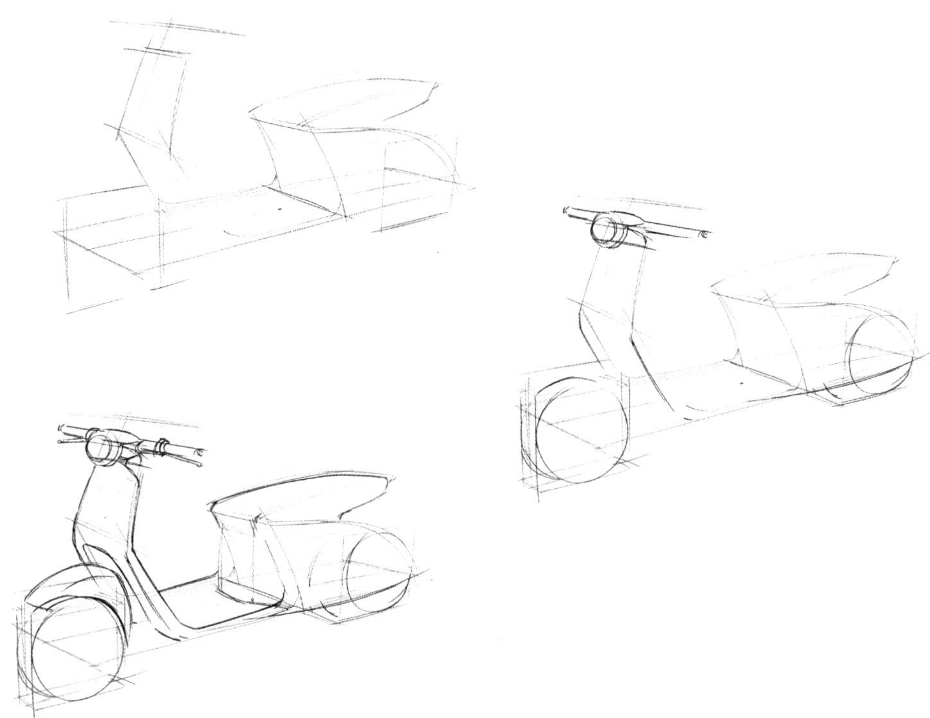

Add Details

After sketching in the wheels, it's time to move on to adding other supplementary details. Draw the front wheel cover, handlebar levers, and any details around the seat that you may want to include. I took time to add a cutout to the front of the scooter where the steering column would meet the wheel. Try not to get too bogged down in details, but also add enough as you go to lend realism.

Next, at the front and rear of the scooter, offset ellipses to give the wheel additional depth. Sketch in an ellipse for the hub of the front wheel. Toward the rear of the scooter, break up the body into panels that are related to the functional pieces of the scooter, such as the rear wheel cover or footrests. At the front of the scooter, sketch in treads on the wheels, emphasizing the steering column, and adding spokes to the front wheel.

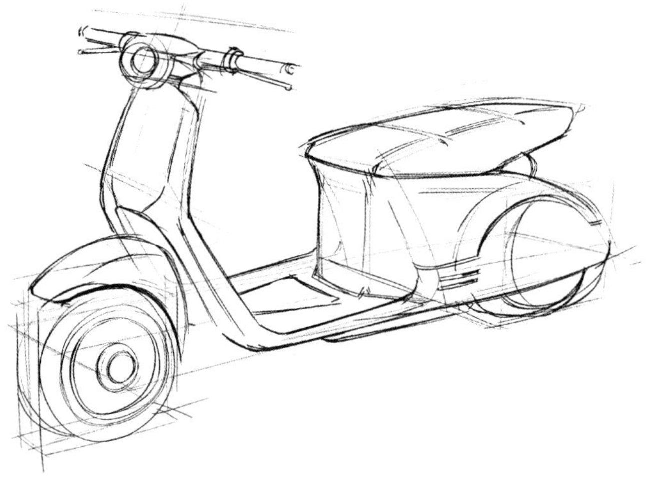

To draw the spokes, simply draw a V shape using double lines, and then repeat that V shape around the wheel hub to create the effect of spokes. Don't forget to add spots for lights or vents or any other relevant functional details. Lastly, with a little extra pressure and repetition, outline your sketch with your ballpoint pen to enhance the line weight and presence of the scooter on the page.

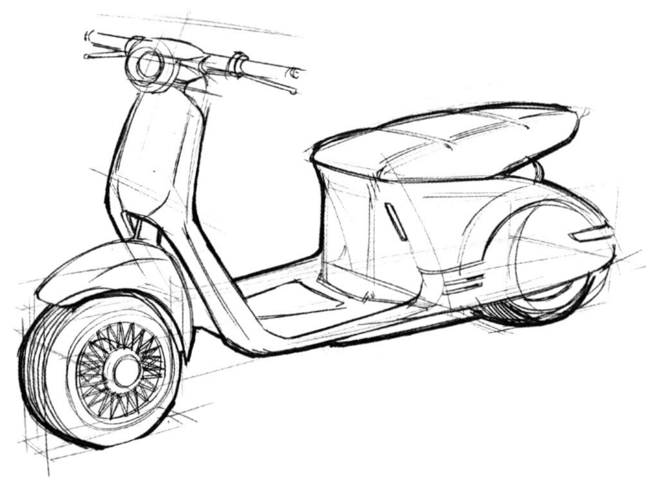

Add Color

If you choose, you can add color to your sketch now (or just continue using pen to shade it). For the example, I used xylene-based markers, also called solvent-based markers. Alcohol-based markers, such as those from Copic and Prismacolor, tend to smudge and smear once their ink interacts with the ink of a ballpoint pen. I find, using a solvent-based marker prevents any bleeding of the ballpoint pen strokes. Before adding color to your sketch, test how your markers interact with your pen on scrap paper. If you are hesitant in adding color to your neatly drawn sketch, you can always scan your sketch or make a copy prior to applying the marker, just to make sure that the original sketch is preserved.

Start by applying your lightest colors. I selected a light and dark yellow to color in areas of the scooter, while I also sketched with two grays. Trace along areas you want to color in with your markers so that you have a visible area to fill in and a way to start and stop applying the color. Work light until you get it right and give your markers a chance to dry before applying more. After the marker is dried, you can reapply another coat in the same spot to get a deeper effect, such as on the seat cushion or the wheels.

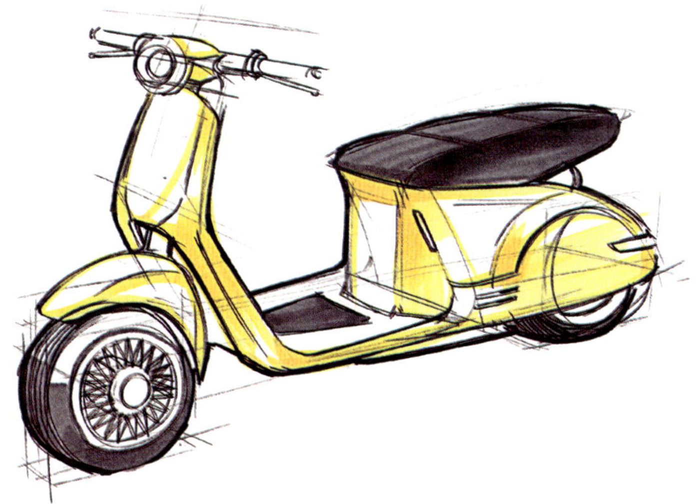

Next, with a midtone yellow and middle gray marker, shade in any areas that would be shadowed by another element in the sketch or the sides of the scooter that would be facing away from the light. Based on the highlights in my sketch, its light source is located toward the top left, while a secondary light source creates highlights toward the rear of the scooter. It's up to you to decide where you'd like to put your light source and highlights as you sketch. Continue to add value and contrast with your markers by reapplying gray or yellow markers once your ink is dried.

As you can see, reapplying the marker has enhanced contrast in the scooter sketch. Notice in the example that the trim on the headlight is shaded so as to mimic chrome by having crisp reflections and highlights, while the seat and wheels are shaded in a more blended way to convey a matte or dull finish for those parts and their materials.

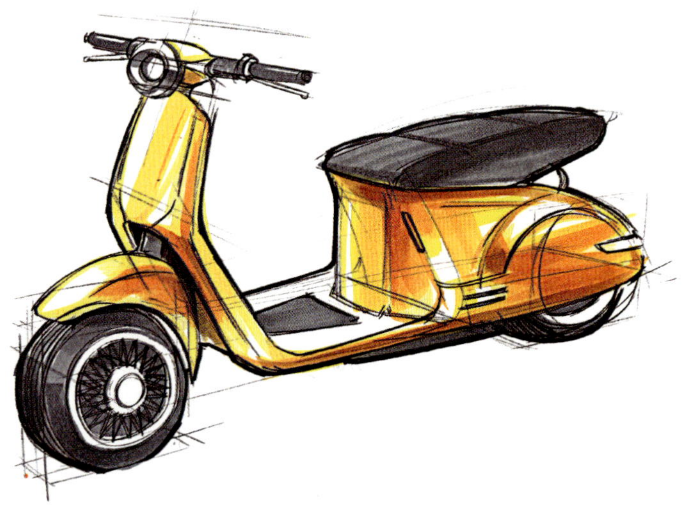

Enhance Highlights on Top of the Color

Once you've established enough contrast and shading, use a pencil to enhance any highlights you may want to pop. For example, on the front wheel, I used a pencil to shade in a bit of a highlight on the rubber portion. Likewise, a few squiggles and shaded areas on the seat added a bit of luster to what is likely synthetic leather.

At a glance, it may seem that I neglected to include the forks for the front wheel. However, one trick you can use when sketching is to place an element on the far side of the object in an effort to save a bit of time. For example, were you to sketch this scooter from another angle or point of view, you could include a detailed sketch of the front to clarify that detail.

To finish up the scooter, continue to refine lines and details on top of the color. By drawing on top of the marker-colored areas with a ballpoint or other pen, you can introduce a crisper break in the structure of the object. Notice the crisp highlights that I added to the example with an opaque paint marker. These are readily available at craft and art stores, and they come in a variety of sizes. Alternatively, you can use a bit of opaque white paint, like gouache, acrylic paint, or correction fluid to add an intense highlight where needed, such as where there is a glossy or shiny surface.

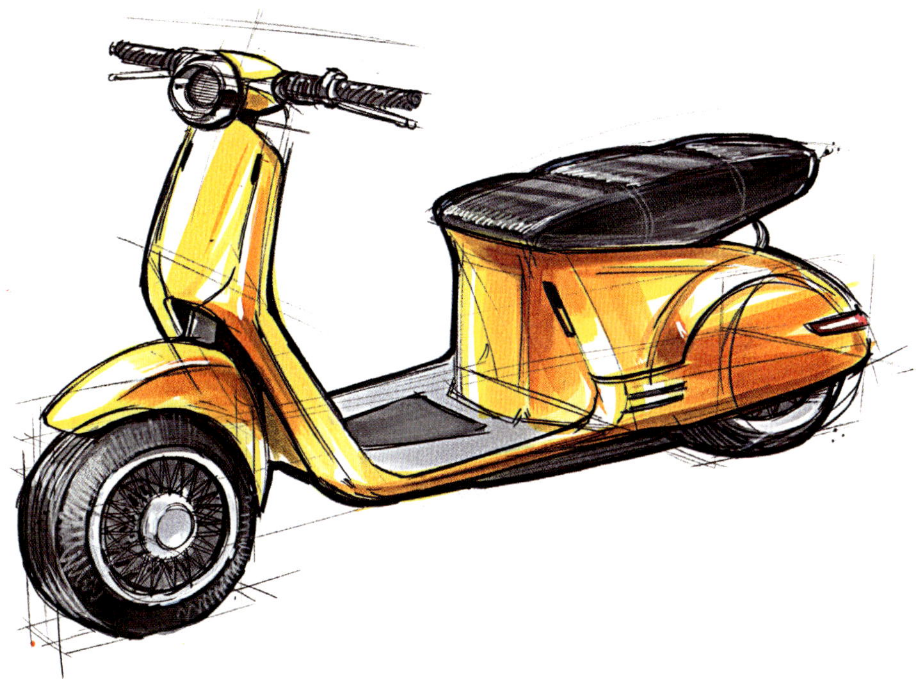

CHALLENGE

Using a ballpoint pen, sketch a few complex objects—a stroller, a shoe, a ride-on mower—that require a bit of thought and planning, like the scooter. Remember to use light pressure to sketch in construction geometry and work your way up from rough construction lines and shapes to a more refined and defined drawing. Don't try to sketch the entire complex object at once— work up to drawing it. If you choose to apply color, remember to work light and test your markers before applying them to your sketch. I've had many painful moments where I exuberantly rushed to apply some color to a sketch, only to discover that I had selected the wrong color or the wrong value in that color family. Don't let your own mishaps discourage you and remember to keep sketching every damn day!

For this exercise, you'll draw a deceptively complex object: a men's dress shoe. I recommend using a Paper Mate Flair pen because it holds up well to alcohol- and solvent-based markers when adding color. If you use a different pen, make sure to test it with a variety of inks on scrap paper—better to find out there if the pen lines bleed or smudge than to mess up your drawing!

Draw Thumbnail Sketches

To start, sketch a few side view thumbnails of your shoe, trying to capture the gesture of the shoe. Additionally, you can draw top- or end-view thumbnails to better understand the structure of the shoe. When consulting a reference (either in a photo or in your closet), notice the general gesture of the shoe's heel, sole, and forefoot. These lines are important when you translate these thumbnails into perspective.

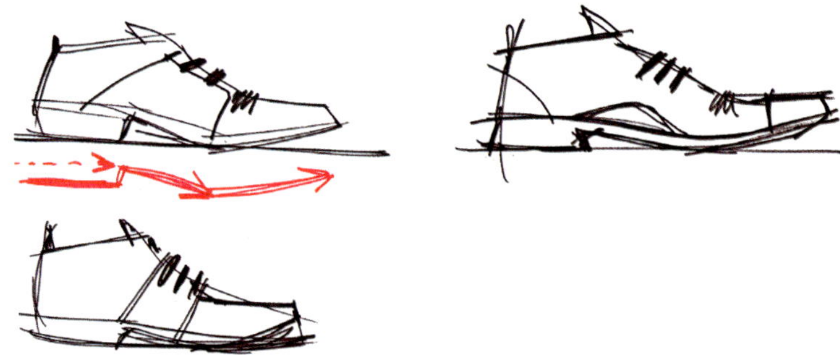

Rough in Perspective

Sketch three lines in perspective that represent the overall gesture of the sole of the shoe. At the intersection points and ends of these lines, extend them to the right or left depending on the orientation of your initial lines. These lines represent the width of the shoe overall. While looking at the first lines you sketched, follow the pattern and complete three rectangular shapes by drawing three additional lines in perspective to intersect your second set of lines. These rectangles now form planes in perspective. Remember, in perspective drawing, things that are closer to you will appear wider or longer than things further away. Pause and check to make sure that your shoe has been sketched in perspective by comparing the lengths of lines relative to those closer to you in your sketch.

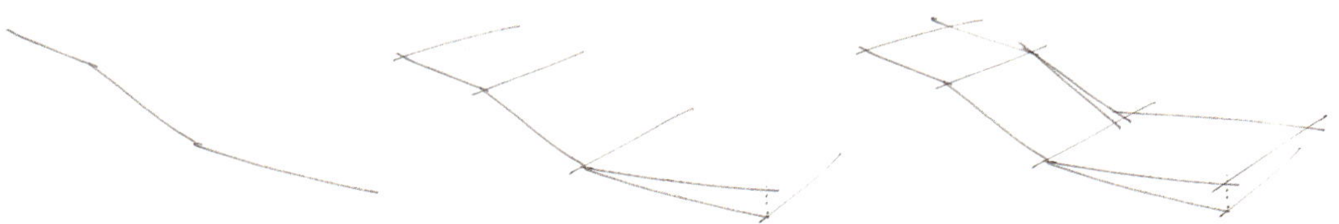

Construct the Heel

Box in the heel of the shoe by drawing a cuboid below the leftmost rectangular shape in perspective. Additionally, scribe two arcs in the line at the rear of the shoe. This will form the rear quarter and collar of the shoe. Toward the front of the shoe, slightly modify the sole to kick up slightly. This way, you can more accurately capture the gesture in your thumbnail sketches. Within this rectangle toward the front of 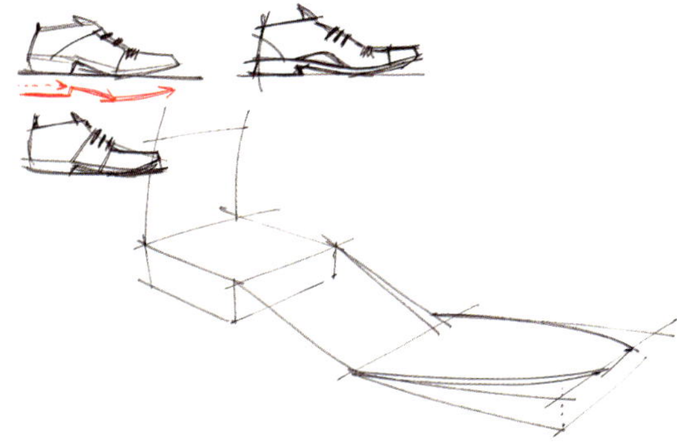 the shoe, scribe two arcs that represent the overall shape of the shoe. Don't get too caught up at this step with getting things completely perfect. You'll be overlaying the sketch in a later step.

Detail the Shoe

Using the planes and construction lines as a guide, rough in the overall shape of your shoe by referencing the thumbnail for the location of details related to the look and feel of the shoe. Detail around the toe cap and vamp of the shoe, as well as locate where your laces will be placed as you sketch. Laces can be a bit tricky, so it's a good idea at this point to take a look at some reference imagery for general proportion and placement of the laces. If you'd like to keep it simple, you can also opt for a slip-on shoe that doesn't require laces. Still, I challenge you to try drawing laces by following along the general shape of the shoe as sketched.

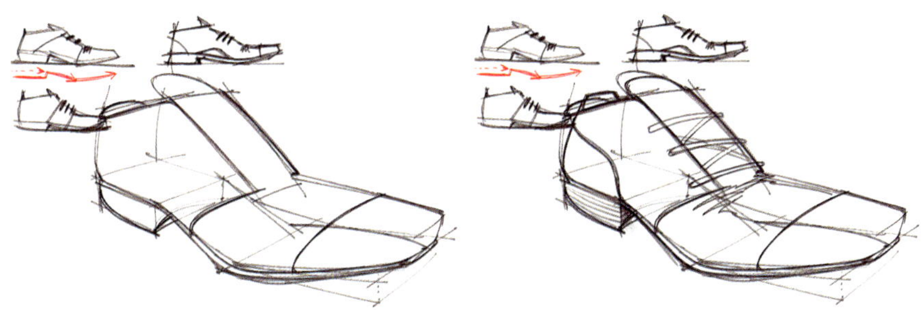

Enhance Line Weight and Shading

Continue adding details and modifying the shoe by enhancing the line weight of the overall silhouette as well as adding light shading and hatch marks. At the heel, draw a few offset lines that are slightly curved to mimic a wood heel. Create a shadow where the heel goes under the sole of the shoe. On the forefoot, or vamp, of the shoe, sketch in a few squiggly lines to indicate a bit of a wrinkle in the shoe leather. Also emphasize the lines that define the collar, tongue, and toe cap of the shoe.

Finalize the Sketch

At this point, I was almost done sketching the shoe and decided to shade a bit with just my pen. To create a shadow core along the lateral side of the shoe, sketch a series of arcs and lines that are parallel and grouped together to create a shadow core. The shadow core runs along the profile of the shoe as shown. A simple way to think about this is to position these lines inset from the overall profile of the area with which you'd like to show some curvature. Additionally, sketch a few hatch lines orthogonally to the shadow core along the forefoot or vamp of the shoe. You can accentuate the wrinkle lines with additional line weight and groupings of lines. To further enhance the three-dimensionality of the shoe, punch up your line weight by sketching with a different pen on the outline of the shoe or by simply sketching in places where the lines exist already to deepen the value and thickness of these lines. I shaded in the laces using hatch lines with my felt pen and, as you can see, the construction lines became less significant and visible overall in the sketch.

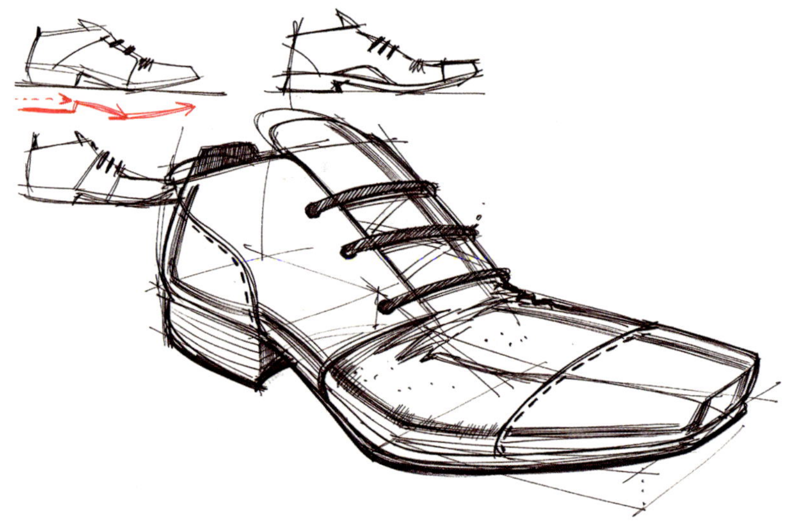

Create an Overlay and Enhance

Sketches like these are a great way to show visual thinking, whether for yourself or for the benefit of others. This is a great place to stop if you are simply sketching something like this to capture an idea. Alternatively, if you wish to enhance your drawing, create an overlay. As you remember, place a sheet of translucent paper above your rough sketch, then re-sketch (not stiffly trace!) the sketch below. On this overlay, you can now apply marker to bring the sketch to life, as well as take a few liberties in perspective and placement of your sketch on the page by re-sketching. You can even rotate the sketch underneath your new sheet of paper for a new perspective.

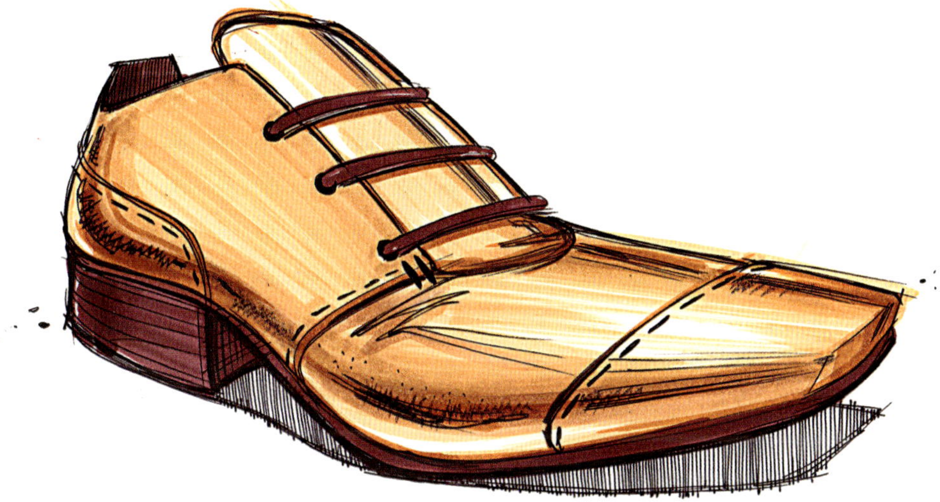

CHALLENGE

Continue sketching a few shoe ideas and focus on creating a few thumbnails to help guide the process. Explore as many ideas as possible and select a few to refine by sketching them in perspective. Consider varying the point of view and perspective of each shoe but use a similar construction method to establish the sole and heel of your shoe. Continue to sketch until the shoes are completed. Feel free to stop at the point where you have a rough sketch completed, or, if you wish to push through a little further, try your hand at completing a more rendered sketch using markers. (See Exercise 43 for tips on applying color to your shoes.)

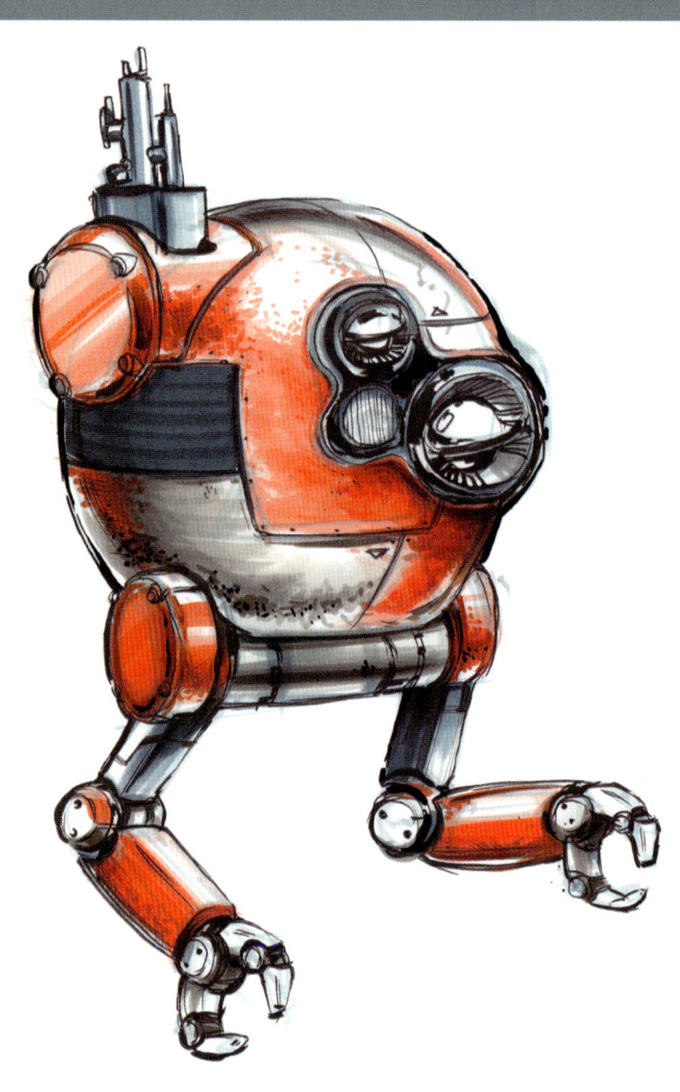

CHAPTER 5

ADVANCED PERSPECTIVE

Sometimes perspective problems can be more complex when an object has a lot of detail or is a combination of many different objects. When tackling advanced perspective problems, try to be patient with yourself. Analyzing the makeup of a given object takes time and thought, but doing so is key to understanding how to sketch it convincingly in perspective. As you consider the object's forms, think about their position in three-dimensional space, evaluate proportion, and assess angles related to the overall object you are drawing.

Observational Drawing

One of the best ways to get better at drawing in perspective is by drawing from observation. As I've mentioned before, pausing to consult a reference, particularly to observe, analyze, and draw a real object, will help you better portray that object or a similar one in your imagination. Drawing from observation will help you become better at drawing from imagination.

Similarly, drawing from observation will help you to understand the complex perspective issues of organic objects, nonlinear objects, and others that aren't defined by rational geometry. As you observe, though, remember that drawing in perspective is more than just tricks used to show scale and relative position. It also involves the cooperation and harmony between line, color, value, saturation, proportion, and point of view.

Yes, that's a lot to learn, but you can do it! Be patient with yourself and keep trying. Practice, practice, practice. Your journey to perspective mastery, like every journey, requires consistent steps and motion, so be sure to draw a little bit every day. Before you know it, you'll be able to look back and see your progress from where you started with your drawing skills.

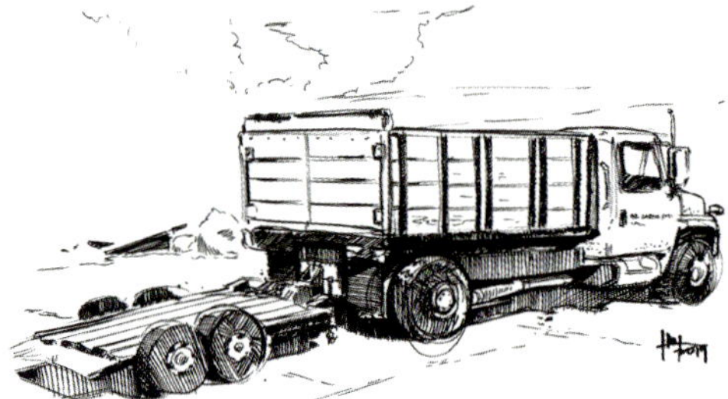

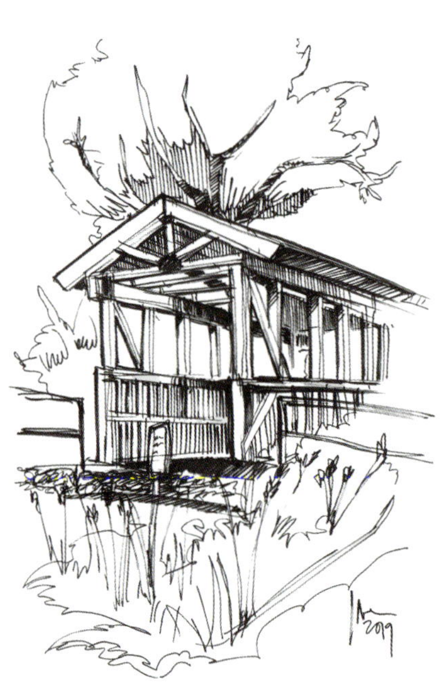

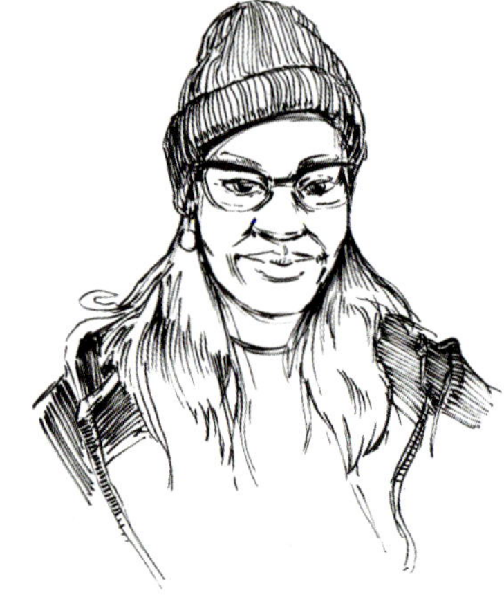

 AIRPLANE

Drawing aircraft is a challenging perspective drawing exercise, so take a moment to analyze some reference photos of various aircraft. Can you identify any basic shape that might help you? Largely, airplanes are comprised of a tubular fuselage, which is similar to a cylinder, with wings, tailpieces, and other fin-like elements extending from this central cylinder. Depending on the aircraft, you can simplify these fins to be squished cuboids or trapezoids. So, with a cylinder, cuboids, and trapezoids in mind and a Paper Mate Flair pen in hand, let's draw an aircraft inspired by the P-51 Mustang, a classic plane with lots of character and nostalgia.

Establish the Base Sketch

To get started, sketch a line that will serve as the central axis of the plane. This process should be familiar at this point, but it is essential for establishing a sense of place, proportion, and scale for whatever you're sketching. Because the fuselage of the plane is roughly cylindrical, sketch two cylinders stacked on top of each other. Make the top one smaller and be sure to taper both cylinders as they recede from you. The upper cylinder will form the cockpit, and the lower cylinder will serve as the main fuselage.

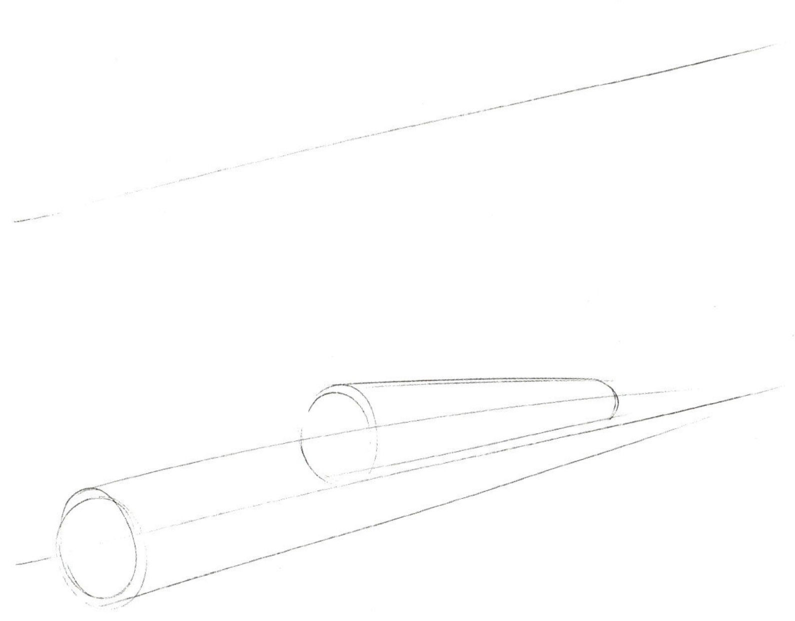

Next, transition from the upper cylinder to the main cylindrical body with a curve. Toward the back of the plane, on the right side of the sketch, add the tail and stabilizers. Now equip the front of the plane with a curved cone to serve as the base for the propellers. Although the fuselage is not exactly cylindrical, sketching in this manner allows you to simplify the process and focus on the overall gesture of the plane.

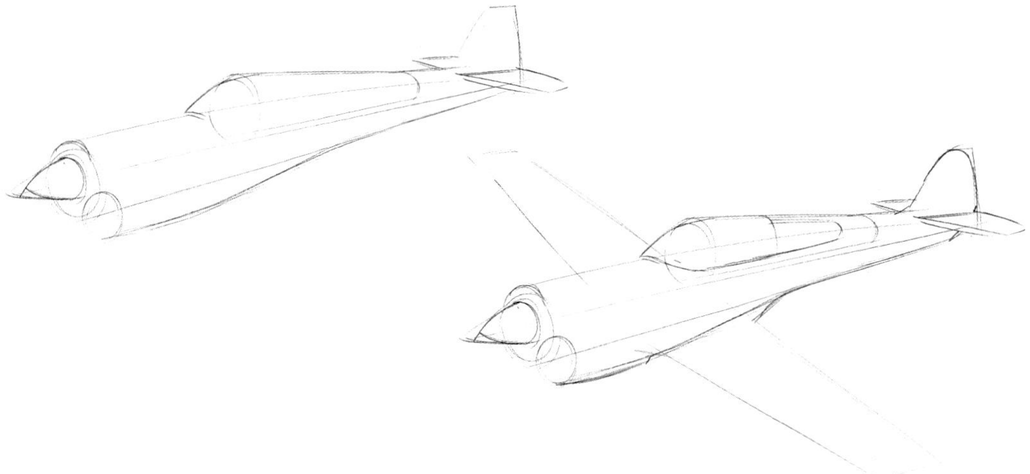

Add Functional Details

Continue by adding details to the cockpit area, such as metal banding over the glass, part lines, and sheet metal breaks on the main fuselage. Classic and modern aircraft often have fuselages made of panels riveted together, complementing the overall 3D geometry shown on paper. You can divide the wings into functional or aesthetic breaks, especially where rudders and flaps are located. Add a double line on the tail to indicate the rudder and add a circumscribed star as part of a graphical treatment on the plane. Feel free to add any additional graphical elements you like.

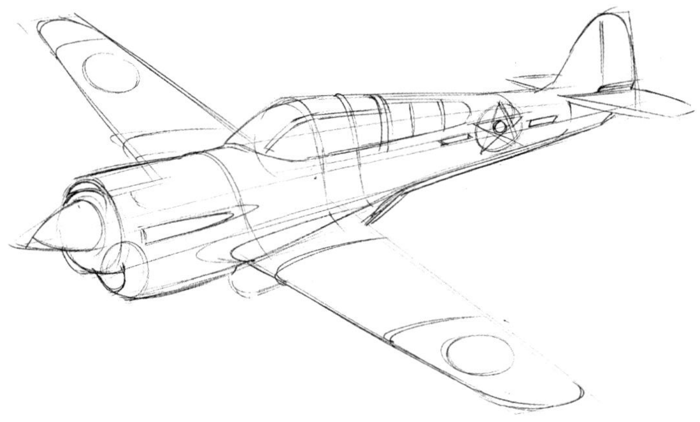

Shade and Refine

To accent the wing tips and tail, hatch in the areas that you want to shade differently than the main body. Attach the propellers to the front cone by sketching an ellipse centered on the central axis. In the areas you want insignia, hatch in a circle surrounding a star surrounding a dot using the pen and directional strokes. Traditionally, the circle was dark blue, the star white, and the dot red. Practice varying pressure and stroke so your hatching suggests the various values. The front of the fuselage and intake are great spots for classic detailing. Sketch in features like an eye, teeth, or flames toward the front of the plane for added fun.

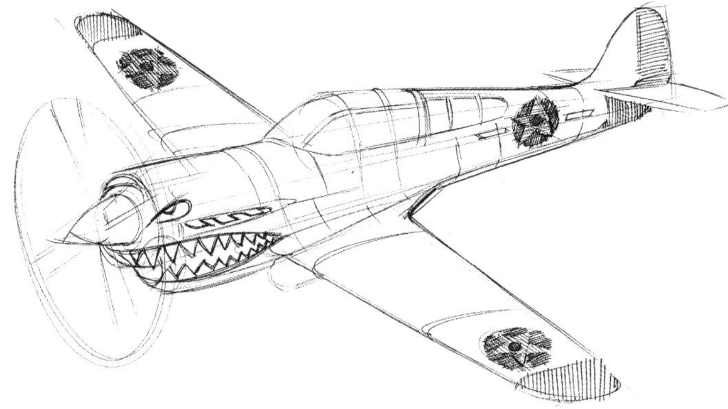

Enhance any line work with additional line weight where necessary around the plane's outline. Divide the fuselage into smaller panels in preparation for detailing with rivets. Continue hatching and refining the outline and include shading on the propeller cone to convey a metallic feel. Shade the propeller to mimic rotational movement, indicating that the plane is in flight.

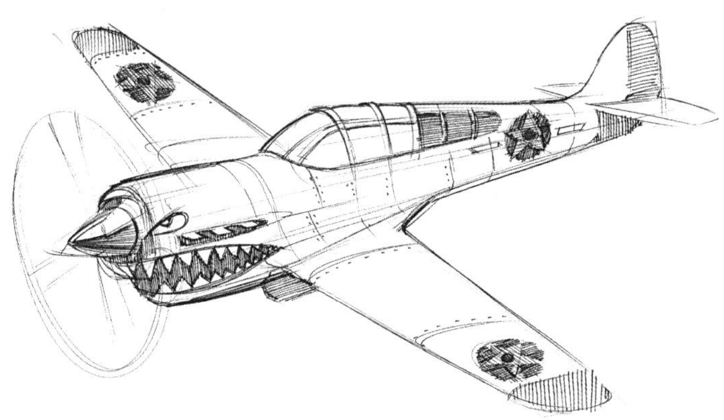

Add Final Touches

Continue refining the sketch by enhancing line weights and adding details. Notice that by adding line weight, the lighter construction lines are less apparent, and the focus shifts to the final lines. Enhance the outline further and add parallel lines in the direction of the fuselage at the top and on the far wing to suggest shadowing.

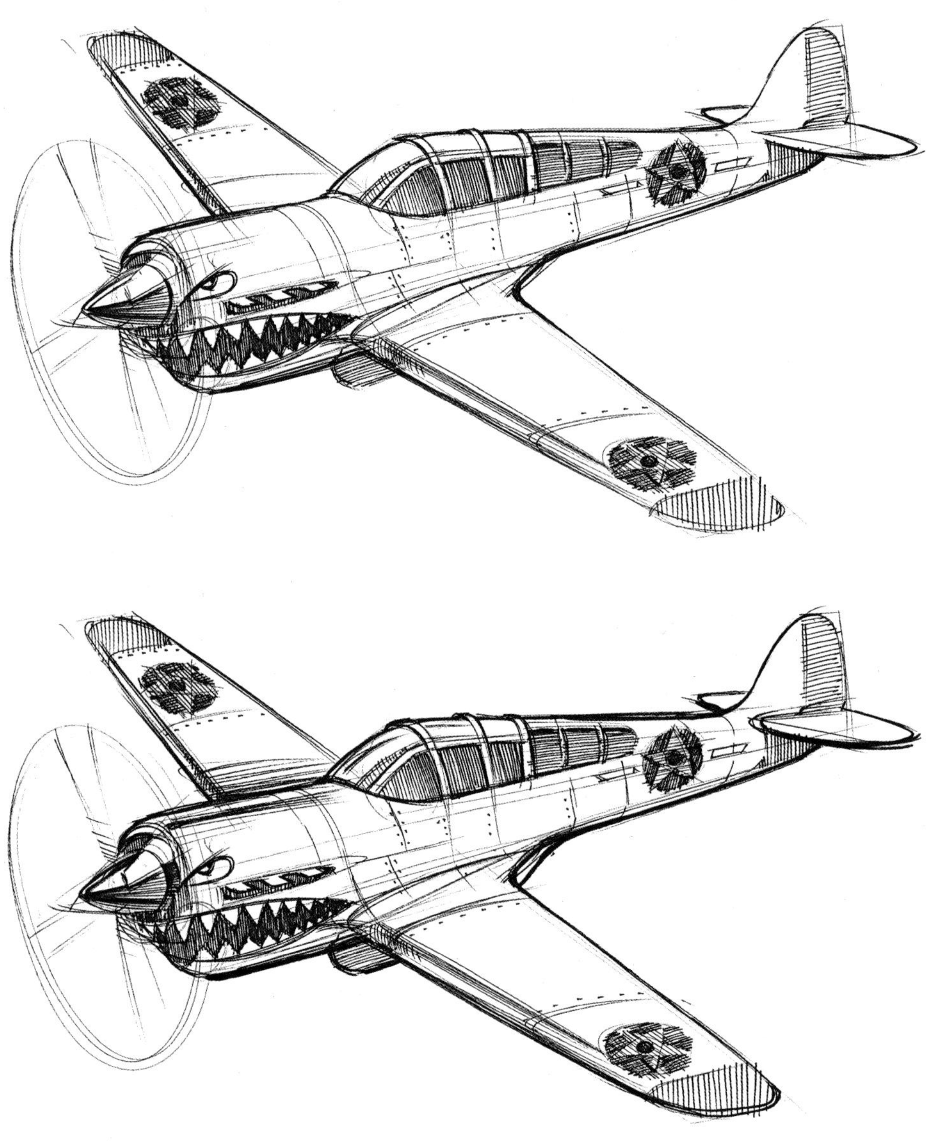

Review your plane sketch and refine any areas that need more detail or precision. To provide context, sketch a few cloud shapes as a background element. Leave these clouds as single-line shapes to support the main sketch without drawing attention with contrast, color, or texture.

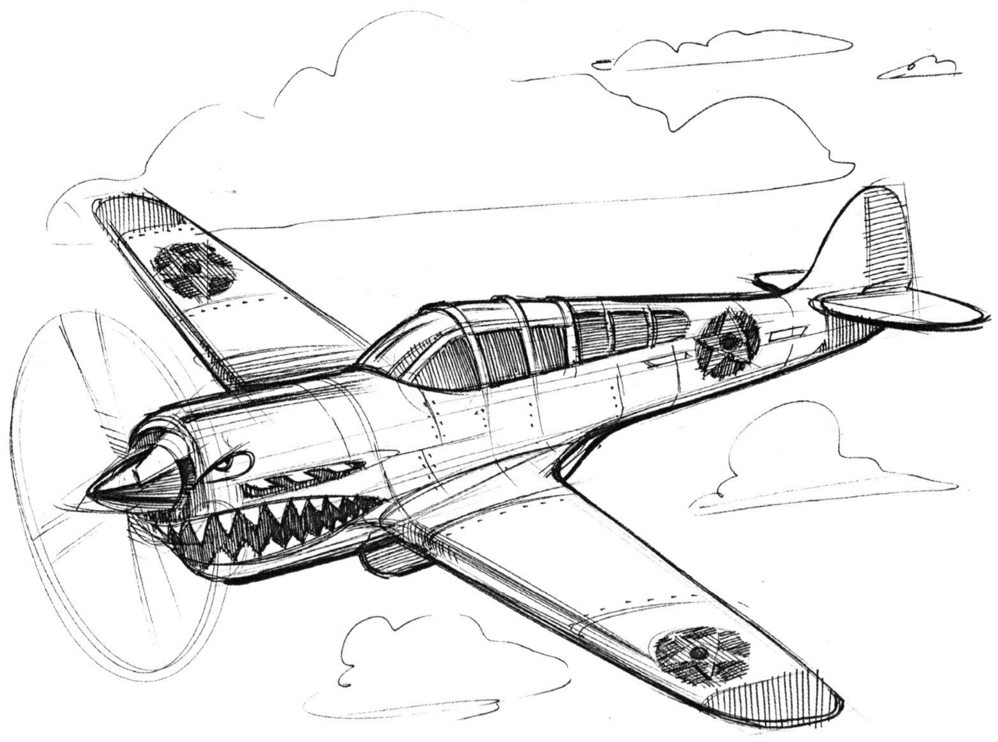

CHALLENGE

Draw more aircraft, specifically focusing on placement and proportion with a more involved perspective. Use simple scaffolding techniques and construction lines to establish the scale of elements related to your aircraft. Research existing aircraft through imagery and understand their functional makeup before sketching. Once comfortable, get creative with your designs while keeping your tools simple, your lines loose, and your sketch muscles ready. Focus on quantity but be mindful of the quality of your sketches as well.

Sketching familiar, everyday objects can be difficult because of our inherent expectations. Practicing advanced perspective drawing with a bicycle can be even more challenging due to its narrow dimensions, technical elements, and features like wheels, spokes, gears, and mounts. In addition, bicycles require careful attention to proportion as they are designed for human use. The key is to balance detail and quick sketching techniques, as you'll practice this week. I recommend using a simple felt pen, but feel free to choose any tool you're comfortable with.

Analyze and Sketch Some Guides

To begin, analyze a bicycle, paying close attention to proportional relationships and patterns. When you're ready, draw two squares on the same plane in perspective. The closer square to the viewer represents the front wheel, while the one further away represents the rear wheel. Sketch lines representing the seat post, handlebars, and the initial position of the frame's front.

Next, divide the squares diagonally into four equal parts by making an X inside both. Start sketching the frame and seat lightly, placing reference lines for construction geometry to ensure proper placement of functional parts.

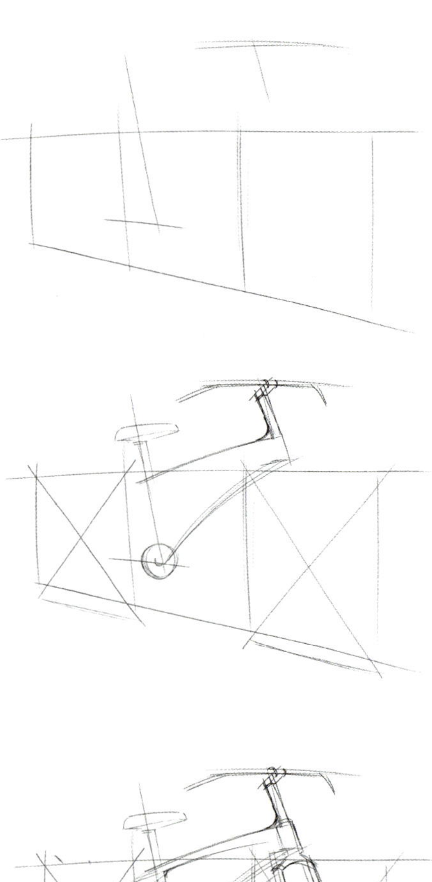

Build the Frame

Continue adding details toward the back of the frame. Sketch double lines to represent the fork and thin axel that will hold the rear wheel. Place ellipses at the center of each X, marking the hub where the wheel will be centered. It might take some practice to get this right, so don't be too hard on yourself if alignment isn't perfect initially.

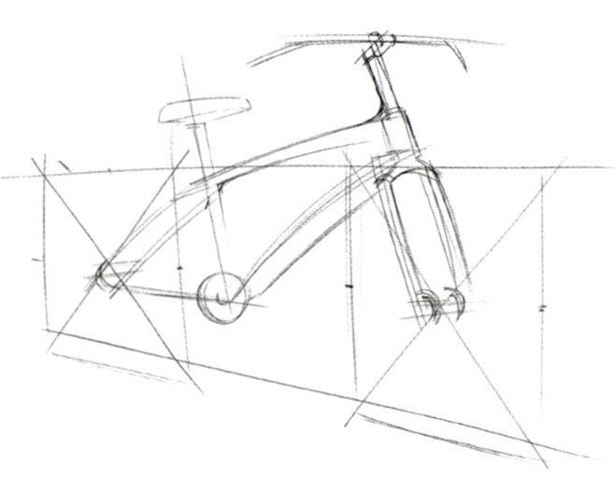

Sketch the Wheels and Additional Elements

Add ellipses inside the two squares to represent the wheels. To help you place them correctly, first add tick marks at the centers of squares' sides. The ellipses for the wheels should be tangent to the sides of the square, touching at the tick marks. Adjust the baseline of the squares if necessary to ensure proper spacing.

Modify the frame to include additional elements, such as a battery for an e-bike. Add line weight and details to the seat and frame components. Sketch in the fork and hub and offset the ellipses to create the thickness of the rim and tire. Lightly sketch the gear shifters and sprocket at the rear of the bicycle.

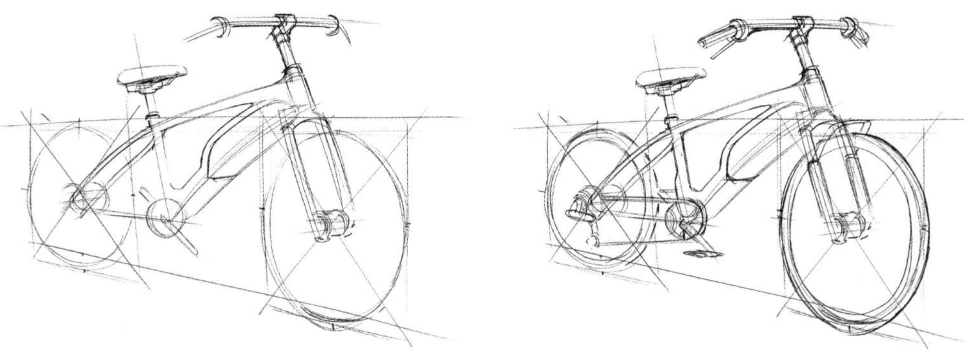

Detail the Bicycle

When sketching technical components, consider the level of detail to include. For the bicycle, sketch some technical components loosely rather than capturing every detail precisely. Enhance the outline of the bike by thickening line weight where necessary. Shade the wheels with hatch lines radiating from the center to create texture. Sketch alternating V-shaped double lines for the spokes, radiating from the hubs to the rim. This might require some practice, but it's just a larger application of the technique you used for the scooter's wheel in Exercise 28. Add a slightly thicker line weight to the chain gear assembly, sprocket, and pedals.

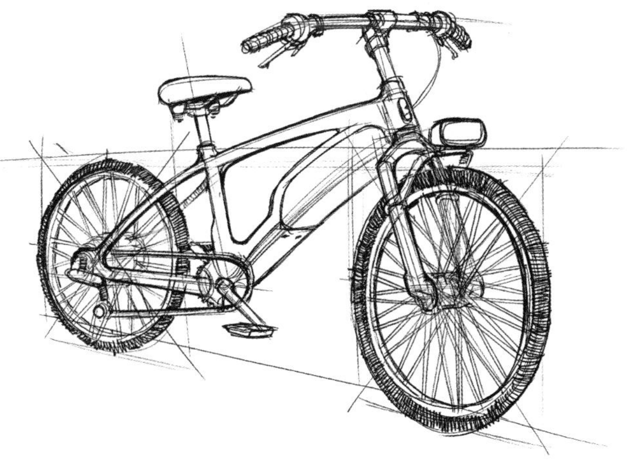

Refine and Shade

Enhance the line weight and refine details with your pen. Add texture to the grips and small details to the levers on the handlebars. Shade the battery section with parallel hatch marks to contrast with the frame. Shade the seat and add a subtle shadow core.

Add shadows to the far side of the front fork to show depth. Shade the hubs and add texture to the wheels. Use parallel lines to shade the headlight lens element. Continue refining the outline of the bike and cleaning up stray elements with carefully applied line weight.

To finish, refine the general outline and clean up any stray elements with line weight and care. Touch up areas that need additional shading or hatching. With these steps, you should have a decent sketch of a bicycle in perspective.

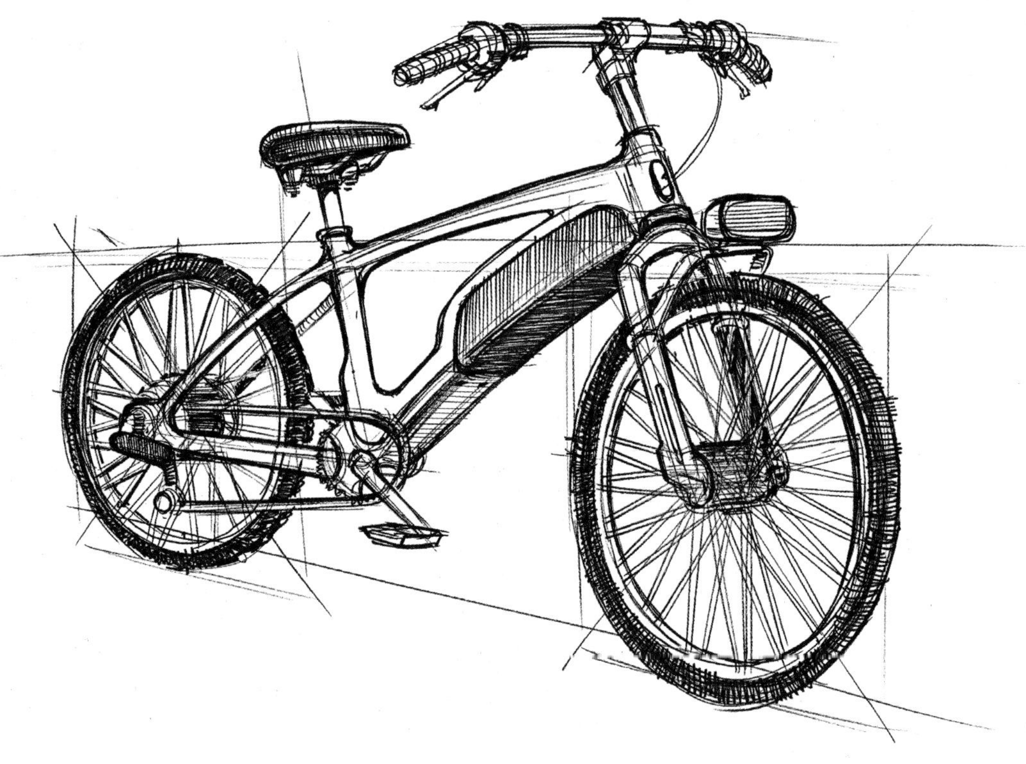

CHALLENGE

Sketch several bicycles or two-wheeled transportation using the techniques you learned. You can thumbnail a few ideas and perspective sketches of bicycles, then refine these sketches with added depth, thickness, and detail. If you're feeling adventurous, add color with markers, ensuring they don't cause your pen lines to bleed. Use good marker paper to prevent ink bleeding.

Study and practice can be tough, so take breaks as needed. If stuck, consider taking a break or going for a walk or bike ride to refresh your mind. Happy sketching, and good luck!

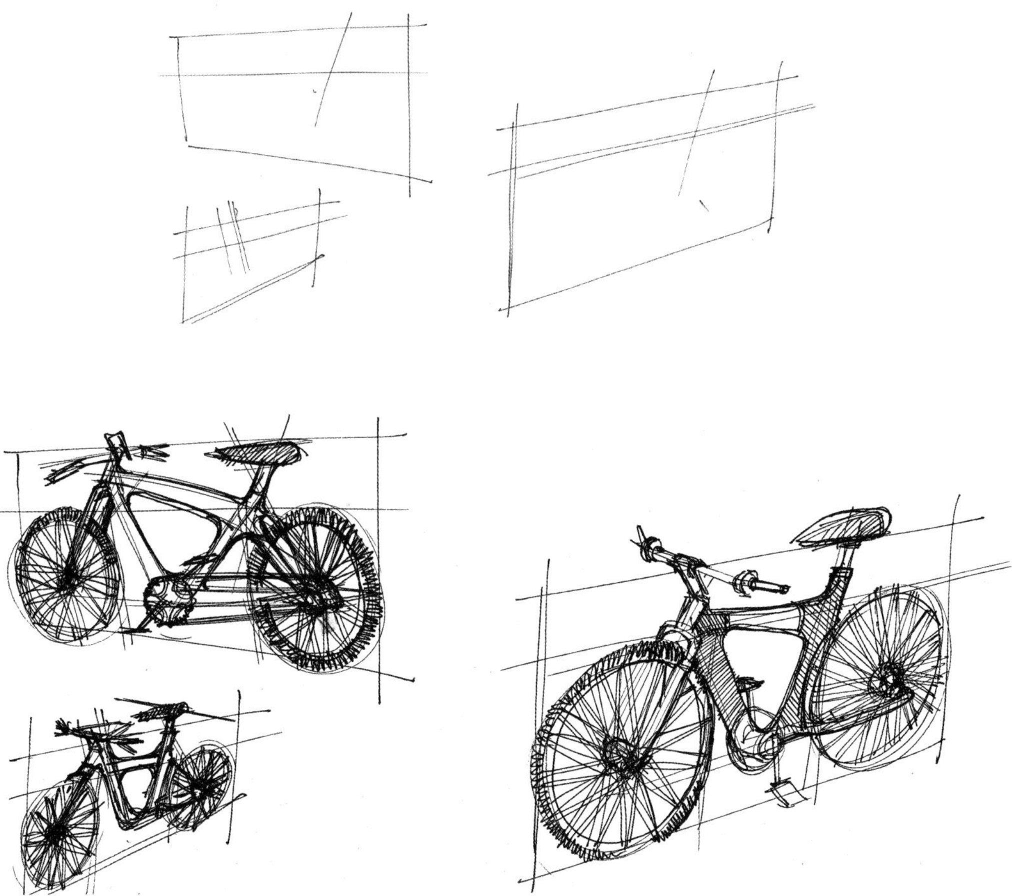

Sketching buildings in perspective is slightly complicated, because it introduces angled surfaces and the need to figure out the proportion of objects in a scene. I find it helpful to start with reference geometry, which is what you'll do in this exercise. You don't need any special tools; I used a Paper Mate Flair pen and printer paper.

Sketch the Horizon and Topography

First, lightly sketch in a horizon line and any topographical details that come to mind below that line. You can use simple squiggles or meandering lines to represent changes in the flatness of the ground on which you'll build the cabin. Think of this as a bit like starting to build a house by preparing the ground.

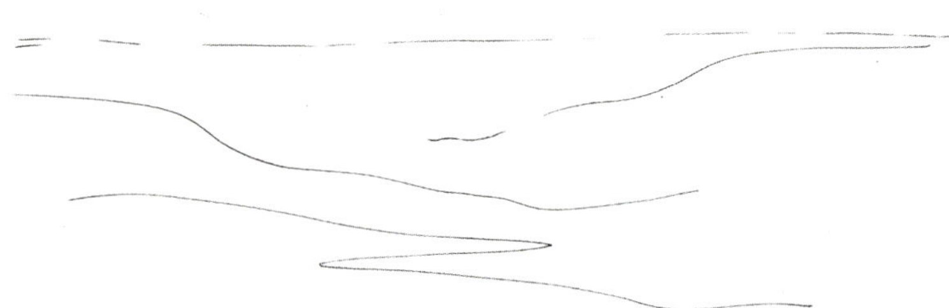

Rough in the Cabin

Next, draw a rectilinear object that straddles the horizon line, slightly above but mostly below it. In the example, notice that the top and bottom lines of the right box are not parallel, but appear to converge as they recede toward the horizon line in the distance. (If not blocked by rising ground, the left wall's lines would do the same.) If you've placed your horizon line too high or too low relative to the cabin, that's okay. These are reference lines and are meant to simply guide the process.

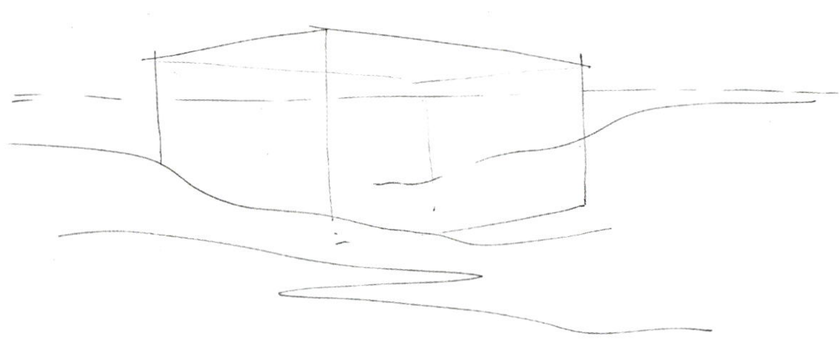

Add the Roof and More Reference Lines

Construct a simple gable roof for the cabin. This step is important, because how you render the angles of the roof can make or break the illusion of depth and perspective. To start, divide the upper edge of the initial box (the front of the cabin) into two equal parts with a tick mark. Project a line upwards from this midpoint to the point where you want the roof lines to converge. This simple sketch, much like the base, will function as guidelines for the rest of the cabin and its details. Connect the upper corners of the initial box to the top point of the midpoint line, and then extend a line (the roof's ridge line) away from the peak of the gable, remembering to angle it subtly as it recedes. To get the right pitch, imagine extending this roof line and the upper edge of the cabin's wall; they should converge at a common point called an *auxiliary vanishing point*. Connect the far-left corner of the cabin to the ridge line. It and the line you drew on the far right to the ridgeline should also converge if extended to an auxiliary vanishing point.

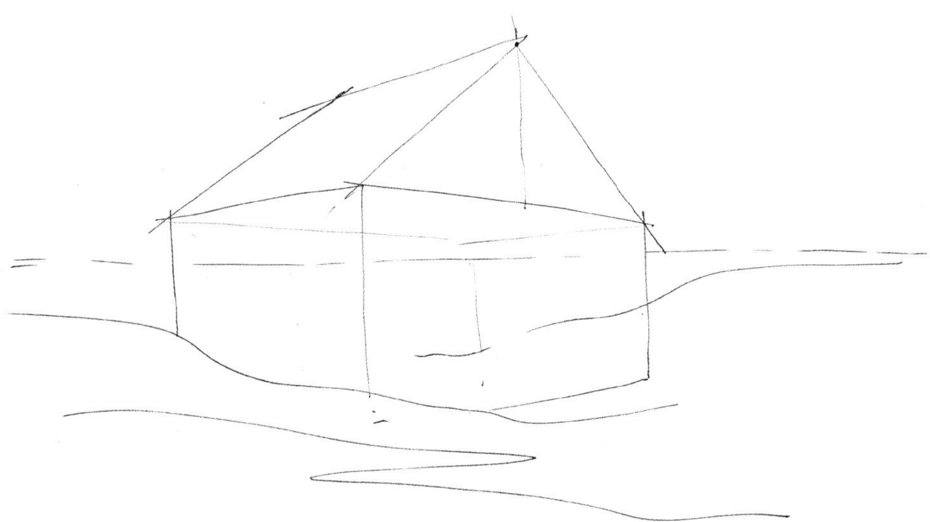

Next, using this base geometry as reference, extend the roof to create an overhang and begin to add thickness to the roof by offsetting these initial lines. Keep your sketch loose and have fun while drawing these lines; you will tighten up the drawing in later steps.

As you can see in the example, I roughed in a concrete slab to the front of the cabin in the form of a very short cuboid on the ground plane. Notice that this cuboid follows the perspective of the base of the initial cabin wall sketch. Add your own, and then lightly divide the front wall of the cabin according to the width of this slab. This line will serve as a guide for later adding a door and window. I typically like to include some construction lines like this along the way, so that I can reference them and sometimes include them in the design—even if they may not appear to fit in at the beginning.

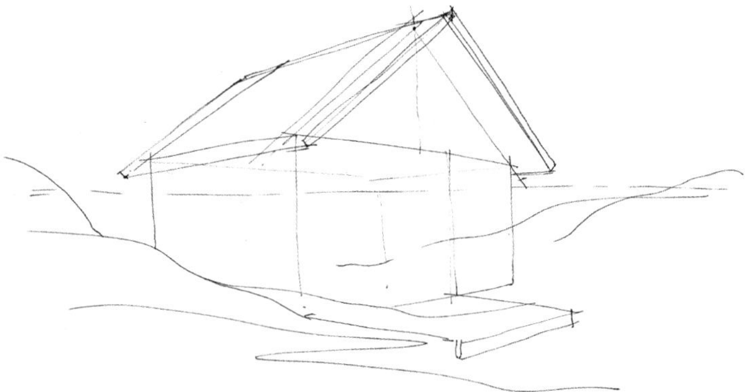

Add Details

Next, consider dividing sections of the cabin into windows and adding features like a chimney. When adding a chimney, make sure its lines follow the surface topography of your roof. Rough in a doorway and add an awning over it. I also added an offset to the far right of my cabin to indicate a window. For architectural-style sketches, I tend to hold my pen slightly further up the barrel to allow myself a bit more deviation and wiggle in the lines. This gives a certain characteristic to the sketch that is in line with typical architectural or landscape sketch styles. Consider taking a look at sketch samples from architects and landscape designers to get a feel for the style should you choose to do more sketches along these lines.

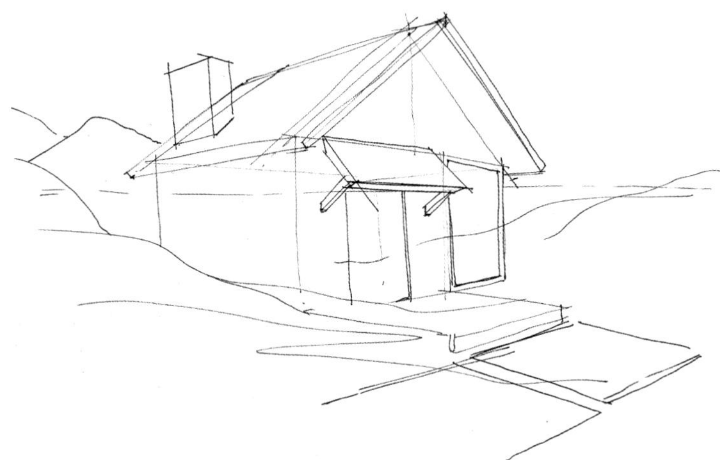

Give the cabin a metal roof by dividing it with parallel vertical lines, and then emphasize the line weight on sections of the roof and the outside of the cabin. Notice that
the line weight you add causes the construction lines to take less importance in the
sketch. Give your cabin a bit more environment: Add mountains in the background
and draw some squiggly shapes to represent shrubs. Practice your squiggles on a
separate piece of paper before incorporating them into your sketch, if you need to.
If the squiggle style doesn't produce the look you're after, experiment a bit to find
something that works for you and then incorporate it into your sketch. In mine, I
added a couple more slabs to the front of the cabin by following the perspective of the
structure itself.

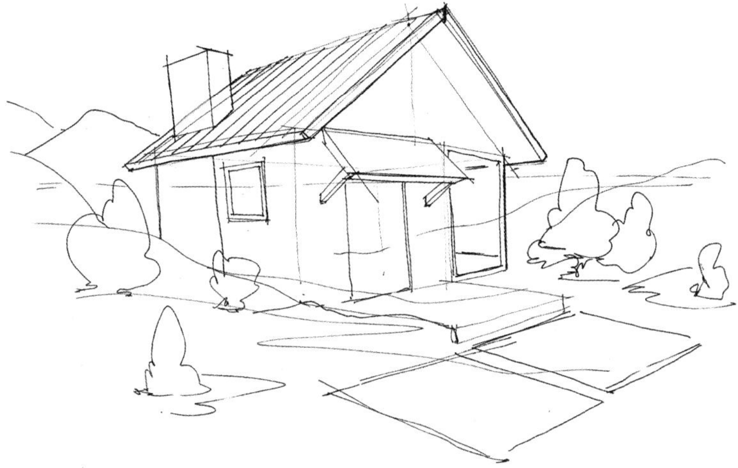

Refine Details

Next, enhance line weight in key areas of the cabin, such as window trim and under
awnings. You can add siding to the left side of the cabin by drawing minimally spaced
double lines. Detail the chimney in a similar fashion using double lines and add a baffle
to the chimney with some hatching. Continue to tweak and enhance the foliage and
consider adding other elements to your environment. I also applied some textural
detail to the door and awning to indicate wood and metal, respectively. Notice the
subtle scribbles under the supports for the awning that convey shadowing caused by
the overhang.

Once you are somewhat satisfied with the overall design, continue to enhance the line
weight on the chimney and other aspects of the cabin that you wish to emphasize. To
the right of the example cabin, I framed a large, beautiful window and added hatching
and a few floor lines on the inside of the cabin to suggest a slight view inside. When

adding context like this in a sketch, be judicious about how much detail you include on the inside. If you put too much detail on the inside of the cabin, it can detract from the overall look, feel, and balance of the sketch. Think about what you're trying to communicate and what's important as you're drawing it. Spend the time on those aspects rather than trying to make everything the same level of finish and detail.

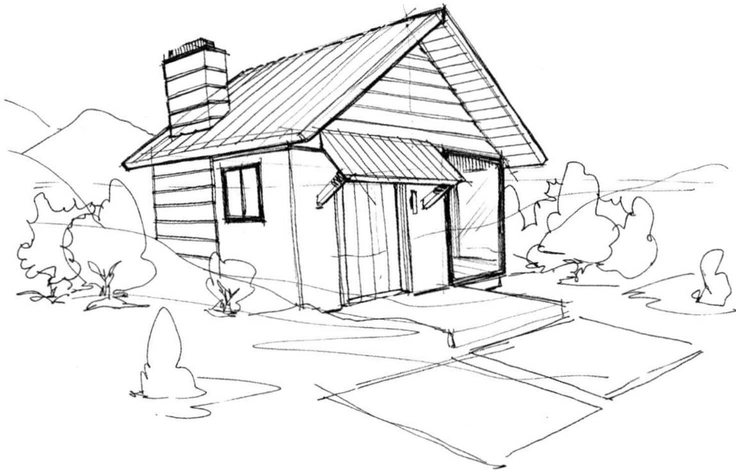

Check for Mistakes

As this is a more complex perspective drawing, now is the time to check and correct any mistakes that may be apparent. As I mentioned earlier, if your horizon line is slightly off at this point, don't worry. The background elements and other details take prominence, and the horizon line has little to any importance in the sketch. It and the initial sketch lines are only minimally visible now.

Enhance Line Weight and Shadows

To wrap up, complete enhancing the line weight in your sketch and begin to add shadows to the vegetation in the scene toward the background. Adding hatch lines to the foliage that is further away quickly creates a sense of depth in the scene along with the scale of these elements. Remember, in perspective, things that are closer to you will appear larger than those that are further away. To show reality without bogging down the sketch, add stippling to areas that are cement, like the front corner walls and slabs in the scene. Additionally, add clouds above the mountains to further contextualize the sketch.

Backgrounds are a useful way of rounding out a sketch and adding supportive elements that give the subject matter context. For example, depending on the type of vegetation used in a sketch like this, a sense of place is established that may be familiar to viewers of your work. For example, if I had added palm trees as opposed to pine trees in my scene, you could assume that the house was located in a tropical or warm area as opposed to a mountainous region. Sketching tumbleweeds or small brush would convey a different sense of place and location, as well.

From here, if you feel adventurous, you could apply some color using a medium of your choice. Or, you could scan the sketch into your computer and print several copies for experimentation as you're learning to use different tools.

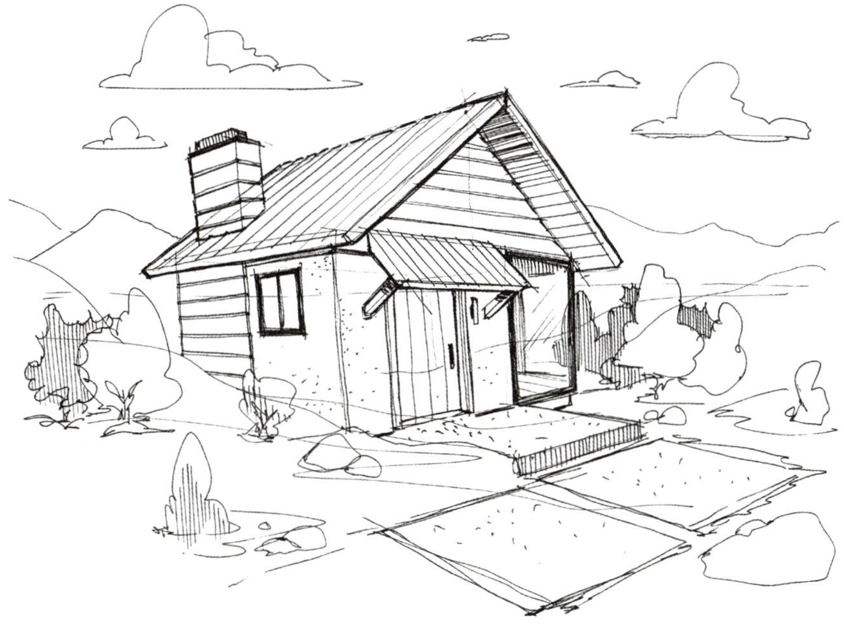

CHALLENGE

Draw several structures in similar fashion by paying attention to the perspective, placement, and background context of the scene. Experiment with textures using simple tools and remember that quantity matters as much as quality. However, don't be too hard on yourself if you're still trying to work on your line quality or fluidity as you draw. With time, you'll get better and more confident in your ability to conceptualize and visualize your ideas. Also, you don't need complex tools for this challenge—just printer paper and your favorite pen should do just fine.

I always appreciate a good challenge, and a car happens to be one of the more challenging things that you can draw. Still, there are creative and simple ways to break down a car into understandable bits so that you can more easily visualize a concept. While your results may not be perfect on the page, creating a strategy around how to approach a drawing is the first step in increasing your confidence.

For this week's exercise, consider using a pen as your primary sketching tool. I find the challenge of a pen forces me to be a bit more thoughtful and conscientious about my strokes and pushes me to sharpen my skills a bit more.

Sketch a Reference Plane

To begin, sketch a rectangle representative of the overall length and width of your car in perspective. Notice that the front and rear lines in the construction geometry example are different lengths; perspective dictates that things closer to you appear larger, so the rear line should be smaller. Additionally, the lines that represent the side of this proportional square taper inwards and would converge to a common point if extended.

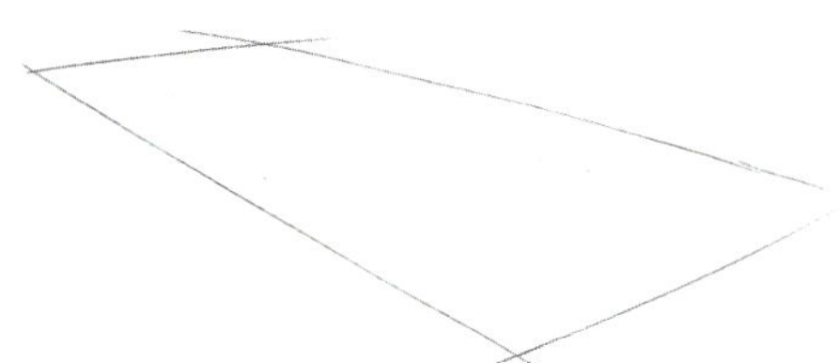

Find Symmetry and Wheel Placement

To find the rectangle's midpoint, draw diagonal lines from corner to corner; where they intersect is your midpoint in this perspective. Now sketch in curves to represent the rear and front of the vehicle as well as a central line of symmetry that passes through the midpoint and splits the car into left and right halves. Finding symmetry by this means is an important step, because to you things appear even from side to side within the car's perspective.

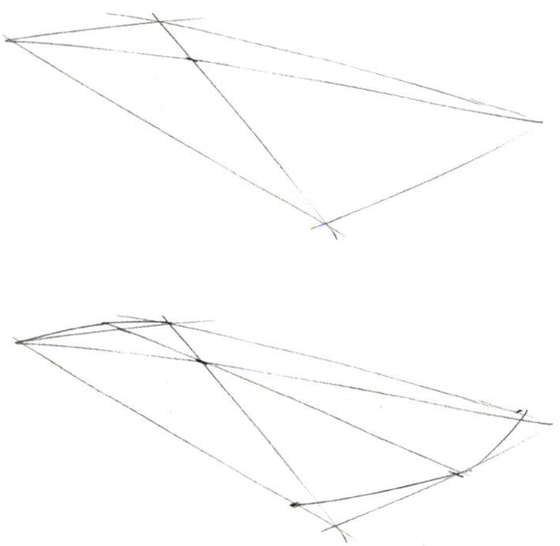

Decide on the wheel placement. Their size and location will vary depending on the type of vehicle you are sketching. As a general rule, I shoot for about two-to-three-wheel widths between the axles of the vehicle. It may be helpful at this point to check a reference (a photo or your car), and practice using one of its wheels as a unit of measurement for the car's proportion.

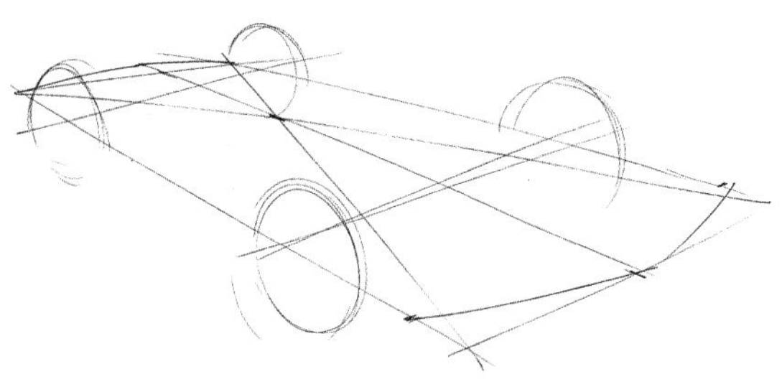

Sketch in the wheels using loosely constructed ellipses. The ellipses closer to the front of the vehicle should appear larger than those further away. Additionally, the minor axis of these ellipses should rest on the virtual line that would travel through each wheel or the axle for the wheels. If your ellipses are significantly misaligned or off, it may throw off the entire sketch, so take some time and care to check your work at this point.

Sketch the Body

Next, begin sketching a rough outline of the body of the vehicle. Generally, this is about one wheel height in its dimension. Notice in the example that I used curved rather than straight lines. Try to be loose and expressive as you sketch in the body lines for your vehicle. Next, begin dividing the general silhouette into functional parts like headlights and a grille at the front of the vehicle. In car design, this is referred to as the graphics on the front of the vehicle. These elements can give your vehicle a unique look and feel. Take a look for a minute at a few different car brands. What similarities or differences do you notice in the headlights, grille, and other details on the front of the vehicle?

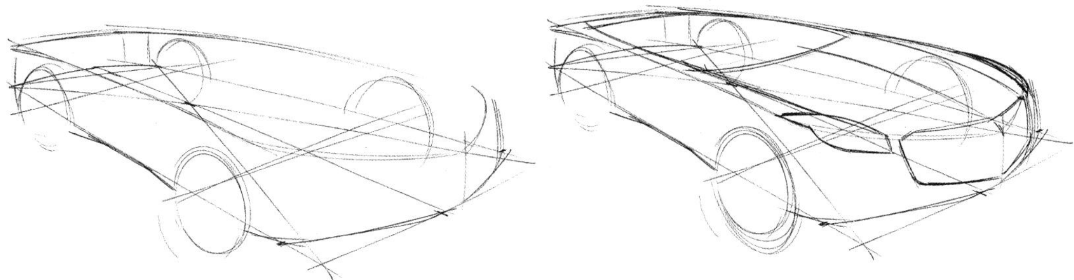

Add Details

Continue building out the shape of the car: Draw from side to side into the rear, creating a rough rectangle on top of the body, and from the rear of the rectangle to the front, roughly sketching in two arcs. Don't get too hung up on this being perfect, but rather try to capture the proportion and gesture of the vehicle. Toward the rear wheel of the car, sketch in the trunk (or boot) and add spokes on the rims of the vehicle. The bottom of the car typically has some trim elements, so lightly sketch in these around the bottom perimeter of the sketch.

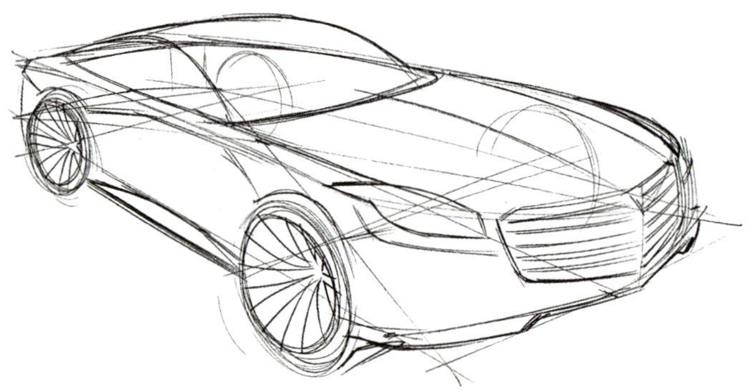

DO A FLIP CHECK

If you'd like to check the perspective of your car while sketching, flip your paper left to right, hold it up to a light source (or place it on a light table), and observe the car. You may more easily notice that certain things feel a little bit off. This technique is similar to holding a self-portrait up to a mirror to see what might be wrong with it.

Sometimes when you look at a sketch too long, you become too comfortable with it and miss opportunities for improvement. Flipping it horizontally or looking at it in a mirror gives you a new perspective on perspective and more.

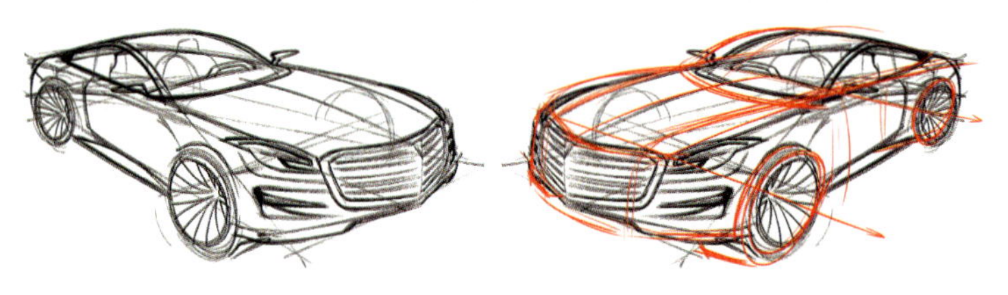

Refine the Sketch

Continue refining the car by thickening and darkening lines that are essential to the functional details you added. A dark line around the car's cabin serves to define that area, but also references the functional trim typically found in this area of a car. Inside the cabin, lightly sketch silhouettes of seats and a dashboard. At the front of the vehicle, thicken and emphasize the intake vents and headlight details. I added fins, too, and emphasized the grille at the front. With car design, details can be exaggerated at times, so feel free to have fun and get a little crazy and expressive with how you decide to define the graphics at the front of the vehicle.

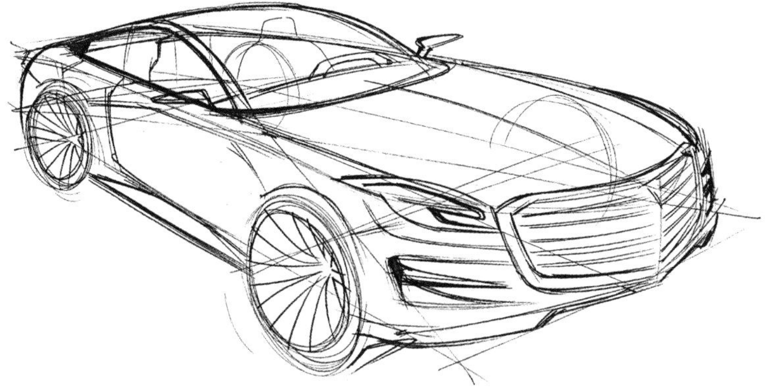

Add Shadows and Finishing Touches

Lastly, add shadows to the rims and loosely sketch in a ground shadow for the car. On the side of the car, sketch lines to represent a reflection or shadow core that may be present in a typically well-lit situation. Don't get too caught up in perfecting your reflection at this point but rather focus on the overall gesture of the car. In the next step, you can overlay your sketch to clean things up a bit and tweak details in your design.

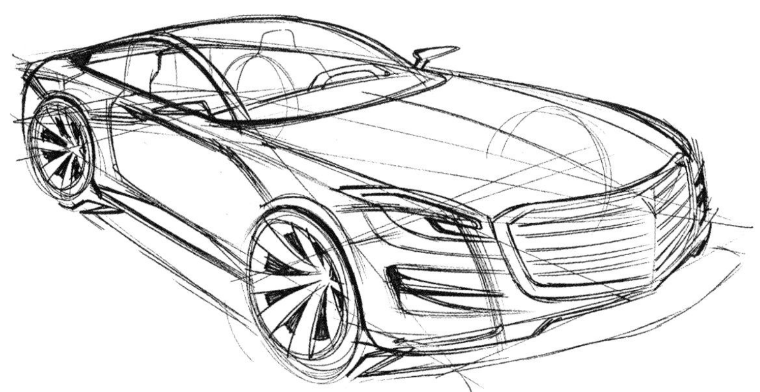

Create an Overlay

For this last step, grab a fresh sheet of paper and loosely re-sketch over your car (For a refresher on overlays, see Exercise 7). By sketching over the rough sketch, you can tweak things in a way that is free and less stressful because you're not having to think about the perspective overall as much. As long as you follow the underlying sketch closely enough, you can continue overlaying your initial sketch to create additional concepts.

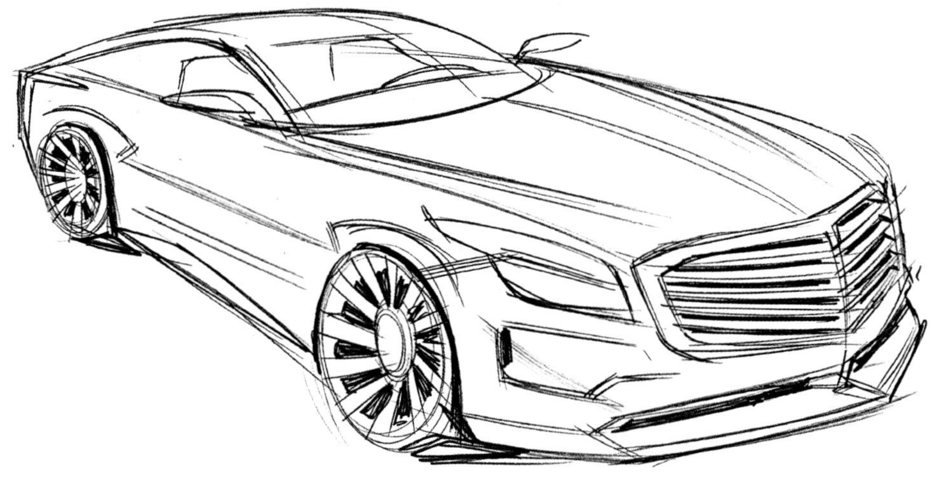

CHALLENGE

Construct another car following this week's techniques. Again, create a rough sketch, and then overlay that sketch to create variations of your initial car. How many different ideas can you come up with? How quickly can you sketch those ideas? Push yourself to think creatively as well as sketch quickly. Study your car and cars around you over the week. As you explore concepts, familiarize yourself with the parts and makeup of various vehicles, and use those observations as a springboard into more creative sketching and think-ing. Focus on using simple tools to create expressive and gestural lines for these sketches. Work on improving your perspective drawing abilities and the gestural quality of your lines as you go through this challenge.

 # HOVERING ROBOT

In Exercise 27 you created a humanoid robot. Now set your imagination free to float—and your robot, too. In this exercise, you'll draw a hovering robot with two arms. Using simple geometry can be a good way to create a unique look for a robot that you're trying to draw. Grab your cool gray markers and pens, and let's get started.

Draw the Initial Sketch

To start, draw a circle to locate the robot on your page. (I used marker paper, but printer paper is totally fine.) Continue drawing in other circles as well as a cylinder across the bottom. This is where the arms will be mounted. These first steps are important because they will help you place your robot and any important elements before you get into coloring or adding details.

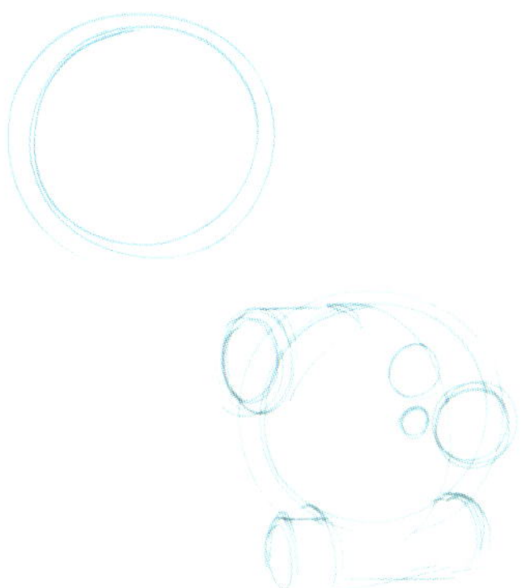

Position the Arms and Some Shading

Loosely sketch in the position of the arms using straight lines and a few ellipses sketched in perspective. Pay attention overall to the positioning you choose for your robot, making sure that each element is sketched in perspective. At this point, I switched to a light peach-orange marker to shade in any material breaks and designs on the robot body itself. I also sketched in optical sensors as well as an antenna array to the top left of the robot. Loosely sketch the robotic arms using the gray marker, which will help establish their placement and give you some idea of how to finish these off.

Add Details

Detail your robot as much or as little as you like. You'll have to use your imagination during this phase, so be creative. For inspiration, look at reference images of construction equipment or automated assembly lines for examples of robotics. If you're a sci-fi fan like I am, check out a movie or two to see how other artists have represented robots.

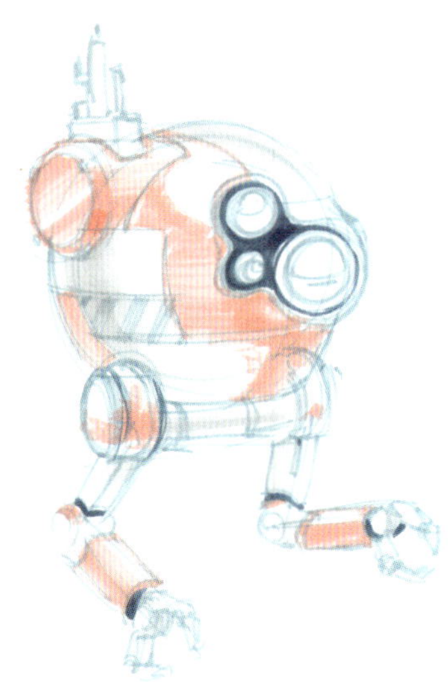

Enhance Shadows and Contrast

With a darker cool gray marker, block out any shadowed areas around the joints. This is a quick way to create some visual separation and lend some functional credibility to your robot design. After shading the area around the optical sensors and the joints on the arm, for example, I then shaded some additional gray areas around the arm mounts. I also refined and clarified details with the gray marker. Grab a peach-orange marker (or whatever color family you're using) that's a bit darker and start to shade in the shadow cores as it relates to the shapes that you've sketched for your base robot. For example, in the top left of the example, you'll notice that the cylindrical section now has a darker orange-peach area, and the shadow core across the arm mounts and the arms themselves have been shaded in. Continue to shade in until you have reasonable contrast.

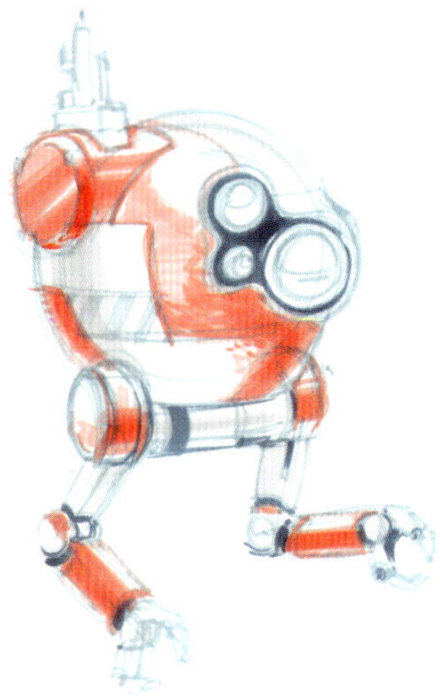 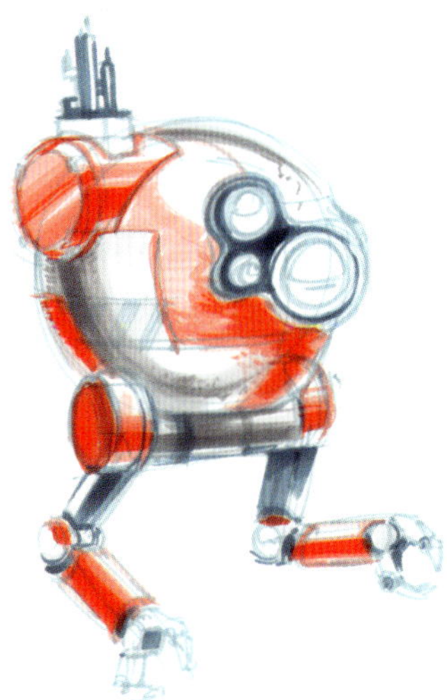

Apply Black Ink

Once you have enough contrast, you can move to applying a bit of black ink. Black ink, of course, will be the darkest element on the page, so it's really going to pop details out on your robot. Be careful and thoughtful as you apply your black ink because it is much harder to correct any mistakes from here on out. Pause and practice on scrap paper before continuing or just commit to doing a few of these sketches until you get it right. Using the black ink, outline the arms as well as add detail to the actuation points and articulation points on the arms, moving up the body of the robot. I also added a bit more contrast to the orange areas using a deeper peach-orange marker and enhanced the gray shadow core areas of the robot.

Refine with Line Work

To refine the line weight, try using a brush marker and felt pen. A brush marker will give you a bit more expressiveness in your stroke as the tip of the marker is flexible but also pointy. While working on this step, I shaded in a couple areas with a deep cool gray marker and changed my design. When working with a light marker, sketching and including details along the way, it's easy to pivot or correct things that perhaps you had not considered earlier on in the sketch. Additionally, in this step, I used stippling to create a bit of texture on the robot body itself. Pay attention to the shading of these dark orange and gray areas. Notice that I tapped the tip of the brush pen as well as the marker in a somewhat randomized pattern to create a bit of texturing. With a felt pen, you can also add some graphics in here like tiny arrows or rivets and fasteners. Just add whatever comes to mind that will enhance the appearance of your robot.

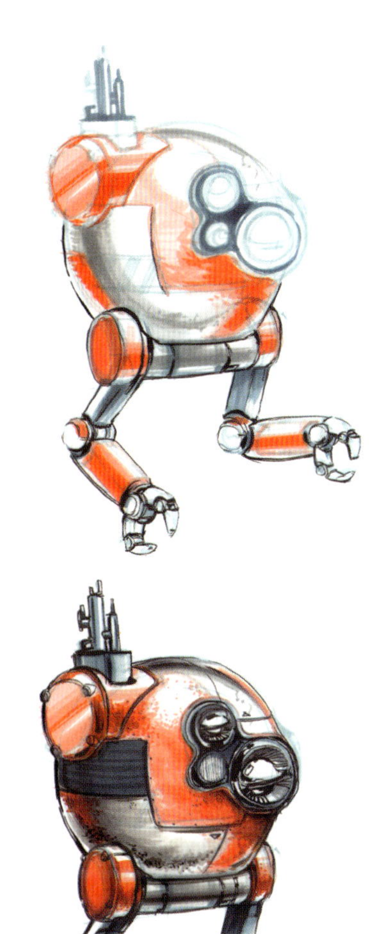

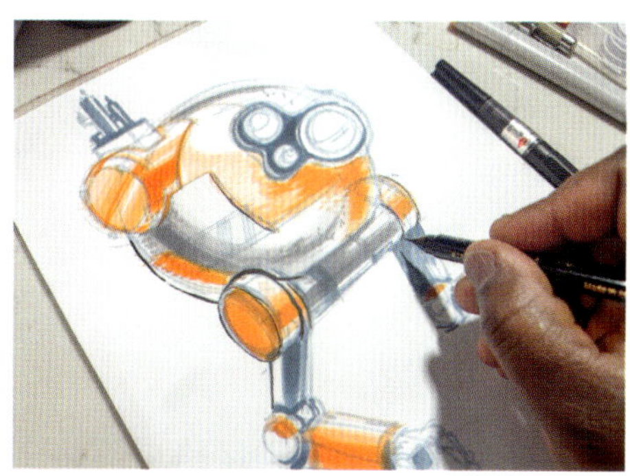

Add the Final Touches

You're almost done—stand back a moment and think about what finishing touches you want to add. One subtle detail I added is orange shading over the gray area on the lower left of the robot. This is an effective way of conveying texture but also a color change when you have two different markers of a very different color family. (You can learn more about this in my book, *The Perspective Drawing Guide*.) Finally, clean up any lines and details on your robot as you please, and when you're feeling satisfied, feel free to call it a day (or a moment).

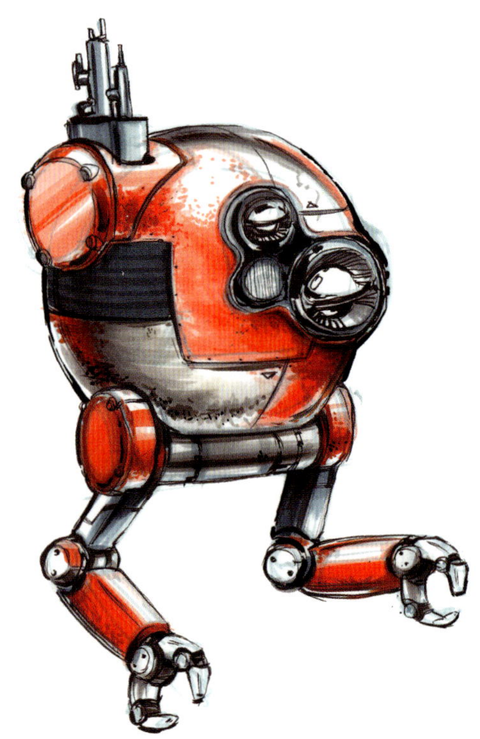

CHALLENGE

Think of simple geometric shapes that you can use to sketch a robot. Some of my favorites are the sphere, cone, cylinder, and even a cube. Try to break up each simple geometric shape into more complex shapes and add details along the way to eventually create a robot of your own. You don't have to add color, but if you do choose to add color, remember to work light until you get it right. You can always do an overlay of your sketch as well in the end to correct any mistakes. As a bonus, if you create an overlay, you get to practice a bit more. Try to sketch as much as you can for the week and seek inspiration around you or by doing some quick online research as well. Remember, practice leads to better results.

At first glance, sketching a dome tent in perspective might seem like a daunting challenge. When I just started drawing, I used to get a bit anxious because I wasn't always sure how to approach things. Try to find a simple element to anchor your process to and build from there. That's the approach that helped me and the one you'll take in this exercise. Gather up some felt pens to create whole lines, as well as markers to add some color and context with background elements.

Sketch the Basic Structure

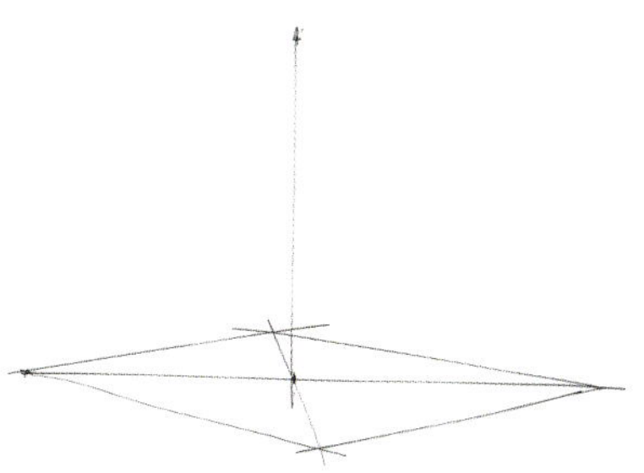

Decide on the proportion of your tent, and then sketch a rectangle in perspective on your ground plane. The rectangle represents the overall proportion and profile of the base of the tent. Next, divide the rectangular shape in perspective by drawing diagonally from corner to corner to create an X, where the two lines intersect is the shape's midpoint. Draw a line vertically from the midpoint upward. You'll use this line to determine the height and overall shape of your tent.

Create the Construction Geometry

This next step is important, and it may take you a few tries to get the hang of it. As you create your construction lines, however, remember to sketch lightly, loosely, and cleanly. Roughly scribe an arc from the leftmost corner to the rightmost corner, with its apex at the vertical centerline. Your arc should look something like the example and intersect your vertical line at the rough height of your tent. In similar fashion, scribe an arc from the uppermost corner on the rectangular base through the intersection point at the top of the vertical line and down toward the front corner of the tent as shown. Again, this may feel a little weird, so take a minute to practice if you're unsure about how to scribe these arcs neatly and quickly.

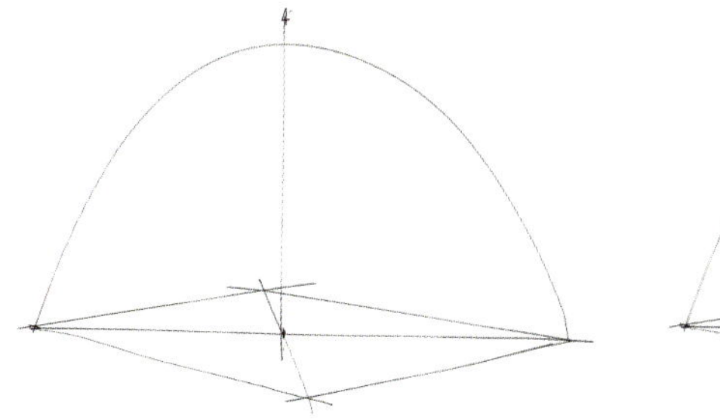 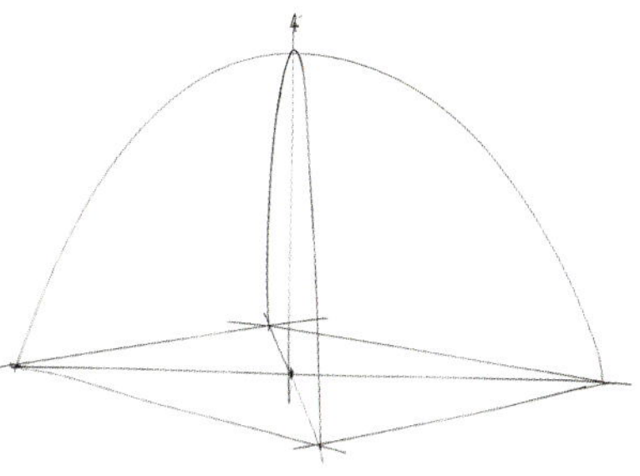

Add Functional Elements

Continue with a subtle arc sketch toward what will be the front of the tent to indicate where the rain cover for the tent's entrance will be located. As you draw this line, think of the height of the opening through which someone would enter the tent.

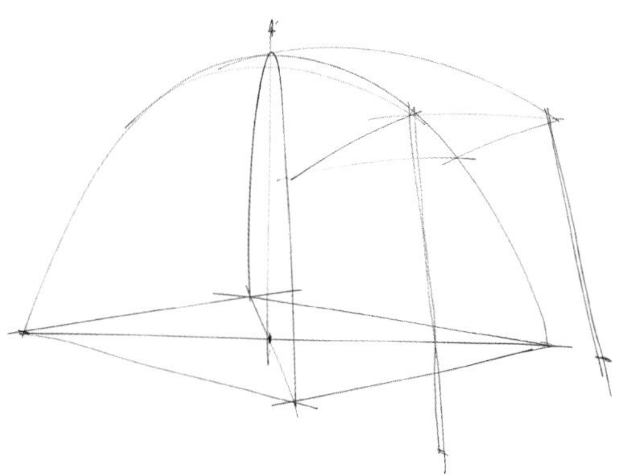

With the arc in place, roughly scribe in a shape for an awning or rain cover that will be mounted onto the tent and supported by two tensioned poles. For the poles, use two pairs of double lines from the awning toward the ground plane at a position of your choosing. Remember to sketch all these construction lines using the tip of the pen to make them as thin as possible so that they don't show up too much in the final sketch.

Detail the Tent

Divide the left side of the tent with whatever design you choose. I added a triangle on the side to represent a mesh window opening. To help you position this, divide the side face with an arc that reaches from the center of the baseline up toward the apex of the tent where the initial arcs and vertical centerline intersect. Now, center your window triangle on this new arc.

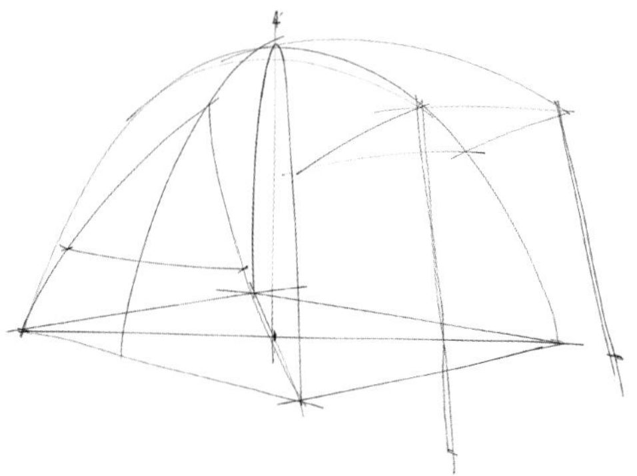

Continue building out the functional elements of the sketch, such as a doorway arc under the awning. Offset the tent's main arcs to create the flexible tube structure of the tent. This double-line approach is a quick way to include that feature, which is a functional and critical component of the tent's structure. Offset any other areas that might require a double line to indicate structural tubing, as well. Notice that on the right side of my example tent the double line stops where the awning is visible, so be mindful of errors that may be obscured in the end as you include these functional bits. Add slight inward curves at the base of the tent to indicate that the tent is made of a fabric that is stretched by the tensioning rods.

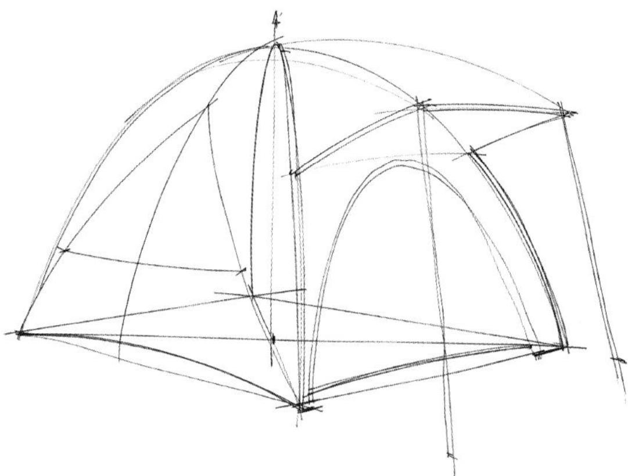

Enhance Line Weight

To pull out the overall shape of the tent, increase the line weight on elements that you have decided on. For example, I sketched in the structural poles, awning, and base of the tent with a slightly heavier line weight. Emphasize the doorway's opening as a parabolic arc and add a zipper to the center of this section. If desired, you can even include fabric tabs that connect the tensioning poles to the overall tent, as shown in the example tent (upper right and front).

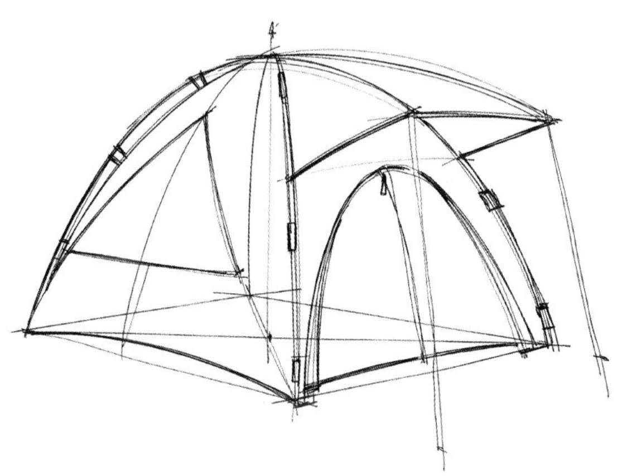

Add Some Background Context

To give the tent sketch some context, add some natural elements around it. For inspiration, think about the landscape where your tent might be located and add those elements in the distance, as well as some supportive elements in the foreground. I added mountains, evergreens, rocks, and small vegetation around my tent to give it some context and a sense of place. Maybe your tent is located somewhere else. For example, what might camping on the beach look like?

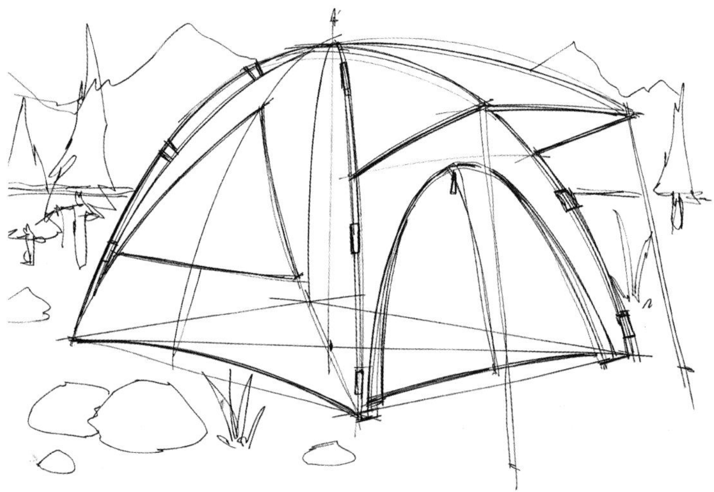

Add Color

Before you begin coloring, scan your sketch visually to make sure you've included all the elements you want, including material breaks on the tent that you want to shade. Select a few colors you'd like to work with; I chose oranges, teals, and grays. Ideally, you want to have three values within your selected color family, each 20–30% different in value. If you're not sure about your colors, just grab some paper and test your markers before continuing.

To start, I shaded a few areas with my lightest gray marker. Remember, work light until you get it right. If you use a dark marker too soon, it's a lot harder to correct and work with any mistakes that may happen. Next, shade with the lightest values of your second and third colors in their desired areas. Be sure to use the lightest value in those color families first. You may find it helpful to outline the area before filling it in; having a border of color can make it a little easier to know where to start and stop when shading with your markers.

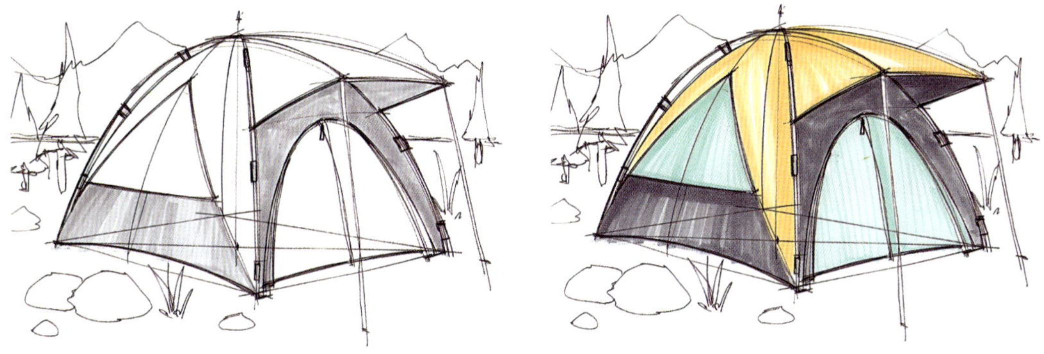

Enhance Contrast and Shadows

With the lighter values now in place, switch to your midtone values. For example, using the midtone markers and a bit of the lightest marker as well, I deepened the value of areas as needed to show shadows and contrast from left to right. To simplify thinking about lighting, I tend to think of one primary light source and shade accordingly. In this case, I decided the sun was located in the top right, meaning that the faces of the tent pointing to the left side of the page should be a bit darker. They would not be receiving as much light as, say, the top of the awning and the front door of the tent. Thinking of lighting this way makes it a little easier to decide what values to use where and how to cast shadows. To shade shadows cast on the tent, use your dark gray.

If you're unsure of how much contrast to add to the tent, squint check. If the colors are blending too well together, that means you need to add a bit more contrast between the light areas and the dark areas. Contrast is your friend and reinforces the three-dimensionality you established by sketching in perspective. Lightest lights placed next to your darkest darks will help the sides of the tent feel more three-dimensional and will make things like overlaps more convincing.

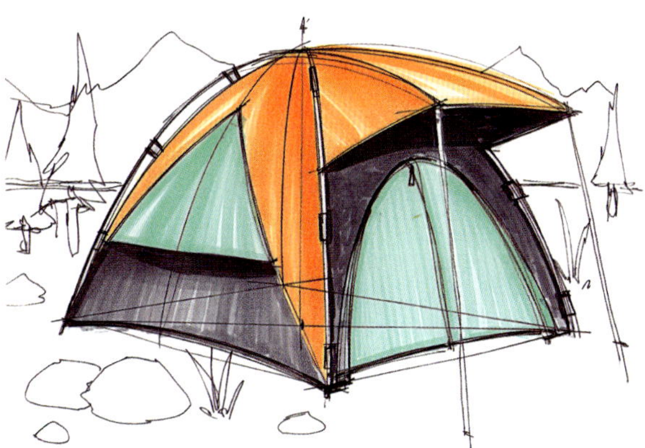

Add Final Touches

Finish up the tent sketch by creating contrast where needed with your darkest values. For example, using my deepest orange on the left side of the tent (facing away from the light source), I created contrast and made the front of my tent appear more three-dimensional. Adding a shadow under the awning and window covering will help you convey a sense of depth, as well. I used a deeper green to add shadows to the mint green areas that have been shaded in. Using a light gray marker, I added a shadow to the ground. When I add shadows in sketches like these, where there is a prominent subject, I try to either go very light with the shadow or have a stark contrasting shadow. In this case, I felt as though having the very dark shadow on the ground would be a bit distracting and opted for a lighter shadow.

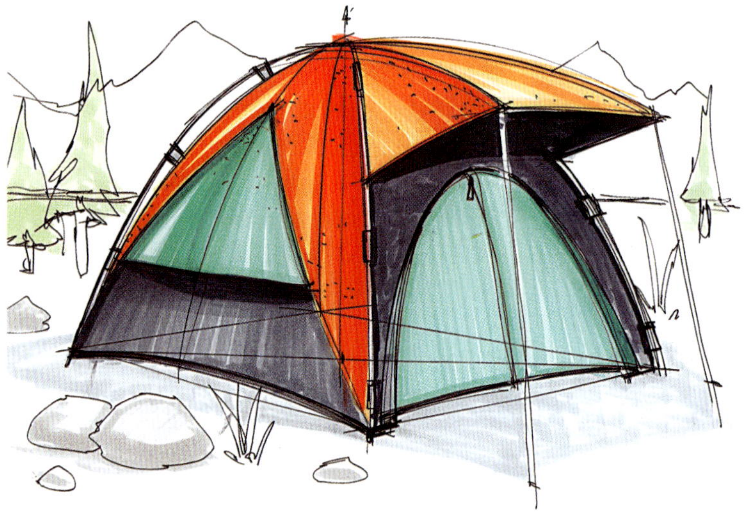

CHALLENGE

Tackle a few more sketches of tents using similar techniques. Try to think about the structure of the tent as well as how the fabric may be stretched and tensioned to create the structure. Keep your sketches loose and vibrant by using colors as you see fit. Remember to try to add some context to your sketches with background elements that are relevant to your scene. You can also play with having different points of view for each tent to continue practicing your perspective drawing skills.

WEEK 36 PICKUP TRUCK

In Exercise 33, you sketched a car using a rectangular plane sketched in perspective as reference geometry. This time let's use the blob method (see "The Blob Method" in Exercise 26 for more tips). Simply put, you'll draw an ellipse (your blob) as construction geometry to help you sketch the rest of the vehicle, in this case a pickup truck. For sketching, try a felt pen. To add shading, I recommend a set of gray markers, with roughly 20% to 30% difference in value. For this truck, you need only one color, so pick three or four shades of it that are similarly spaced in value.

Sketch the Base Ellipse

To start, sketch an ellipse that's roughly the length of your pickup truck and at a slightly off horizontal angle. The angle of the ellipse represents the general perspective in which you will sketch the truck. The longer dimension of the ellipse will form the side of the vehicle and also function as a way to locate the truck's wheels.

Next, loosely sketch in two ellipses (the wheels) along the longer side of the ellipse. Place them generally in line with a virtual axis, similar to the axis you used for the car in Exercise 33. On the far side of truck at the front, sketch a partial ellipse to represent the portion of the passenger-side front tire visible from this perspective.

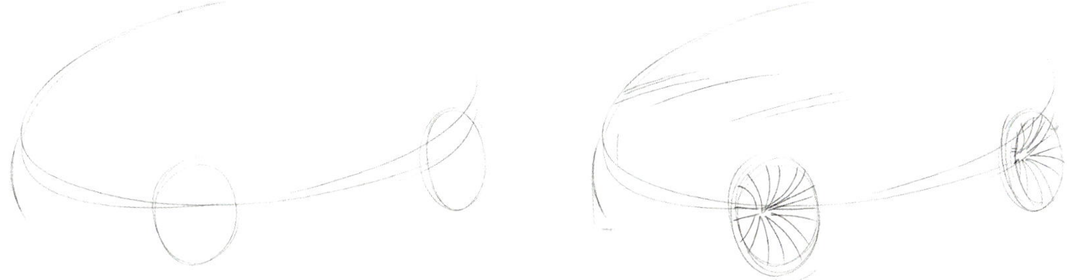

Outline the Truck Body

Begin sketching in the general body line features of the truck: the hood, cabin, and bed. It may seem as though the ellipses are slightly off-kilter here. Adding detail as you sketch will help balance the addition of the angled/cambered appearance of the wheels. If you need to pause and reference a photo of a pickup truck, feel free to search for one.

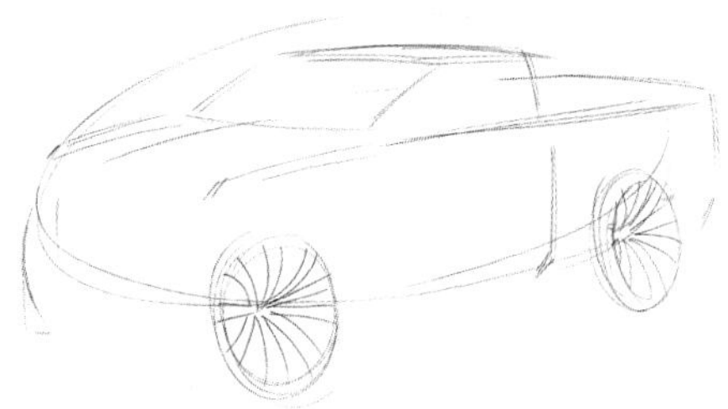

Add Details

Next, sketch in headlights and any lines on the body that would define the surface characteristics of the vehicle, like wheel flares or running boards along the side of the truck's body. I filled in my wheels a bit with spokes that radiate out from their center. To sketch the spokes in, imagine a central point that is inset from the outer ellipse. If you need to sketch this as construction geometry, feel free to do so. Decide on a number of spokes and simply sketch curved lines inward. You can also take a look at rims on vehicles, see if you can simplify their design, and include that in your sketch style. I tend to keep my rims simple and quick.

Loosely sketch the mirrors, door handle, and taillight on the truck. In addition, increase the line weight and definition where you are confident about your design and wish to sharpen up any details. You can do this with the same pen or grab a pen with a thicker tip to enhance the line weight. Add any cut lines for the door and hood as well as take some time to hint at the interior of the truck. Still keep things a bit loose and fluid while sketching.

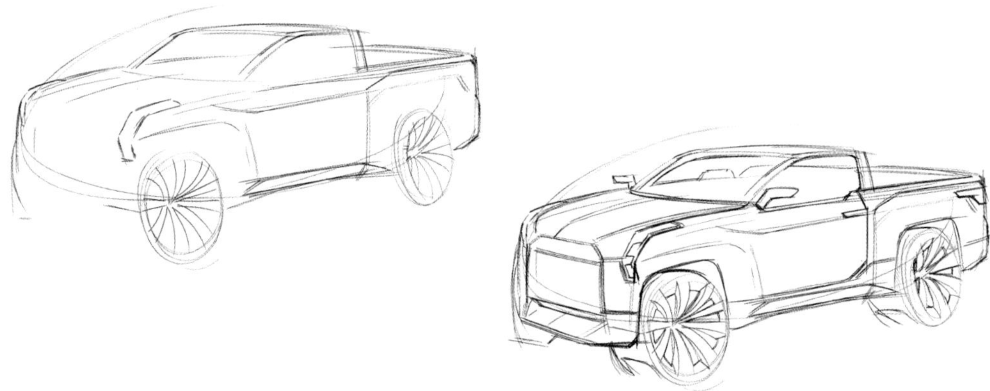

Refine the Sketch with an Overlay

Now that you have a base sketch in place with key details like the headlights, grille, wheels, truck bed, and running boards, grab an extra piece of paper to create a quick overlay of the truck. Remember, re-sketch following the rougher rendering underneath—don't do a stiff, lifeless tracing. (For more tips on overlays, see Exercise 7.) You no longer need the blob as a guide, so leave that out and make any adjustments you'd like. It's a lot easier to make changes now than after you apply color to your sketch. For example, I decided to also change the rims on my truck and adjust a few other details.

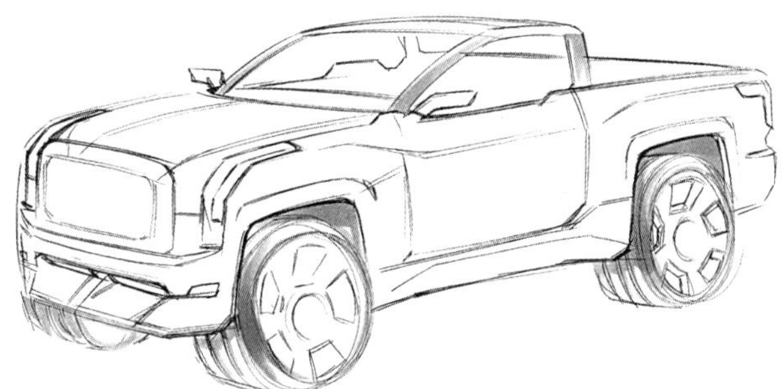

Apply Grayscale Shading

To begin shading, outline the dark areas of the vehicle (tires, wheel housing, pillars of the cabin, and so on) with your lightest gray marker. Continue shading by deepening the values of these grays and following the contours of the surfaces on the truck. These shadows and highlights help describe where the primary light source is located. Where do you think it's located in the example based on my shading so far? If you guessed the top left, you are correct!

Shade the inside of the cabin with your darkest gray and also darken the tires by using your midtone and darkest gray markers to shade them in. You can mimic a tire tread pattern by shading grooves in the tires with a dark marker to create a shadowed appearance.

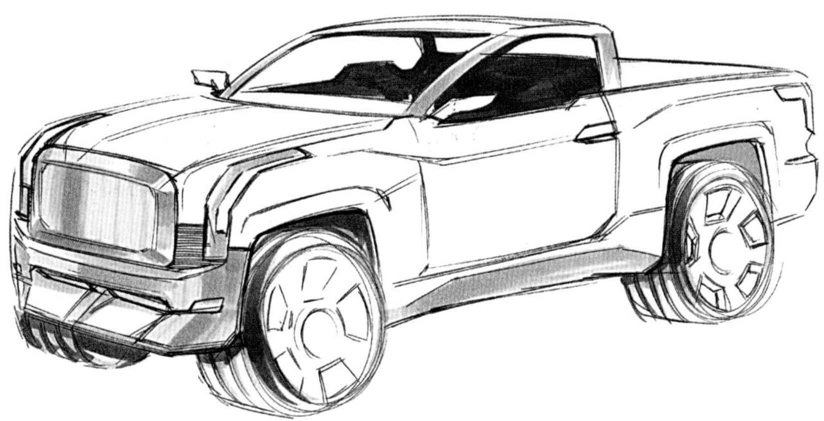

Add Color

Once the grays are in place, you're ready to add color. I used a blue set of Copic markers. With your lightest marker, shade in the surfaces on the body of the truck that would be painted blue (or whatever color you chose). For the most part, leave the surfaces facing upwards, such as the wheel flares, hood, roof, and small light-catching edges, white to simulate light reflecting off these surfaces.

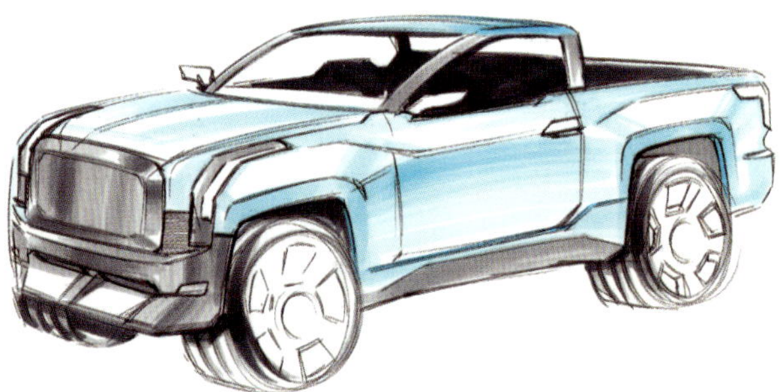

Along the midpoint of the body, use your midtone marker to shade in a reflection of a horizon line or element off in the distance. Curves on an automobile can be a complex thing to visualize with markers, however. Try to think of it in simple terms: Imagine that each facet and surface is a mirror, and like any mirror, the body of the truck will reflect whatever is off in the distance relative to it. If you feel stuck or unsure, study your reference imagery, trying to spot reflections in the side of the truck depicted and then practice on a spare overlay. (I discuss the mechanics of reflections more deeply in my book, *The Perspective Drawing Guide*.)

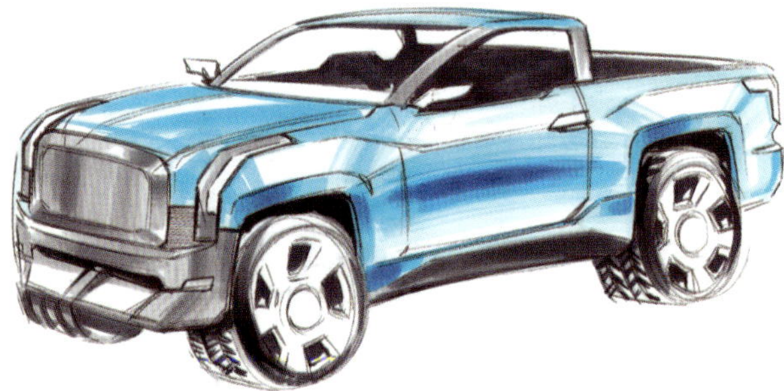

Add the Final Touches

Continue to shade in parts of the truck, such as the running board and the front bumper, by using your midtone gray markers. Additionally, if you need to touch up any details (as I did), use a pen to enhance line weight to further define the silhouette and parts within the truck.

To finish up the truck, use your darkest marker value to add a few deeper tones in the core of the reflection on the body side as well as on the hood as shown in the example. Because the wheel flares have a flat surface relative to the surface facing upward, I shaded this surface with my midtone and dark blue markers by imagining something off in the distance being reflected into the wheels.

Do a squint test to help you focus on the values rather than the lines and small elements in your sketch. Can you identify any opportunities to enhance contrast? I did and subsequently used my felt pen to further refine the part breaks and outlines for the headlights, grille, and front clip, as well as capture a few details on the rims and tires. I also added a few lines somewhat like a chevron pattern to create a texture on the tires that makes them feel a bit more plausible. Finally, I added a bit of red marker to fill the taillight and shaded the bed of the truck with a dark gray.

Now that you've completed the truck sketch, check out your work and see if there are any small tweaks you want to make, like enhancing the line weight or correcting any details that don't feel right.

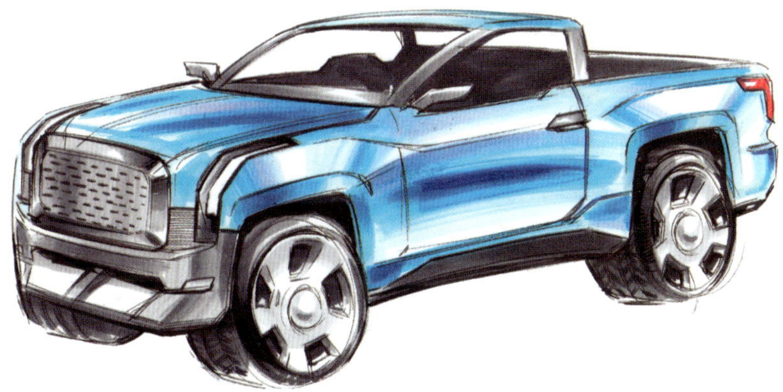

CHALLENGE

Use the blob method to sketch a few more vehicles in a variety of positions and points of view. The blob method actually works well for other products and objects as well, so feel free to get creative and see if this technique works in other instances. For this challenge, slow down a bit and focus on quality over quantity. Aim for clean lines, and think through lighting, color, and shadow for each of your drawings. The more you practice, the better you'll get.

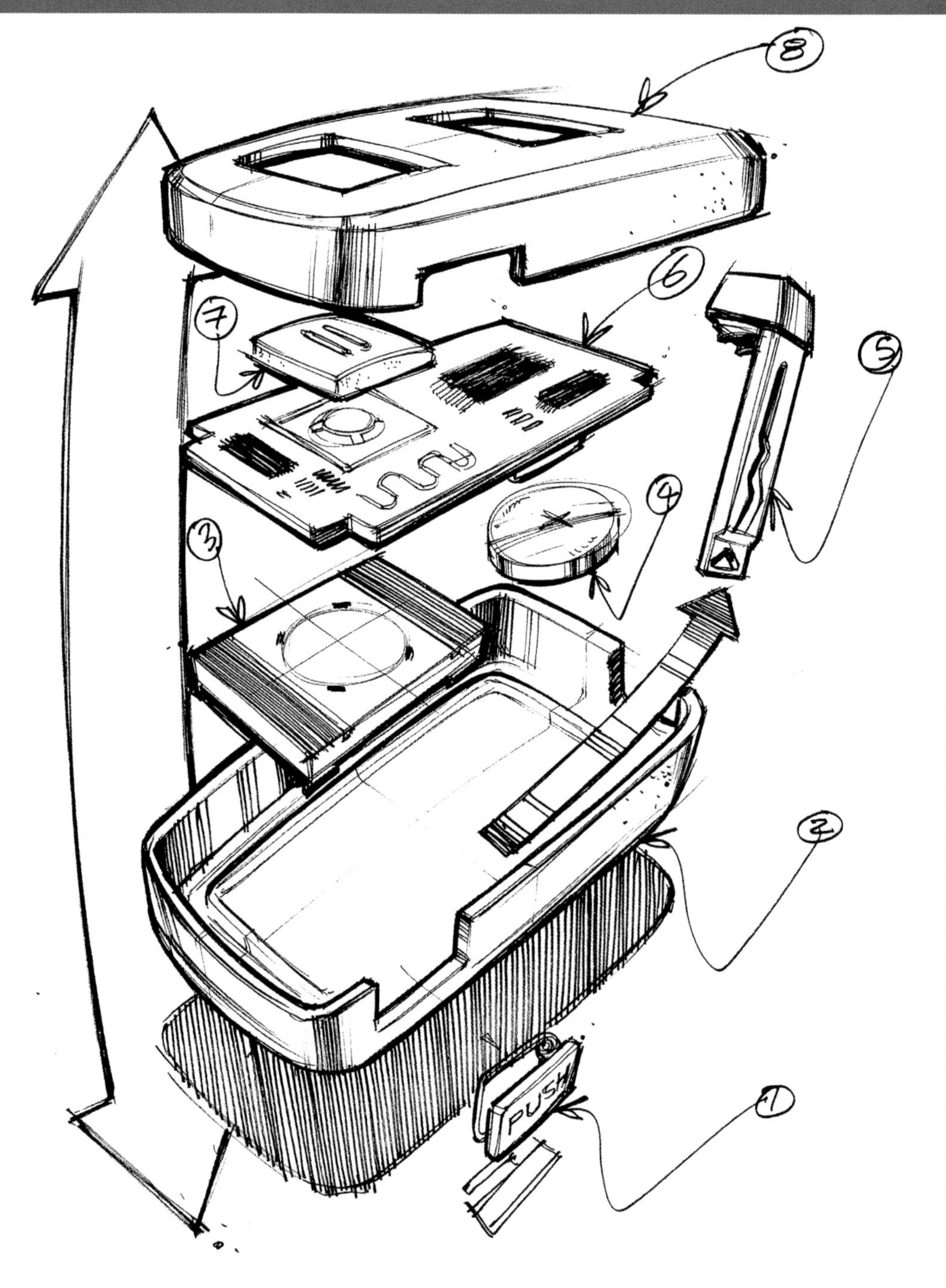

PUSH

CHAPTER 6

THE EXPRESSIVE POWER OF LINES

Lines express a multitude of things. At their simplest, lines are the limit of what you can see from a particular viewpoint. When drawing a table, for example, you can draw the outline of the table as well as any details on the table. Those lines are symbolic representations of the ridges in the wood grain or the shape of the table. They represent the limits of what you can see—but they can also convey a lot more.

For example, lines can have different weights: The outline of an object might be thicker than the lines inside the silhouette of the object you've sketched. This hierarchy in line weight helps convey a sense of depth and importance. When combined, lines can mimic textures or convey value.

Even the type of line you draw can have its own quality. I like to think of lines as an extension of my own personality or drawing style. What do you notice about your lines? Are you more of a fast sketcher or a slow and thoughtful scribbler? Think of your line quality in a drawing as akin to how well you speak or your choice of vocabulary when explaining a concept. These lines are the building blocks and foundation of the shapes and objects you'll be drawing, whether you're drawing something natural and organic, like a tree or an animal, or something more technical, like a house or a tool.

Geometry tells us that the shortest distance between two points is a straight line. Even though the distance may be short, you can pack a lot of expression and emotion between those two points. This chapter is your opportunity to practice.

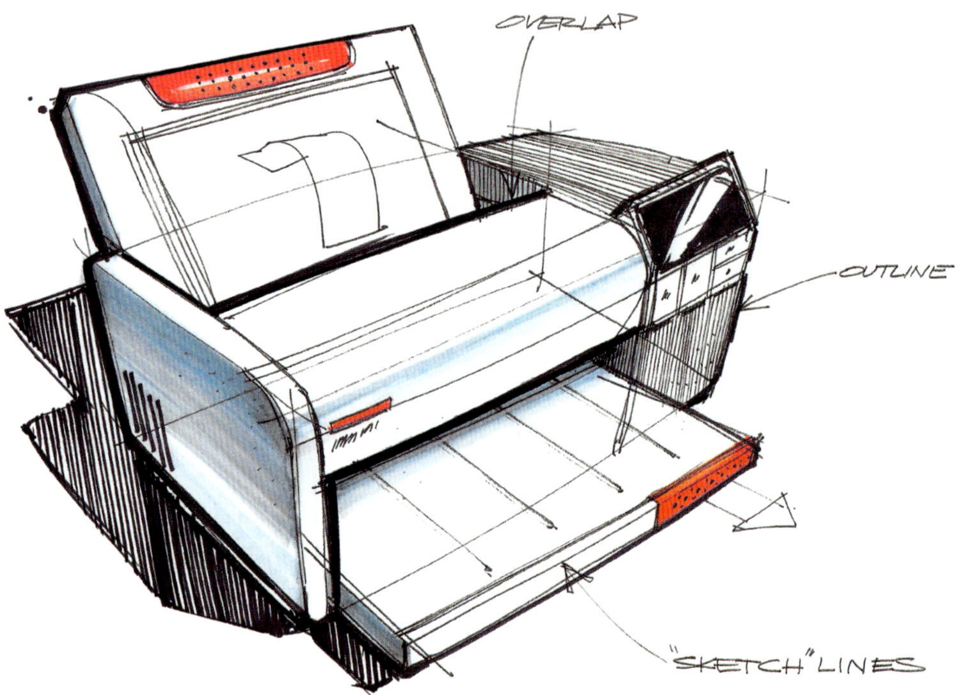

In this exercise, you will draw a side view of a screwdriver and then translate it to a perspective drawing using the power of lines. Lines are a powerful way to simply represent your ideas on paper because they are simple and quick. With a few lines, you will see how simple it is to draw the screwdriver from the side and top views to then sketch it in perspective. For this example, I used a felt pen and simple printer paper. Grab what you have and follow along!

Set Up the Page

First, sketch a side view. Because this screwdriver is cylindrical and symmetrical around the central axis through the middle, you can start by drawing a straight line. Whether you place it vertically or horizontally on the page is entirely up to you.

Sketch the Basic Structure

Take a good look at your screwdriver. What basic shapes represent the major sections of the screwdriver along this axis? Sketch these in. Notice in the example, I sketched the screwdriver shaft and neck lightly with construction lines, and I rounded out the handle on end with a circle. This way, I have general lines to guide the proportion of the screwdriver as I'm sketching.

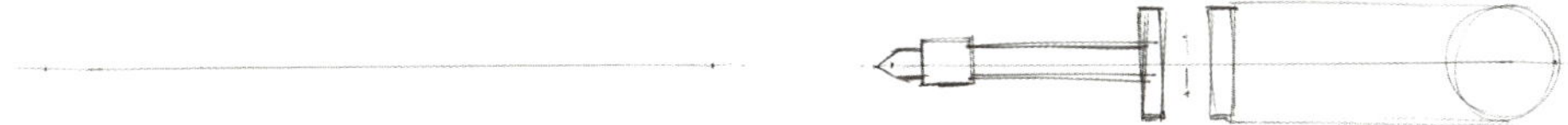

Add Details

Add grooves on the side of the handle to represent a grip surface, then sketch in a semi-circle between the shoulder of the handle and the handle itself. With your rough sketch complete, you can proceed to use line weight to pull out details in the screwdriver. To finish the side view, add shading to indicate the shaft is chrome, refine the bit (tip), and also add shading to the handle. Notice in the example that the line weight helps the screwdriver sketch feel less messy. Additionally, add hatching where you need a shadow, such as in the handle grooves and on the butt of the screwdriver.

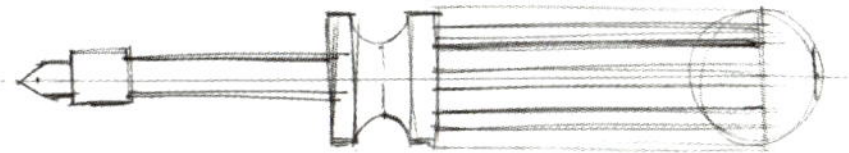 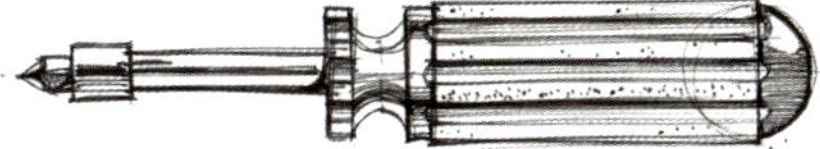

Transition to Perspective Drawing

Now that you have a side view of the screwdriver, it's fairly simple to translate the sketch into a perspective drawing. Because the screwdriver is symmetrical and cylindrical, you only need one view. For more complicated objects, however, you may find drawing several views of the object helpful, giving you more information to transfer to your perspective drawing.

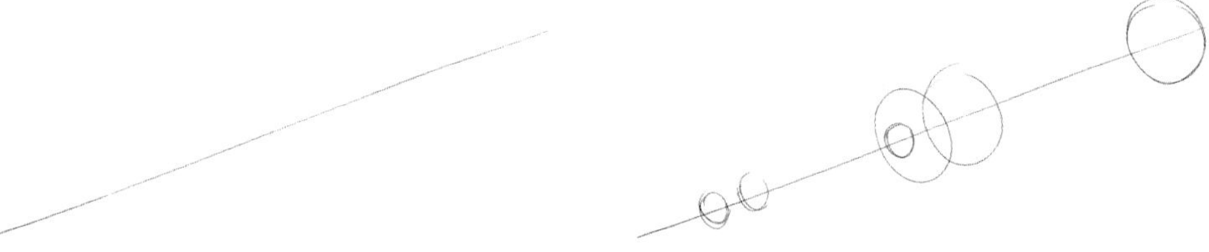

For the perspective drawing, again begin by drawing a central axis line at any angle on your page. Next, sketch in a few ellipses along the axis to indicate key transition points of the screwdriver: the tip of the tool shaft, the shoulder of the handle, along with the smaller neck on the handle, and the general body of the screwdriver. Remember that in perspective, things closer to you should appear a bit larger than those further away? In the example, notice the size difference in the ellipses from left to right on the page. Although subtle, it enhances the illusion of depth and distance.

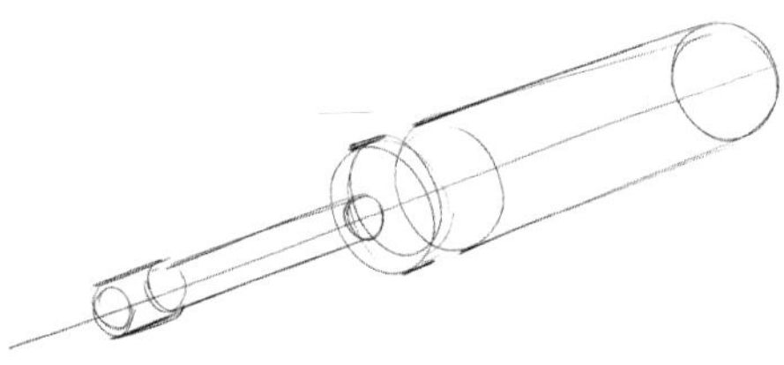

Connect the ellipses to each other as shown. By drawing lines tangent to the ellipses and connecting the ellipses, you now can show a three-dimensional form in perspective.

Enhance the Outline

With the ellipses connected by tangent lines, enhance the outline of the screwdriver with additional line weight or by drawing repeatedly in the same path.

Add Details to the Handle

Make several tick marks on the handle ellipse to serve as construction references that define the grip and ensure the handle grooves feel somewhat realistic. Sketch in the grooves by drawing lines consistent with the overall perspective of the handle and connect the ends of those lines with a small arc. These arcs are effectively the section of an ellipse that would define in perspective the subtle edge you would find here on a physical handle.

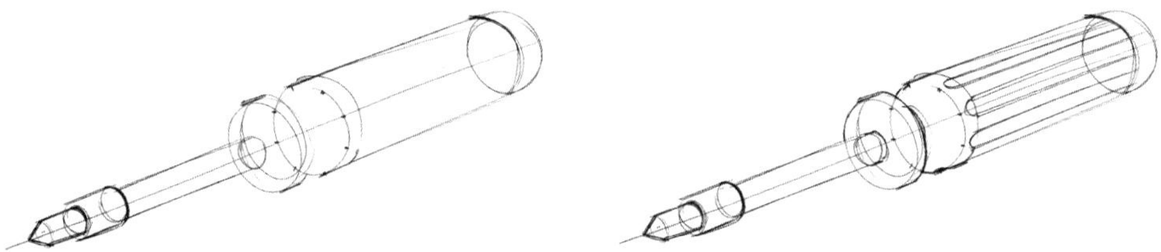

Add Shading and Finishing Touches

With the grooves in place, continue sketching and emphasizing the silhouette of your screwdriver by drawing a slightly heavier line on the outside silhouette. I also sketched in a line for a small cast shadow on the neck of the screwdriver. Next, add some shading to the shaft tip and handle of the screwdriver as shown. Shading in this way will convey a sense of materiality as well as help reinforce the screwdriver's three-dimensional appearance.

Observe the Shadow Cores

If you're not sure where to shade on the screwdriver, do a little visual research. Look for a cylindrical object nearby, and see if you can observe a *shadow core*, a slightly shadowed dark area on the outside of the cylinder. If the object you found is shiny, you may see reflections of yourself or things around you reflected in the surface. The more you observe and learn how real-world objects are affected by light and shadow, the easier it is to add shading and highlights in your drawings.

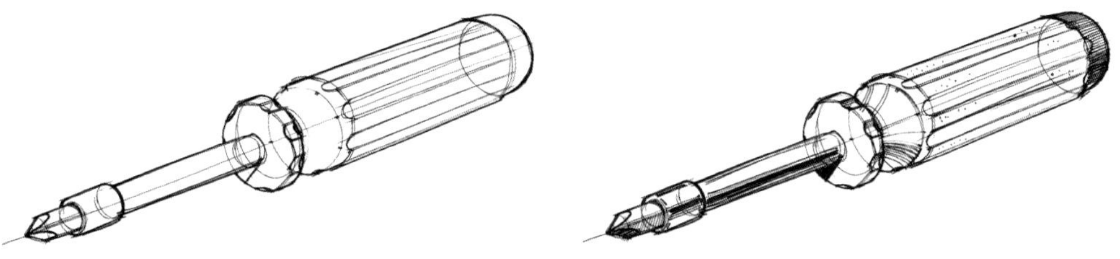

Add Final Enhancements

Once your reflections and shading are in place, take some time to look over your screwdriver and add any additional shading you may want. For example, I added some shading to the butt of the screwdriver by using hatching lines that are placed fairly close together to create a tonal difference in appearance. Finally, use a much thicker marker to create an outline on the bottom portion of the screwdriver, which is an effective but subtle way of indicating lighting within your scene. Because this sketch uses simple tools, it's important to pay attention to the direction, quality, and weight of your lines.

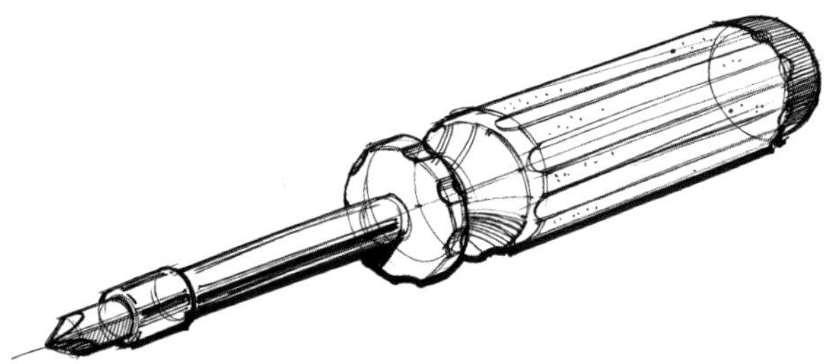

CHALLENGE

Sketch several screwdrivers or cylindrical objects in a similar fashion by focusing on the perspective of each object and its placement on the page. Think of creative ways to quickly shade and indicate materiality and three-dimensionality as you go. I highly recommend at this phase that you use a felt pen, which will force you to be a bit more thoughtful about your drawing style before committing to the final sketch.

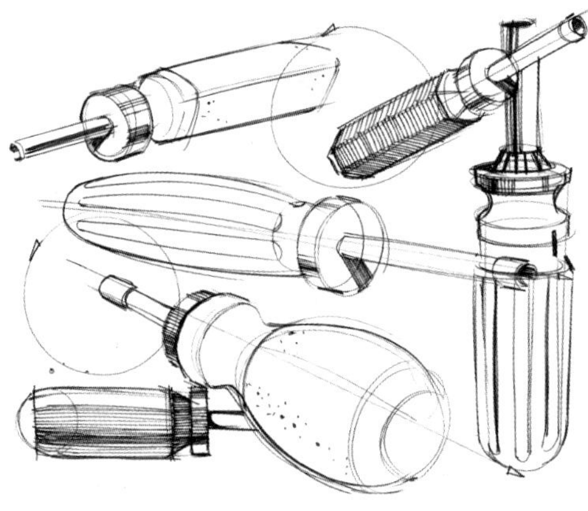

Let's draw some fish this week. Drawing life is a great way to practice basic skills, as well as try different techniques and line styles to represent your subject. All you need is a felt pen and printer paper.

Start with a Blob

Decide where on your page you want to draw your fish and draw a blob that encompasses the overall shape of your fish. Remember, this blob will guide the rest of the fish. If you don't have a specific fish in mind, you can draw a shape similar to the example.

Add Fins and Tail

Next, loosely sketch in the fins on the fish as well as the tail. You can lightly sketch a few construction lines as well for the extent of the body and the tail as it is moving. It may be helpful to take a look at some aquatic life if you're feeling unsure of the process or skip ahead a few steps to get a sense for the look of this fish.

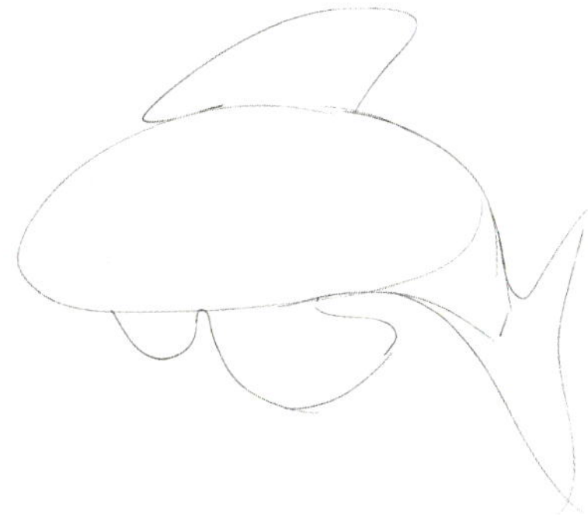

Detail the Fish

Lightly sketch details like the eye and mouth. Notice that the outline of the example fish doesn't exactly follow the initial blob. That is okay, because adding line weight and texture will help create the emphasis needed to clean up the sketch.

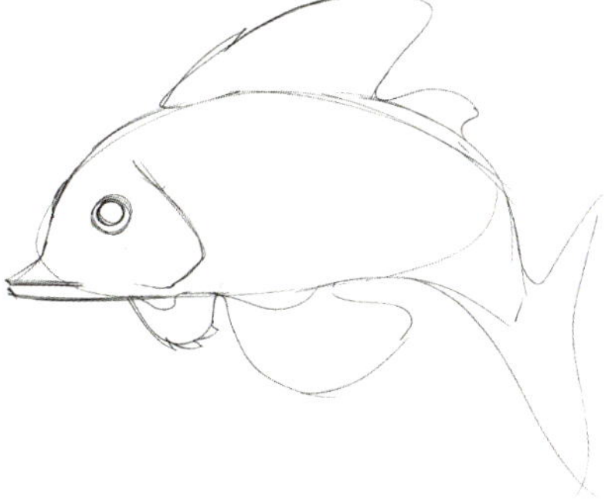

Enhance with Texture

Now that the body and silhouette are largely sketched in, move on to adding texture to the fins. Use slightly curved lines that follow the overall shape of the fins to create a texture on them. This is a quick way to effectively add some richness to an otherwise simple sketch. Now is also a good time to correct any body shape issues that you want to tweak.

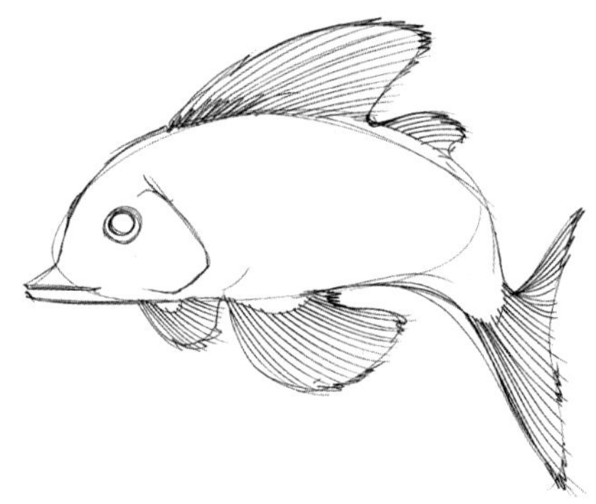

Add Scales and Shadows

Using a finer point felt pen or by rotating the felt pen to the vertical position, sketch in scales along the body of the fish in a position where you would naturally find a shadow core or where the curvature of the body relative to your point of view would be maximized. This way you can hint at the scales without committing to completely shading in or texturing the entire fish. Shade in the eyes and enhance any textural elements along the tail, as well. To finish up, use a very fine point pen to add a shadow core along the outer perimeter of the fish. In doing so, be careful not to shade all the way to the edges as this will work against you in communicating volume and depth with your fish.

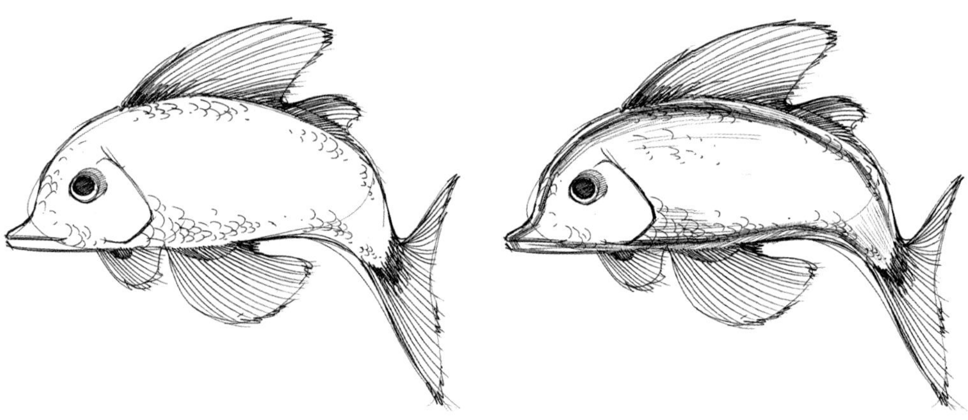

Sketch Another Fish

Try another fish using a similar technique. Just as you did before, start by drawing a blob shape. This time I imagined the fish swimming towards the viewer. Next, sketch in the tail and mouth. If desired, sketch in construction lines for the tail. These can be very light, because you again will use line weight to create emphasis where needed.

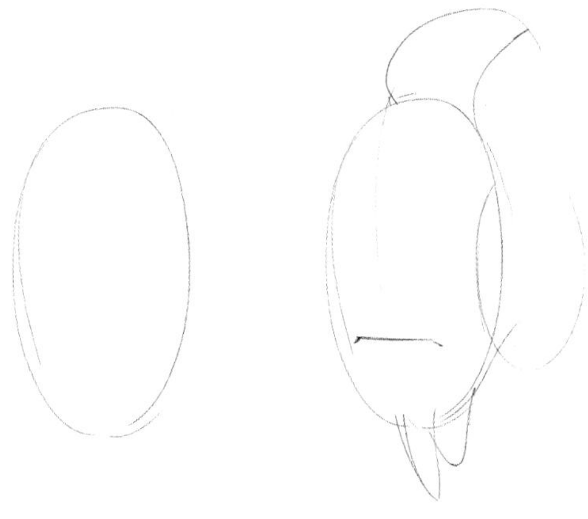

Refine the Second Fish

Sketch in a slight deviation from the initial blob shape to form the face of the fish. Sketch in the eyes, add a touch more definition to the mouth, sketch in the tail, and add fins on either side of the fish. Notice that the initial ellipse I used to locate the example's tail is starting to appear less significant because of the added line weight and definition added to the rest of the fish.

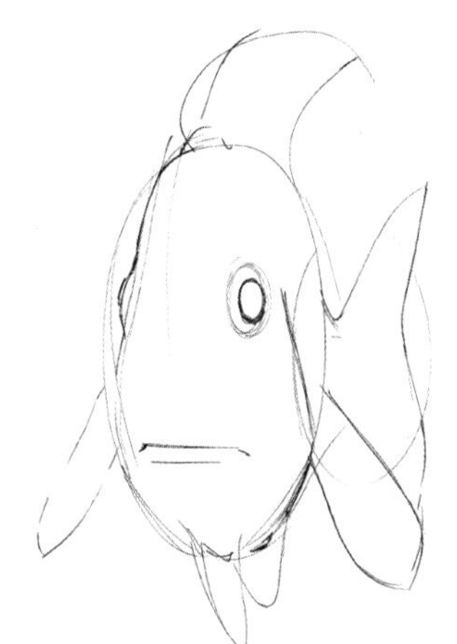

Shade the Second Fish

Next, shade in the eyes. I intentionally left a white spot to communicate a bit of a reflection on the eye based on what might be a potential light source for the fish. I decided to sketch the mouth of the fish open and made a small tweak using a few curved lines related to the initial mouth line. If yours is more of a closed mouth fish, that's fine too.

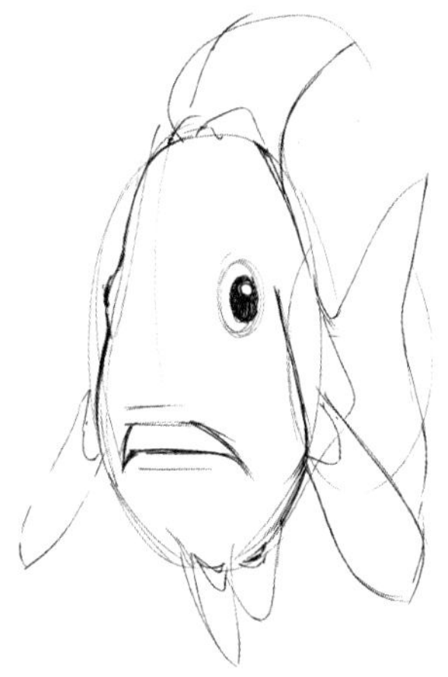

Shade in texture on the fins and mouth, and then continue to refine the outline of the fish by enhancing line weight. Notice the variations in line weight in the example. These variations relate to the relative position of elements on the fish. For example, to the right of the fish, I used a heavier line weight between the tail and the fin to suggest that the fin is closer to the viewer than the tail. Additionally, I used an even heavier line weight for the main body of the fish. This interplay of line weights is used to convey a sense of depth without having to use color or other elements to communicate that depth and perspective.

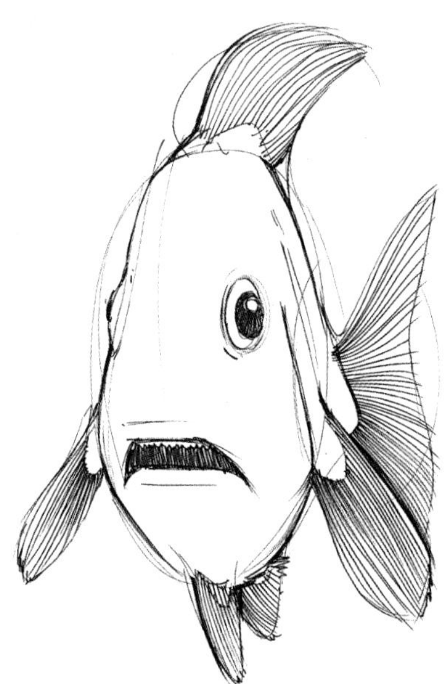

CHALLENGE

I bet you've already guessed the challenge this time: more fish! For inspiration, search out photos of fish, study other artists' drawings of fish, or sit in front of an aquarium awhile. Remember, observational drawing is a great way to fill your visual vocabulary as you figure out ways to observe, simplify, and execute in a way that is convincing and confident. Push yourself to draw as many blob-method fish as you can and focus on quantity over quality. When you get comfortable, feel free to shift to drawing a bit more slowly and refining your results.

In this exercise, you'll draw a pair of hairbrushes in two orientations: one facing up and the other down. To color them, you need only a few simple markers, including a set of grays and some warmer brown tones.

Sketch Reference Lines

Start by drawing two lines that will represent the central axes of the brushes. Decide which line you want to place your upward-facing brush on and which side you want to place your downward-facing brush on.

Next, sketch in cross sections for the handle of your hairbrush. (Don't hesitate to take a quick look at a reference, if you need to.) I chose to do simple handles, so my cross sections are ellipses drawn in perspective. Don't get too hung up on the shape of the cross section. If adding lines or a couple of dots is enough to help guide your sketch, that's alright, too.

Rough in the Brush

Roughly sketch in the shape of the head of your hairbrush using a combination of straight and curved lines. If you need to establish another cross section, particularly where the head of the brush meets the handle, now is a good time to do so. Continue sketching in the shape of your brush roughly by connecting your cross sections with curved lines that are tangential to them and soften the corners of the hairbrush itself. To prepare for applying marker to your drawing, finish out the rough volume of the bristle area of the hairbrush.

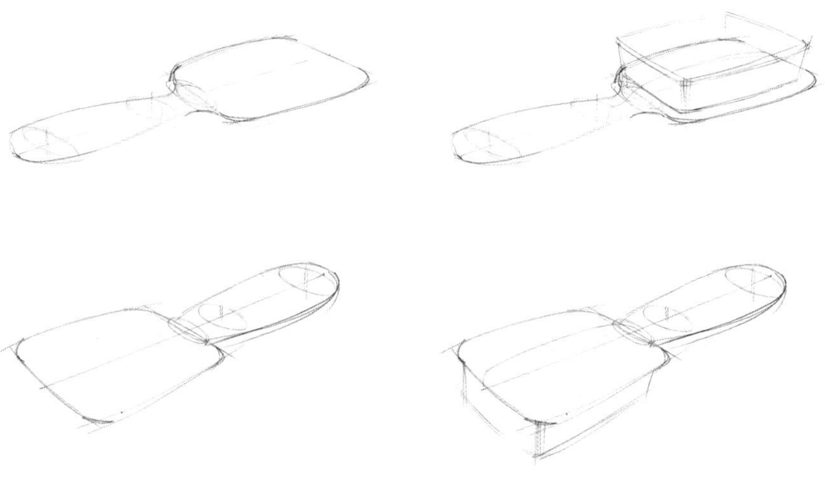

Shade with Color

Sometimes it can be difficult to represent black with markers without going too dark. For that reason, it's important to start with lighter tones so that there's room to correct any mistakes you make along the way. Shade in the handle and head of the brush with a gray marker and outline the bristles with a dark brown marker. Outlining is good preparation for shading in larger areas more confidently.

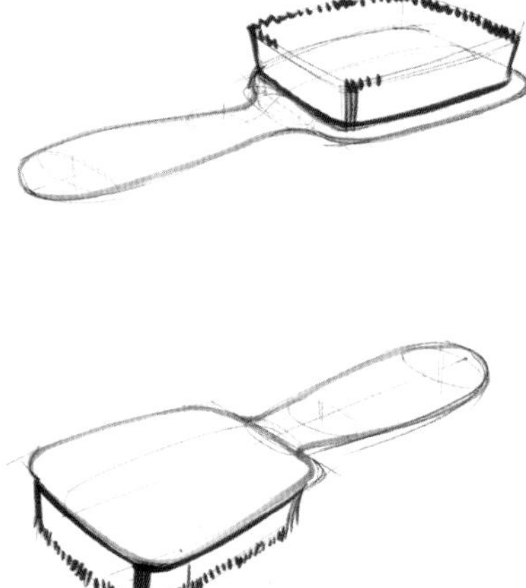

Next, shade in the bristles of the brush by applying marker in a way that's consistent with the direction of the bristles. For the upward-facing example brush, notice that I left the bristle area white for now. This is to leave some room for correction should there be a need to tweak something.

Continue filling in the bristle area of the brush with the brown markers. Alternate between a darker brown and a lighter brown marker to create a texture using short strokes. By carefully including light and dark strokes, you can make the texture of the bristles of the brush start to pop a bit more in the sketch. At the same time, shade in the handle of the brush and the head of the brush by introducing your midtone grays. Remember to consider the reflections in the handle if it is shiny. Also, think about your light source and how that may be impacting the overall look and feel of the brush.

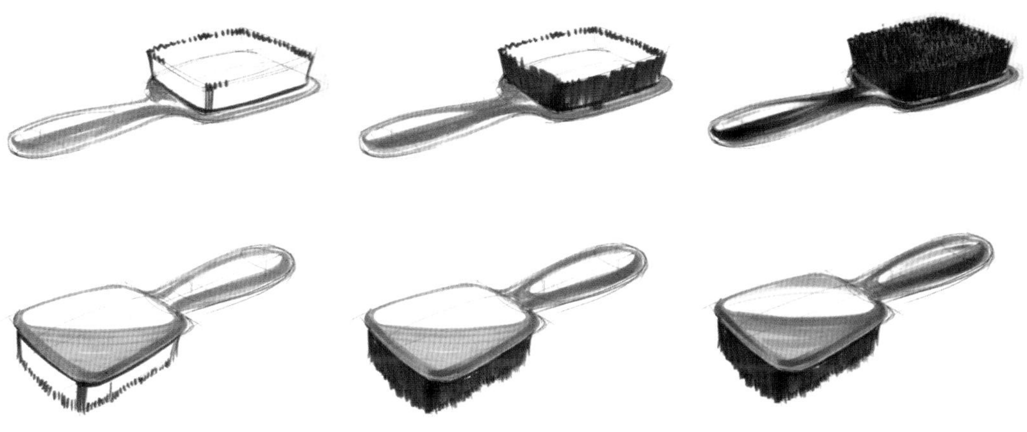

Refine Contrast and Line Weight

Continue to deepen the value of the dark gray areas by introducing your darkest grays. Be mindful of the white unfinished areas in your sketch, as these highlights are important in communicating the glossy material. Using your darkest gray for the compressed reflections in the handle is a good way to reinforce the shiny material for the handle. With most of the shading in place, turn your attention to the outline of the brush. Thicken the outline of the brush by either using repeated strokes along the outside that are consistent with the sketch or by switching to a slightly thicker pen or marker tip. The key here is to figure out what is most comfortable for you. Work consistently with the tool that works best for you.

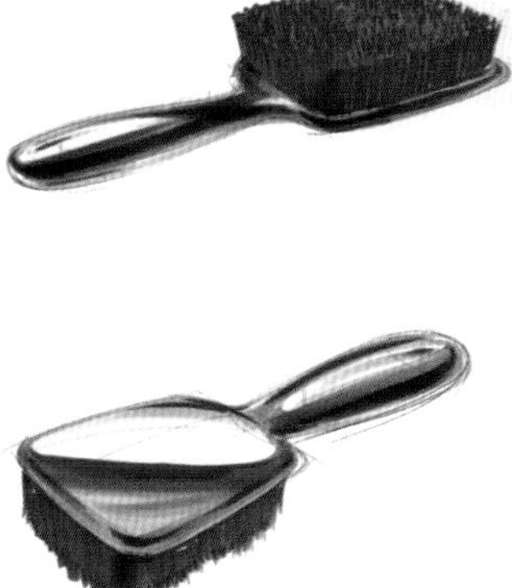

Finally, to finish up the brush, add a slight shadow. While your shadow can be a variety of tones, I chose to keep the shadow light to create a sense of depth but also to not distract from the drawing of the brushes themselves. Notice that I also textured the brush head a bit more by using white and black pencils on top of the marker to bring additional details into the brush head and bristles. Because pencil is waxy and your marker ink is thinner, it's important to not apply pencil over the marker unless you are certain that this is the look and feel of the drawing that you're after.

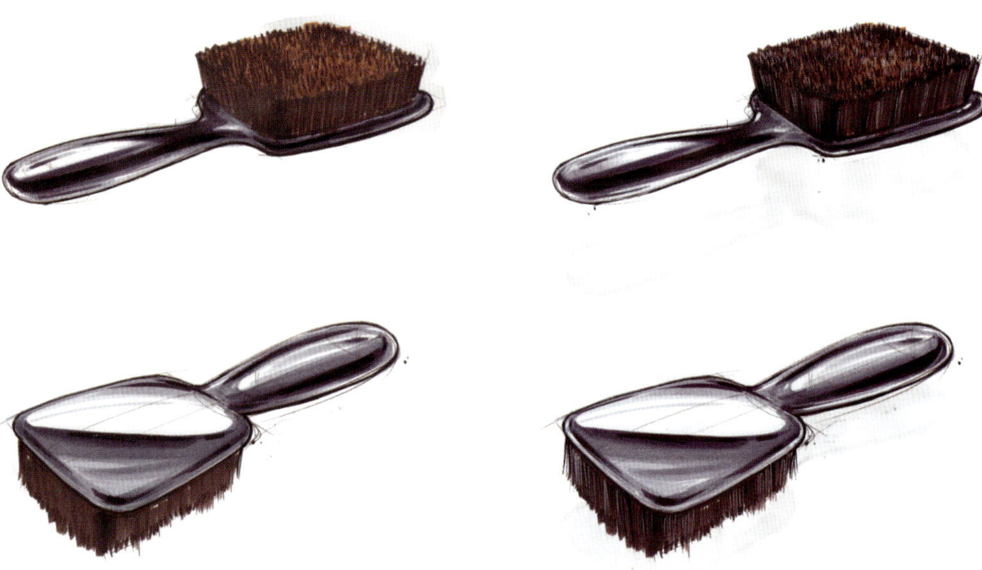

CHALLENGE

Focus on shiny materials: Sketch objects or ideas that incorporate some very shiny glossy elements. As you sketch and color your shiny objects, remember to be careful about not filling in highlights and to apply your marker strokes quickly. The gesture in your stroke will either help or hurt your drawing. Materials can be simple to draw if you get creative and resourceful with the tools you have. Pay attention to patterns in the behavior of that material as you rotate it relative to a light source or as you look at the material up close.

Drawing goggles is a fun, challenging exercise that will teach you how to deal with curved lines, including ellipses and other organic details in your sketch. To draw the example pair of googles, I used a Paper Mate Flair pen and some markers.

Establish Proportions

Start by drawing two ellipses, one on top of the other. Because of the slight difference in point of view between the two, your top ellipse should be slightly narrower top to bottom (across the minor axis) than the bottom ellipse.

Identify a region between the top and bottom ellipse to represent the width of the goggle's lens and mark it with two vertical lines. You'll use the rest of the ellipse to create a stretchy strap. Divide the lens region in half, and next add a simple sketch of a potential nose piece or nose. If you're sketching goggles for snorkeling, for example, you may need to include a molded nose piece. Even if you're not, sketching a nose-like shape can help you plan out your object and its design as you draw. After all, if someone's going to be wearing this thing, they need a place for their nose to go!

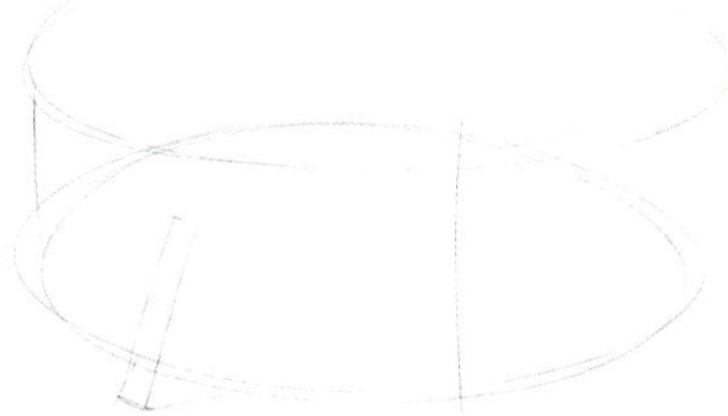

Sketch the Lens

It may not be immediately apparent, but starting your sketch with two stacked ellipses immediately establishes perspective and the sense of place on the paper. Consider the relationship between the far-right side of the top ellipse and the bottom ellipse. What do you notice about the two curves? The

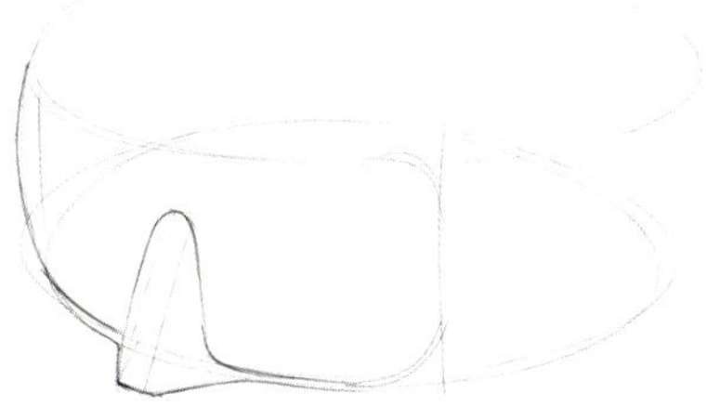

bottom ellipse being a bit more open appears to curve a bit more rapidly towards the top ellipse. It's similar to the phenomenon observed with straight lines in perspective where lines appear to converge to the same point.

Next, start to outline and rough in the
portion of your goggles that will make up
the lens. I sketched some curved lines and
softened the transition of the nose portion. If
you feel comfortable, start enhancing the line
weight slightly. As always, work lightly until
you feel confident about the direction and
details in your sketch before enhancing line
weight. If you're having trouble with rounded

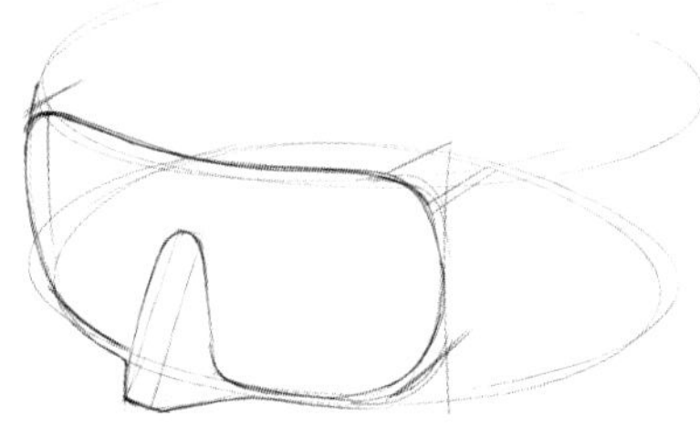

or curved lines in perspective, try to think of them as sections of an ellipse—much
like the transition between two lines at 90 degrees to each other in two dimensions
is a quarter circle. By warming up with ellipses, you can familiarize yourself with the
position of these ellipses relative to your lines in perspective.

Create Depth

Next, offset the front lens with additional
curved lines to create the thickness of the
goggles' frame. Notice that by offsetting
these lines, you create an impression of
depth in the sketch. When you are satisfied
with the appearance of the major elements,
take a minute to rough out some details that
you may want to include down the line.

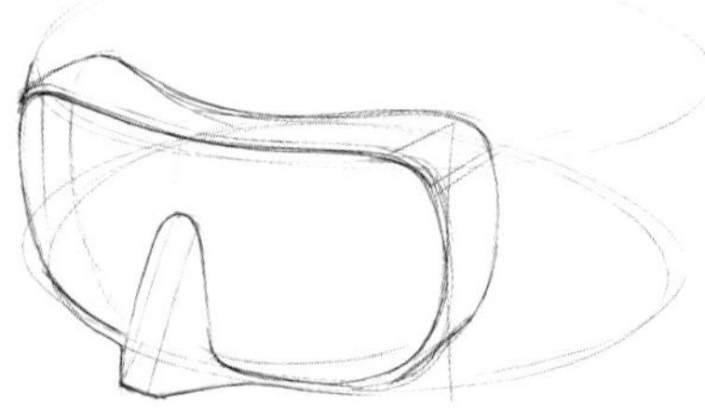

Sketch the Strap

To sketch the strap, follow the overall curvature and placement of the ellipse on the top
and bottom. As you can see in the example,
the strap largely follows the shape of the top
ellipse with some deviation and variation
included. By leveraging the ellipses, you can
sketch a more organic feeling strap while
having a nice guide to follow. As you sketch in

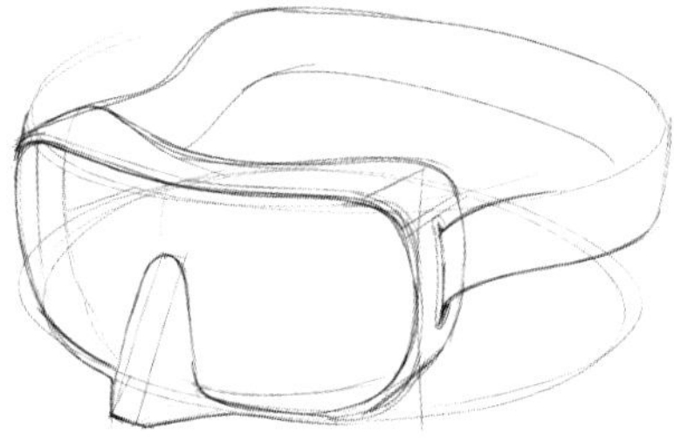

the strap, enhance the line weight and outline of the strap as well as include details for
where the strap attaches to the body of the goggles. I sketched in a slot on the side of
the frame as the strap's mounting point.

Refine the Sketch

Before you add color, texture, and shadows, take a minute to review the lines and details that you've included. Clean up any lines that you find bothersome. If you sketched some lines that are out of place, you could create an overlay, re-sketching fluidly and loosely while following your original design.

Add Initial Color

Next, grab some alcohol-based markers. I used Copic markers in shades of yellow, red, orange, and mossy or dark sea foam green. Start by outlining areas you wish to shade in with your lightest marker. Outlining with your lightest marker gives you a point of reference to shade—almost like coloring between the lines in a coloring book. It may seem counterintuitive because the sketch lines are already there; however, I find it very helpful to have this visual reference in the color that I'm using. For my goggles, I outlined the nose and frame trim with a 30% gray marker, as well as outlined and shaded a portion of the strap with my lightest green tone.

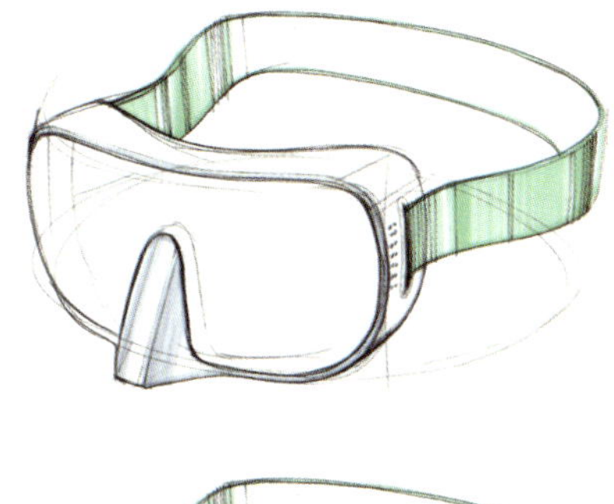

Continue shading in the frame material with your gray marker. Be careful to leave a few spots of white as these spots will act as highlights on the rounded

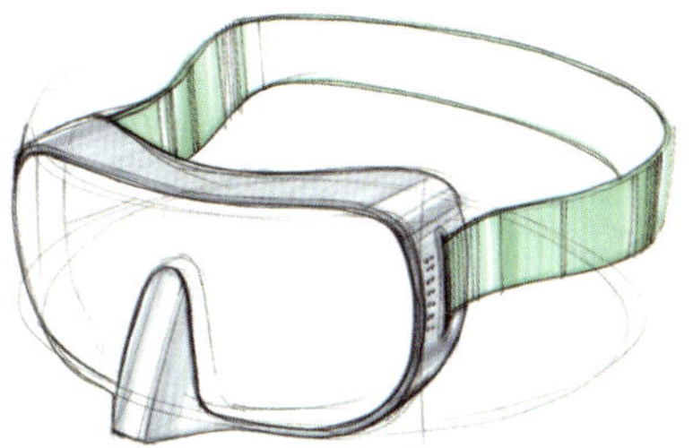

corners. You can see this on the top corners of the frame. These spots indicate the primary and secondary light sources that may be illuminating these goggles. Try to get in the habit as you color and shade your sketches of thinking about your light sources and which direction they may be facing. Understanding where your primary and secondary light sources are makes decisions easier when considering how to shade surfaces and how light or dark to make things.

Shade the Strap

Switch to your midtone marker (midtone green for me), and shade in the strap, particularly in areas where there would be additional shadows. Shade portions of the strap closest to the frame a bit darker. Do the same for the portion of the strap that returns from the right to the left, because this area would be slightly obscured as it bends and wraps around. Where there's the absence of light, there is shadow, and so shading in a bit darker helps reinforce this idea as well as helps make your pair of goggles seem more three-dimensional. Once your marker is dried, you can also reapply it in the same spot to get a deeper tone or value should you choose to.

Notice I added vertical lines with a pen on top of my green marker to begin creating a bit of texture that mimics the rigidness of an elastic strap.

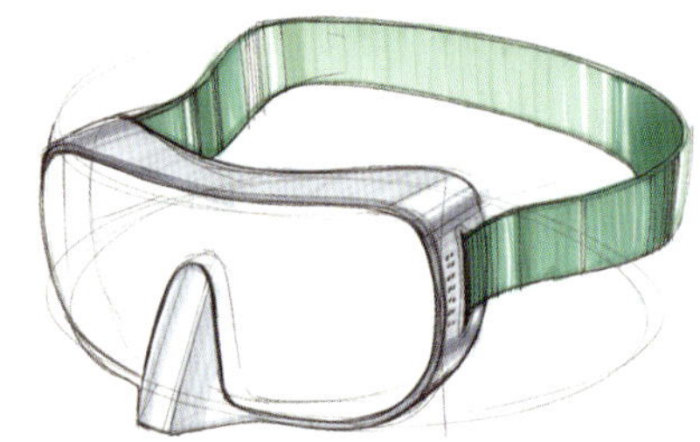

Color the Lens

Continue coloring by outlining the main lens portion. Next, you're essentially going to color a sunset or sunrise on the front of the lens. What would you see during a sunset or sunrise? I imagine orange and yellow skies with a deep, dark horizon with details such as trees or buildings perhaps distorted by a curved surface. This gives us at least a conceptual starting point for coloring the goggles.

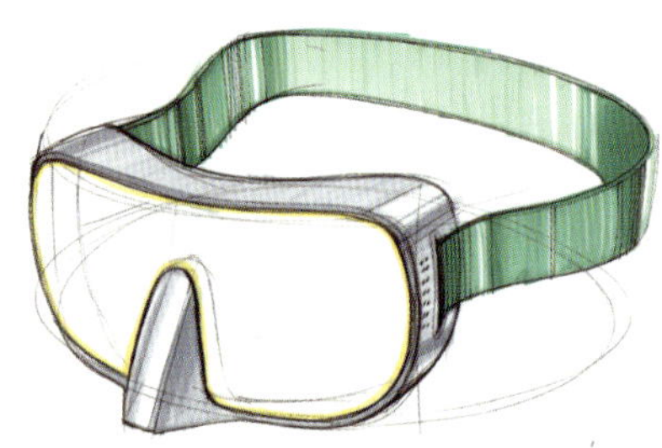

Using your lightest yellow, shade a section arced over the nose piece. This arc is meant to represent a distorted horizon or other details in the goggles that you'll be filling in a bit later. Even though the construction lines are visible with semi-translucent objects, I tend to either sketch in lines, such as those around the example's nosepiece, or by drawing through the rest of the object to show that there is frame material behind the plastic lens. You can see this in the construction lines to the left of the lens as well as the lower right portion of the lens on my goggles.

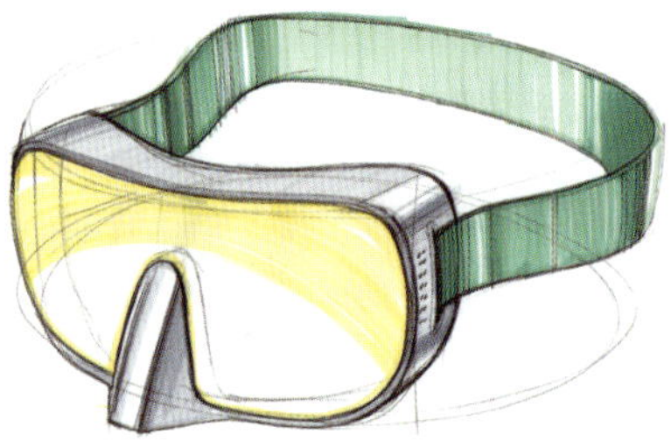

Switch to an orange that complements your yellow (I chose a peachy orange), and with a few strokes blend the yellow into the orange.

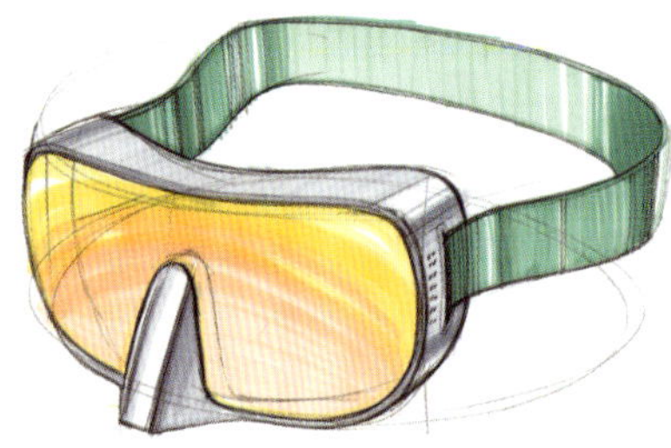

Follow the yellow's arc with your orange strokes to convey directionality and the visual effect created by a curved lens. You can blend strokes with other colors as well should you choose to, but the most important thing here is to work light until you get it right. Progressively increase the contrast as you go, all while keeping in mind the overall look and feel that you're trying to achieve in shading. Continue building up value, saturation, and intensity with your markers to help the lens pop. With a few applications of yellows, reds, and oranges along with pinks, the front of the lens begins to take shape.

Add Texture and Shadows

Use your green marker on the strap to create a slight texture by angling its chisel tip horizontally to complement the flow of the strap (look closely near the inner left and right curves). These contrasting marker strokes help communicate a bit of relief and depth, making the strap a bit more convincing.

In addition to shading with a green marker on the strap, add line weight to its outside to help the construction geometry fade into the background and pull the main sketch lines to the forefront. Compare the right side of the example's strap now with the previous step. Notice the contour line on the silhouette is slightly curved now to suggest that the strap is a soft and flexible material. Subtle changes in your lines like this can help lend credibility to elements that are soft versus hard in your sketch. This is just one example of a symbolic gesture that you can include that comes from observational drawing and simplifying what you see into these gestural elements.

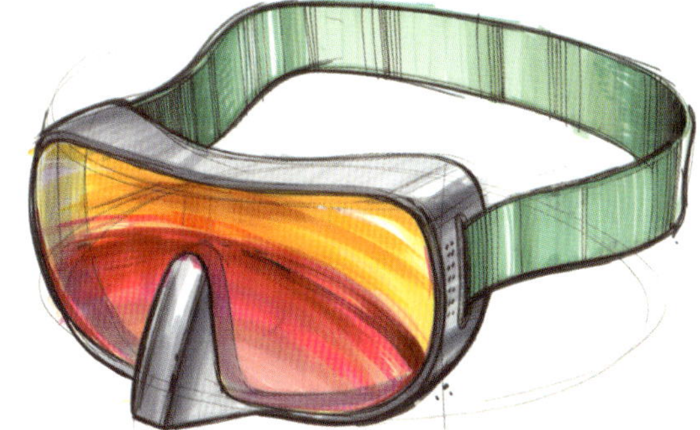

On the gray frame and nose piece, use a midtone gray, usually a 40% to 60% gray, to shade in shadow cores where necessary, particularly where the highlight is located on the top-right corner of the goggles. Shading with the darker gray creates a bit of contrast and a subtle shadow core that helps reinforce the round appearance of this corner. Layering with markers and pens in this way is an effective and quick step to creating a convincing three-dimensionality in your sketch.

Create Translucency

Using a gray marker, shade over the colored lens to indicate the frame behind that's seen through it. By simply showing some of the material behind the lens, you create the look and feel of translucency or transparency of the lens. Using grays over colors in this way is a great way to introduce depth and translucency with materials when sketching with markers. You can achieve a similar effect with pencil by shading in lightly over the lens in this last step.

Add Highlights and Final Details

To add a few highlights, you can use the pencil for more subtle blended white areas and use a white pen for crisp high contrast dots on the top edge of the strap. Remember, if you are using a pencil or any sort of opaque white in your sketch, be sure to do this last, because the opaque areas will not readily receive marker

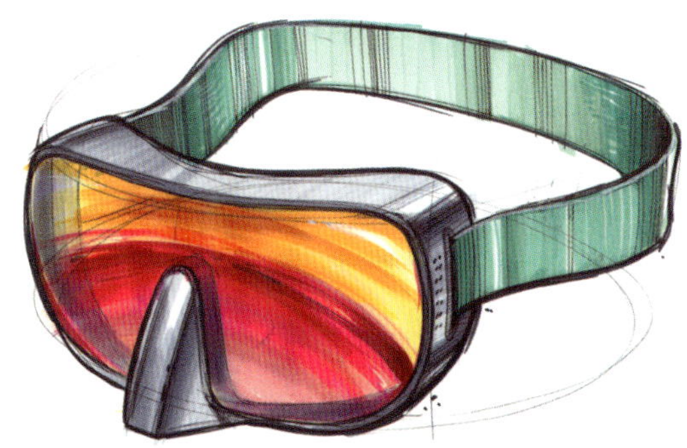

after you apply the white. Additionally, you could add a few other details, such as vent holes on the frame, hatching, or stippling marks to help add warmth and texture to your sketch. Think about the expressiveness in the overall outline, then adjust as needed. Finding balance with the line quality and marker technique is a skill in itself and something that will take some consistent practice.

CHALLENGE

Sketch a series of goggles or other eyewear. Review the initial steps and techniques used in the exercise and try to apply them to a few designs of your own. Consult reference imagery or objects as needed and look for ways to visually break down the geometry in a way that makes sense to you. Leverage the skills and knowledge you've learned about point of view to rotate and position your goggles in a variety of ways. As a bonus, focus on trying to find the balance between being gestural and expressive in your line work with the overall communication and cleanliness in your sketch.

PUFFY COAT

Lines in your sketches can set the mood and tone for what you're sketching. They can connect with an audience and convey emotion. With that in mind, let's soften things up. In this exercise, you'll practice line quality when drawing something soft and fabric-like, specifically a puffy coat. For this example, I used a felt pen and a set of Copic markers in the orange color family. When choosing your color family, select markers that have around 20% to 30% difference in value between each.

Sketch the Coat

To start, sketch a trapezoid to represent the general proportion and perspective of the coat. Using the trapezoid as a guide, sketch an ellipse for the neck, a few curves for the base of the coat, and a centerline for the zipper. These lines are your construction lines and will help orient things as you sketch. Sketch in the sleeves. If you think about the sleeves as slightly bent cylinders, you can get a sense of how and where to place them. Notice that the bottom of my sleeves are ellipses that I sketched in a similar perspective to the bottom of the coat.

Add Puffiness

With the coat's basic structure established, you can move on to adding its characteristic puffiness. To do this, simply sketch along the overall shape of the initial construction geometry. Transform the sleeves' cylinders into puffy sections by sketching a series of arcs along the perimeter of the coat and across the width of the sleeves. Treat the main body of the coat similarly, with arcs running the length of the zipper's

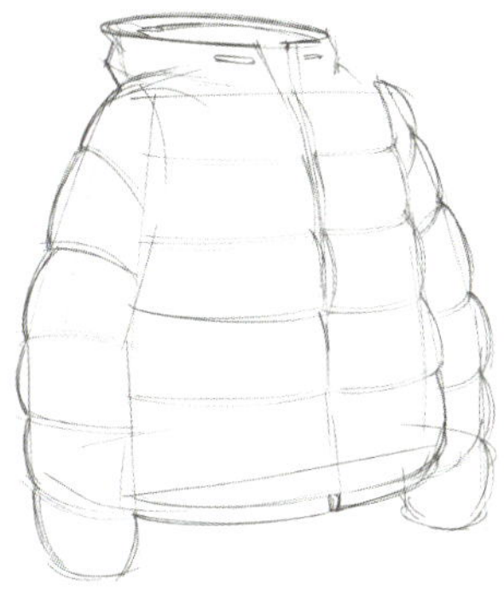

centerline. Additionally, segment the body into five sections, adding arcs on the outer perimeter of these sections to help reinforce the coat's puffy appearance.

Sketch Details

For the hood or neck of the coat, bump up the line weight and add a few squiggles to represent the folding of the material that makes up the coat. Add a few loosely sketched rectangular shapes at the neck of the coat to serve as eyelets for a potential drawstring. Finally, at the bottom of the coat, sketch a double line to serve as a bit of trim to finish things off.

Color and Detail the Coat

To begin coloring the coat, grab your lightest hued marker (light orange for me) and continue to add expressiveness to the lines you've sketched so far. For contrast and to create a shadowed interior, add hatching to the slightly open inside of the coat around the neck and down toward the zipper. You can also sketch in the zipper loosely at this point. I even added an upper zippered pocket (for the wearer to stow goggles, perhaps). Notice the squiggles I placed on the left and right of the coat's body. These squiggles indicate where to add some dark shading later to show the wrinkliness of the coat material and add to the overall appearance

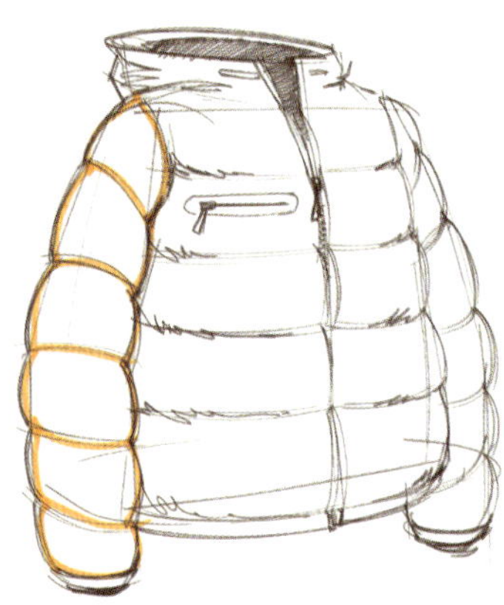

and texture. This is one example of how lines and line quality can be used to convey a certain materiality and feeling in your sketch. If you're not feeling confident at this step, pause and experiment with a few of your own strokes to see if you can get the hang of it before proceeding. Likewise, if you're ever unsure about a color or marker, test it on scrap paper before coloring your drawing.

Shade with Markers

As you begin shading, outline the main silhouette of the areas you want to color, giving yourself a guide as to where to start and stop with your alcohol markers. Using the lightest color, shade in portions of the coat that would likely have a core shadow, such as the outermost left side of the left sleeve, the inner and outermost sides of the body, and where the left sleeve comes in contact with the body of the coat. Shade quickly and confidently, but also loosely, to give your coat some life in its appearance. Follow the general contour and shape of the main body and the sleeves as you shade to help reinforce the three-dimensionality of the jacket and show the puffiness of the coat. Continue filling in with the strokes until the majority of the coat is filled in. I intentionally left a few white spots as highlights that are related to the relative position of the primary light in the scene, which is to the right and above the coat. Therefore, surfaces that face upward or are more to the right will receive highlights or shading with the lightest of colors. When shading with markers, be sure to let your markers have enough time to dry before proceeding.

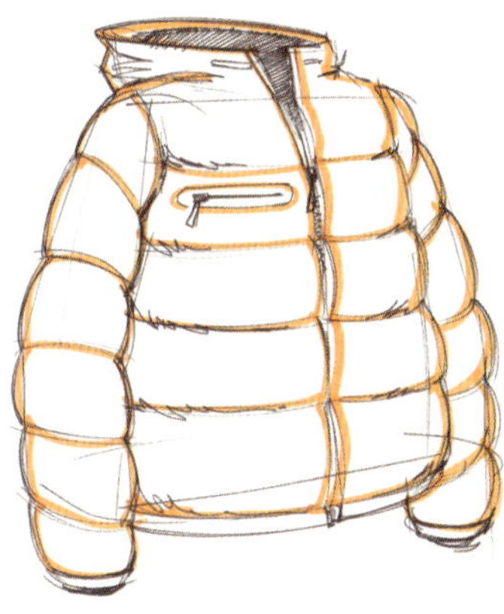

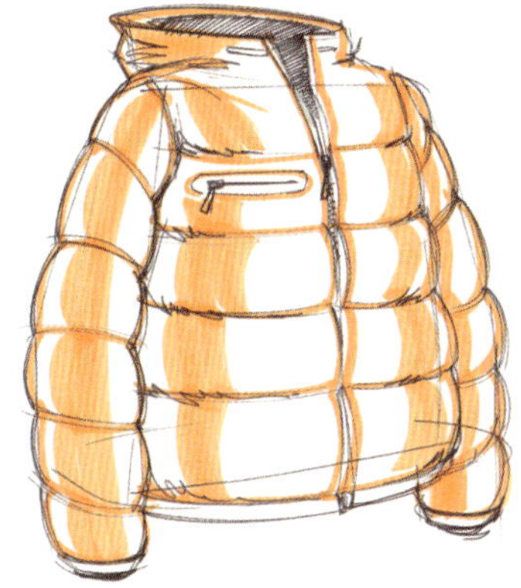

Enhance Shadows

Switch to your midtone color marker, and begin enhancing areas that are in shadow, such as wrinkles, creases, and the shadow core on the far side of the coat. Keep these strokes loose, confident, and energetic. Things should be starting to come together for you now. As you add more color, you'll need to beef up the initial lines in the sketch a bit. So, enhance your lines as needed, or address them as the final step. Continue shading in with your midtone marker, but do not cover the entire area that you initially shaded. You want to make sure

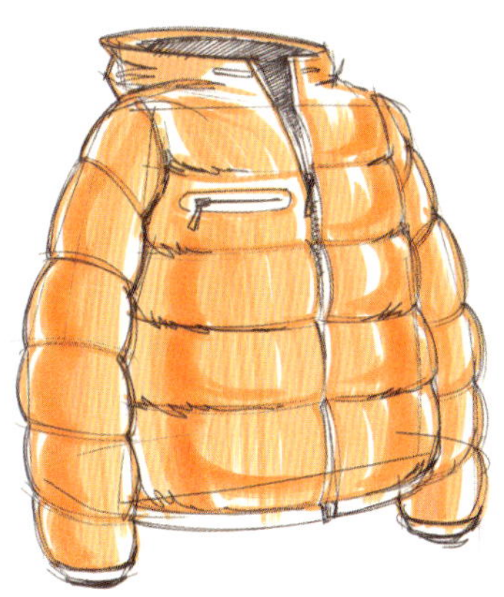

that those initial tones and colors show through. Be judicious and exercise restraint in how much you color and where you apply your color. If you're finding it difficult to achieve that balance, that's okay. With practice, you'll get better and your confidence and precision will improve.

Add Materiality

To further enhance the appearance of the marker and convey a sense of materiality, use a stroke with the marker that is a bit like an M or W in motion. Notice on the example's sleeve that I repeated this M or W shape up along the outermost left side to serve as a shadow core of sorts. Take a minute to enhance the overall line weight on the sketch on the outside perimeter. Rather than a solid whole line, I opted to repeatedly sketch over my lines, because I wanted to maintain a certain level of warmth and roughness with the sketch; this coat is made of fabric after all.

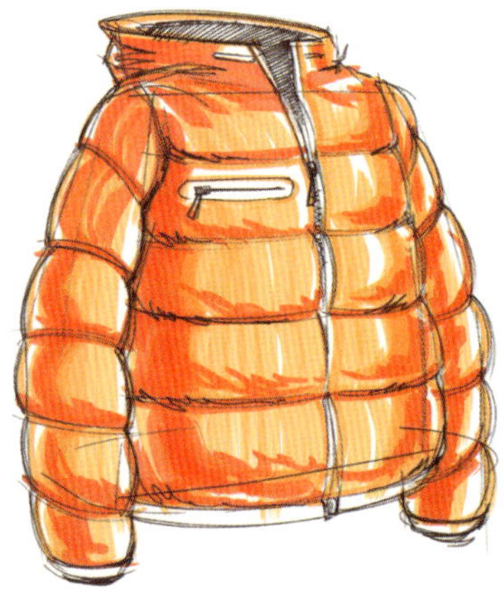 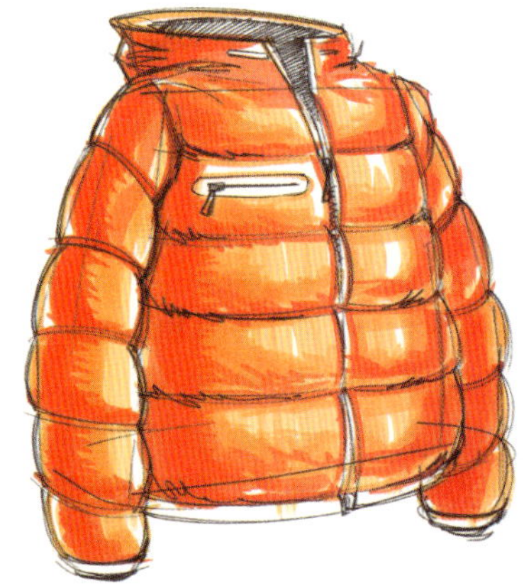

Apply Finishing Touches

Use your dark gray marker to shade in the pocket zipper, the inside of the coat, and elastic trim at the bottom of the coat and sleeves. To make the zipper feel more zipper-like, scribble on the zipper down the center of the coat using a zigzag stroke. Because of the scale of this coat, it would not be the most efficient use of time or skill to sketch every tooth on the zipper. Sometimes when sketching, you have to decide how much detail to include based on the scale of what you're drawing. Additionally, I added

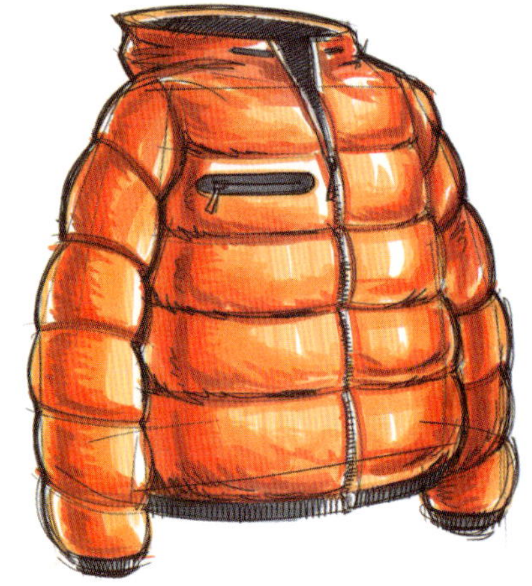

a few more scribbles to the fabric of the coat using my black pen and went one value deeper on my oranges to get a more distinct shadow and shadow core in the orange section of the coat.

As I mentioned, lines are a key part of this style of sketching, and as you can see, I used lines intentionally to convey a fabric-like texture and feel overall. While the color markers do a lot of the heavy lifting, perspective plays an important part in the overall appearance of the lines in the sketch. Stay loose and have fun, and you too will be able to create lively and engaging sketches.

CHALLENGE

Create a series of sketches of a soft object like this coat, and work on the expressiveness of your lines. Try to find a balance between color and line quality in your sketches. Think about your light source and where your shadows might be. As always, feel free to grab some reference imagery to better understand what's happening.

 # KITCHEN MIXER

This week, let's sketch a countertop-style kitchen mixer. In this exercise, you'll focus on techniques for sketching in perspective as well as line quality and surface finish using markers.

Rough in the Initial Sketch

To begin, use a thin pen to lightly sketch three planes that represent the base, neck, and head of the mixer. More specifically, the top plane references the underside of the mixer's head or motor. Next, lightly sketch in the mixer's overall body while trying not to get too caught up on its exact details. This step is more about capturing the essence of the mixer rather than precisely defining everything about it.

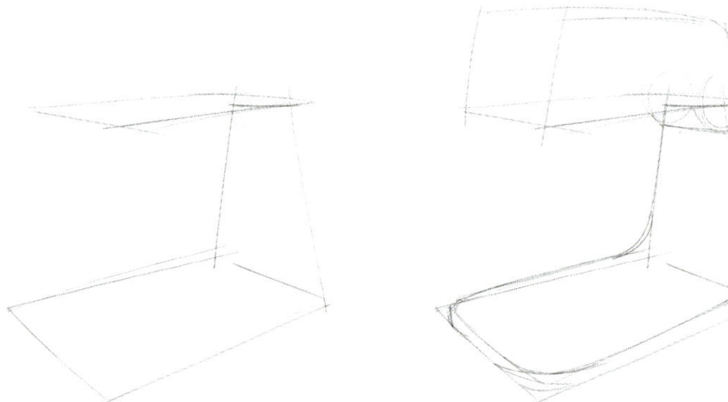

Add Transitions and Details

Still sketching very loosely and lightly, add a few transitions where the initial planes meet, as well as round the corners of the mixer's base. Sketch two ellipses at the top of the right trapezoidal surface to indicate a hinge. Quickly rough in the shape of the head, as well as the mount for the mixing attachments, a bowl, and the rest of the body.

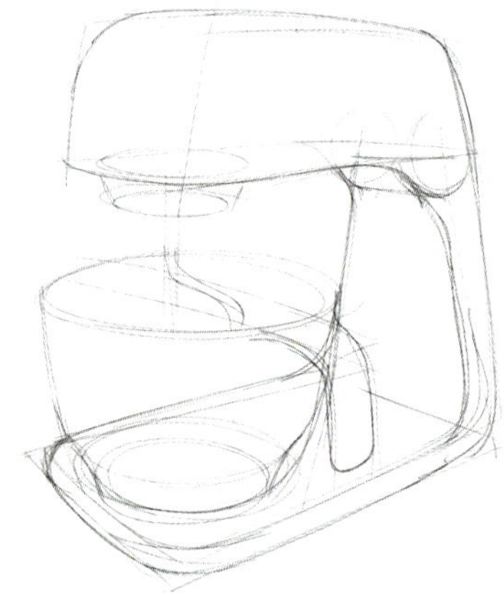

Next, continue adding functional details: a handle on the bowl, an attachment mounting point at the front of the mixer, a control switch on the side of the motorhead, and any other details you want to include. Pause a moment and evaluate your progress: Have you forgotten any details? Are you satisfied with the perspective? When you're happy, proceed to the next step.

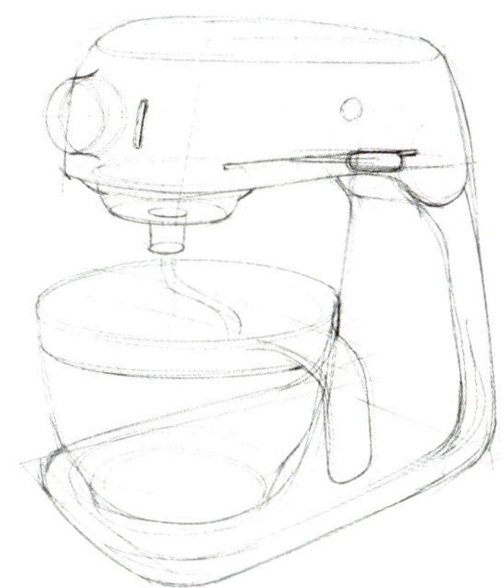

Create an Overlay

Place a thin translucent sheet of paper over your initial sketch, and re-sketch your mixer to create an overlay. Not only will this breathe new life into your sketch, but it also gives you a chance to modify details about in the undersketch, as well as correct any perspective errors you spotted. (For more tips on overlays, see Exercise 7.)

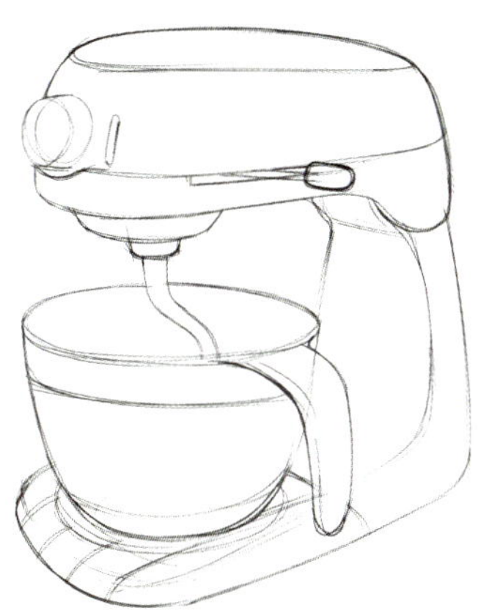

Start Light

To add color to the mixer, select a color family that you like for which you have a highlight, mid-tone, and shadow tone marker. I chose a minty green, red, and gray to shade in the mixer. Start by outlining the areas you want to color with the lightest color and fill in accordingly. Be mindful to leave small areas of white where applicable as you shade. Notice that I intentionally left white areas on the base, the handle of the mixing bowl, and the upper-right side of the mixer. These areas function as highlights in the final drawing by allowing the white of the paper to show through. By starting with your lightest markers, you can more easily build up to the tones and values you want in the end rather than having to correct things later on.

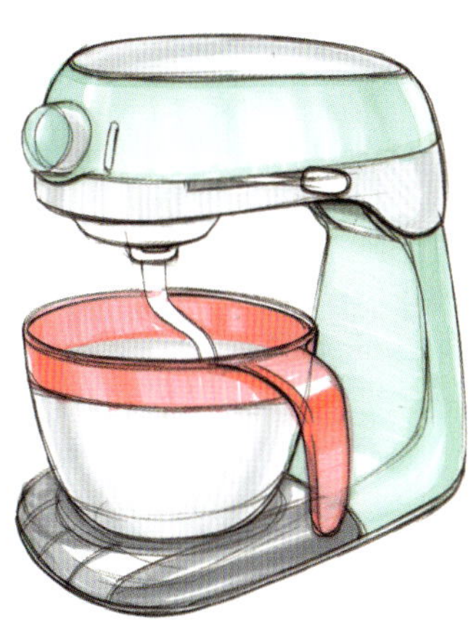

Enhance with Midtones

Next, where needed, switch to your midtone value markers and enhance the shadow cores of rounded areas on the mixer, such as to the far right of the base or the upper right of the motor housing. Take a minute to compare the example in this step and the previous step to observe the differences. This may help you determine where you want to apply additional darker value marker strokes. Where the handle on the bowl extends outward, add a shadow using the same marker you used to shade in the base (in my case, a red marker). Additionally, add a shadowed area to the lever on the motor housing where there is a recess.

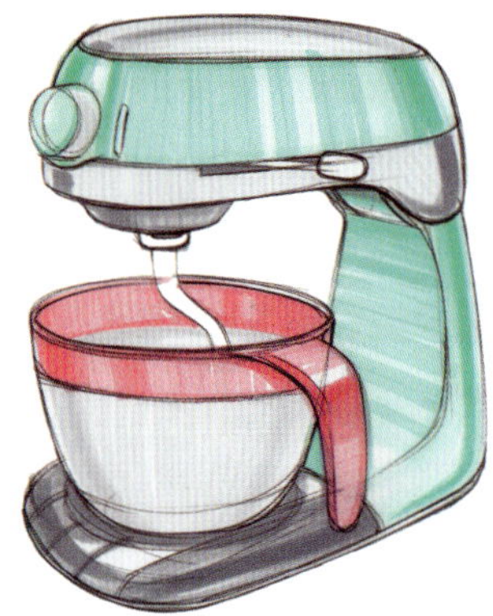

Continue sketching and enhancing color by applying your midtone values. For example, I sketched on the bowl using the midtone marker to further enhance the contrast between the upward and outward-facing surfaces and those that are facing away from the light. Be careful when shading the bowl if you want to achieve a lighter finish on it. Stick to using a lighter gray marker rather than switching to a midtone color. At this point, I also enhanced the metallic finish of the motor housing by using a midtone marker, specifically a Copic Cool Gray No. 5. marker.

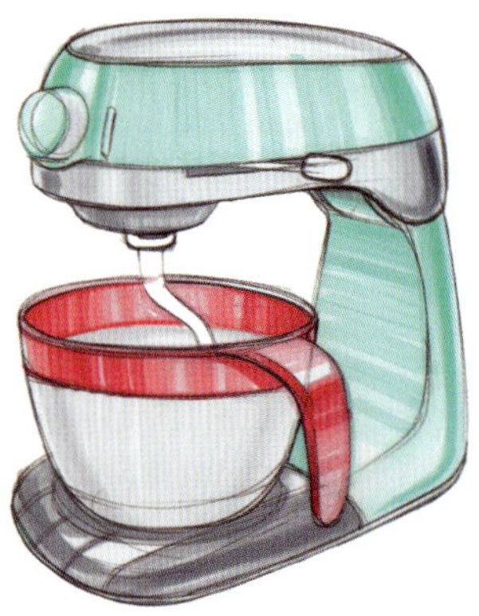

To further enhance the materiality of the base, use a midtone marker to apply strokes in a way that complements the surface and suggests reflectivity. As the surface of the motor housing wraps around in a somewhat pale shape, orient the strokes vertically with a slight curve to convey reflections that may be picked up in this glossy surface. Additionally, you can enhance the metallic finish on the motor housing with dark and crisp marker strokes to suggest a metal finish.

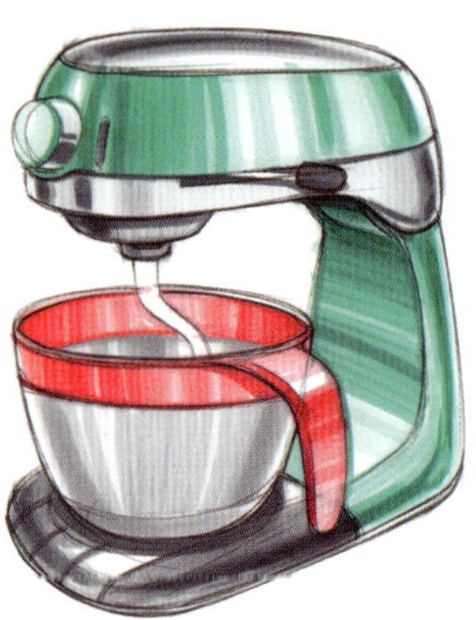

As needed, continue touching up the colored areas of the mixing bowl sketch with darker marker values, using your midtone or dark marker as needed. If you have additional markers that provide in-between tones, you can use those as well. Try a squint check to gauge whether you have enough contrast. Another way to check contrast is to place your sketch on a wall, take a few steps back, and look at your drawing. Much like atmospheric perspectives, the additional distance between you and your work will give you a chance to focus on the overall effect rather than the details in the sketch.

Finalize the Drawing

For the final step, refine the outline of the mixer by adding a heavier line to your drawing. Notice in the example that the heavier outline is largely located to the right and lower portion of the sketch. My aim was to reinforce the direction of the scene's primary light source by placing the dark lines opposite the direction of the light source. You can also shade in recesses slightly darker and refine the overall line quality if needed. Finally, I enhanced the reflective portions on the head of the mixer with strokes of a Copic Cool Gray No. 9 (90%) or Cool Gray No. 8 (80%) marker in their reflected core.

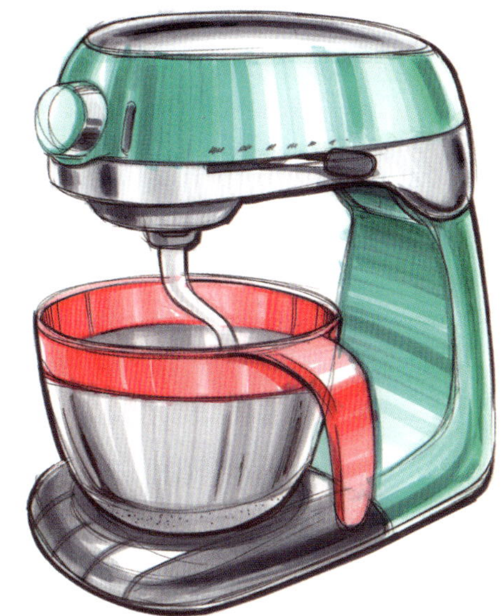

Take a close look at the accessory mounting point toward the front of the mixer head, and notice that the way I shaded the colored portion of the mixer head complements the way that I shaded its gray portion. This is to avoid any sort of confusion as to the directionality of the surfaces when shading with a marker. To wrap up, add text or hatch lines where necessary and any additional textures, shadows, backgrounds, or contextual information you'd like to add.

CHALLENGE

Sketch a somewhat larger object using perspective that is functionally more complicated than the simpler objects you've sketched so far in this chapter. Pay attention to your surface finishes, line quality, perspective, proportion, and shadowing with line length. Try several pages of these, whether by repetition of the same sketch or by varying the view of each object. Remember to stay loose, relaxed, and draw with your shoulder. The more fun you have and the more positive you are, the better your sketches will be in the end.

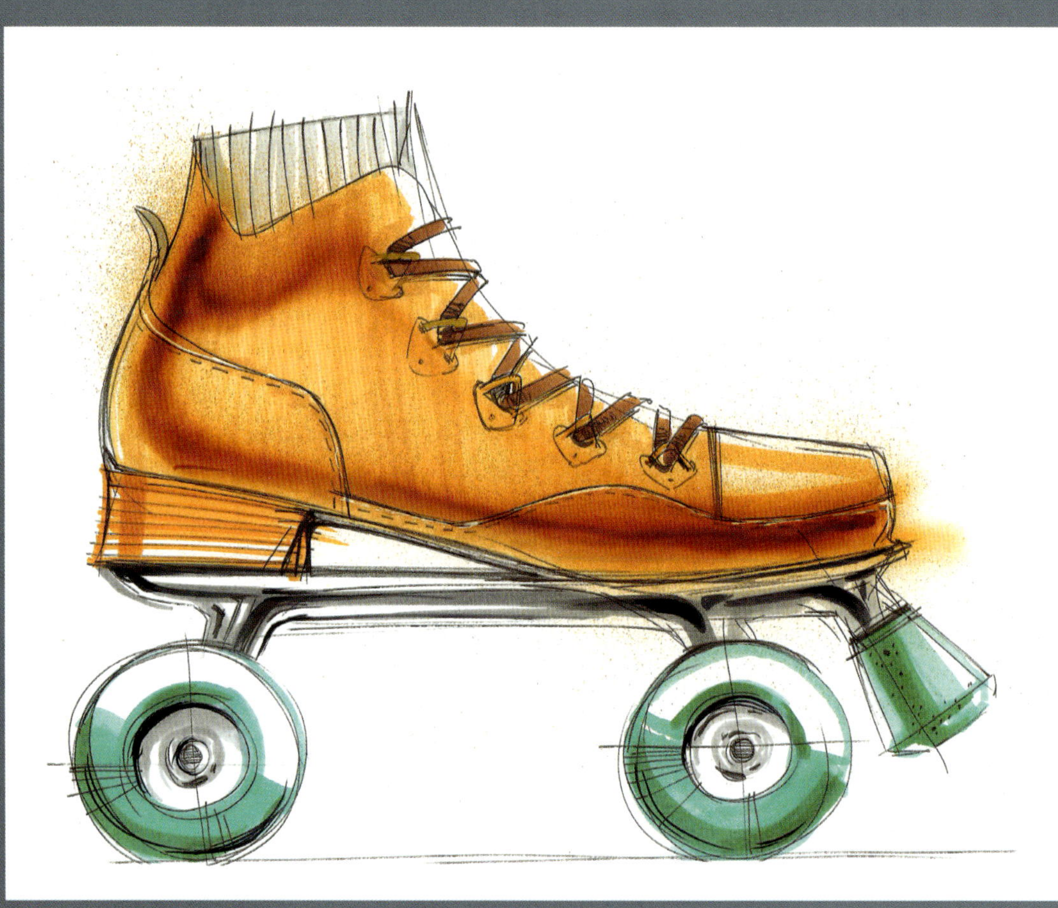

CHAPTER 7

COLOR, TEXTURE, MATERIALS

When you're drawing, perspective, line weight, and gesture help communicate three-dimensionality, but the color you use as well as the texture and materials that you convey will make your drawings feel more realistic.

Color can command focus in drawing and also anchor a composition. Colors can create warmth and realism, enhancing the overall feel of your drawings. Color can even help you convey texture. Pay attention to the world around you. How does color reflect off other objects? How does light interplay on surfaces? These clues will help you represent real textures, colors, and materials as you sketch.

How can you replicate what you see? Get creative, and play with your pen and pencil strokes, shading, and gestures while sketching. Think of ways to symbolically show the depth in a material, whether it be through a surface effect, like reflections or shadows, or small details, like cracks or wrinkles in leather or concrete.

Remember, contrast is your friend and helper. If you want to show depth in a drawing, layer contrast on your perspective as you add color. Contrast helps to enhance the depth and feeling of your drawings, making them more engaging and realistic. In this chapter, you'll have plenty of opportunities to focus on improving your skill with colors, materials, and textures—starting with drawing a watch.

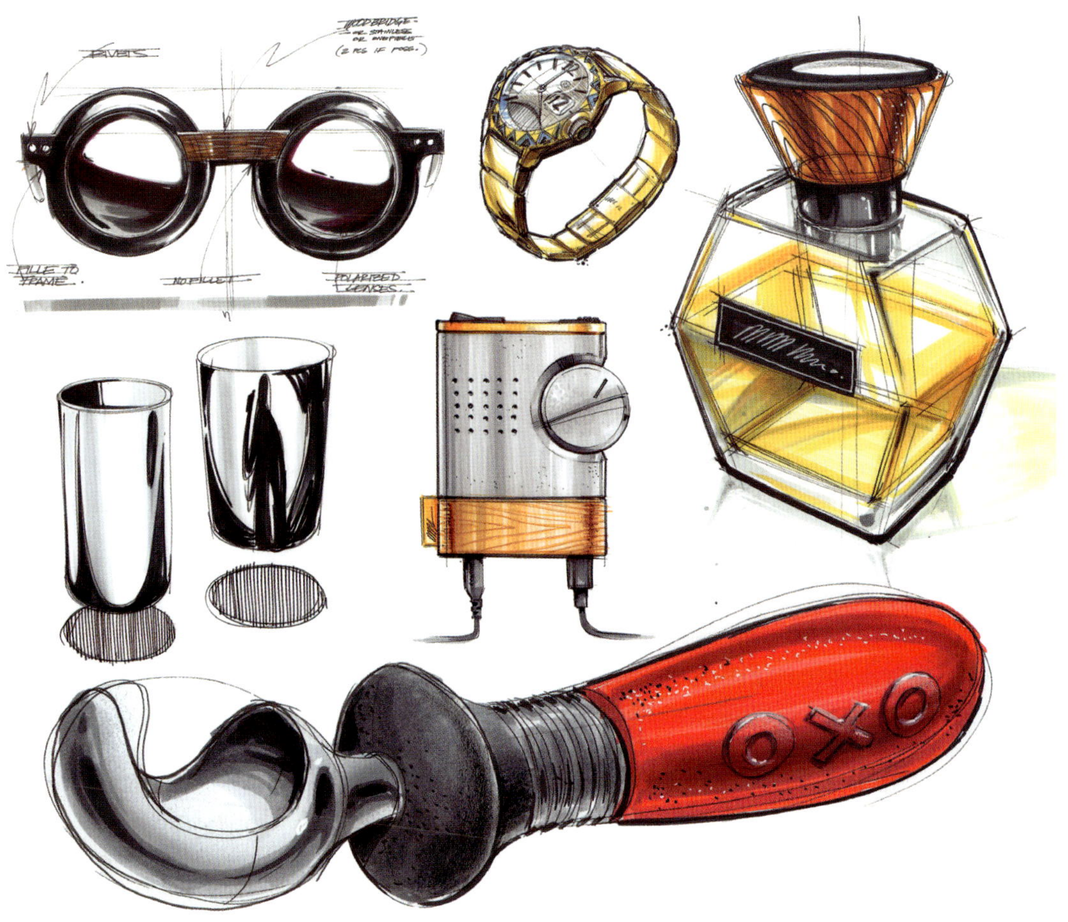

As always, understanding the underlying structure of the object you're sketching will make your task easier. A watch, this week's subject, is comparable to a cylinder in some ways. Basically, it's a very short cylinder with straps that are meant to wrap around a wrist. Thinking of a watch this way enables you to structurally understand it and identify a way to begin to draw it.

Because you'll be applying color to your watch, I recommend using a Paper Mate Flair pen. Markers do not cause bleeding with this pen (or others like it), so you can apply the marker directly over your sketch without creating smudges or having sketch lines bleed everywhere.

Establish the Central Axis

The first step is to establish a central axis for the main cylindrical form of the watch. Draw a shallow line relative to the virtual horizon in your scene. Next, draw two ellipses perpendicular to your axis, side by side but spaced apart. These ellipses will serve as guidelines to further refine the straps of the watch.

Sketch the Face

To sketch the face of the watch, pick a point between the two ellipses, and draw a line to indicate the axis that goes through the face of the watch. Remember that in perspective, the minor axis of the ellipse will follow the perspective system and appear to converge to the same vanishing point as other relevant lines.

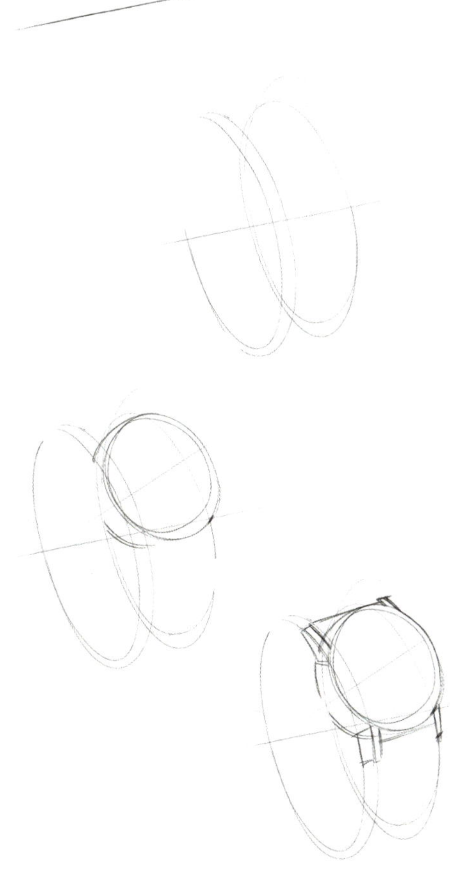

Add Thickness and Mounting Prongs

Offset the watch face ellipse, and sketch in a few arcs to represent the thickness of the watch's body. Next, begin sketching in its mounting prongs. Pay attention to perspective in the scene, but feel free to take some liberties as needed; you can correct mistakes later. As you sketch in the details, try to think of where things would go based on how they would work. If needed, take a look at some reference images or watches.

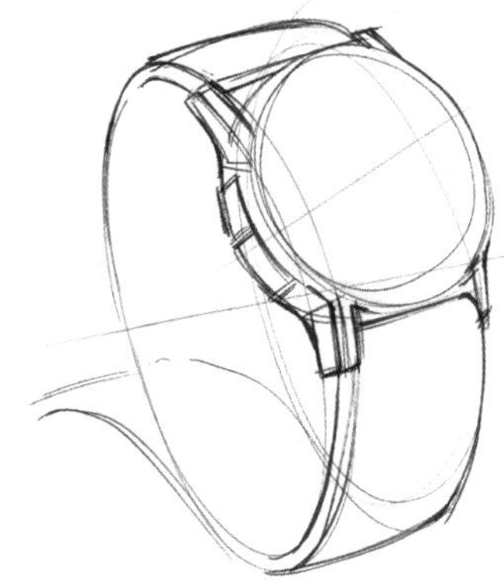

Enhance the Outline

Enhance the overall outline of the sketch and important areas within the sketch. Notice that adding the line weight to the strap, face, and body of the watch begins to pull out its overall look and feel. Begin thinking about potential materials. What is the strap made of, and how might you re-create that material's look and feel?

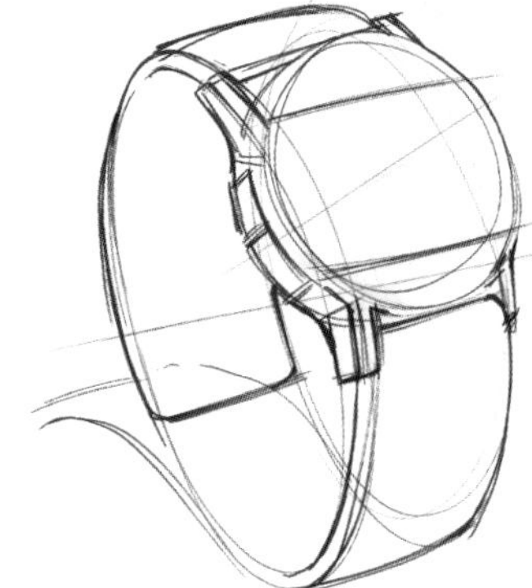

Define the Strap and Add Line Weight

Use the initial two ellipses as construction geometry to further define the watch strap. Where appropriate, add a solid line to break up the ellipses into two sections. In the example, notice the extension toward the lower left of these ellipses. This extension functions as a way of introducing a closure method to the strap (I imagined it as an adjustable strap with a hook-and-loop closure).

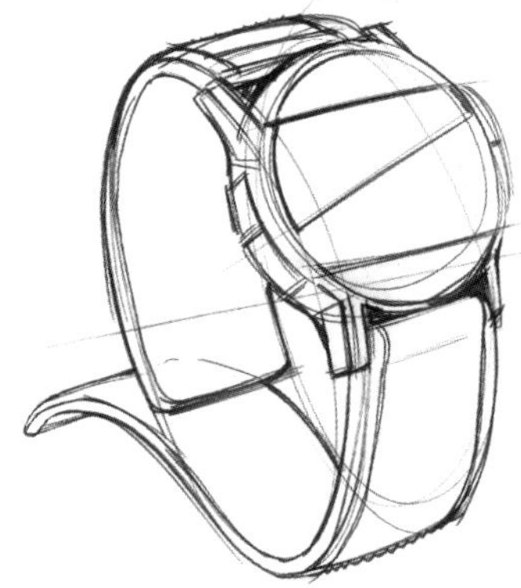

With your pen, sketch over previously drawn areas and emphasize lines in preparation for adding color. If you feel the need, you can create an overlay of your sketch before you move on.

Apply Color, Highlights, and Textures

To start, decide on the materials and colors for your watch band and face. For my band, I chose light, midtone, and dark value markers in a brown color family. Outline areas where you plan to apply color, then evenly shade the straps. For the watch face and buttons, I chose an olive green and orange, respectively. In some cases, you can use the same marker to deepen value where necessary. Wait for the color to dry slightly, then reapply the marker in the same spot to achieve a darker tone. I used this technique for the housing of my watch face.

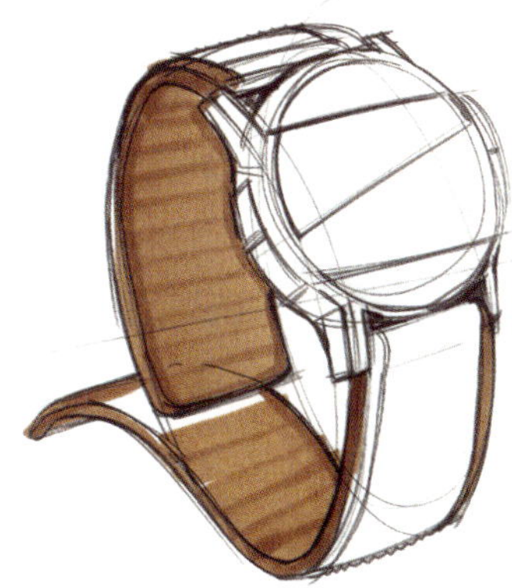

When adding color to the buttons, leave a sliver of white paper showing through at the top right of each to create the impression of highlights. Shade the middle section of the strap with a randomized pattern, using the marker to create a textured look in addition to coloring the material. Next, continue shading by deepening values in the shadowed area of the strap as well as any overlapping areas.

Do a squint check: Have you included enough contrast? If not, touch up where necessary. Additionally, shade in the face of the watch. Notice I drew a diagonal line across the watch face and added some hatching. The diagonal line and white area represent a highlight across the face.

Refine the Sketch

Lastly, continue to refine the sketch by emphasizing the line weight of the outline to help the sketch pop on the page as well as clean things up. Now is also the time to add textural details with pencil on top of the marker, if you want to. For example, I applied a white pencil to the dark brown areas of the strap to enhance the textural look. Toward the inside of the band in the tan area, I used a very fine pen to create a hook-and-loop texture on the material. Additionally, you can use the same scribble technique to reinforce the three-dimensionality of the strap by mimicking a shadow core toward the lower right of the strap.

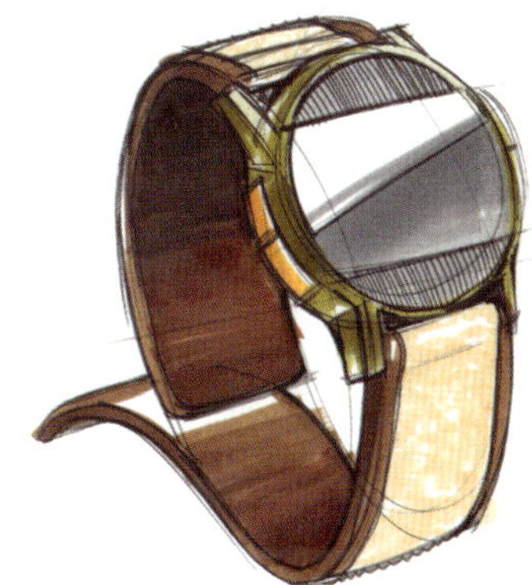

On the watch face, use a dark gray marker to deepen the reflection in the face. You can also use a black marker to create striking reflections in a shiny surface or simply enhance using a pencil. Well done!

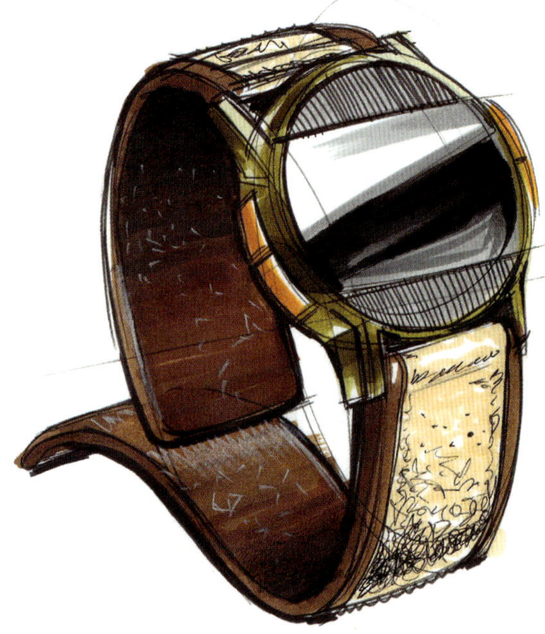

CHALLENGE

Experiment with wearable tech—watches, bracelets, or other items that might be worn on the wrist. When sketching these objects, pay close attention to the perspective and consider which of the strategies you've learned would be best to construct them. Add some color and texture to each object and consider line quality and clarity in each of your sketches. As an extra challenge, push yourself to draw a little faster to inject some energy into your sketch style as you practice. Focus on quality, but remember that quantity will be the most beneficial aspect of your practice. So, try to create as many sketches as you can and enjoy the process.

 # AIR PURIFIER

In this exercise, you'll explore a quick and efficient method of applying texture and enhancing your drawing. To sketch and apply texture to this week's object—an air purifier—you'll need pencils, a set of gray markers, and paper that is thin but can hold up to marker ink. I used marker paper that is coated on the back so that the markers won't bleed as I sketch. Marker paper also has a subtle texture, or tooth, that makes for great pencil shading.

Sketch Reference Geometry

Lightly sketch a set of ellipses toward the top and bottom of your page. I oriented my page vertically so I can use the size of the paper to my advantage for the design I have in mind. When drawing the ellipses, think about the point of view from which you are illustrating the air purifier. The ellipses toward the top should be narrower than the ellipses at the bottom.

Next, connect the sides of the ellipses tangentially from top to bottom, using a light hand for these construction lines. Offset the ellipses at the top to create a small lip, and also offset the ellipses on the bottom to create a foot.

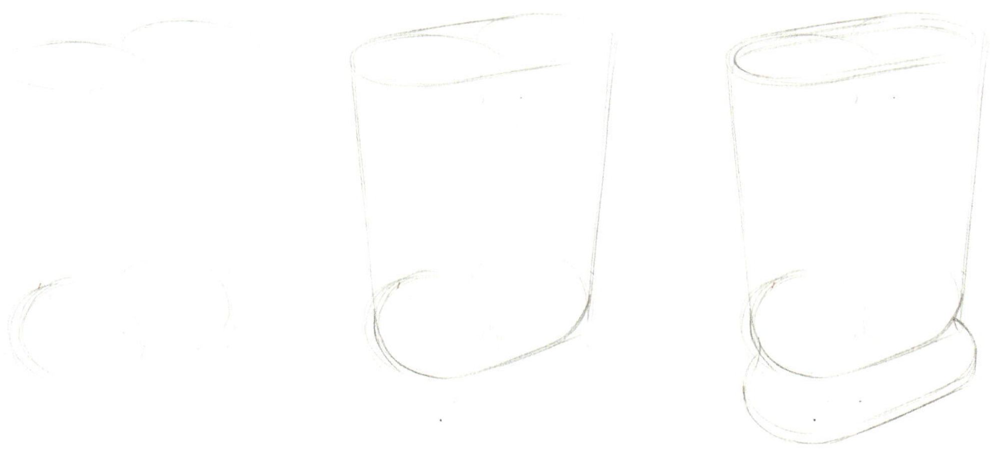

Apply Color

At this point, you have enough light pencil
applied, so you can begin applying some marker.
(Remember to work light until you get it right.)
Rather than working with three distinct values
for this sketch, you'll use a wider range of markers to better show differences in material and
value between the foot of the air purifier and
the upper portion. Because the upper portion
is meant to be white, use a very light marker
here, such as a 10% or 20% gray, and a shorter
stroke because the surface will be perforated
for ventilation. If there is a region that needs
to be excluded from marker shading, like the
power button, outline that area and then shade
around it. Creating an outline makes it easier to
fill in the marker and have a cleaner application
in your sketch.

Continue shading in the base of the air purifier
using longer marker strokes that are consistent
with the surface shape and topography for the
base. Continue shading and fill in the regions
to communicate the different parts of the air
purifier.

Wait, then Continue

Give your marker ink time to dry, then deepen
values in your shaded areas by going over each
again; use the same marker (or markers) as for
the first layer. Notice that the base of my air
purifier now has more distinct shadows, while
its top has a bit more contrast compared to the
rest of the unit. This is a result of applying the
same marker after the marker ink has dried, as
well as using a darker marker in a few specific
areas.

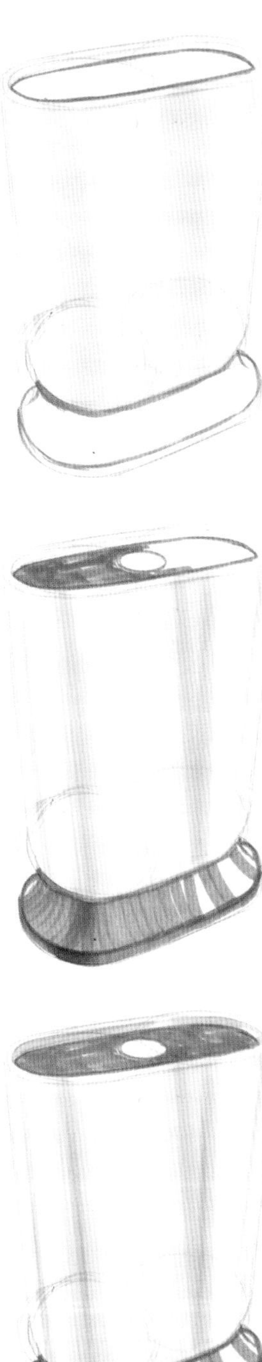

Adjust Line Weight

Once you're satisfied with the marker shading, use confident pencil strokes or, with the aid of a ruler, sharpen up
and pop your sketch with heavier line weight by applying
heavier pressure to your pencils.

Create Texture with Marker

To begin creating a texture on the top of the purifier,
apply a series of short marker strokes in a consistent
pattern across the top. If you are creating a pattern like
the example's, pay attention to the number of strokes
you use across a given dimension so that the pattern
may appear consistent when complete. Finish up the pattern by filling in the area and
addressing any other details that need to be added.

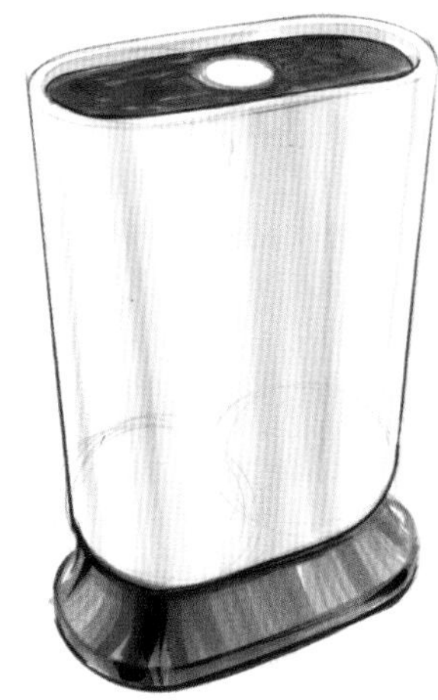

For example, you could use a white opaque marker pen to add a single point of light
on each of the vent holes. Similar to the pencil, an opaque marker pen can create contrast with the dark areas of the perforations in the top. This further strengthens the
appearance of three-dimensionality in the sketch and is a great way to show that the
pattern on top is three-dimensional.

To further ground the sketch on the page, shade in a shadow and continue to enhance
line weights around the perimeter of the purifier.

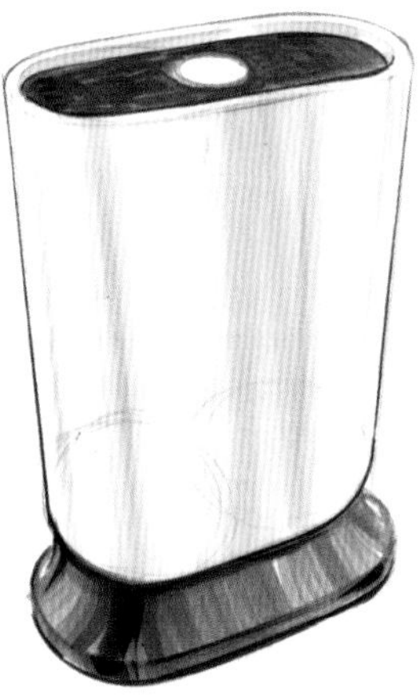
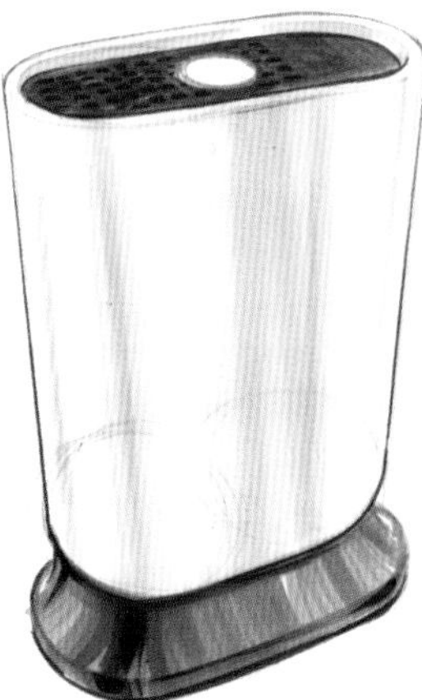
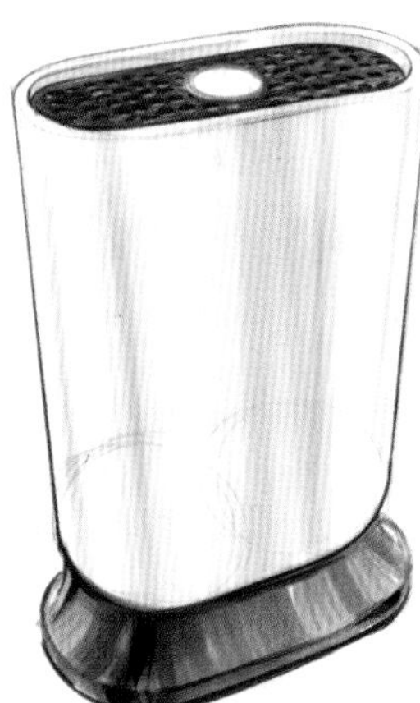

Create Texture with Shading

To add a bit more texture to the outside of the purifier, place a piece of material with a consistent, repeatable texture under your paper (see why you needed thin paper?), angle your pencil to the side so it lays fairly flat, and shade. If you don't have a fabric swatch, you can simply find something with an appropriate texture in your environment that you could use. If you're unsure of the shading pressure needed to transfer the texture into your sketch, practice on a piece of scrap paper before committing to shading on top of your sketch.

Notice that the shading that I added to my sketch is consistent with the overall shape of the purifier. As you continue shading, try a squint test. Is there enough contrast in the sketch? If not, make some final adjustments.

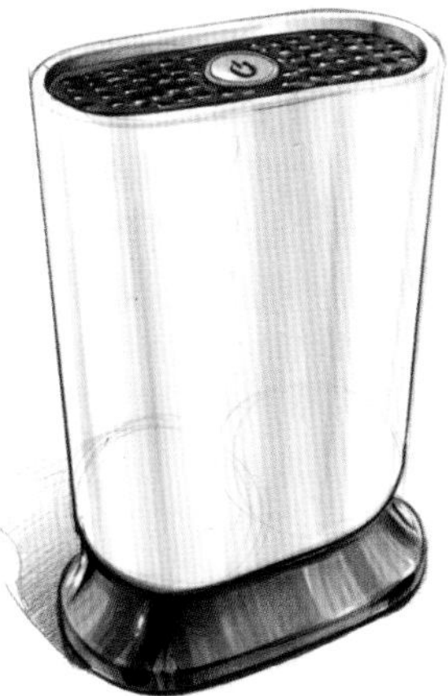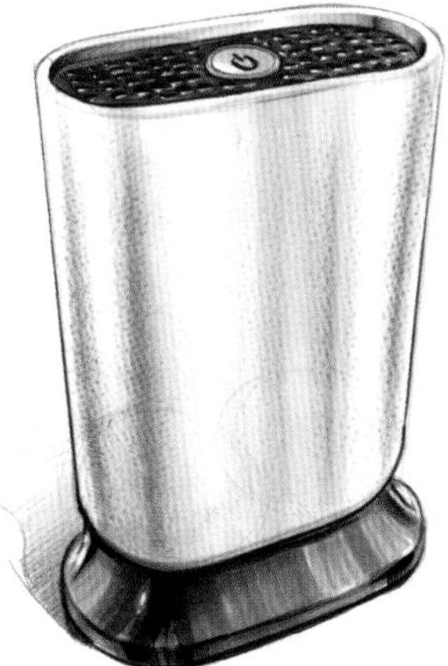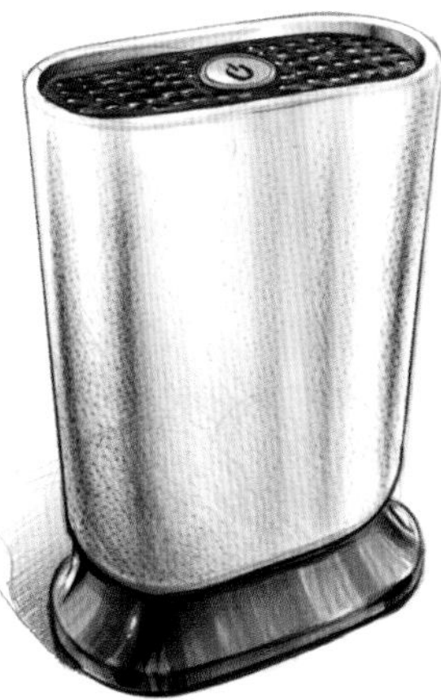

CHALLENGE

Now that you've added a bit of texture through shading, think about other textures that you could add. Sketch some objects, and then get creative with textures that you can transfer into a sketch. Experiment with real objects by placing them under a piece of paper and shading on top of the paper to transfer that texture into your sketch. With enough practice, you'll be well on your way to adding this extra dimension of realism to your sketches.

What's that saying? "Measure twice, cut once," or maybe it's, "make sure you have the right markers before you start sketching." Either way, in this exercise, you'll sketch and color two tape measures. You'll need to grab a few markers, a pen, and some paper (I used marker paper). The colors you select aren't important; just make sure that you have a set of colored markers that are about 20% to 30% different in value and within the same color family. I used alcohol-based markers in a green family and a red family, as well as a set of grays.

Shape the Body

To start, sketch a line on your page at a slight, shallow angle. This line will be the baseline of the side of your first tape measure. I started with the bottom of a side, but you could start with a vertical line or the side's top line. Next, sketch two vertical lines that intersect the baseline, and then complete the side of the tape measure by sketching another line above that tapers slightly toward the left. These two shallow, almost horizontal lines should appear to converge from right to left. This will help communicate perspective in your drawing.

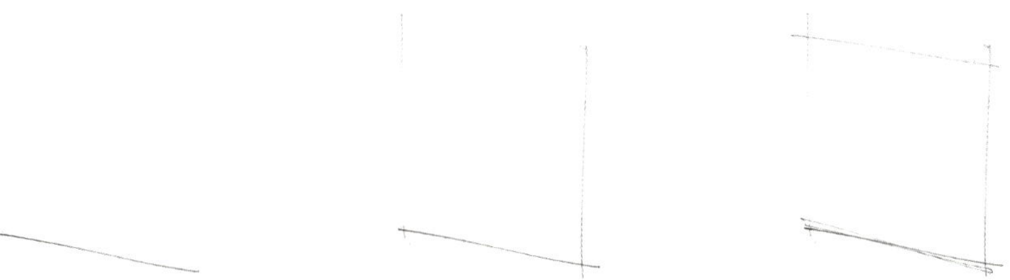

Next, from the top left, top right, and bottom right corners of your side, sketch three short lines that represent the depth of your tape measure. Complete your shape by connecting and completing the far side of this box by sketching in lightly. (Remember, work light until you get it right.) This way, these lines will serve as construction lines for your overall drawing.

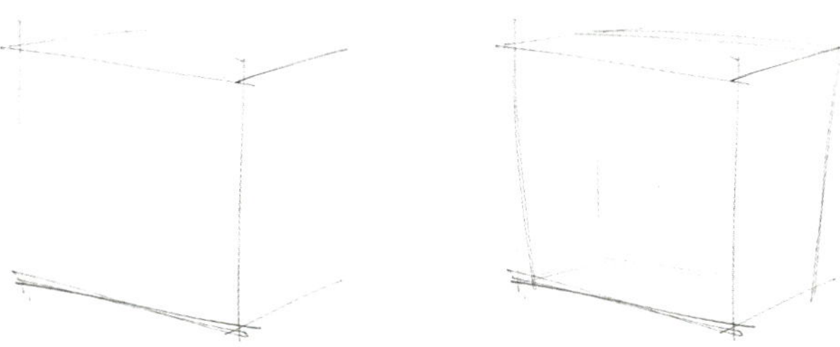

With the overall proportion of your tape measure established, add curved lines to transition from the top of the tape measure down toward the front. These curves are actually a section of an ellipse.

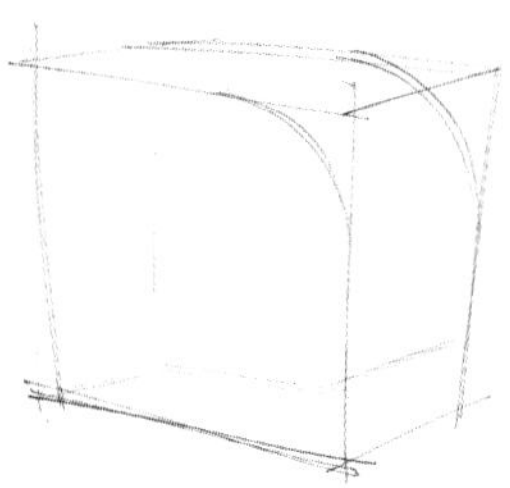

Complete your sketch by sketching in additional lines. These lines can be light and rough but should be sketched fairly quickly to maintain the energy in your drawing. Remember to think about functional parts of your object and think about where you may want certain elements to go. As you compose the tape measure, should you need to outline additional areas, such as the tape itself, feel free to add additional construction geometry by sketching lightly. For example, I added a slot area in the lower front, where the tape will extend and retract.

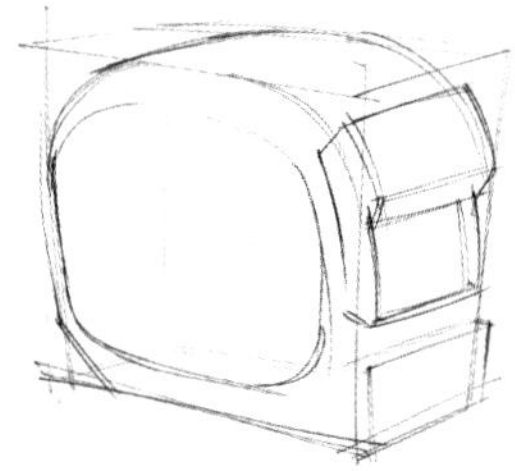

Add Details

Continue to break up your tape measure by adding details such as a locking mechanism and ridges for a grip. You could also add a belt clip or fasteners as needed.

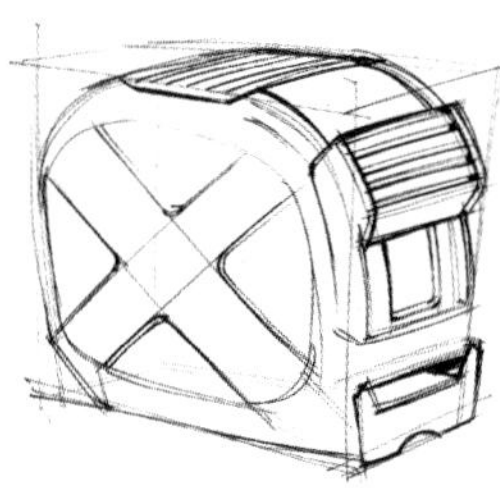

Sketch the Second Tape Measure

Once you have your first tape measure sketched in, sketch another tape measure using the same method. If you're comfortable sketching without construction lines, you can move a bit more quickly, as I did, and simply sketch your object lightly and cleanly in preparation to add color.

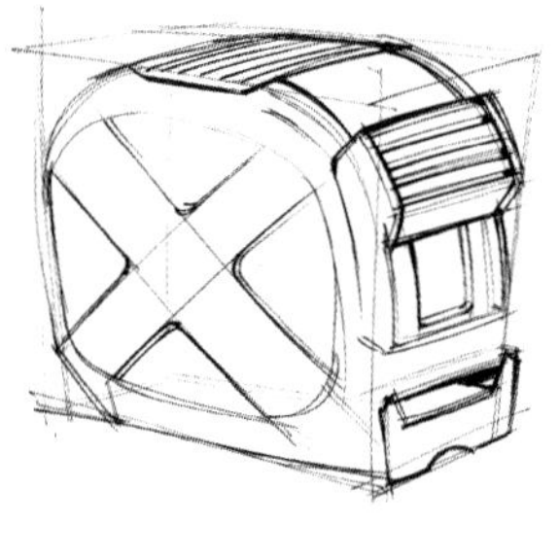

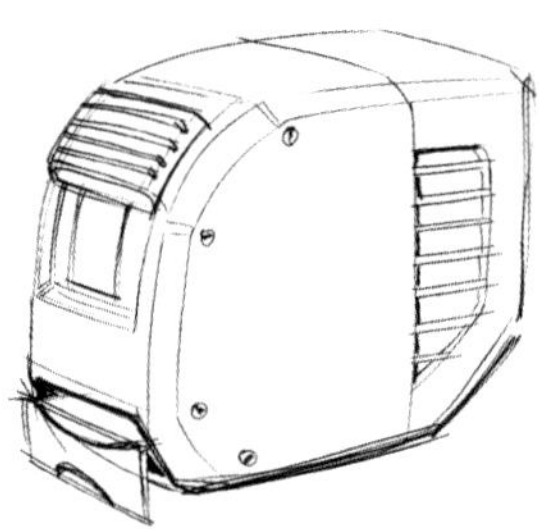

Add Shading and Highlighting with Marker

When coloring with markers, it's important to start with your lightest marker and work your way up to your darkest marker. Begin by coloring in areas that you want to remain lightest, using the lightest marker in each color family. I find it easier first to outline the area I plan to color because it gives me a visual indicator of where to start and stop as I shade. If you're having trouble with shading or drawing with the markers, take a minute to pause and familiarize yourself with how the marker feels as you use it, as well as each end of the marker (if yours has multiple tips).

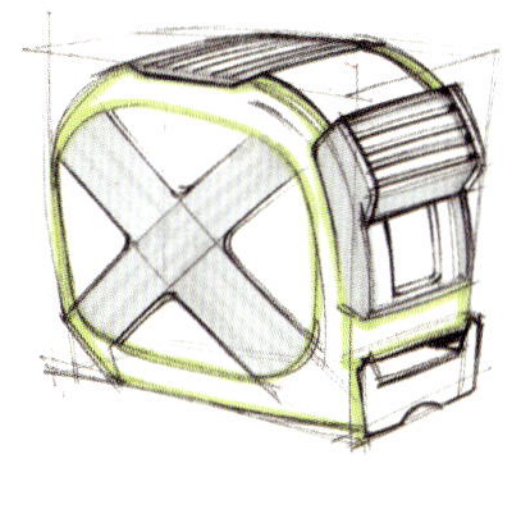

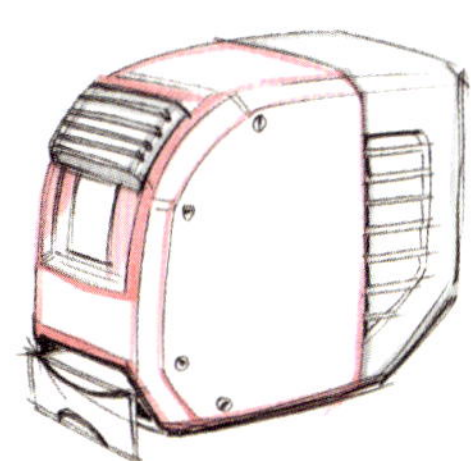

Next, add light shading using your lightest gray marker to those areas that will be gray. I find that a gray color is useful for things like plastic, rubber, or metal. Continue shading in your colors with your lightest marker. When shading with your markers, it's important to consider the lighting of the object you're shading.

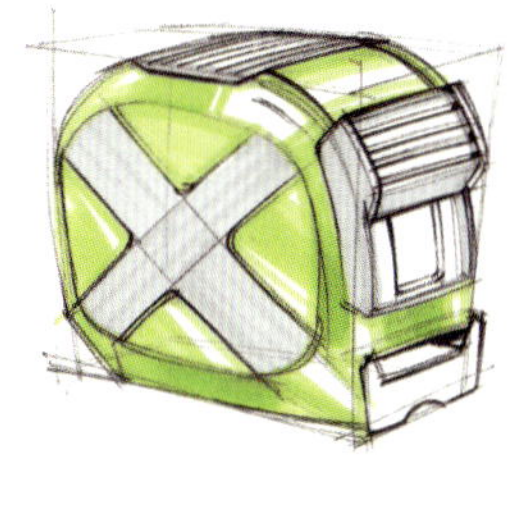

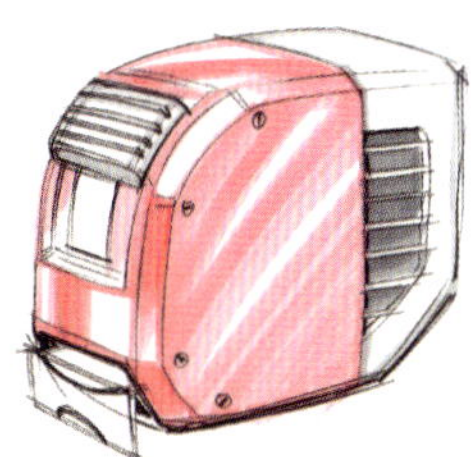

Because these tape measures are typically made from plastic or have shiny finishes, intentionally leave white spots to act as highlights. To figure out where highlights would go on each of your tape measures, think about the overall shape of the object and where a light source may be placed relative to each. Typically, the darker shaded areas will be opposite in relative location to the highlights in your sketch. For example, if there is a highlight to the top right of the tape measure, the bottom left portion of the tape measure would be a bit darker. Of course, there are exceptions to this, but this is a general guideline that I find useful.

Apply Midtones

With the lightest color and lightest gray shaded in, jump to your midtone markers. These will be the middle value in the color set. For grays, this is typically a 50% gray marker. Use your midtones to add contrast where necessary and to enhance the three-dimensionality of the underlying sketch.

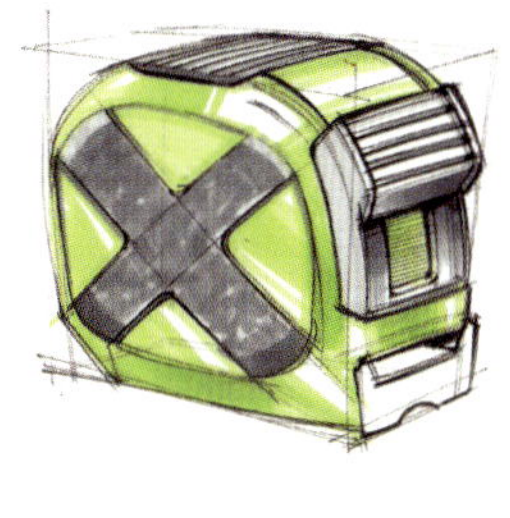

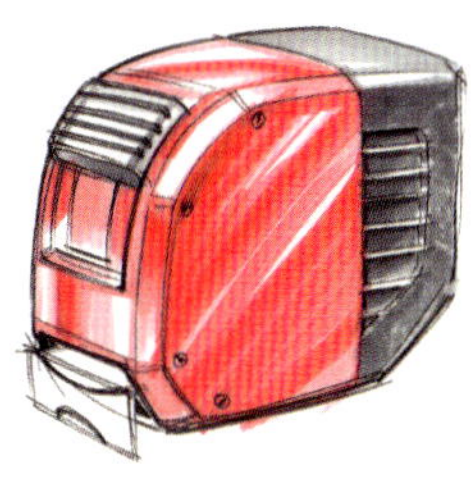

Deepen the Contrast

Step back, take a look at your drawing, and see if there are any additional areas that need more contrast. You can apply the same marker to your sketch a few times, as marker ink is translucent, and multiple applications will help you build up the value and the appearance of the colors on paper. Watch out, however: If you're not using marker paper and you apply the marker several times in the same spot, you may find that your marker ink begins to bleed into sheets of paper under your main drawing.

Use Your Darkest Values

Next, switch to your darkest value gray and color markers. With these markers, you can cautiously add deeper value to the colored areas of the tape measure. For example, on the red tape measure, I added a deeper red right next to the highlight on the beveled edge of the tape to enhance the contrast and help punch up the three-dimensionality. On the green tape measure, I added slight hints of the deepest green in specific areas to indicate a bit of a reflective element in a shiny surface. Finally, I applied the gray marker in a stippled or dappled way to convey a rougher texture or a more matte finish.

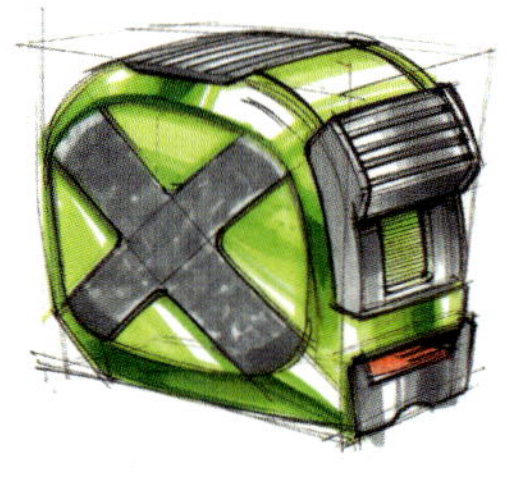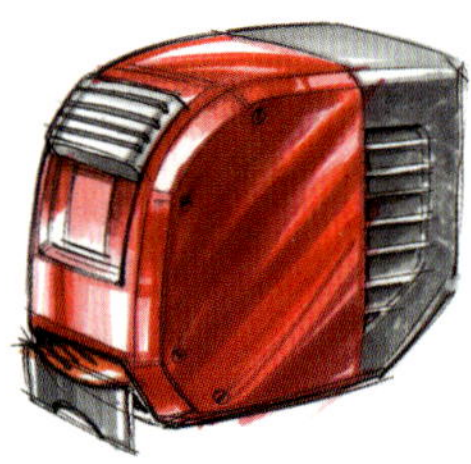

STYLE

Your style is a combination of your choice of tool, gestures, favorite colors and elements, perspective, and preferences. Your mood and demeanor will often transfer into your work. Pay close attention to the attitude of your drawing strokes.

As you work on your style, seek out inspiration from other artists' work. Try not to directly copy someone's work, but rather take time to experiment and understand what it is that makes their work look different from yours.

Refine with Final Touches

At this point, should you need to clarify aspects of your sketch, you can use a pen to clean up areas. Additionally, should you need to deepen a color or gray within the sketch, now is a good opportunity to do so once the marker ink has dried somewhat. Because the light source is coming from the top above each of these concepts, I added a shadow under each tape measure by way of enhanced line weight and a slightly extended shadow. Again, this helps ground the object on the page, gives it a sense of presence, and reinforces the perspective. Additionally, should you need to explain an aspect of your drawing, consider adding notes indicated by an arrow and script text.

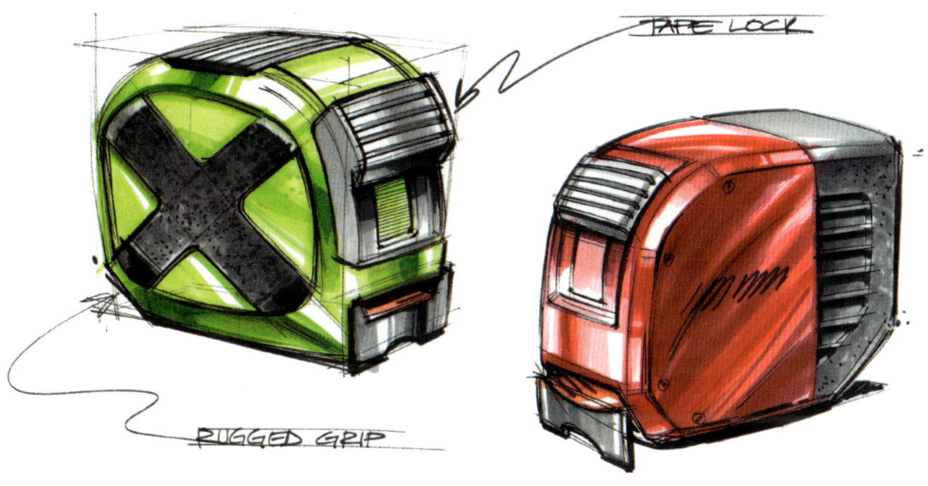

CHALLENGE

Continue sketching similarly simple yet detailed objects using pens and markers. Practice observing the interplay of colors as you apply your marker to paper, as well as understand how you best draw with the markers. Focus on line work and balance cleanliness with expressiveness, experiment with adding annotations or notes to your sketches, and include textures where necessary. As a bonus, try sketching the same object in different points of view but with a single light source. Pay attention to the shading of each object and its placement on your page. Remember, measure twice, draw once.

 # LEATHER SOFA

To sketch a leather sofa and mimic its texture, you'll use the "when in doubt, rough it out" technique, first discussed in Chapter 4. You'll also use one-point perspective for your sketch (see the sidebar "Perspective Points" in Chapter 2 for a refresher). Creating a rough sketch is a great way of reducing stress and tension when you're a bit unsure of what you want to draw or how you want to draw it.

Create and Refine the Rough Sketch

By now, you've had plenty of practice lightly drawing perspective and construction lines, as well as using them as guides to sketch an object. So, I'm not going to walk you through the initial steps this time. Use my example as a guide to roughly sketch your sofa, and then create an overlay, re-sketching to refine the roughness.

As you can see, a rough sketch should be very loose but also show hints and indications of the intent behind the way you're going to draw the object. Notice that although the second sketch (my overlay) is true to the rough sketch in terms of composition and placement, the back of the sofa now has a slight curve to it, and the cushions are refined. I also took some liberties with the frame of the sofa, as should you if you so desire. Your overlay is a chance to correct errors or tweak the drawing for your final linework.

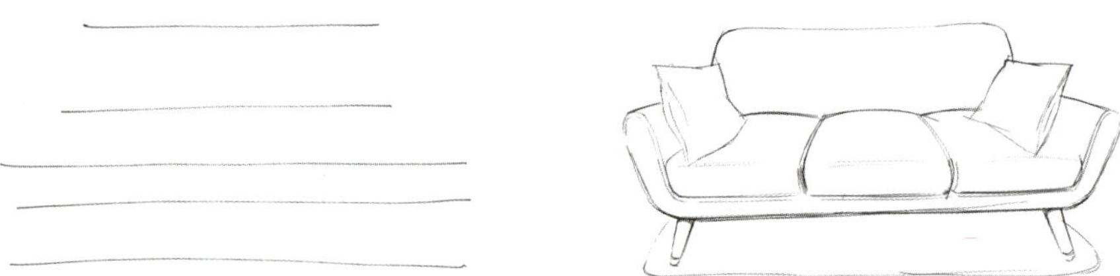

Select and Test Markers

To start coloring the sofa, select three markers from the same color family that vary 20% to 30% in value. This will ensure that you have enough contrast to work with while staying in the same family. If you are unsure of what color to pick, checking out your marker manufacturer's guidelines or color guide is a good place to start. More importantly, test your markers on scrap paper to make sure that you have the right spread of color family and that your markers are fresh.

Shade the Sofa

Ready? Outline the sofa with your lightest marker, then loosely and roughly shade it in. Because this sofa is upholstered with leather, scrub your marker by moving back and forth in a randomized motion against the paper to create a loose texture. Shading in this way creates a more natural and textured feel as opposed to shading by making parallel lines with the tip of your marker. Wait just a second to let the marker ink dry, then reapply it to deepen the value in a few key areas.

Add Midtones and Textures

With the sofa mostly filled in, jump to your midtone brown marker. Using a scrubbing motion, shade the gaps between the cushions as well as a small shadow behind the pillows. Continue to scrub with this marker to shade the front of the cushions and to begin texturing the seat cushions. It's important to use the same shading technique so that the texture builds on itself rather than contradicts or interferes with earlier layers. Continue filling in with the midtone marker (after a quick drying break) to enhance the texture, as well as concentrate around the shadow cores at the top of the couch and edges of the cushions.

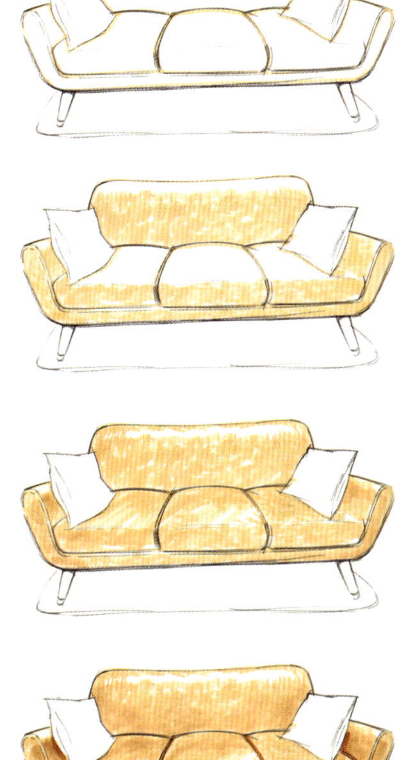

Emphasize Shadows with the Darkest Marker

Now switch to your darkest brown marker to emphasize shadows and pop the shadow cores a bit on the sofa. Again, move the tip of the marker in a somewhat randomized fashion to create a general texture. If you want to get creative with your material presentation, you may also include pencil or paint to show wear on the couch, a specular highlight, or simply opaque variations in the color of the material. Remember, however, don't switch to pencil until you're done with the markers.

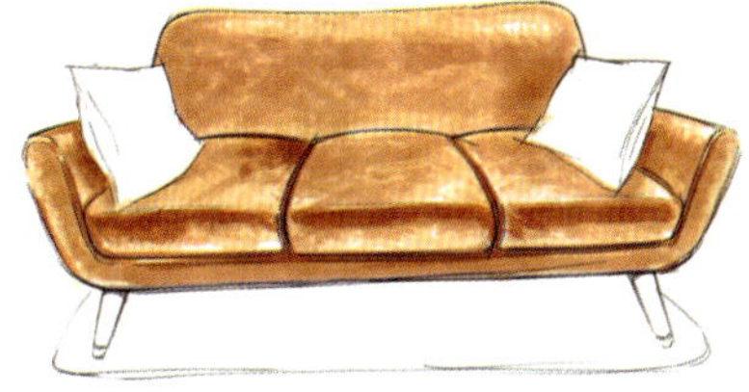

Shade the Cushions

Shade in your cushions with an accent color. I chose a very light blue to complement the more reddish-orange tones of the brown. As you shade the pillows, try to shade in a way that suggests the undulating surface of the soft pillow covers. As you can see, I used a 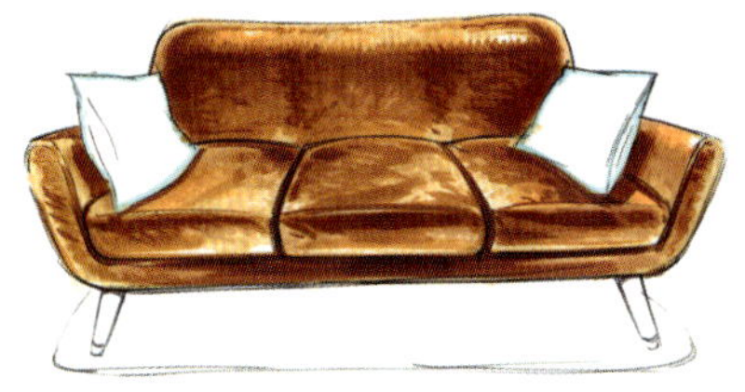 series of patterned lines to convey fabric on these pillow covers. To finish up, use a slightly darker blue marker to enhance the pillows' texture. Additionally, you can add a few highlights to the sofa with a white pencil and a few wrinkles with a black pencil. Adding pencil at the end of your marker coloring can be a nice touch to help highlights pop or for you to bring out other details that may have been missed.

Add a Bit of Chrome

Shade in the legs of the sofa to make it look like chrome, and then finish off the sofa by shading in the shadow as well. Give yourself a high five, a hug, and a handshake. You did it!

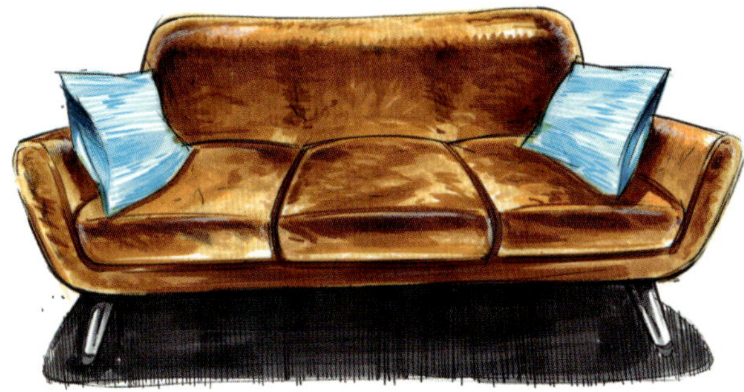

CHALLENGE

Try to draw some furniture of your own that, while simple, includes some interesting materials like wood, leather, chrome, and so on. Remember to warm up and practice before jumping right into the sketch. Get creative and see what interesting material and color combinations you can come up with. As you're coloring, if you're unsure of how bold of a color to use, do a squint check to remove some of the business and detail in your field of view so you can better focus on the contrast in your sketch.

Unlike the leather sofa you just finished, this exercise focuses on shiny manmade materials. Specifically, you'll draw a bicycle helmet and mimic its semi-reflective plastic texture. Shiny materials will be more reflective and present challenges such as leaving a bit of white space as you sketch to create highlights or using contrast to show reflections of objects in the virtual environment around the helmet.Continue to be mindful of reflections and lighting as you shade. Practicing reflections by observing what happens with real objects and then sketching what you see will help you make the necessary connections to draw shinier things. This helmet is a good practice in abstracting those real reflections in a way that is simplified for sketching.

Sketch the Initial Shape

Draw a simple egg shape, sort of an elongated sphere or an oval. Now you have a sense of the helmet's place on the paper. You can play with the composition of your sketch by creating thumbnails, or simply dive right in.

Next, sketch panels on the sides, elongate the front to look more helmet-like, and add straps. I also added a few lines to further define the shape of my helmet.

Continue to break up the overall shape by adding details, such as a vent cutouts as well as surface transitions. You can create surface transitions by simply offsetting shapes that you initially sketched. As you can see in the example, the size differences in the shapes help create the illusion of depth. Feel free to explore in thumbnail form or on a rough piece of paper if you're unsure where to place your cutouts on the helmet.

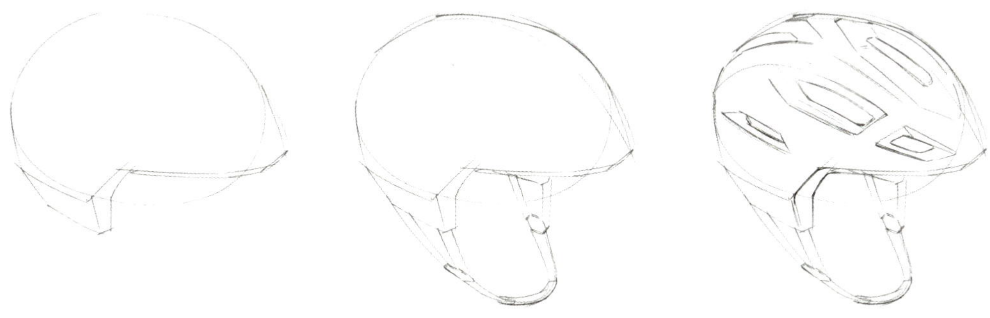

Add Values with Marker

With your rough helmet lines and details in place, you can start adding some value with marker shading. Remember to start with your lights and work up to your darker colors, so mistakes will be easier to handle if you happen to make them. I started with a Copic Cool Gray No. 3 marker.

Enhance the contrast by moving to a darker tone. Apply the darker shading in areas where the facets or surfaces on the helmet are turned away from the light source. Even if you haven't decided if the light source is to the left or the right, you can still apply some darker marker to show that there is a change in the direction of the surface. The most important thing is to make sure that there is enough contrast between the values so that the shading complements and enhances the perspective in your sketch. (Squint check if you need to!)

Continue to darken and add deeper value to the gray areas of your helmet. If you are using color, you can also darken and deepen the color of the spot. Now that you have your gray values in place, try out some colors on a test piece of paper. When drawing with markers, I quite often take a minute to test my colors just to make sure that they are representing my design intention as I sketch. You should have an assortment of two to five markers in the same color family with varying values. I typically sketch with three markers in the same color family.

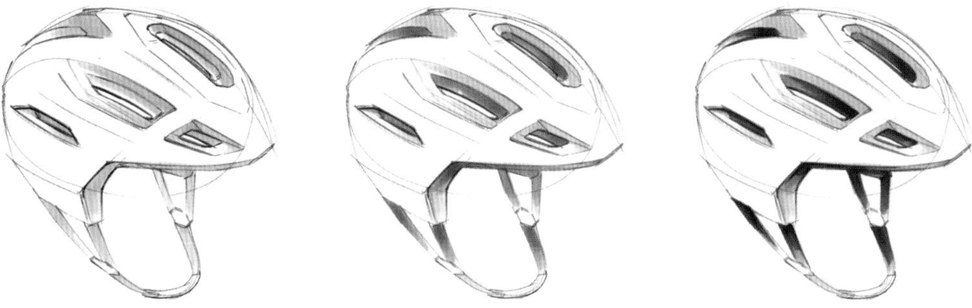

Apply Color

After you decide on colors, start with the lightest color and value so you can more easily handle mistakes and have a loose exploration as you sketch. Once the light marker strokes are down, you can move on to your midtones.

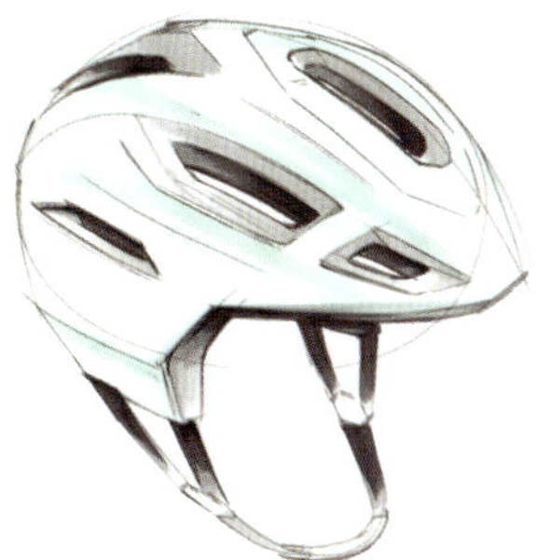 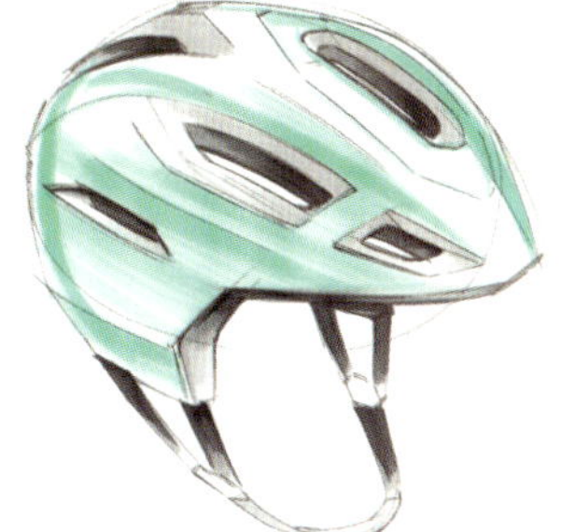 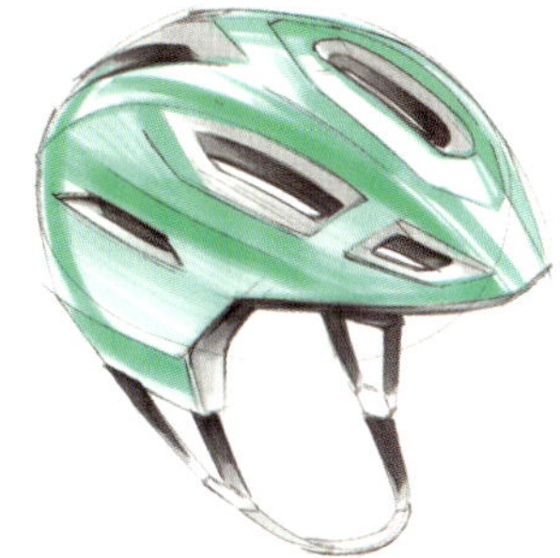

Use your midtone marker to further deepen and enhance the saturation and value along key areas of the helmet. If you think of the helmet like a sphere or an egg, you can observe how a ball or an egg reacts to light. Drawing by observing is a great way to understand how things work and focus on those differences.

Continue to darken and deepen surfaces that are key to communicating the form. Typically, on a shape like this, I have a shadow core as well as a highlight that are my areas of focus. Deepening the shadow core will help you add depth to your drawing.

Refine the Shading and Line Weights

Even when working with color, I like to go back and forth between my grays, pen lines, or other elements in the sketch. At this step, work to deepen the value as needed. For example, I chose to darken regions within the helmet cutouts to further help the design and sketch pop. Line weights are a great way of separating your object from the background if you're doing more traditional design sketching. Having this outline helps establish presence, helps the viewer focus on your drawing, and cleans up your drawing by taking care of those stroke ends that are just dangling.

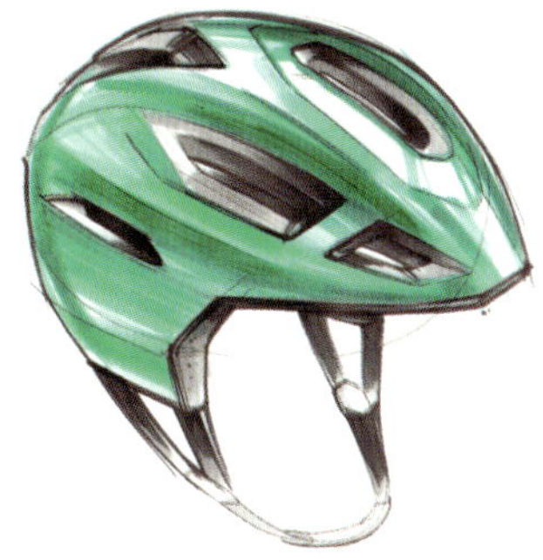 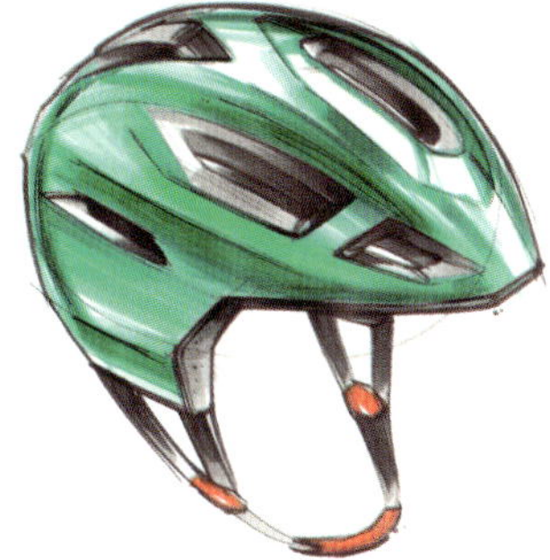

At this final stage, I added some color as well as continued to refine my line work and elements of the sketch. Remember, constantly monitor your contrast to make sure that you're not drawing things that blend seamlessly into the environment but rather are supported by an environment.

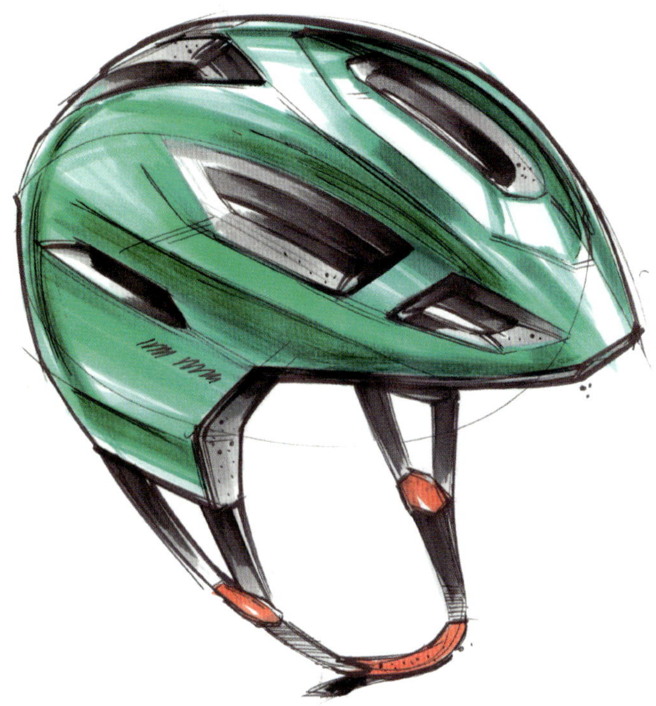

CHALLENGE

Sketch your own helmets or other shiny plastic shapes. If you need to, find a reference and study the reflections you see. Sketch observationally first, then take some time to sketch from your imagination. What other shiny plastic objects can you think of to sketch? Remember to work light until you get it right and use contrast to show reflectivity where needed. Quantity is always great, but for quality, focus on using your markers to accurately capture the material qualities of the plastic.

 # HIGH-HEEL SHOE

With all its styles, shapes, and sizes, footwear can be fun to draw and an interesting challenge. For this exercise, you'll draw a shiny leather, high-heel shoe, focusing on its material finish. I used a Paper Mate Flair pen, but any pen that will hold up to markers will do. If you want to work on your speed and expressiveness, I caution you against getting too comfortable with pencils. Sometimes pencils can be a little too forgiving; a pen doesn't forgive and doesn't forget—but does challenge you. For the shoe's color, I used alcohol-based Copic markers. When choosing your color family, remember you need three or four makers that are each 20% to 30% darker than the previous tone.

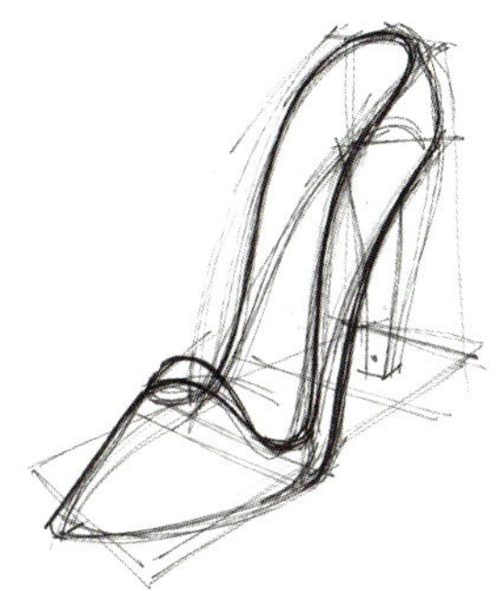

Create a Thumbnail Sketch

To start, thumbnail or rough out a sketch of a high heel in whatever perspective you choose. Remember, when in doubt, rough it out. As you can see from my unedited attempt, a rough sketch helps you think through some of the details of the object prior to creating a final version of the sketch.

Analyze and Tweak the Perspective

To start your final sketch, analyze your rough version and decide on the perspective you'd like to draw the shoe in. Now's a good opportunity to make any tweaks that you need to your primary view of the shoe. Orient your paper vertically so you can take advantage of its height, and sketch in a base plane for your shoe. Next, divide this plane into three parts to help you locate the forefoot area and heel of the shoe while you sketch in perspective.

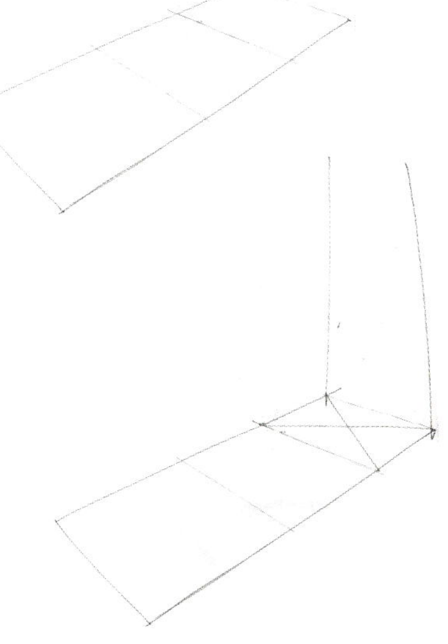

Construct the Basic Shape

Draw two diagonal lines from corner to corner in the rightmost section of the base (the heel area). From each of the rear corners of this rectangle, extend two lines upward to roughly the height of the shoe you plan to sketch. Notice in the example that I have sketched these lines with a slight curve. This allows some flexibility but also is a nod to the shoe itself which is composed largely of curves rather than straight lines.

Divide the base rectangle in half lengthwise and add tick marks along the base edges to indicate where the forefoot of the shoe will contact the ground. Add tick marks at the tops of your vertical lines to indicate where the top of the heel will be located.

Create the Geometry

Time to connect the ticks and build the shoe: From the left tip of the base's center line (the shoe's toe), scribe an arc to each of the tick marks on the base rectangle to shape the forefoot. From the same ticks, scribe two arcs up to the heel's corresponding vertical tick marks. Connect these upper tick marks with a straight line at the back of the shoe. You should begin to see the high heel take shape with these simple curves.

Next, scribe an arc to represent a cross section along the forefoot of the shoe. The design or your shoe determines the height of this arc. Offset the curves you initially sketched from the base to the back of the shoe to create the side walls of the shoe's toe box. These curves are placeholders and will guide you in your process of sketching the rest of the high heel. Next, create transitional lines and arcs between the cross section toward the toe and the new offset lines that represent the side walls of the shoe.

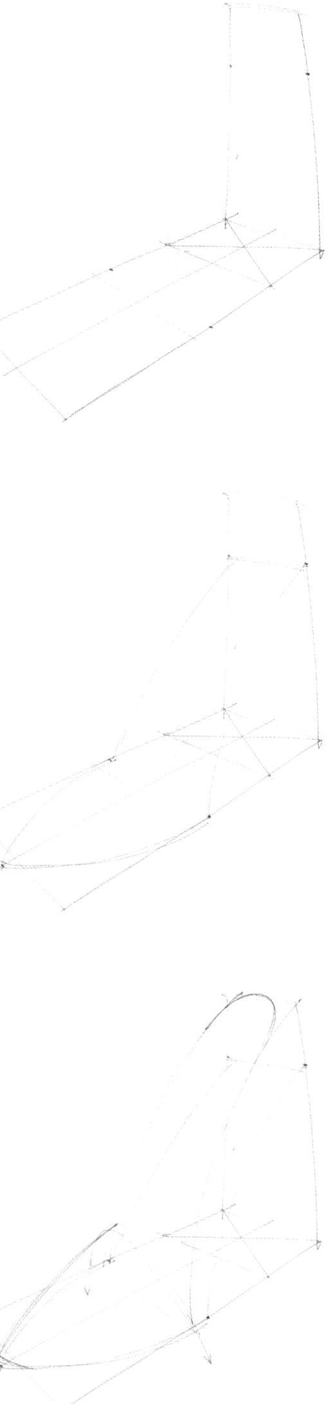

Refine the Shape

During this phase, I like to keep things loose as oftentimes I'm actively deciding on details of the shoe that I may want to tweak along the way. Next, roughly sketch in a heel by scribing curves toward the center of the rear rectangle of the base plane. As you can see in the example, these three lines travel downward to this central point to form the base for the heel of the shoe.

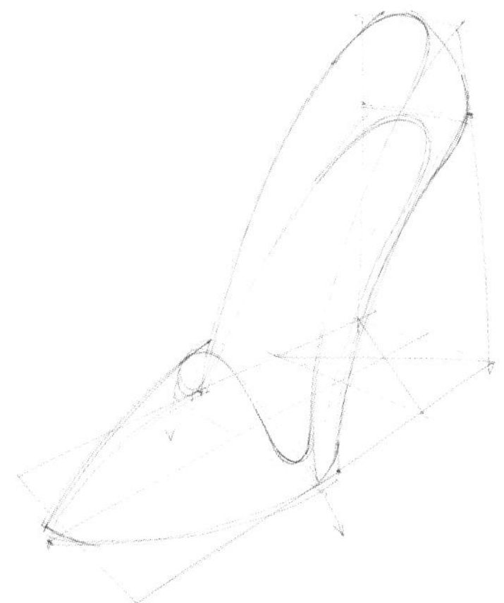

Enhance Line Weight

Add line weight to the outline and side walls of the shoe. This should help define the shape of the forefoot as well as the general silhouette of the shoe. You may notice at this point that the forefoot of the shoe seems a little tight or potentially uncomfortable—mine did. To address this, I essentially cut into the geometry that I already sketched. Here you can see the original curve as well as a new curve defining the opening for the forefoot of my shoe.

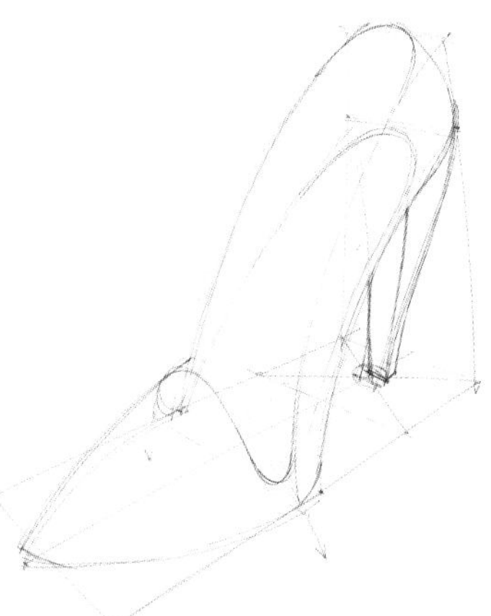

Create an Overlay

Grab a piece of translucent paper and create an overlay to eliminate your construction geometry and rough sketch lines and provide a fresh, clean, energetic, and loose sketch to receive your marker work. I took some liberties in the expressiveness of the shoes while re-sketching. This is totally fine and one of the tricks that many artists use when drawing. Think of rules as guidelines; as you gain more experience, you'll be able to take some creative liberties as well.

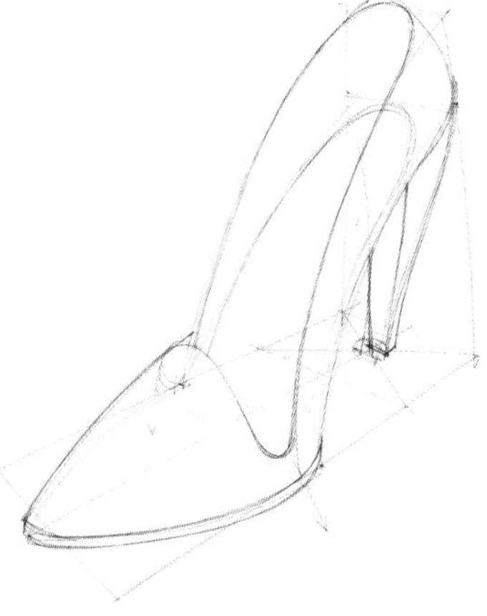

Add Color

Start by outlining the upper of the high-heel shoe with your lightest marker of your preferred color (red for me). Additionally, add marker strokes where there may be reflections on the shiny shoe finish.

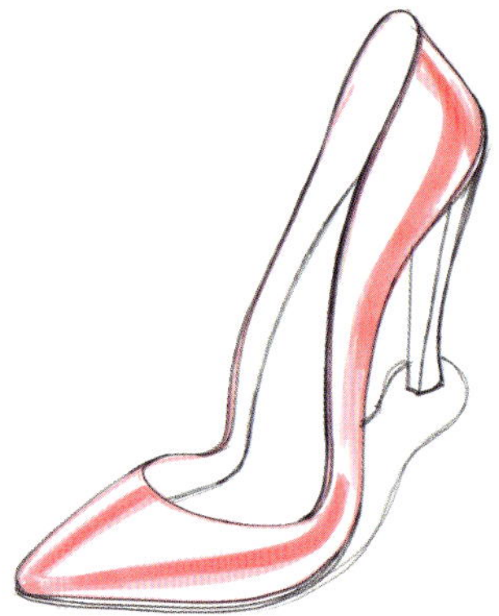

Continue by using the light marker to fill in the upper of the shoe, leaving a white area untouched at the forefront of the shoe as a highlight. As you can see, my marker strokes are fairly expressive here. By leaving the white region showing, I created a sense of reflectivity. (Practice this on scrap paper first, if necessary.)

Add Midtone and Dark Values

With your midtone marker, deepen the value of shadow cores along the reflective portion of the shoe on the outside. If you need to, take an observation break: Find something shiny in your environment and rotate the object relative to your point of view. What do you notice about the reflections? How do they change and move over the surface of the object? Continue deepening these values on the shoe's shadow core by allowing the ink to dry and reapplying your midtone marker.

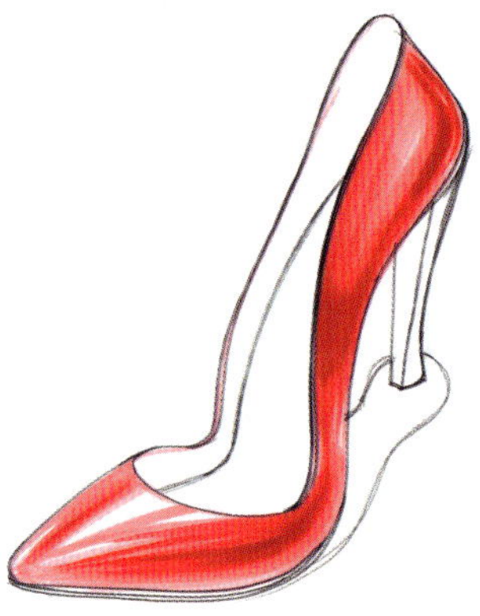

With your darkest marker, color over the red that you've already applied, focusing on the shadow core of the upper portion of the shoe. As you imagine the cross section of this upper portion of the shoe and its roundness, you should have a good sense of where to place the darkest values. One way to think of it is slightly inset from the outer perimeter of this upper, allowing a blended transition to the perimeter of the silhouette of the upper.

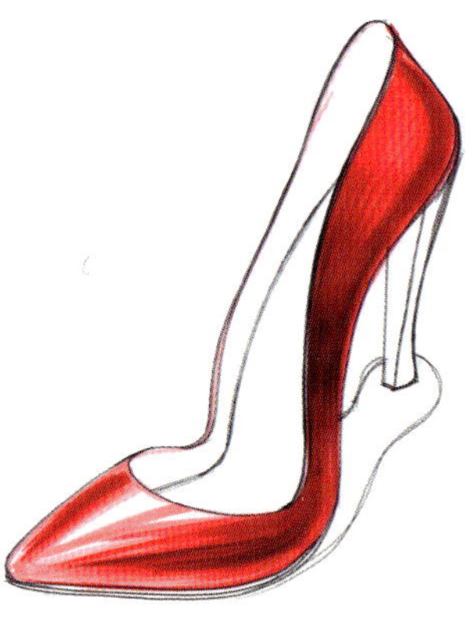

Shade the Inside

For the inside of the shoe, I selected a tan marker color to shade. Shade in the shoe's lining using evenly spaced strokes to create a consistent look and feel. Shade the heel with a gray marker (outside) and a tan marker (inside). Additionally, you can use pen to scribble in a shadow that the shoe is casting on the ground, then shade it with gray.

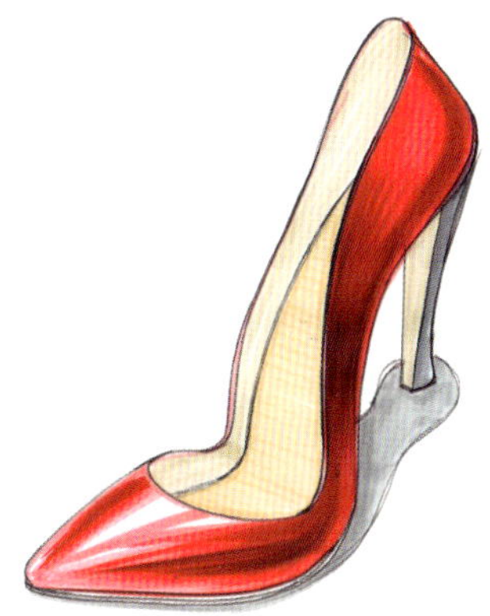

Finalize the Shading

Deepen the value of the shoe's lining with a darker tan marker, let the ink dry, then re-apply the color again to deepen the value of the tan lining. Applying additional gray marker to the heel also helps with the overall contrast. To finish up, make the outline of the shoe slightly thicker by using a different pen or thickening the outline by repeatedly drawing over the same line. Now the shoe pops a bit more off the page.

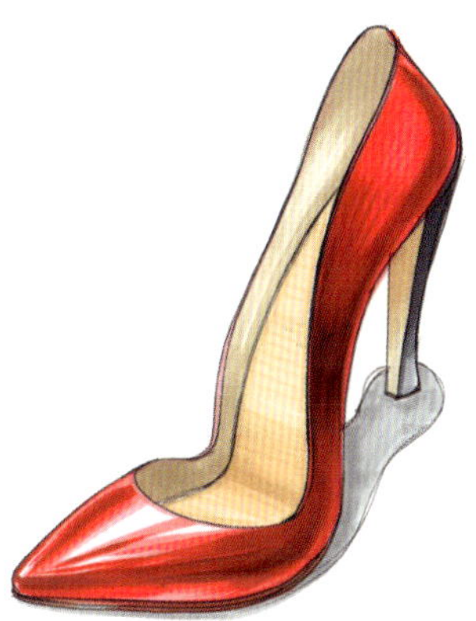

Add Highlights with White Pen

To help with the reflectiveness of the red material, use an opaque white pen to pump up the highlights at the front of the shoe. If you're having trouble thinking of how to draw your highlights, try the thought process I followed: Imagine what lights might be in the scene. Are they artificial or from a window? Now imagine those light sources wrapped onto the surface of the shoe and somewhat abstracted.

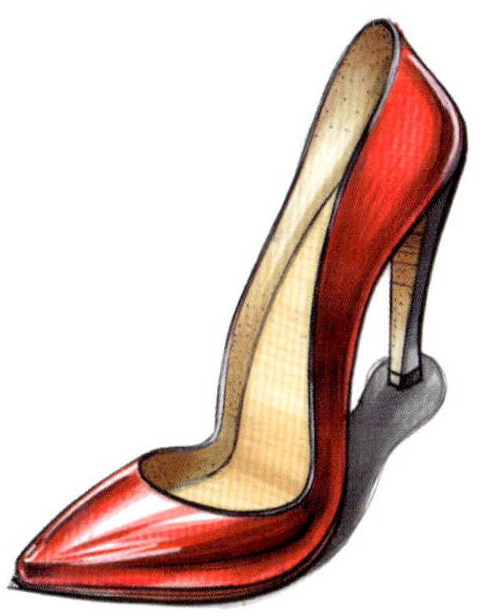

Using your pen, stipple the shoe's lining to create a bit of a texture on top of the color. Similarly, you can add details to the heel, such as a heel cap, as well as to thicken the sole of the shoe and add a shadow between the heel and the sole of the shoe. Finally, I added a touch of white marker to the thickened lip of the upper of the shoe. This thin white region helps contrast against the saturated red sides of the shoe to make even that thin region appear three-dimensional. Done—give yourself a high five!

CHALLENGE

Sketch more shoes—any design but those shown in this book. Think about the underlying geometry and identify proportional breaks to sketch the shoes. Use markers to add color and emphasize material breakups on your shoe concepts. This is a good opportunity to practice expressing different types of materials by combining your pen strokes with marker colors. Marker paper would be a good investment for this challenge and help prevent ink from bleed through to the underlying papers in your sketch deck or onto your work surface.

DRAWING SPEED

The faster you draw, the less likely it is that you will make mistakes as you work. Try to find the right balance between speed and accuracy for yourself as you sketch. To improve your sketching speed, warm up and practice the basic elements of drawing, like lines, circles, ellipses, and curves. (The Introduction offers some sample warmups to try.)

At times, you may want to slow down to create an intentionally wavy or more expressive line. This is fine; however, be sure to be proactive and test your stroke before jumping right into your drawing. If you're unsure of what to do, relax and try holding your pen or pencil a bit higher on the barrel or body.

Continuing with the theme of fashion, let's sketch a handbag. By this point in the book, you should be comfortable with the construction phase, so I will simply give a quick overview of that, then go into more detail on replicating the materials of the handbag: faux alligator skin, fabric, brass, and wood.

Create a Rough Sketch and Overlay

To construct the handbag, create a rough sketch in perspective of the body of the bag. Start with two pairs of vertical, diagonal lines that taper toward a common point in the distance. Don't make them ruler straight; think of a handbag's slight slouch. Connect these lines into a rough trapezoidal box, and then sketch in handle straps, feet, top zipper, and any other details you think a high-end handbag needs (check out some fashion photos if you need inspiration).

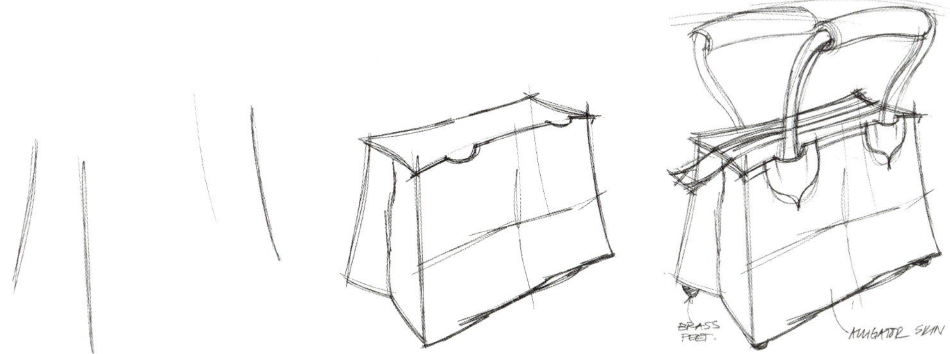

Create an overlay, re-sketching your idea while giving the new sketch a life and energy of its own.

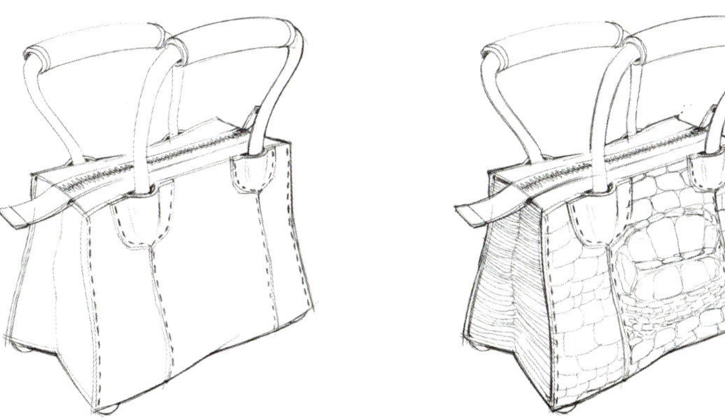

Apply Texture

To prepare for the texture, divide the outside of the bag into panels. These panels are design features that are layered onto the bag to create a premium feel. For the final step in the line work, sketch in two textures: faux alligator and woven fabric.

To apply the alligator-like texture to the front of the bag, sketch small cells as shown in the example (yes, I needed some visual inspiration and looked up photos online for this).

The side panels are meant to be stretchy, woven fabric that allows the bag to expand slightly, as indicated by the crease in the side of the bag. Roughly sketch some horizontal lines radiating from the center crease to simulate fabric grain.

Color the Bag

With the sketch done, take a minute to think about what colors you want to apply to your bag. Perhaps it's a favorite color or perhaps you can draw inspiration from your immediate environment. I chose an olive-green color scheme for the majority of the bag, tan for the wooden handles and the side panels, and red for the top of the bag and zipper. To add brass accents, I grabbed a couple yellow and brown markers.

Start by shading in the leather portion of the bag with the lightest tone in that color family, then do the same for the other elements to help you quickly color in the next step. In my sketch, I used a light olive green for the handles, a light tan for the wood accents, brown for the side panels, and for the top of the bag, a pink.

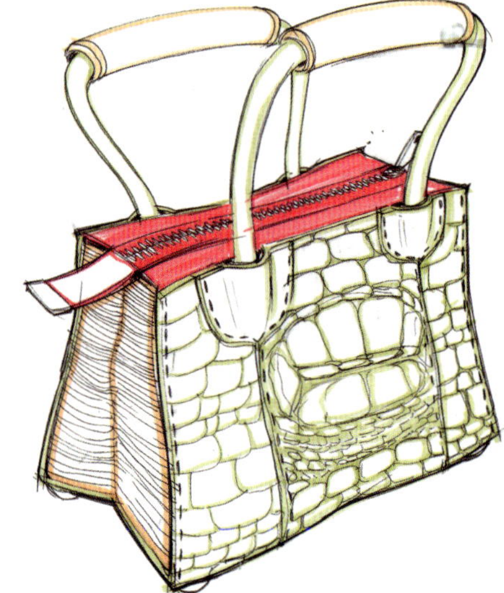

Using the same light markers, fill in the regions for your materials. Be sure to leave white spots for highlights where applicable, such as the intentional white spots I left on the bag's leather material. These will come in handy later to help with contrast and showing three-dimensionality.

With your midtone markers, shade the straps as well as the leather body of the bag. To create three-dimensionality in the side panel, I applied the darker green to the edges of the leather panels; I also used this darker green to shade in the straps of the bag. Remember to work light to dark as well as to place dark values next to lighter values. This juxtaposition will create a three-dimensional appearance for your subject matter.

Apply the Final Touches

Continue deepening the value of your colors and use your midtone markers to create a textural relief as you sketch. Color in the shadow cores on the handles of the bag, and also add shadows, such as under the zipper tab or toward the bottom of the bag. On the top of the bag (the red section for me), shade over the initial light tones with your midtone marker to create some variation in the appearance and indicate this part of the bag is soft and flexible. I also shaded the bottom of the bag with a light tone to create a different effect.

To finish up the sketch, refine the outline of the bag overall and especially thicken the outline toward the bottom of the bag—a quick way to help ground the sketch on the page without having to shade in an actual shadow. If you feel adventurous, however, you could add a shadow here or perhaps a background element to give your handbag some context.

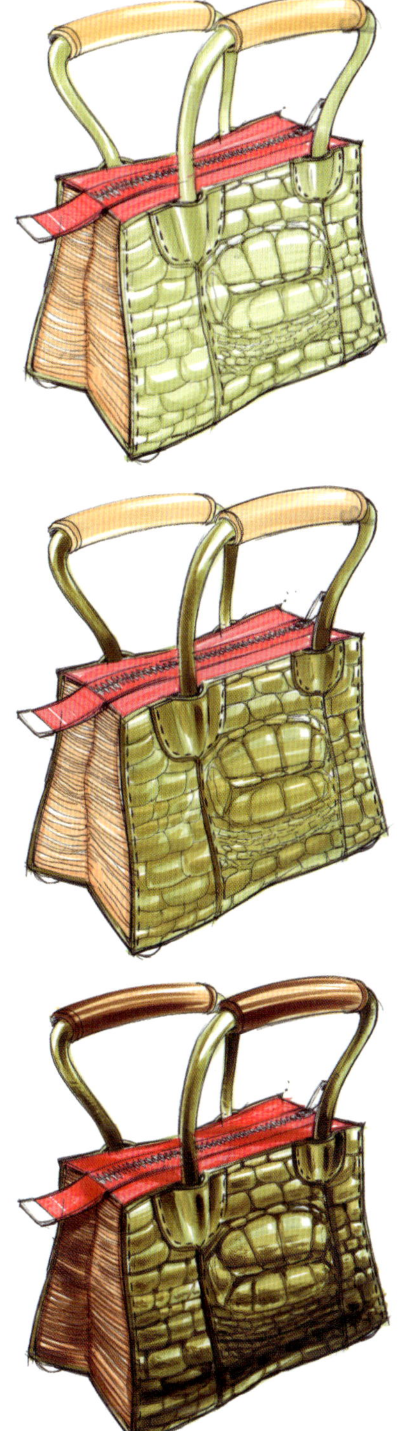

Finally, shade the brass tab on the zipper and the bag's feet with mustard yellows, then a deeper yellow to give them a brass metal look and feel. To help the cells on the leather panel pop, I also used white pencil and white pen to create small highlights where I sketched in these textural elements. Notice that the contrast between these intense white spots and the rest of the panel help the leather bag feel a bit shinier.

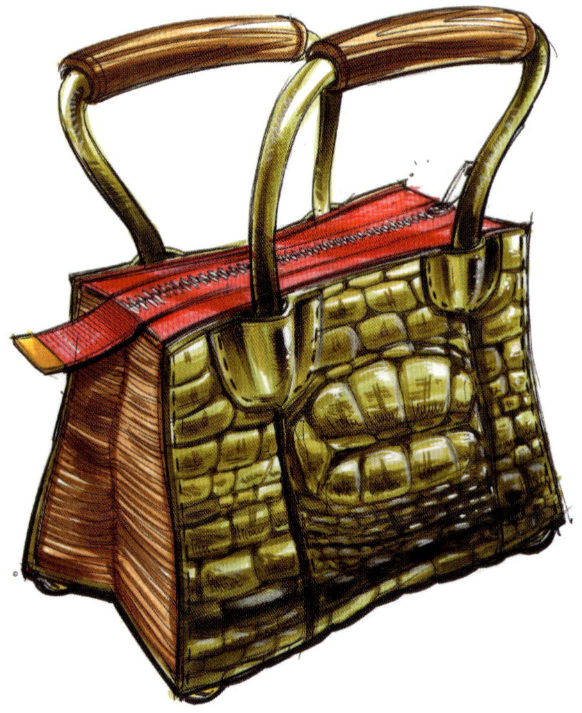

CHALLENGE

Sketch a few accessories, such as this handbag, and play with their materials. Experiment with your materials, focusing on both sketching the coloring them. If you use reference imagery, try to mimic the materials you see as closely as possible. When you're ready to get creative, venture out on your own and come up with unique ideas to sketch. Remember, when in doubt, rough it out!

WEEK 50 STILL LIFE

Can you believe it? You've made it to Week 50 and almost completed a full year of sketching. Great work. To keep your progress going, in this exercise you'll create a still life. Still life drawing is a great way to focus on observational drawing skills while honing a host of fundamentals. In one drawing, you can practice perspective, placement of the objects within your view, proportion, color, texture, reflections, lighting, and more. In this exercise, you'll use pens (I used my trusty Paper Mate Flair and a Micron) to sketch a still life scene that includes multiple textures and reflections.

Set Up the Scene

For this example, I gathered a quick arrangement of objects in my vicinity that varied in proportion, texture, shape, and details. My goal was to create an interesting scene that wouldn't be boring for you to draw, but that would challenge your perspective drawing skills. Notice that the placement of the objects is meant to be a bit difficult in terms of overlap, proximity, and even point of view. The bananas, for example, are facing the viewer (and, therefore, you the artist), and that can be quite a difficult perspective to sketch. Use the photos here as a reference or set up a scene with similar challenges using objects that you have handy.

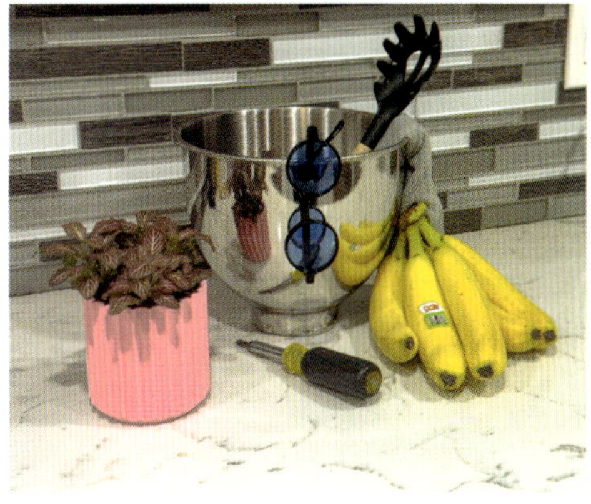

Create a Rough Sketch

With your Paper Mate Flair, quickly create a rough sketch of the scene using some gestural sketching. Your goal is simply to establish the overall placement of objects in the scene, which can help guide you later in the rest of the sketching process. If you'd rather challenge yourself, skip this step and jump right into your main sketch.

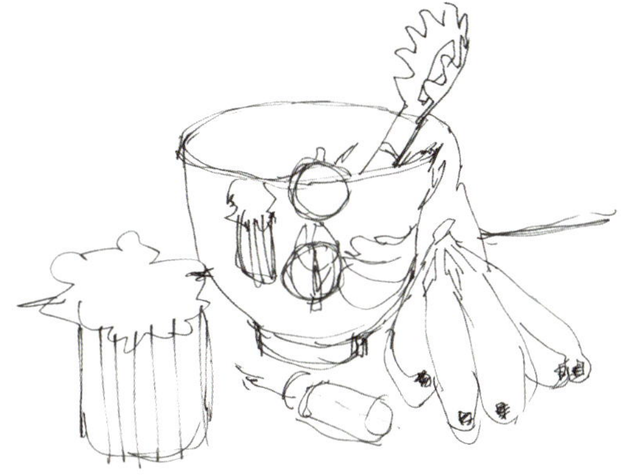

Sketch the Main Objects

While working on that main sketch, remember to
consult your reference as you go along, whether
a reference photo or an object grouping in front
of you. Drawing from a photo presents different
challenges than having the actual objects in front
of you. Sometimes it can be more difficult to
perceive depth in the photo the same way that
you would in real life. Neither way is "wrong"
or "best," but the difference is something to
consider and perhaps experiment with along your
sketching journey.

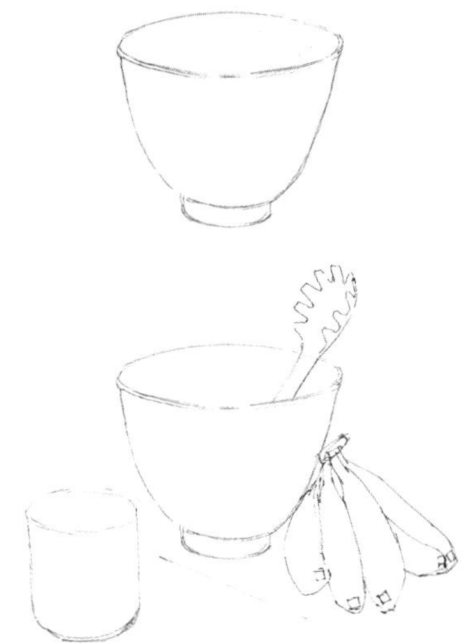

Switch to a slightly finer-tipped pen for your
detailed sketching. I used a Sakura Micron pen;
if you don't have a set, a regular felt pen like a Papermate Flair will do just fine. With
your rough sketch as a guide, lightly sketch the general shape of the bowl that is
central to the scene. Next, sketch in the utensil, some of the bananas, the plant's
pot, as well as a line indicating the direction of the screwdriver. Having these objects
sketched in anchors the drawing, so make sure to check your work against the placement of each object in the perspective scene.

Add Details

With the anchor points in place, sketch the glasses and the body of the screwdriver
along with the details on the pot. Use thin lines as construction lines for the scene, but
don't overextend the lines too much as this is meant to be more of a fairly accurate
representation of what you see. Continue sketching in details like the reflections on
the bowl and glasses, as well as details on the utensil. Add the towel in the bowl to
your scene as well.

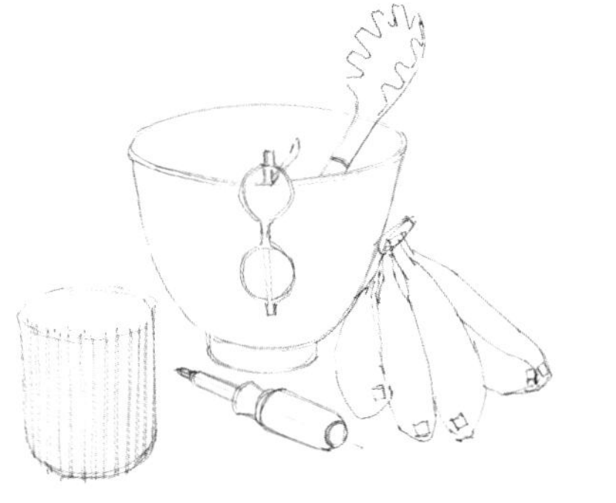

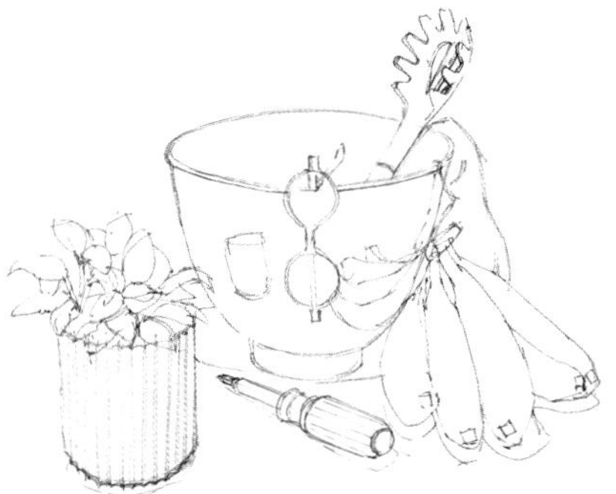

Sketch the Leaves or Take Artistic Liberty

When it comes to details like the leaves of the plant, I frequently take artistic liberty. Drawing details like the leaves accurately can be overwhelming. If you have the time, patience, and desire, give a detailed version a try. I, however, opted for a general representation. (Let's face it, will anyone notice whether you rendered an exact replica of the third leaf from the left?) Instead, spend your attention and energy on accurate placement

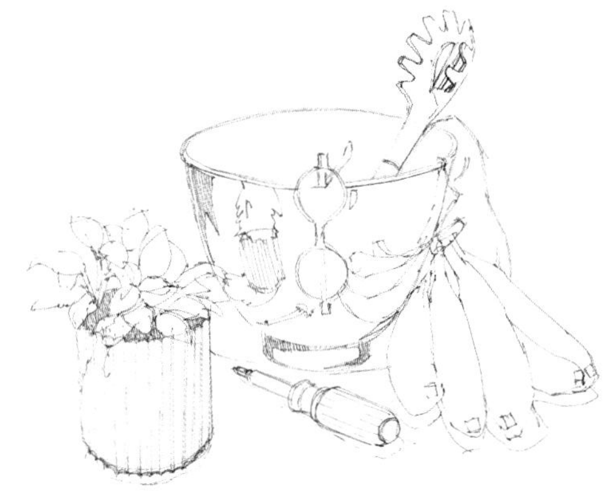

and perspective of each element in your scene. Getting these right will factor into the drawing's success more than whether you included the exact number of spots on the bananas or perfect leaf positions.

Hatch Shadows and Add Texture

With everything loosely sketched in, start hatching in shadowed areas on the bowl, planter, and banana. To do this, outline the area first and then fill with hatch lines. Sketch in the shadows for the screwdriver, planter, bowl, and bananas, and then hatch these shadows using a series of quickly sketched parallel lines. For the reflections in the bowl, pay close attention to the curvature of the objects in the scene as reflected and hatch with a slight curve as well.

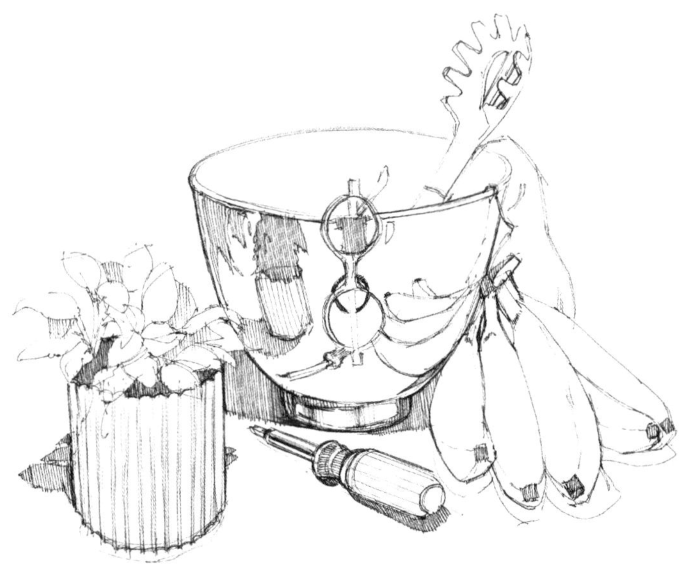

Enhance Line Weights and Shading

To add more definition to the still life, don't forget to enhance line weights where needed, as well as sketch a bit loosely and expressively depending on the object that you're drawing. For example, I sketched the bananas a bit more loosely than I did the screwdriver or utensil. The expressiveness in your lines can help reinforce the appearance and nature of the object itself. Next, sketch in a bit of texture on the towel, as well as shade in the shadows on the banana. Don't forget the sticker on the banana, but much like with the leaves, feel free to sketch an artistic interpretation rather than an exact representation of the bar code. When drawing a still life, you have to balance realism with gesture, expression, and artistic looseness. To me, the most interesting and effective still life drawings convey a sense of emotion and the artist's intention.

Continue shading the texture on the towel by using short scribble marks in the shape of a W or V in a repetitive fashion. At this step as well, take some time to shade in the utensil and any other areas that need to be a bit darker.

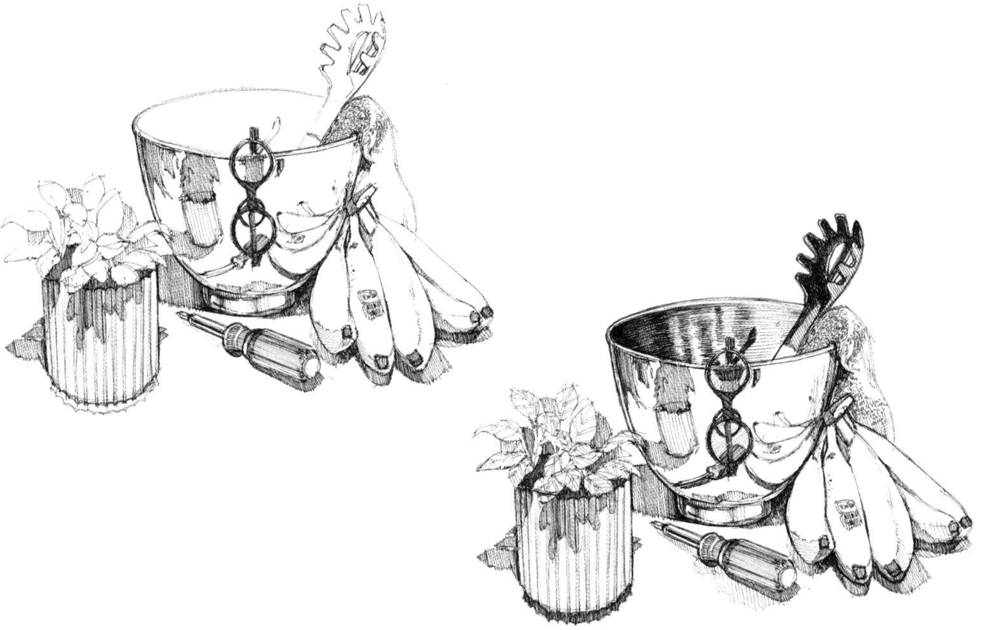

Squint Check Your Shading

As you are shading, try squinting your eyes to minimize detail and focus on the values and tones. Are you shading with enough contrast? Additionally, you can squint at the objects you are drawing to get a sense for the major groupings of values in what you see.

Make Final Refinements

To finish up, shade in the leaves of your plant, as well as correct any minor wandering lines in the main scene. Check the outlines and textures on the towel, banana, bowl, and plant for refinements you could make. Shade the inside of the bowl using lines that mimic the brushed stainless-steel finish. When creating a texture, try to find a way to interpret the texture rather than getting bogged down by creating an exact representation of it—think feeling over precision.

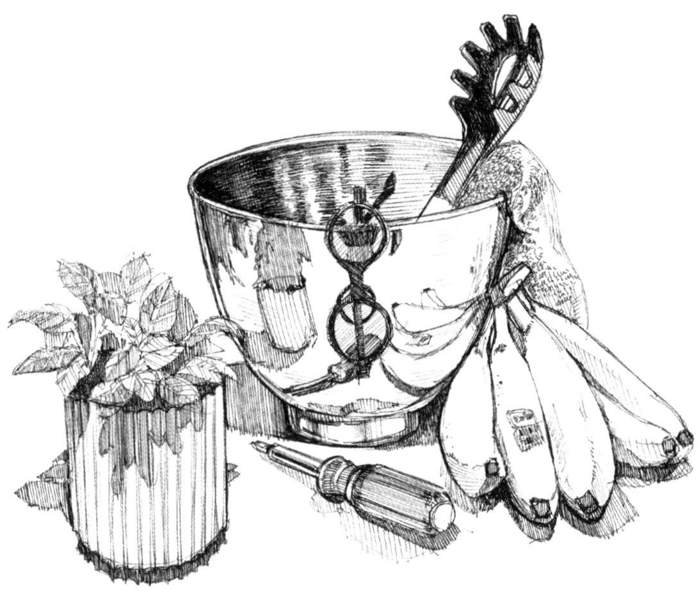

CHALLENGE

Create a series of observational drawings based on objects in your environment. One of my favorite things to do is to visit a coffee shop or restaurant, and while waiting for my food or relaxing after a meal, I draw people and objects in the vicinity. I try to draw what I'm seeing as quickly as possible and to capture it in a gestural way. You could also set up still life drawings to practice your perspective, proportion, placement, lighting, shadow, and texture skills using your pens. You should find that if you complete this exercise and continue to practice, your skills in each of these core areas will improve, and you will have increased confidence in your drawing abilities.

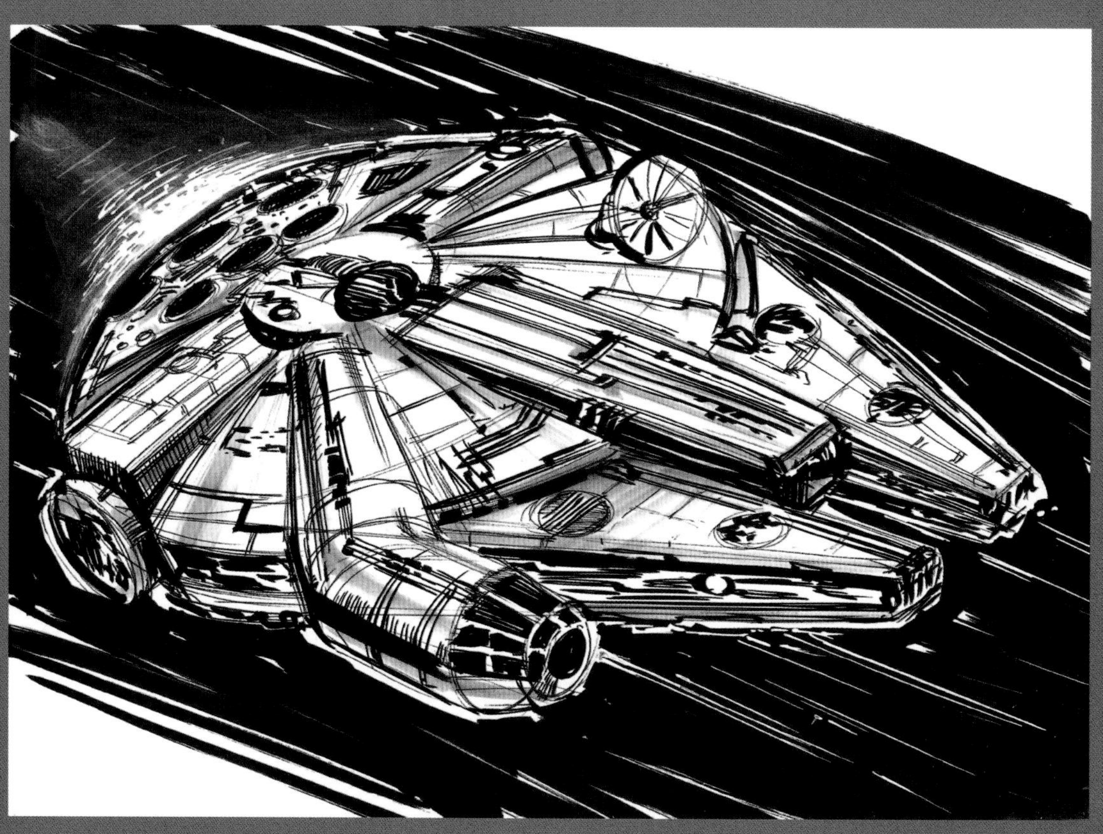

CHAPTER 8

BACKGROUNDS AND SUPPORTIVE ELEMENTS

Backgrounds contextualize the subject of a drawing to make it more relatable. For example, a product designer might include a background or supportive elements to add context to their sketch, perhaps subtly suggesting a use case, market, or mood for the product, or simply to make a new concept seem more familiar. If you were working on a comic illustration, still life, or architectural sketch, you might include a background to provide a sense of place for a scene or to hint at additional information about the subject.

Backgrounds don't need to be elaborate to be effective. A simple rectangular shape with a wood texture behind a concept sketch of a screwdriver or hammer hints at the tool's purpose, while a gestural mountain range behind a drawing of a building gives the viewer clues to its location. (Remember how the background in Exercise 32 helped locate the cabin?) In fact, simple is better. A background should never be the center of attention. When sketching, make sure that your background and supportive elements are less prominent than your main subject. Color, line, scale and patterns should be generally subdued when used as a background. This way, they won't compete for the viewer's visual attention.

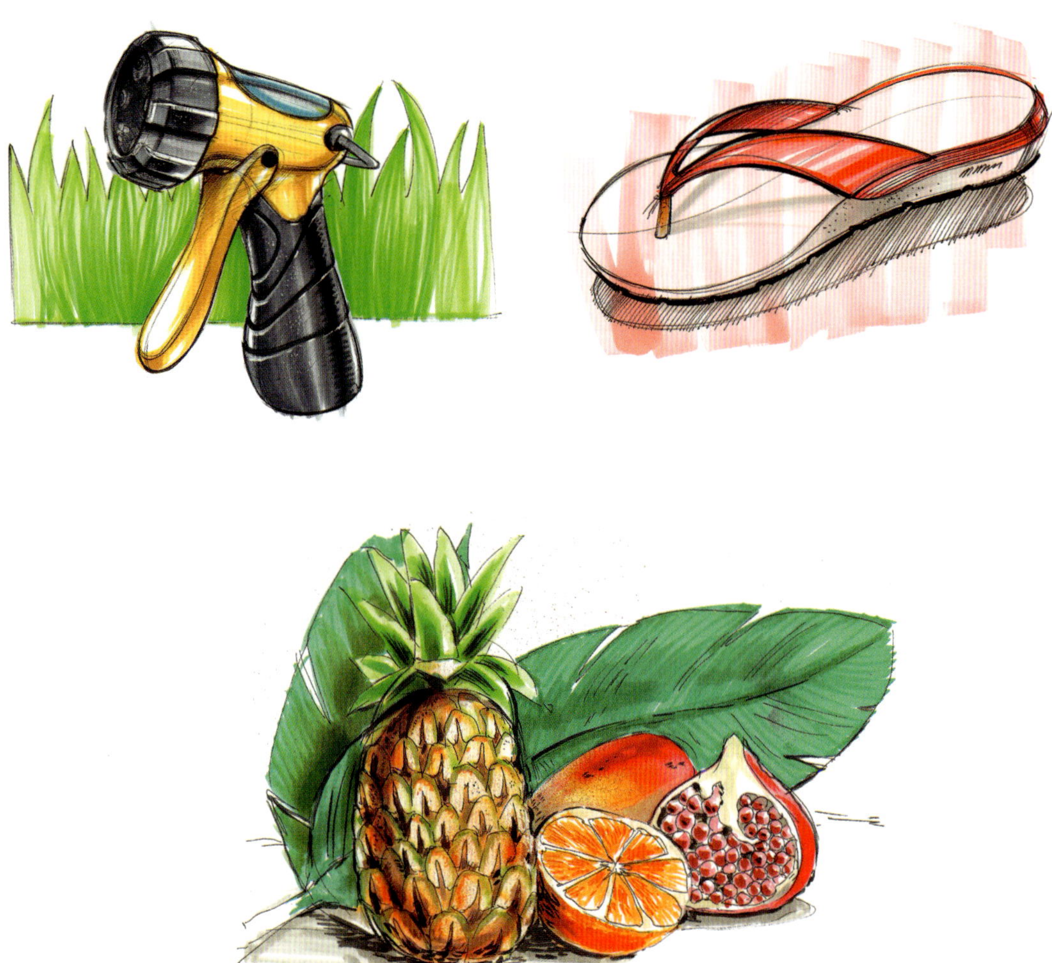

   SKETCH EVERY DAMN DAY

In this exercise, you'll sketch an electric screwdriver or drill and add some context through the use of a background. Gather your pens, markers, and marker paper. You can use whatever colors you have available.

Establish the Sketch

Start by drawing a slightly angled line that will function as the central axis through the driver's cylindrical body. Next, sketch a circle toward the front or lower left of the line. This circle will function as the sphere-like ball end of the electric driver.

Continue sketching in construction geometry, such as elliptical cross sections along the central axis of the driver. Be sure to sketch these in lightly before committing to them as part of the final design.

Complete the Silhouette

Next, connect your cross sections with straight lines and curves to complete the outside silhouette of the driver. Toward the front of the driver, sketch a few additional ellipses in a downward fashion to create the functional working end of the tool. Be sure to keep these lines light and loose as you define the rest of the driver.

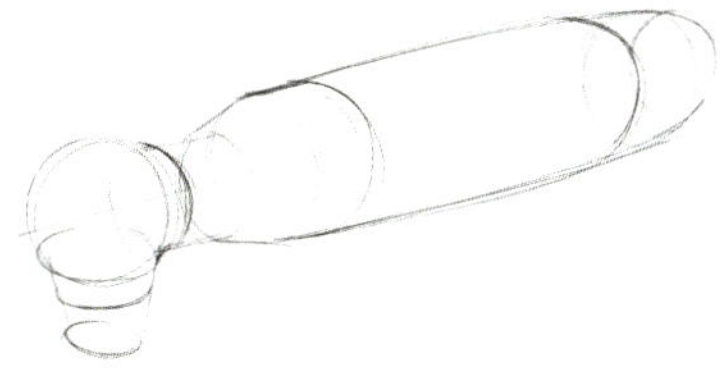

Continue dividing the tool into functional pieces. At the driver's spherical business end (lower left) where the bits would be housed, for instance, add jaws to hold the bits and a ring of short, vertical lines to imply the ridged chuck to adjust them. On the handle, loosely sketch a switch, following the overall perspective of the driver. Define the material breaks in the handle with sketch lines, as well. Because I knew I

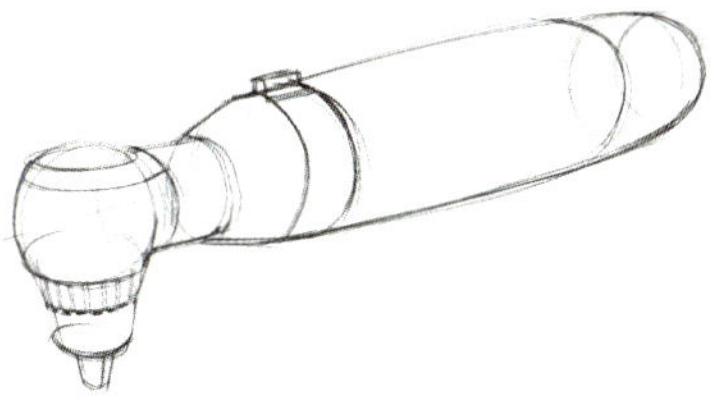

would be adding color to this sketch, I wasn't concerned about having the cleanest of lines. If you want to clean up your sketch at this point, however, feel free to grab an extra piece of paper and re-sketch or overlay what you've done so far.

Add Texture and Details

Next, loosely sketch in knurling in a grid-like pattern on the handle. To sketch this detail, think of these lines as cross sections or slices taken through the handle at an angle. Slicing through the handle that is largely cylindrical and at an angle results in an elliptical profile. Therefore, each of these lines is slightly curved in a way that is reminiscent of an elliptical section. Use a double line to give yourself some space to later shade in grooves that will help this feature feel three-dimensional. When sketching the texture on your grip, be sure to think about the perspective and angle at which these ellipses would be drawn. Try to be as consistent as possible, but also be loose and have fun with it.

Next, shade in lightly any shadow cores on the bit end of the driver that may help communicate the materiality of that portion along the grip. I also added slicing to a small section by the switch and a scribble at the butt of the electric driver. This scribble is a simple way to suggest that there is some text on the tool.

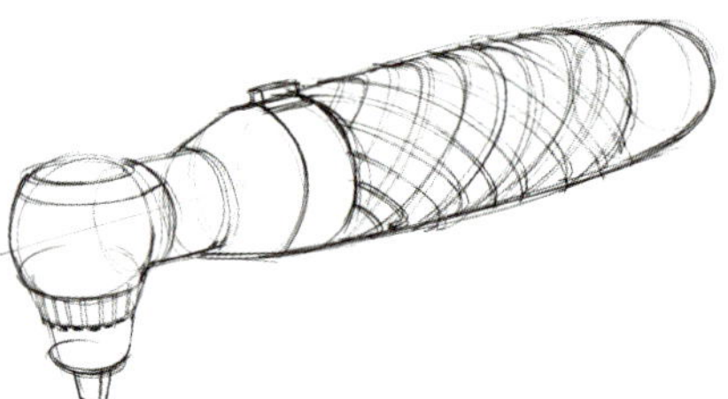
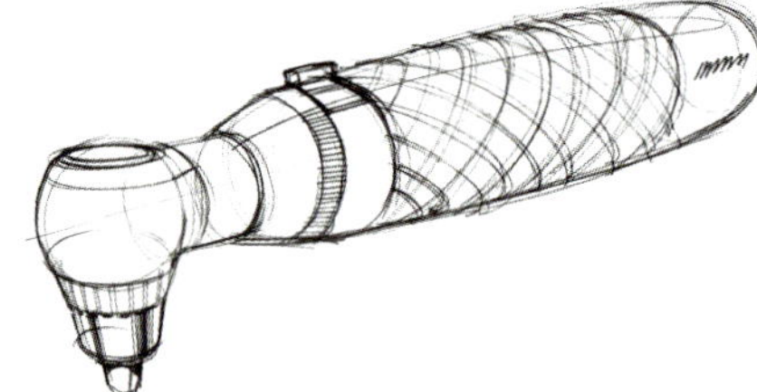

Add Color

Time to add some color to the driver. For the example, I used a yellowy mustard green, a set of three gray markers, and red for the switch. When coloring, I find it helpful to outline the areas in marker first. Also, start with your lightest marker, and work light until you get it right. Create outlines

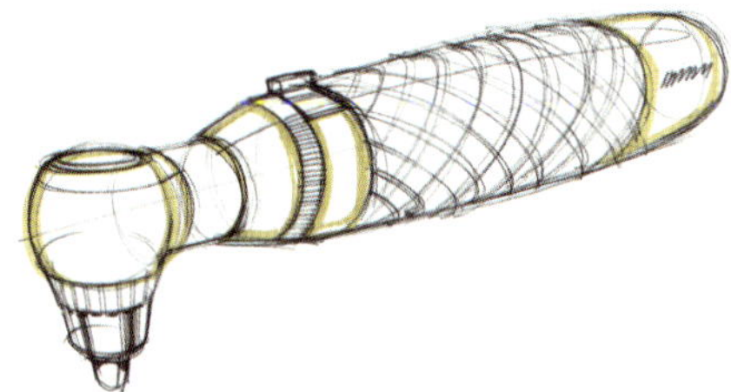

with the lightest shade of your accent color (the yellowy mustard green for me), and then fill in each region. Do the same with the grays that will represent the bare metal. Shade the handle grooves twice to emphasize their depth (remember to let your ink dry between applications).

Continue deepening value and doing squint checks along the way. You can reapply marker to the same area or switch to deeper value within the same color family. I used my deeper colored markers to enhance the shadow core of the colored sections and my deeper grays for the metal areas. Pay attention to how the shadow core on the colored section of the driver lines up with the shadow core on the grip section of the driver. It's important to be consistent with details like this; if the details are not in line with each other, the drawing will feel more chaotic.

Add red to the switch and use a white pen to enhance highlights. Depending on how shiny your material is, you can use more or less white to mimic reflections. Add white on the grip where edges of the raised areas point toward the light source or are in line with the highlight to help those areas pop. With contrast comes depth, as the lightest lights are placed next to dark darks. The arrows in the example sketch, as well as dots, are stylistic elements that I chose to add. As you gain experience and sketch more, you may find that you adopt certain stylistic elements that you like to include. Feel free to do so by experimenting on the side and including these elements in your sketches.

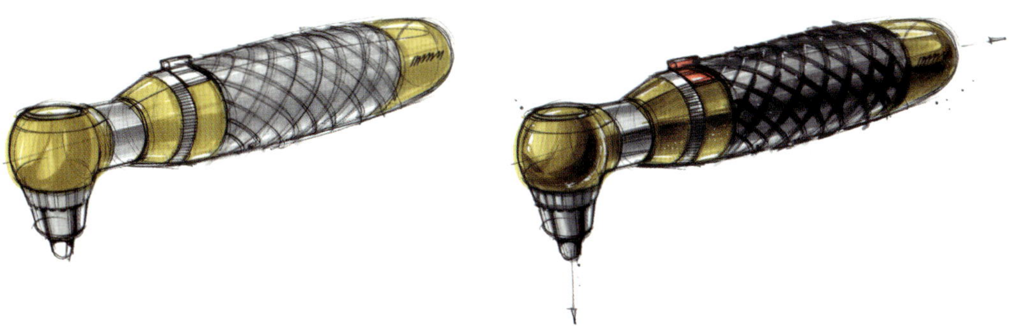

Create the Background

With the driver itself in good shape, you can start working on the background element to suggest some context. Backgrounds are a great way to ground an object to the page as well as minimize the amount of white space on that page. When using a background, try to keep it simple but also relevant and contextual to the object itself. More often than not, my backgrounds tend to be simple shapes like a rectangle. Because this is a powered screwdriver, I decided to make a rectangular background element reminiscent of wood.

To do so, draw a rectangle, and then use what you learned about simulating wood grain in Exercise 5 to create a wood grain texture. Sketch lightly and try to avoid sketching over the object itself.

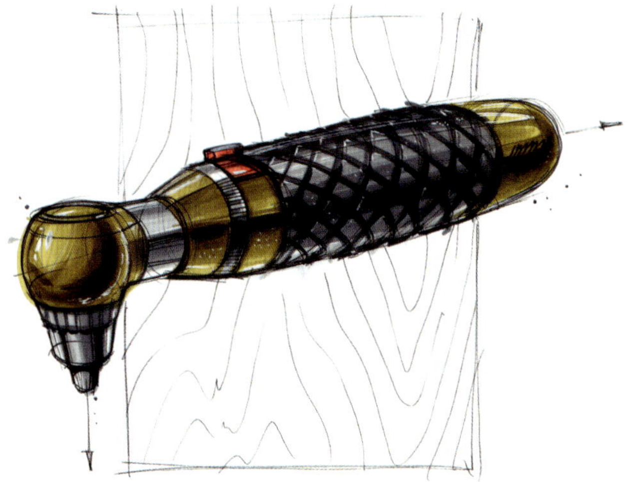

Shade your rectangle with a light brown or tan marker leaving some intentional gaps that reveal bits of white in the texture. Already with the addition of color, the back-ground begins to take shape and come to life.

With a midtone marker, accentuate the grain of the wood by tracing along the pen lines. Don't worry if the marker stroke does not line up perfectly with the pen lines. The idea is to create a difference in value that is subtle and not overbearing when compared to the sketch of the driver.

Add a shadow with the midtone brown tone to represent that the driver itself is in front of the background. This shadow is not meant to be taken literally; it functions solely as a hint as to the scene's depth and the relative positions of the driver and background.

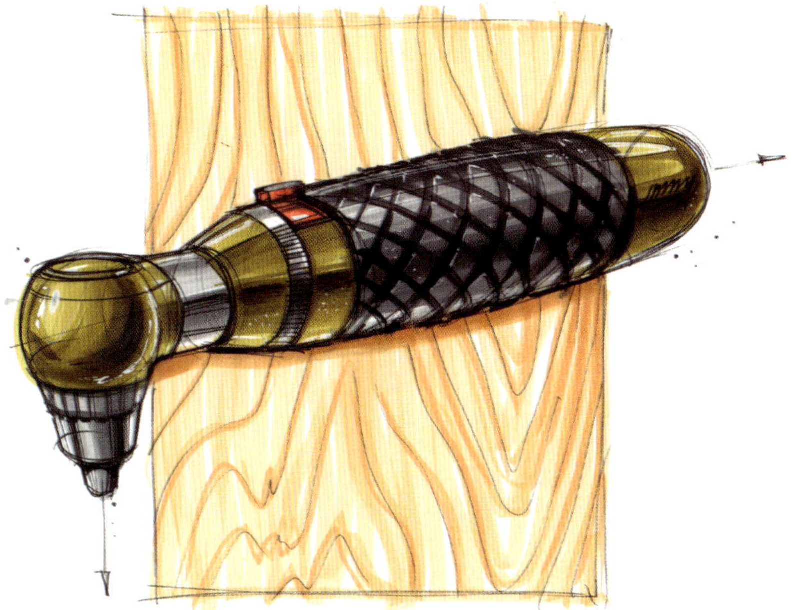

Add Finishing Touches

To wrap up, clean up any line work and elements that you need to in this sketch. I decided to emphasize the bottom contour of the silhouette by enhancing the electric driver's line weight. Good work—you've created a sketch you can confidently present to anyone.

CHALLENGE

Find a similar object to which you can add context by using a simple rectangular background. Try to keep the proportion and placement of the background from overpowering your subject. Play with the size and scale of the background either in thumbnail form or final sketch form to get a feel for how big or small you would like to make it. Feel free to explore other two-dimensional shapes that add context to your chosen subject, too.

In this final week, you'll sketch a lantern and add a background for context. Whether it's simple and gestural or more detailed, your background should not overpower your main sketch. Your background is there to support the sketch and not take away from the visual presentation of what you're drawing. To sketch and color the lantern, I suggest a felt pen as well as several markers. I used maker paper, because it helps prevent ink bleeding.

Sketch the Lantern

With your paper oriented vertically, draw a vertical line to be the central axis for your lantern. Next, sketch a series of offset ellipses at the top, the bottom, and about a quarter to a third of the way up from the bottom. You will use these to outline the general shape of the lantern. Notice that the ellipses vary in degree moving down the page. The upper ellipses are narrower than those nearer the bottom because of the difference in the degree of the ellipse relative to the viewer. Next, begin sketching in a handle on the top of the lantern. You can keep these lines fairly simple; you will have the opportunity to refine them later on.

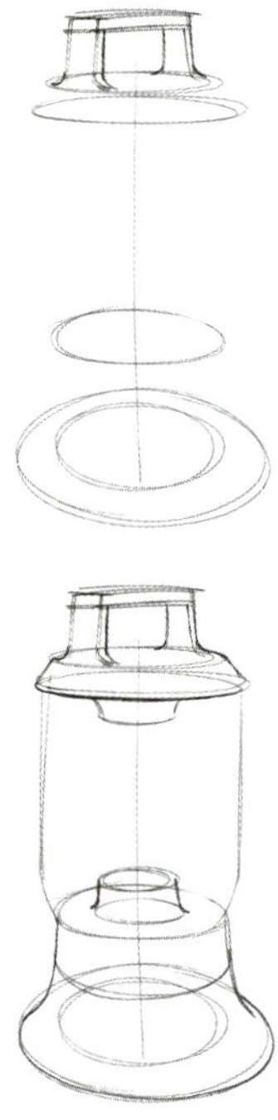

Draw the Outline

Connect the offset ellipses with straight lines to sketch the outline of the lantern, including the top cover. Draw downward from the top cover and handle toward the base of the lantern, curving your lines to meet the base tangent at the ellipse that is the top of the base housing.

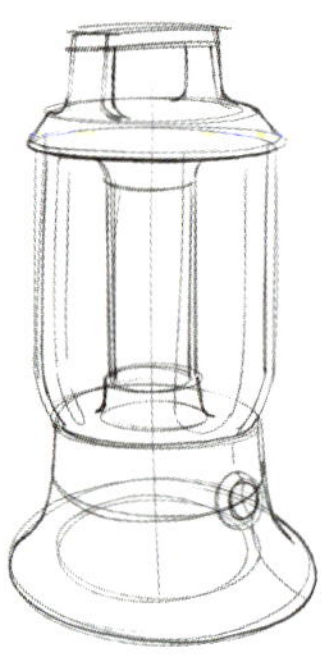

Establish Transparency and Details

The lamp housing must be some sort of transparent material, so the light can shine through. To convey this, sketch
a double line at the perimeter of the glass portion of the
lantern. Sketching a double line is a quick way to establish transparency when sketching with a single tool. In the
center of the lamp area, sketch in two ellipses and transition
them into the lantern's base as well as its lid. Connect these
vertically to form the bulb and its connectors. Add an ellipse
on the front of the base to serve as the power button.

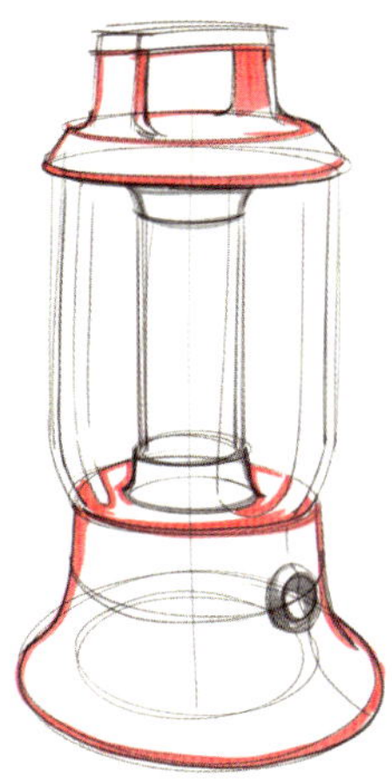

Add Color

It's time to add some color. When choosing your color, make sure your markers
include a decent spread of values in your color family. Not all reds are the same, and
not all blues are the same. If your markers are not in the same color family, your final
shading may look a bit off. After selecting your markers, test them on scrap paper just
to make sure they work well together.

Outline the areas you want to shade using the corresponding marker. For this example, I outlined the base and upper portion of the lid with my lightest red, as well as
outlined the bulb housing and power button with my lightest gray. Shade with your
lightest red marker. Notice that I intentionally left a few areas untouched to communicate the three-dimensionality of the subject by way of contrast. Make sure your
highlights shine to contrast with the shadows that will darken portions of your lantern.

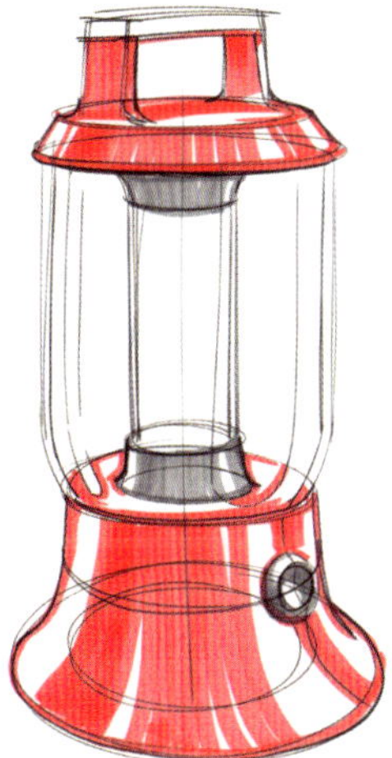 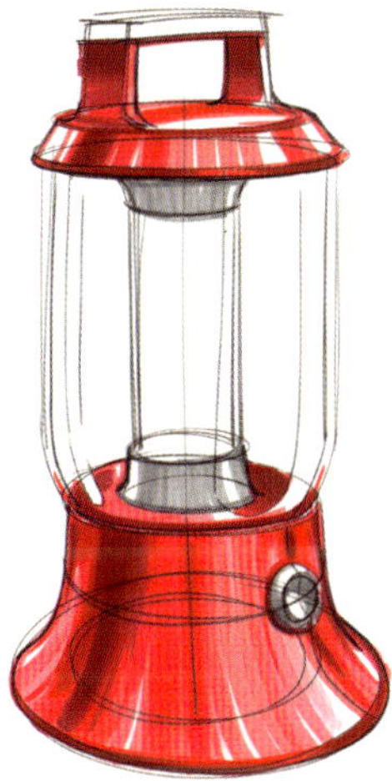

Add Depth

Once your base color is in, start shading with your midtone red marker. Shade any areas that will be away from the primary light source in your scene and allow these surfaces to have enough contrast against the light surfaces to make your sketch look three-dimensional. In the example, look closely at the handle as well as the base. I shaded in a shadow core on the base as well as a deeper value for the handle, as the side surface is away from the light source.

Shade the Glass

Next, shade in the gray trim pieces with additional value at the top, middle, and bottom of the lantern. Before shading the transparent glass material, observe some glass of similar thickness to better approximate its refraction. *Refraction* deals with the bending of light as it passes through different materials. As the light passes through the lamp, it may pick up some of the reds in the base. At the top of the base, I extended a bit of red into the glass, for example, to mimic this phenomenon. Give it a try when you're ready.

Add Blue Tones

To shade the glass without making it seem too heavy, use a very pale blue to add some subtle tones to it. If you don't have a very light blue, you can also use a very pale gray; something like a 10% or 20% gray marker would do just fine here. Notice now that you've introduced the marker colors, your construction lines simply fade away into irrelevance on the page. I think sometimes construction lines can add a certain degree of charm and warmth to whatever it is that you are sketching.

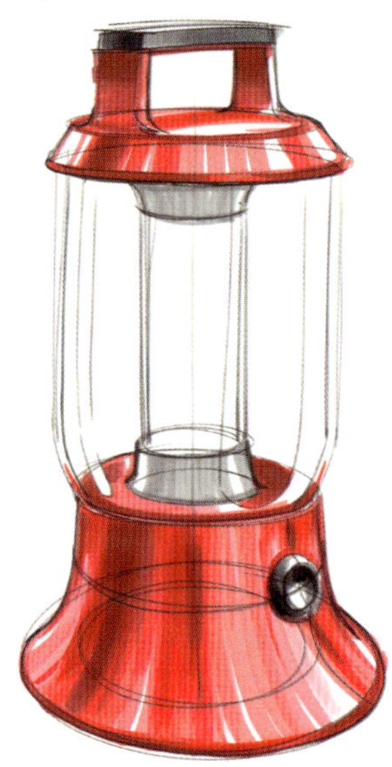

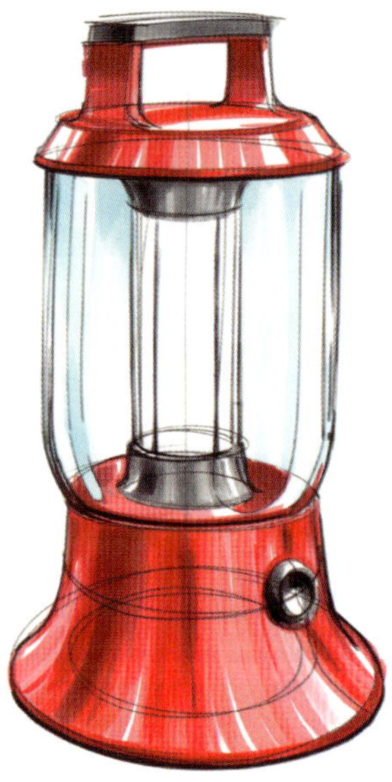

Create the Background

First, think about what type of background would help give context to the lantern. Perhaps someone would use it while camping, so try that as the theme for your background. Loosely sketch in a few evergreen trees to form a field of trees that resembles a forest. With the green you plan to use for the trees, shade in some more refractions in the glass of the lamp. This may be uncomfortable and take some practice but stick with it. Simply apply some color to the glass as if these green marker strokes are refractions in the glass. You can take some artistic liberties here, but don't hesitate to check some reference imagery for how glass might look if color is viewed through a thick edge.

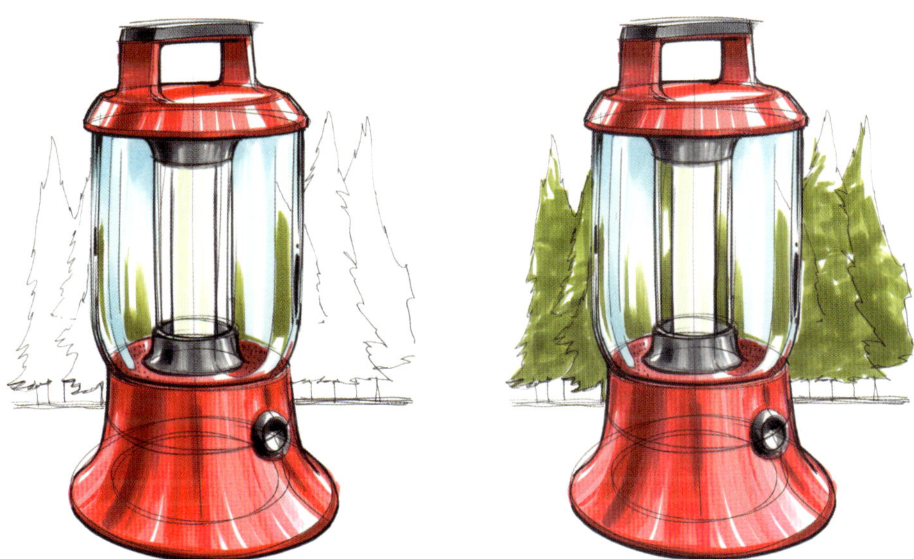

Apply Final Touches

Using your felt pen, add additional details to the bulb and also refine the lid and the glass a bit. Shade the lantern button, leaving the upward-facing surfaces more white or untouched. Continue filling in the background by shading in the trees with your lightest green marker. Notice the color interplay between the lantern and the trees in the background. The background does not have to follow the sketch in terms of the sketch's perspective. In the example, you may notice that the trees are set on a horizontal ground line while the base of the lantern is not a perfectly horizontal straight line and is constructed from an ellipse. This visual contrast is appropriate in this instance as, again, the background serves to give the sketch context as well as elevate it.

For one of the final steps, add deeper tones to the background trees. I also used a deeper green to enhance the shading of the colors peeking through the glass as well as add shadows to the background trees. Touch up any outlines you may need to by drawing over the same spot a few times or switching to a pen with a slightly thicker tip. And you're done—one presentable, refined lantern.

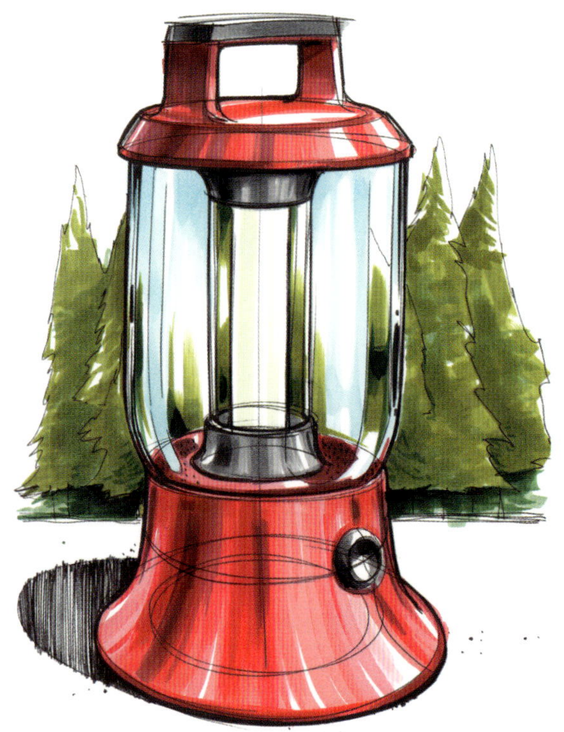

CHALLENGE

Work on backgrounds for your sketches and balance those backgrounds with the subject matter. Sketch a few lamps and add context by using backgrounds that relate to the concept. Be mindful that the background does not overpower the sketch but rather complements it. Be sure to err on the side of caution as you decide how complex or interesting to make the background. Most importantly, however, is to relax and have fun. Play with these tools and techniques to see what you come up with.

CONCLUSION

Well, you did it!

If you made it this far, you've completed the exercises… or maybe you skipped ahead and focused on a few. Either way, you've gone through a series of exercises and challenges that have enhanced your *perspective* on sketching or introduced you to a different style of sketching. I hope that they've pushed you to be just a little uncomfortable, too. If things aren't just a little bit uncomfortable for me, I feel I'm just coasting and not really working to improve my skills and abilities. Challenging yourself is one of the best ways to improve.

Don't feel you have to stop just because you've reached the end of the book! Redo the exercises with new subject matter. Try a tool or an approach (or both) that you're less familiar with this time. For example, if you're used to drawing with a gray marker first and working light until you get it right, experiment with sketching with a pen only. If you're used to creating overlays of your drawings, perhaps push yourself to be a bit more precise in the process of your original sketches and see how that feels.

Take some pride in the fact that you have risen to the challenge of trying something new and made it this far. Believe in yourself and think of all you've accomplished by working through these exercises and whatever artistic challenges and frustrations you faced along the way.

As you continue to draw and add beauty to this world, be bold and brave enough to show up, show off, and share your work. Many times, it's in that sharing process that we grow in our ability to receive critique, as well as improve aspects of our work. Putting your work—a little piece of yourself—out there can be a scary thing at first, but

I will tell you that much of my growth and development has happened because I was willing to get out there, share, and incorporate the feedback from others.

In fact, I hope to see your work, whether online or in person. If you see me out in the world, feel free to say hello as well. Much love to you and good luck on the next stage of your journey to becoming the best artist or visual communicator you can be.

And so I end as we began, with a reminder to sketch *every damn day*, be *gentle* on yourself, and, most importantly, be *consistent*. The more consistent and committed you are, the more you will continue to see those results and improvements along your journey.

ABOUT THE AUTHOR

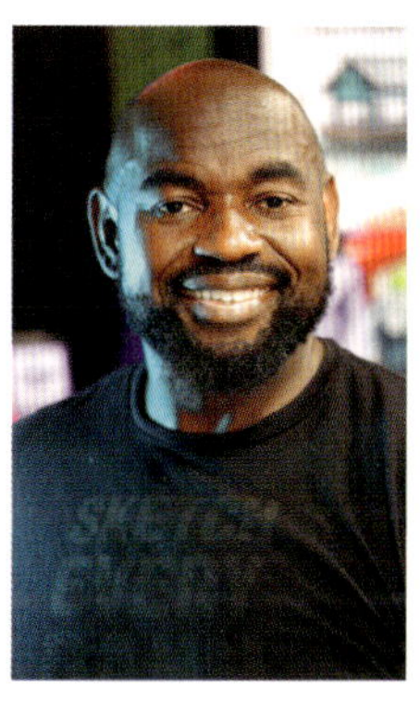

Spencer Nugent is a Jamaican-born creator, maker, educator, and author currently based in Salt Lake City, Utah. The founder of Sketch-A-Day.com, Spencer has been providing free, high-quality online design sketching tutorial content and on-site sketch workshops since 2008. He has created an extensive online network and following within the industrial design community and continues to connect with students and design professionals via his online properties. With his educational videos on YouTube, Instagram, Facebook, and TikTok, he continues to share his passion for creating and drawing.

Spencer's professional experience includes working at General Motors in Warren, Michigan, and San Francisco–based design firm Astro Studios. He also headed up his own design consultancy, Studio Tminus, where he worked with clients primarily in the consumer electronics and apparel industries. Spencer has worked with brands such as Microsoft, Intel, Hewlett Packard, BodyGlove, Adidas, Verifone, Kyocera, Altec Lansing, Hasbro, Dell, Tupperware, Motorola, and Vivint Smart Home. Spencer has also led workshops and presentations for many higher educational institutions and corporate clients, including designers at Adidas HQ, Herzogenaurach Germany, Apple Retail, LG, and Adobe MAX, and he frequently presents on Adobe Live on Behance.net.

In 2020, Spencer was awarded the Industrial Design Society of America's Individual Achievement Award for his consistent work producing online educational content and his overall passion for industrial design education.

Because of his love for education, Spencer also is an active instructor at Offsite, an online program that offers a real-world view of the design profession through instruction by several design industry leaders.

Spencer has published *The Perspective Drawing Guide* as well as *Digital Sketching* to help beginners understand how to approach drawing and to help professional creatives level up.

Spencer currently leads 5050.design, where half his time is dedicated to personal projects and the other to client work.

Links:

Website: www.sketch-a-day.com
YouTube: @sketchadaydotcom
Instagram: @sketchadaydotcom
Facebook: facebook.com/sketchaday
Threads: @sketchadaydotcom
TikTok: @sketchadaydotcom

Acknowledgments

Special thanks to my friends and family and mentors, including: My wonderful sons, Oliver and Leo. You've been a wonderful light and inspiration along the way.

Camille Nugent: Thank you for always believing in me and being a should for support and an amazing cheerleader. www.camillenugent.com

Hector Silva. My wonderful friend. Your heart, advocacy, and commitment to education are an inspiration to me. www.advdes.org

Thank you all for being amazing humans.

Resources

The stuff I use to draw:
https://www.Sketch-A-Day.Com/Stuff

Sketch-A-Day Workshops and Tutoring:
https://www.sketch-a-day.com/workshops

Digital Sketching: Digital sketching tools, techniques, and tips for product design and Illustration by Spencer Nugent.

How to Draw: Drawing and sketching objects and environments from your imagination by Scott Robertson and Thomas Bertling.

How to Render: the fundamentals of light, shadow and reflectivity by Scott Robertson and Thomas Bertling.

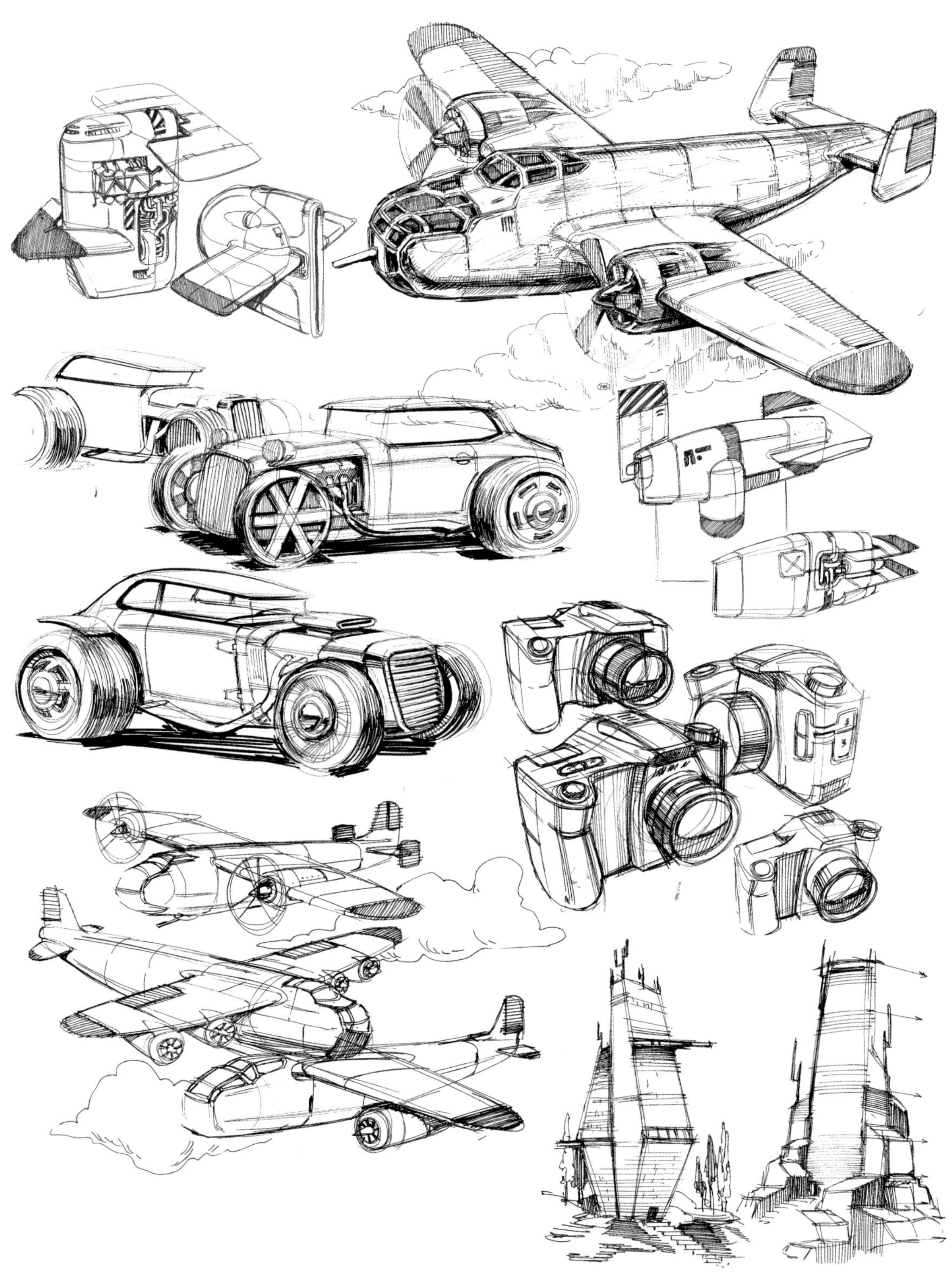

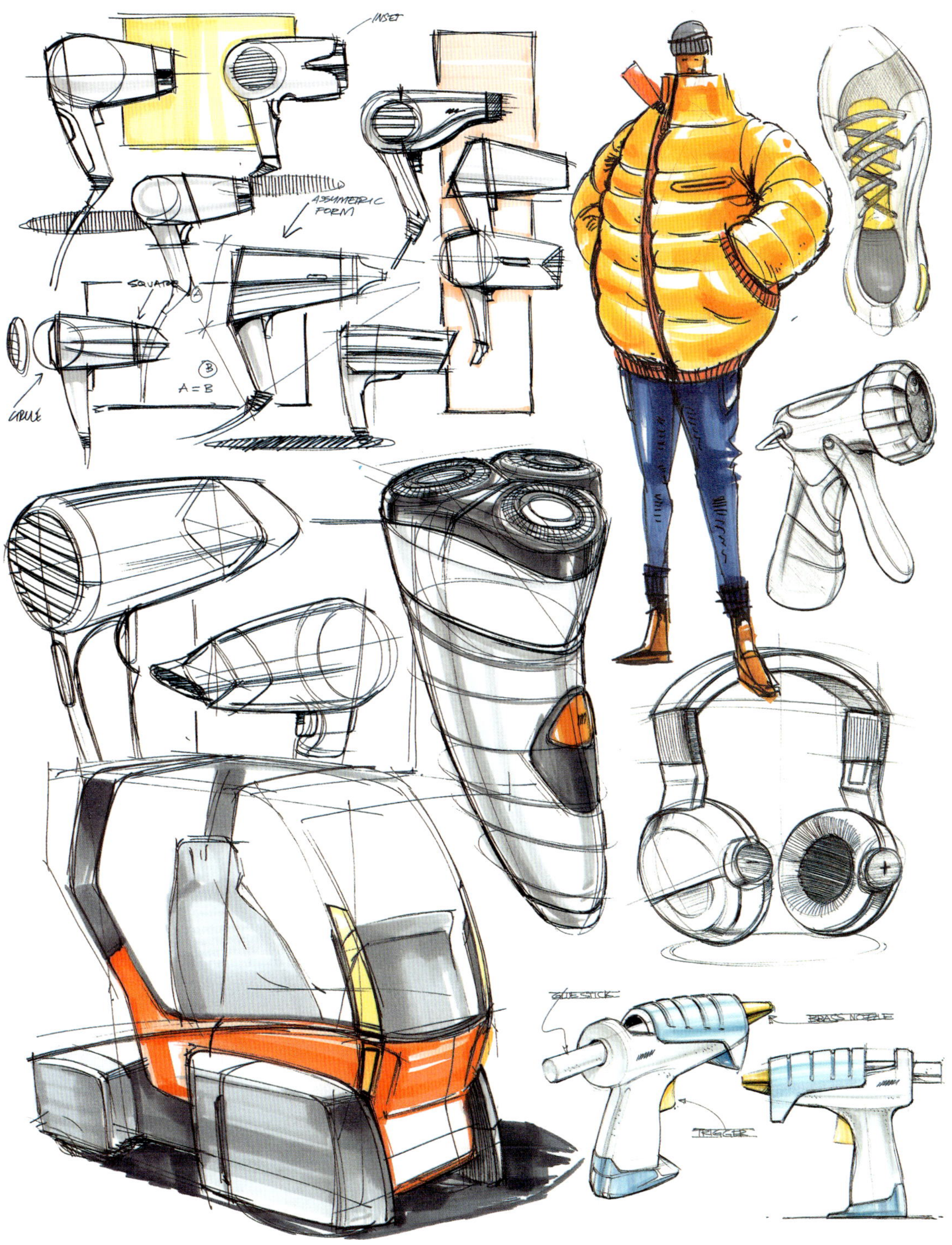

INSET
ASYMMETRIC FORM
SQUARE
A
B
A = B
GRILLE
GLUESTICK
BRASS NOZZLE
TRIGGER

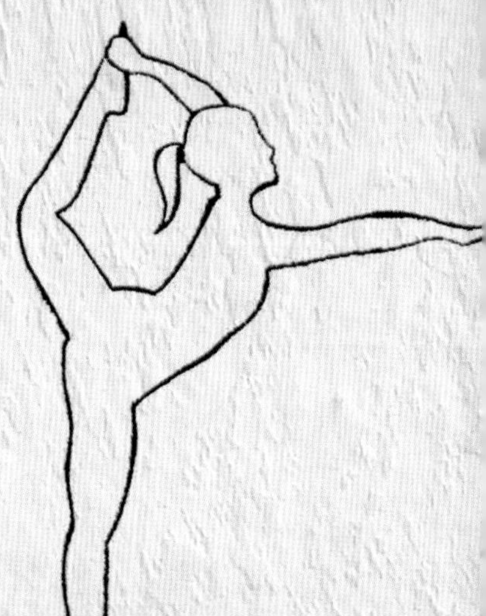

Don't Close The Book On Us!

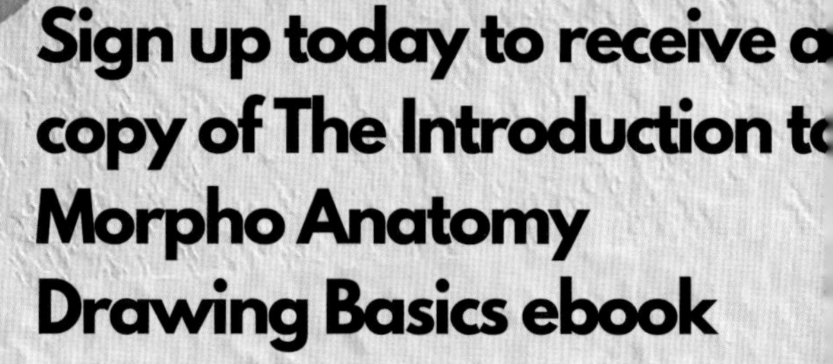

Sign up today to receive a copy of The Introduction to Morpho Anatomy Drawing Basics ebook

Plus access to:
- Discounts
- Free Online Events
- Exclusive Content
- And More!

www.rockynook.com/drawing-newsletter